Famous Gunfights of the American West

By Dave Southworth

Front and back cover design by Chip Southworth

Library of Congress Cataloging-In-Publication Data

Southworth, Dave
Famous Gunfights of the American West

    Bibliography: p. 367
    Includes index: p. 381

    1. West (U.S.) — History — Biography. 2. Outlaws — West (U.S.) — Biography. 3. Peace Officers — West (U.S.) — Biography. 4. West (U.S.) — History — Sources. 5. Frontier and Pioneer Life — West (U.S.) — Sources.

ISBN: 978-1-890778-13-2
      1-890778-13-3

Copyright: 2010 by Dave Southworth
Printed in the United States of America

All rights reserved. Without limiting the rights under copyright reserved above, no part of this book may be reproduced, stored in or introduced into a retrieval system, or transmitted, in any form or by any means (electronic, mechanical, photocopying, recording or otherwise) without the written permission of the copyright owner.

CONTENTS

Preface		Page 7
Chapter 1	The James-Younger Gang	Page 9
Chapter 2	Doc Holliday and the Earp Brothers	Page 33
Chapter 3	Coffeyville: Last Raid of the Dalton Gang	Page 45
Chapter 4	The Pleasant Valley War	Page 51
Chapter 5	Jim Courtright and Luke Short	Page 59
Chapter 6	Terror in the San Joaquin Valley	Page 65
Chapter 7	John Wesley Hardin: Deadly Son of a Preacher	Page 73
Chapter 8	Billy the Kid and the Lincoln County War	Page 79
Chapter 9	Shootout at the Tuttle Dance Hall	Page 95
Chapter 10	Raid on the Doolin Gang at Ingalls	Page 99
Chapter 11	Hanging Bell	Page 103
Chapter 12	Mysterious Dave Mather	Page 107
Chapter 13	Feuds of the Horrell Clan	Page 111
Chapter 14	Will Hicks Graham, Duelist	Page 125
Chapter 15	The Black Jack Ketchum Gang	Page 129
Chapter 16	Jack Slade and the Julesburg Vendetta	Page 135
Chapter 17	The Arizona Rangers	Page 139
Chapter 18	Wild Bill and the Naked Bull	Page 145
Chapter 19	Bad, Bad Clay Allison	Page 151
Chapter 20	Misfortune at Medicine Lodge	Page 153
Chapter 21	Dodge City: Frontier Cow Town	Page 157
Chapter 22	Shootout at Round Rock	Page 163
Chapter 23	Henry Plummer, Renegade Sheriff	Page 167
Chapter 24	Bully Brooks	Page 171
Chapter 25	Dee Harkey: Guts and Grit	Page 175
Chapter 26	Fort Smith and Indian Territory	Page 181
Chapter 27	Battle for the Gray County Seat	Page 189

Chapter 28	The Dewey-Berry Feud	Page 193
Chapter 29	Black Bart, Poet Bandit	Page 101
Chapter 30	The Jaybird-Woodpecker Conflict	Page 205
Chapter 31	The Hoodoo War	Page 213
Chapter 32	Bill Tilghman, Peace Officer	Page 219
Chapter 33	Trouble in Hays City	Page 225
Chapter 34	Bulletproof Killer and the Pecos Grudge	Page 229
Chapter 35	The Johnson County Invasion	Page 231
Chapter 36	Joaquin Murrieta: Bandido	Page 237
Chapter 37	Aurora: A Tough Mining Town	Page 241
Chapter 38	Bodie: Reddy or Knot	Page 245
Chapter 39	The Sutton-Taylor Feud	Page 249
Chapter 40	Cullen Baker: Fugitive	Page 273
Chapter 41	He'll Hang Again, and Again	Page 275
Chapter 42	Colorado Potpourri	Page 279
Chapter 43	The Alvord-Stiles Gang	Page 287
Chapter 44	Tom Horn, Assassin	Page 291
Chapter 45	Vaudeville and Vengeance	Page 295
Chapter 46	Wanted: Harry Tracy	Page 299
Chapter 47	El Paso's Fighting Marshal	Page 303
Chapter 48	The Deadwood Stage: Easy Prey	Page 307
Chapter 49	Butch Cassidy and the Wild Bunch	Page 311
Chapter 50	Reprisal in Bell County	Page 319
Chapter 51	The Mitchell-Truitt Conflict	Page 323
Chapter 52	Belle Starr and Her Bad Boys	Page 327
Chapter 53	Relentless Harry Morse	Page 337
Chapter 54	Rowdy Joe Lowe	Page 341
Chapter 55	The Lee-Peacock Feud	Page 345
Chapter 56	Shootout on Christmas Day	Page 349
Chapter 57	Laredo: The Botas and Guaraches	Page 355
Chapter 58	The Battle at Dry Creek	Page 359
Chapter 59	Chronology of Frontier Firearms	Page 363
Bibliography		Page 371
Index		Page 385

OTHER WORKS BY DAVE SOUTHWORTH

BOOKS: NON-FICTION
Famous Gunfights of Texas
Feuds on the Western Frontier
Colorado Gold Dust: Short Stories and Profiles
Ghost Towns and Mining Camps of the San Juans
Colorado Mining Camps
Gunfighters of the Old West
Gunfighters of the Old West II
Leadville

BOOKS: FICTION
Franklin Hall
Rhymes of a Storyteller

VIDEOS
Colorado Mining Camps: A Pictorial Treasure of
    the Gold and Silver Boom
Leadville: The Boom Years
Mining Camps of the San Juans
Cripple Creek and the Mining Camps of
    Teller County
The Mining Camps of Northwest Colorado
Boulder County Mining Camps: A Look Back
The Mining Camps of Gilpin and Clear Creek
    Counties
The Mining Camps of South Central Colorado

AUDIO BOOKS
Colorado Gold Dust: Short Stories and Profiles
Gunfighters of the Old West
Billy the Kid and the Lincoln County War
Jesse James and the James-Younger Gang
Doc Holliday and the Earp Brothers

Preface

Gunfights in the early American West usually resulted because of mutual hostility between two or more individuals, clans, tribes, families or other groups. Or, they occurred because one party infringed upon the rights and property of the other, as was the case when a robbery, or attempted robbery, took place. Sometimes the gunfights were spontaneous. Sometimes they occurred because of prolonged hostilities between the parties involved. Often they were marked by murderous assaults in revenge for some previous insult or injustice. In many cases a quarrel would intensify, as ill will and animosity increased, until both parties engaged in battle. Basically, each participant strived for satisfaction or gratification for what they thought was some unjust deed. That deed could have been something as simple as an insult, or an offense to one's honor or pride. Many gunfights erupted due to a seemingly insignificant incident. Conversely, its origin can sometimes be traced to an episode of serious magnitude. There were feuds that lasted for months, even years, during which many confrontations might occur. The roots of such feuds took many forms. The Lincoln County War, with its famed participant Billy the Kid, was an economic struggle. The Pleasant Valley War was a conflict between families. The communities of Cimarron and Ingalls battled for the right to be county seat. There were disputes over land rights or claim rights; conflicts between political parties; clashes with ethnic overtones; discord between large and small cattle ranchers; hostilities between cattlemen and sheep herders; and labor wars.

The gunfights which unfold throughout the following pages were selected for inclusion based on interest, renown, variety and historical significance. Many of the participants are individuals of much notoriety. The cast of characters includes Billy the Kid, John Wesley Hardin, Jim and Bat Masterson, Jesse and Frank James, Commodore Perry Owens, Deacon Jim Miller, Wyatt Earp, Pat Garrett, the Dalton brothers, Bill Tilghman, Jim Courtright, Doc Holliday, Wild Bill Hickok, Butch Cassidy, Luke Short and Cole Younger. Much of the action, however, is created by those with lesser reputations.

At the root of each conflict are two or more people, with different opinions, certain that they are right and their opposition wrong. Common sense, litigation and mediators usually did little to resolve unwavering differences. Guns were often the last resort. Actually, they were sometimes the first resort as well. Indifferences that have become historically prominent usually have done so because of their gunfights and bloodshed.

Animosity, from whatever the cause, would usually grow and then blossom to its fullest. Rarely would it simply wilt and die. Sometimes it had to be cut off by intervention of a third party of greater strength, or by mutual extermination.

"An eye for an eye and a tooth for a tooth" is the oldest code of law enforcement known to man. It was also the code of revenge and retribution across much of the early Western Frontier. To what degree could one consider lawless the act of "taking the law into one's own hands" in places where reasonable legal redress could not be obtained? For example, there were no lawmen, nor was there a judge, in Pleasant Valley when the Grahams and Tewksburys went to war with each other. After considerable mutual extermination, outside law enforcement stepped in to end the feud. To arm one's family or group, or to establish a committee of vigilance for the purpose of self-preservation, did not necessarily constitute disrespect for the law. The disrespect occurred when the feudists or vigilantes overplayed their role as "frontier lawmen." Usually when men take the law into their own hands, they do so until they commit atrocities under the guise of doing what is "lawful." Hostilities developed with different scenarios, with both factions believing they had the right to be lawmen, judge and jury.

Conflicts have occurred around the world, throughout recorded history. There were many in the early American West. This book presents some of the more significant encounters, predominantly during the post-Civil War period (from about 1865 until shortly after the turn of the century). There is no order to the following chapters, either chronological or geographical. The author has attempted to present the workings of frontier justice in these conflicts strictly as historical events without any bias or judgment toward any faction involved. There were always two sides to every story.

Jesse Woodson James, leader of the James-Younger gang was daring, humorous, and had much bravado. *Wild Horse Collection.*

Chapter One
The James-Younger Gang

The Kansas-Nebraska Act of 1854 created a struggle between abolitionists from the North and slaveholders from the South in their efforts to settle Kansas. Northerners flocked to Kansas, hoping to establish a free state where slavery would be prohibited. It wasn't long before vicious fighting broke out on both sides of the Missouri River. Anti-slavery Jayhawkers, or Redlegs, from Kansas raided farms in Missouri. They burned, looted, and carried off slaves in order to set them free. Pro-slavery Bushwhackers from Missouri invaded Kansas to recapture their slaves and to intimidate Northern settlers.

Missouri, although it was a slave state, did not secede from the Union when the Civil War broke out. There was much tension between pro-slavery and anti-slavery factions within the state, as they grappled with each other. The first state constitution of Missouri required that "free" blacks be kept out of the state so they wouldn't be a bad influence on slaves. The state was indeed divided.

Cole Younger's father, Henry Washington Younger, was a

Union sympathizer, even though he was a slave holder. When the Kansas-Missouri border troubles heated up in 1861, Kansas Jayhawkers raided the Younger homestead in Lee's Summit, Jackson County, Missouri. Seventeen year-old Cole urged his father to take a more active position against the Jayhawkers and to support the cause of the Confederacy. Circumstances that followed dictated that the Younger clan would do so.

Cole, his brother Jim, and two of their sisters attended a dance during the fall of 1861. While at the dance, Cole felt the necessity to defend his sister against the advances of a Union soldier. Heated words turned into fisticuffs. Cole struck the soldier, who immediately drew his revolver. Several other young men at the dance stepped in and broke up the fight.

Later that night, Cole informed his father of the incident. Concerned for Cole's safety, Henry suggested that the lad leave the area for a while until the matter had time to blow over.

The Confederate raiders of William Clarke Quantrill were beginning to take shape. Quantrill's band of guerrillas, sometimes called Missouri Bushwhackers, grew rapidly. Quantrill, a former schoolteacher, strengthened his ranks with the leadership capabilities of George Todd

Alexander Franklin (Frank) James had a passion for literature and often quoted Shakespeare. *Wild Horse Collection.*

and William Gregg. Many Jackson County youths who were anxious to battle the Jayhawkers joined forces with Quantrill. John Jarrette was Cole's brother-in-law and close friend. John, who was married to Cole's sister, Mary Josephine, had suggested to Cole that they both join Quantrill's band. They armed themselves, left Lee's Summit, and joined the guerrillas. Their allegiance to the Confederate States of America was official.

Robert and Zerelda James had a farm near Kearney, Missouri, a small town in Clay County. By 1850, the James family owned seven slaves to help with the duties of the farm. Robert devoted much time to his position as pastor of the New Hope Baptist Church, and their two sons Alexander Franklin (Frank) and Jesse Woodson were too young to be of much assistance with the chores. Robert's ministry soon carried him to the gold fields of California, where he hoped to establish some Baptist missions. Shortly after he arrived on the West Coast, he became ill and died. A year later, Zerelda married again. Benjamin Simms did not get along well with the children, and the couple soon separated. In 1855 Zerelda married for a third time. Dr. Reuben Samuel was a mild and easygoing gentleman. His personality meshed well with the strong-willed Zerelda. Reuben was a fine stepfather to Frank, Jesse, and their younger sister Susan. Zerelda and Reuben had four more children of their own: Archie, John, Sallie and Fannie. As youngsters, Frank and Jesse James learned to care for horses. They became excellent riders and adept with firearms.

Because of the inability of Confederate forces to hold Missouri, many defeated soldiers joined the ranks of Quantrill's raiders. One such soldier was Frank James. Frank and Cole Younger would initiate a friendship that would last until their deaths.

While driving his wagon near Kansas City on July 20, 1862, Henry Younger was shot three times and killed. His death devastated his widow, Bursheba, and the children. The assailants were never apprehended. The murder was attributed (at different times) to different individuals, including Irvin Walley (the soldier that was struck by Cole at the dance in 1861), James Madison Smith (a neighbor of the Youngers), and a Captain Stephens.

Quantrill's guerrillas were highly trained and very active. They put fear into the hearts of many Union soldiers. Confederate soldiers under the command of Colonel Upton B. Hayes teamed up with Quantrill's raiders for an attack against the Seventh Missouri Cavalry at the Union post in Independence. The Confederates, who were badly outnumbered, needed to know in advance how many federal troops there were in town and where they were located. Two days prior to the attack, Cole Younger entered Independence dressed as an old lady, complete with shawl and bonnet. He (she) sold apples and vegetables while carefully calculating the best locations for their attack. At the break of daylight on the morning of August 11, 1862, Hayes, Quantrill and their men completely surprised the troops at the Union post. The attack was a success for the Confederates. Many Union soldiers fled the wrath of the rebels. Others surrendered or were killed. The Confederates took possession of much needed firearms, ammunition and food. After the attack at Independence, Cole Younger and several other guerillas were sworn into service in the army of the Confederacy. Cole was commissioned First Lieutenant in Upton B. Hayes' Missouri regiment, although he continued to ride with Quantrill.

    Union authorities tried everything to bring the rebels to their knees. They decided that by arresting the female relatives of guerillas they would be crippling one form of their aid. Approximately one hundred females, including Josie, Caroline and Sally Younger, were transported to a prison in Kansas City. The guerillas realized that it was time for a real show of force.

    The separate factions of Quantrill's raiders led by George Todd, "Bloody" Bill Anderson and John Jarrette assembled for an attack on Lawrence, Kansas. Cole Younger and Frank James were among the group. On the morning of August 21, 1863, the infuriated rebels rode into Lawrence with blood in their eyes. Any male old enough to carry a rifle was shot. Union soldiers and others pleading to be taken prisoner were assassinated. Food, arms and ammunition were confiscated. Buildings were torched, regardless of whether they were stores or homes. When John Jarrette had his horse shot out from under him Cole Younger came to his assistance. The guerillas rode out of town leaving Lawrence in shambles.

    Union authorities retaliated. An order was issued to all citizens of Jackson, Cass and Bates counties, as well as a part of Vernon County who could not prove their loyalty to the Union, that they had fifteen days to evacuate their property and homes, and relinquish all rights to their crops. Cole's mother, Bursheba, was sick in bed when soldiers arrived to carry out the order. She was allowed to remain at home that night under the condition that she would burn her home and buildings the following morning. She agreed, and did so.

At age 16, Jesse James signed on to ride with Bloody Bill Anderson's band of Quantrill's raiders. Like many of the guerillas, Jesse had the capability of handling revolvers with both hands while riding full speed with the reins grasped between his teeth.

The war was not going well for the Confederacy. Feeling the heat, the guerillas believed they could be more effective further south. Most of the raiders headed to Texas or Louisiana with missions already predetermined. Cole Younger, now a captain, rode to Louisiana under the command of his brother-in-law, John Jarrette. While Jarrette and Younger moved about on one assignment or another, Quantrill and most of the raiders returned to Missouri in the spring of 1864. Jim Younger, now 16 years-old, joined Quantrill at that time.

Shortly after joining Quantrill's forces, Jim Younger traveled with his leader and a small detachment of men to Louisville, Kentucky. Some of the men bunked one night in the barn of a Southern sympathizer near Louisville. They awoke to a surprise attack by Union soldiers. The outmanned guerillas surrendered. Quantrill, who had been shot, was transported to a military hospital at Louisville where he died within a few days. Jim Younger, along with the other prisoners, was sent to a federal prison at Alton, Illinois, where he remained until several months after the end of the war.

Cole (left) and Jim Younger were an integral part of the James-Younger gang. *Wild Horse Collection.*

On September 27, 1864, Bloody Bill Anderson led his band, which included Jesse James, on a raid into Centralia, Missouri. After pillaging the town, they robbed a train of the Wabash, St. Louis & Pacific Railroad, and executed 25 unarmed Union soldiers who were aboard. Union forces under the command of Major A. V. E. Johnson gave pursuit. Anderson's band joined forces with the Quantrill raiders led by George Todd. Together, with a force of over 200 men, they set an ambush for Major Johnson. One hundred Union soldiers were killed during the ensuing battle. Jesse James was credited for slaying Major Johnson.

Facing the reality of eventual defeat, many of the guerilla forces disbanded and the irregulars either headed home or elsewhere to lie low. Cole Younger was visiting his Uncle Coleman in California when the war ended on April 9, 1865. He remained there for several more months.

Jim Younger knew that he would not be released from prison unless he agreed to sign the loyalty oath of Missouri and the United States. He agreed to do so. Cole, on the other hand, was considered a fugitive of the law. Both men returned to Missouri in late 1865.

Following the Civil War, many Missouri guerillas were denied amnesty. Frank James turned himself in to Union authorities and was paroled. Jesse James also attempted to surrender but was shot by soldiers near Lexington, Missouri, while carrying a white flag. Jesse escaped to Rulo, Nebraska, where his mother and step-father had been staying because they had been driven from their farm in Kearney, Missouri. Jesse remained there for about two months. He encouraged his mother to take him back to Missouri so he wouldn't die on strange soil. She agreed, and they traveled by boat down the Missouri River. When they arrived in Harlem, a community north of Kansas City, they stopped at the boarding house of Jesse's aunt, Mrs. John Mimms. There Jesse was further nursed by his cousin, Zerelda, who was named after Jesse's mother. Zee, as she was called by Jesse, cared for him until he gained enough strength to be moved to the family farm at Kearney. It was the beginning of a romance that would last for nine years before they were married.

In January of 1866, John and Bob Younger (ages 15 and 13) hitched up a wagon and drove their mother to Independence for supplies. John had just picked up a revolver from a gunsmith who had repaired the weapon for Cole. While loading the wagon for Bursheba, the boys were accosted by a former Union soldier named Gilcreas who made some derogatory remarks about the older brothers of John and Bob. John stepped to their defense, but was slugged by Gilcreas with a frozen wrapped fish which Bursheba had just purchased. John grasped the loaded revolver (the one he had picked up for Cole) and shot Gilcreas between the eyes. The shooting was considered self-defense and John was not charged.

Frank James approached Cole Younger to discuss an idea expressed by his brother Jesse. Jesse James believed that they could gain some measure of revenge by robbing banks that held Union dollars. Cole liked the idea because he was also, like Jesse, a wanted man who was unable to live a normal civilian life.

With the exception of a Confederate military operation, no bank had ever been robbed in broad daylight prior to February 13, 1866. On that date, the Clay County Savings Bank at Liberty, Missouri, was the target of 12 men dressed in blue Union Army coats. It is generally believed that the robbery was masterminded by Jesse James, but that he was still too weak to participate in the raid. The bandits who escaped with approximately $60,000 stuffed into grain sacks were predominately former guerillas, believed to be Cole Younger, Frank James, Donny and Bud Pence (cousins of the James brothers), Oliver and George Shepherd, and possibly Joab Perry, John Jarrette and James Wilkerson. A college student, George Wymore, who happened to be on the street following the robbery, was shot dead by the bandits as they galloped out of town.

Outlaws raided the bank of Alexander Mitchell and Company at Lexington, Missouri on October 30, 1866. Jesse was able to ride by then and probably participated in the holdup. The bandits were not able to get into the vault, and fled with the proceeds from the cash drawer which amounted to about $2,000. A posse pursued in a brief and futile attempt to catch the outlaws. It was led by Dave and John Pool, former Confederate guerillas who may have recognized Frank or Jesse and possibly led the posse astray.

Judge John McClain was shot down after refusing to open his vault during an attempted bank robbery at Savannah, Missouri, on March 2, 1867. Six bandits rode away empty handed. Two were assumed to be the James brothers. Judge McClain eventually recovered from his wounds.

Each of the robberies (or attempted robberies) basically followed the same pattern. Gang members would ride into town, usually in pairs from different directions. They would converge on their target. Usually, two or three from the group would enter the bank as if to conduct some business. After assessing the whereabouts of the employees, they would draw their revolvers in unison, announcing their holdup in such fashion that all would be alerted. The other gang members would remain outside at strategic locations where they could head off impending trouble.

On May 22, 1867, a dozen men rode toward the Hughes and Wasson Bank at Richmond, Missouri. Jesse and Frank James were joined by Cole Younger, Payne Jones, Thomas Little, Andy McGuire and others. The Richmond raid didn't unfold as smoothly as usual. While the bandits inside were stuffing their grain sacks, with over $4,000, the others who were waiting about the town square looked suspicious to local citizens. Several of them grabbed their guns and began shooting. The gang members quickly returned their fire. Frank Griffin, who crouched behind a tree near the courthouse, was shot through the head by one of the bandits. He died instantly. As Griffin's father ran toward his fallen son, he took two shots and was killed as well. Mayor John Shaw was dropped by another slug. Meanwhile the other gang members dashed from the bank, leaped onto their horses and spurred them out of town. Those who had remained outside were right on their heels.

During the ensuing months, the trail ended for several members of the James-Younger gang. Thomas Little was captured and jailed at Warrensburg, Missouri. While he awaited trial, an angry mob broke into the jailhouse and hanged him. Payne Jones and Dick Burns were assassinated. Andy McGuire and James Devers were arrested and sent to Richmond to stand trial. They received the same fate as Thomas Little. Incensed townspeople dragged the pair from jail and lynched them both.

With the heat on, the gang decided to move a little further away from home. Cole Younger and Bud Pence suggested that they venture to Kentucky. Younger had spent some time there during the Civil War. Bud's brother Donny was now sheriff of Nelson County and could possibly offer some help should the gang get into trouble. On March 21, 1868, Jesse and Frank James, Cole and Jim Younger, Oliver and George Shepherd, John Jarrette and Jim White looted the Southern Bank of Kentucky, at Russellville. They netted between $12,000 and 14,000 dollars. Nimrod Long, the bank's president, suffered a superficial head wound during the robbery.

A private detective, D. G. Bligh, was hired by Long to investigate the robbery. Bligh was able to obtain enough evidence to implicate Oliver and George Shepherd. The evidence was passed along to Jackson County, Missouri authorities, who dispatched lawmen to the Shepherd farm. There, deputies shot and killed Oliver Shepherd during an exchange of gunfire. George Shepherd was eventually arrested in Kentucky, stood trial, and served three years in prison for the robbery at Russellville. Still, no proof existed that would incriminate the James brothers or Younger brothers in any of the holdups to date.

Cole Younger traveled to Texas to visit family and friends. Among the friends was the family of John Shirley. Cole had met Myra Maybelle Shirley in 1864 while riding with Quantrill. Myra Maybelle, who would later be known as Belle Starr, was 16 years-old at the time. When Cole saw Belle in 1868 she was married to former guerilla Jim Reed. Belle later claimed that her daughter Pearl (born in 1869) was sired by Cole. Cole Younger vehemently denied the accusation throughout his lifetime. With Cole's mother Bursheba, and other members of his immediate family now living in Texas, Cole decided to remain there for a while. He became involved in the cattle business.

On December 7, 1869, two men entered the Daviess County Savings Bank at Gallatin, Missouri. As Captain John Sheets changed a $100 bill for Frank James, Jesse approached Sheets and shot him twice, in the chest and head. William McDowell, a clerk, was shot in the arm as he ran out of the bank shouting for help. With their grain sack full, the brothers rushed to their mounts. Jesse's horse was spooked, and he had to climb up behind Frank and ride double out of Gallatin. Before long they encountered a farmer named Daniel Smoot and stole his horse.

Supposedly, Jesse had recognized John Sheets as the man who had killed Bloody Bill Anderson during the war, and he was avenging the loss of his leader and friend. Identification of the spooked horse led straight to the Samuel farm. For the first time the James brothers had been a little careless. Governor Joseph McClurg offered a reward of $3,000 for the capture of Sheets' murderer. Eight days after the Gallatin robbery, Deputy Sheriff John Thomason, his son Oscar, and two other men surrounded the Samuel farmhouse. As they did so, Jesse and Frank spurred their mounts out of the barn nearby and galloped safely away.

Newspaperman, Major John Newman Edwards, an editor of the *Kansas City Times*, published a letter presumably written by Jesse James indicating his innocence in the Gallatin affair. It was the first of many letters written in Jesse's name to appear in the *Times*. The letters were possibly written by Edwards himself, who had met and befriended the brothers during the Civil War. Edwards, through these letters and his editorials, helped Jesse James emerge as a sort of folk-hero. Additionally, the people of Clay County were sympathetic toward the James brothers and helped protect them. Jesse and Frank James were probably as safe hiding out at the farm near Kearney as they would have been anywhere.

Bursheba Younger, whose health was failing, had been living in Dallas. She wanted to die in Missouri so she could be buried with Henry. Within days after the family returned to Jackson County they were again badgered by lawmen. John and Bob were pushed around and harassed. A rope was placed around John's neck and he was hoisted from the ground four times, but refused to give the authorities any information as to the whereabouts of Cole and Jim. The tormenting didn't help Bursheba's health. She died on June 6, 1870.

The next target for the James-Younger gang was the bank at Corydon, Iowa. Jesse and Frank James were accompanied by Cole Younger, Clell Miller (an old friend from Kearney), and Jim Younger, as they rode into town on June 3, 1871. The Ocobock Brothers' Bank was a pushover. Most of the townspeople were listening to a speech by Henry Clay Dean at the Methodist church and were unaware that the bank was being robbed. The bandits left with several thousand dollars in their sacks. Before leaving town, Jesse saw the opportunity to have a little fun. In his brassy way, he entered the church and interrupted Dean's speech to announce that the bank had been robbed. The crowd told him to hush so they could hear the speaker. By the time anyone investigated, the gang was long gone. Clell Miller was later arrested near his home in Kearney and returned to Iowa to stand trial. He was eventually released due to a lack of evidence.

Five members of the gang (probably Cole, Jim and Bob Younger, Jesse and Frank James) raided the Columbia Deposit Bank at Columbia, Kentucky, on April 29, 1872. The bandits cleaned out the cash drawer, but when cashier R. A. C. Martin refused to open the vault, they fatally shot him and departed. The gang had ridden a great distance, and murdered, for a meager take of a few hundred dollars.

Frank James declined to participate in the next robbery. It just didn't appeal to him. On September 26, 1872, Jesse James, Cole Younger and John Younger raided the front gate at the Kansas State Fair. In broad daylight, with thousands of people milling about, they boldly approached Ben Wallace at his ticket booth and seized the cash receipts from a tin box. The trio fired several shots as they galloped away. One hit a young girl in the leg. Their take was less than a thousand dollars, as most of the gate receipts had been deposited into a bank shortly before the robbery.

Cole's brothers went in separate directions for a while. Following the Columbia, Kentucky raid, Jim headed to Dallas to do some ranch work. Bob traveled to Louisiana where he worked temporarily at the port in New Orleans. After the Kansas State Fair heist, John Younger went to California where he remained through the spring of 1873.

The next objective for the gang was the Ste. Genevieve Savings Association at Ste. Genevieve, Missouri, on May 27, 1873. The four bandits who participated in this heist were probably Jesse and Frank James, Cole Younger and Clell Miller. Two gang members stuffed a grain sack with approximately $4,000 while the other two remained outside. After the outlaws had galloped out of town, one of them accidently dropped the grain sack. As he dismounted to pick it up, the clinking of coins spooked his horse and the animal darted away. At gunpoint, he flagged down a farmer who was riding past and ordered him to retrieve his horse. The farmer quickly brought back the runaway. The bandit mounted with the sack and spurred away to catch up with the rest of the gang.

Jim, Bob and John Younger reunited with Cole and the James brothers as the gang turned their attention to the railroads. On July 21, 1873, they struck the Chicago, Rock Island & Pacific Railroad near Council Bluffs, Iowa. The outlaws had heard that the train would be carrying a substantial shipment of gold. They selected a spot where the locomotive was forced to slow down for a sharp bend in the track. A rail that had been loosened by the bandits caused the locomotive to flip over on its side crushing the engineer, John Rafferty. The hooded robbers helped themselves to over $2,000 from the express car's safe and whatever cash and jewelry they were able to collect from the passengers. They had raided the wrong train. The shipment of gold had already passed through safely on a prior train. Following the Iowa train robbery, officials from several railroads gathered to face this new danger. They decided to enlist the services of the highly effective Pinkerton National Detective Agency. By robbing the railroads, the James-Younger gang had created for themselves a new nemesis.

Jesse James was the newsworthy leader of the gang. He was daring, humorous, and had much bravado. The news media seemed to put him on a pedestal. The exploits of the gang enhanced their growing legend as southern heroes. On January 15, 1874, during a stagecoach robbery near Malvern, Arkansas, Cole Younger returned one man's cash and pocket watch declaring that the gang never robbed Southerners, especially former Confederate soldiers. When the gang struck the Iron Mountain Railroad at Gad's Hill, Missouri, on January 31, 1874, they checked the palms of the passengers refusing to rob those whose hands were calloused from hard work. Before departing with over $12,000 in loot, the gang left a press release with the conductor that described the holdup that had just occurred. Such brazen and audacious acts were characteristic of Jesse James.

Pinkerton agents tracked the James brothers and the Younger brothers relentlessly. Jim and John Younger had been staying at the farm of Theodoric Snuffer in March of 1874 when two men strangely appeared asking directions. The Youngers, who were hiding, decided to follow the men when they left. A short distance down the road, the two inquisitive individuals were joined by a fellow named John Boyle whom the Youngers believed to be a Pinkerton agent. The brothers confronted the trio. Boyle quickly fled. After some discussion, a gunfight erupted. Jim Younger shot Edwin B. Daniel, an ex-deputy sheriff, through the neck. John Younger traded fatal shots with Pinkerton agent Louis J. Lull. John Younger and Edwin Daniel were dead. Louis Lull held on for about six weeks before he also succumbed from his wound. Jim Younger was unscathed.

The Pinkertons decided to plant one of their men as a worker on the Samuel farm. On March 10, 1874, John Wincher arrived at Liberty, Missouri, and set out on the road toward Kearney. Late that night, the ferry operator at Blue Mills was awakened by three men who had a bound and gagged prisoner. The ferryman transported them across the Missouri River to Jackson County. The following morning a body was discovered several miles from Blue Mills. The dead man, who had been shot in the chest and head, was identified as John Wincher.

Following a nine-year courtship, Zerelda (Zee) Mimms and Jesse James were married. The wedding ceremony which took place on April 24, 1874 near Kearney was performed by the Reverend William James, an uncle. While on his honeymoon in Texas, Jesse recruited some help and robbed a stagecoach near San Antonio. One of the passengers, Bishop Gregg, an Episcopalian, pleaded with the bandits to keep his watch that had been given to him by a friend. The bishop was advised that he shouldn't need a watch for his Master never owned one.

Jesse James and Cole Younger struck separate stagecoaches simultaneously on August 30, 1874, near the Missouri River. In December, the James-Younger gang robbed the Tishimingo Savings Bank in Corinth, Mississippi. They also looted an express car of the Kansas Pacific Railroad near Muncie, Kansas (now a part of Kansas City, Kansas). The raid netted the outlaws about $30,000.

The Pinkertons were persistent. An undercover agent named Jack Ladd obtained a job as a field hand at the farm of Daniel Askew, which was adjacent to the Samuel farm. It was a position from which he could watch who arrived at, or departed from, the Samuel home. After being tipped off by Ladd, Pinkerton men arrived at the Samuel place on the night of January 25, 1875, and crept toward the house. They hurled two flambeaus through the windows which Dr Samuel alertly scooped into the fireplace. The spheres exploded, spraying metal fragments across the room. Archie Samuel, a nine-year-old half-brother of Jesse and Frank was killed instantly. Zerelda Samuel's lower right arm was badly damaged and eventually had to be amputated. The Pinkerton agents fled the scene, but as they did one of the detectives dropped his pistol. It was later found with the initials P.G.G. clearly etched into the handle, which stood for Pinkerton's Government Guard, the name by which the agency was known during the Civil War. There was no doubt as to who was responsible for the casualties. If Jesse and Frank were at the farm, they escaped to safety. Newspapers across the state condemned the Pinkerton raid. The attack led to an outflow of sympathy for Jesse and Frank.

Following the incident at the Samuel farm, Jack Ladd disappeared; Daniel Askew was shot to death on his front porch, on April 12, 1875. Samuel Hardwicke, a Liberty lawyer through whom Ladd passed his information to the Pinkerton office at Kansas City, feared for his life and fled to Minnesota.

After laying low for about a year, during which time Frank married Annie Ralston and Zee gave birth to a boy, the first of two children, the James-Younger gang struck again. During the evening of July 7, 1876, they flagged down a Missouri Pacific Railroad train at Rocky Cut, near Otterville, Missouri. The gang consisted of Jesse and Frank James, Cole and Bob Younger, Clell Miller, Charlie Pitts (alias Sam Wells), Bill Stiles (whose real name was Bill Chadwell), and a new man, Hobbs Kerry. While the bandits cleaned out the contents of two safes, the passengers sang hymns to the leadership of a minister from New York. Following the robbery, the gang divided the loot which totaled about $17,000. Then, as always, they headed toward their respective homes.

After receiving a tip that Hobbs Kerry had been seen with an unexplainable sum of money, St. Louis police picked him up for questioning. Kerry, who had no criminal record, broke down under pressure and confessed. He described the robbery in detail and identified each of the bandits.

Zerelda Samuel, mother of the James boys, had to manage in later life without the use of her lower right arm, which was amputated following an injury during a Pinkerton raid on her farm. *Wild Horse Collection.*

On August 11, 1876, Pinkerton agents raided the home of Annie Ralston's parents believing that Frank James had been hiding there. Again, as in the past, they came up empty-handed. Disaster was soon to strike the James-Younger gang, however.

Bill Stiles was formerly a resident of Minnesota, and had convinced the others that the area would be easy pickings. Eight gang members set out into unfamiliar territory, far from their Missouri homes, and had to rely on Stiles' judgment with regard to the terrain and their destination. The group had originally decided to hit the bank at Mankato, but they were discouraged by a large group of people gathered in the street in front of the bank. They moved on toward Northfield, a sleepy little town about forty miles (64 kilometers) south of St. Paul. The First National Bank of Northfield seemed like the perfect target. Indications were that its bank vault might be bulging with an estimated $75,000 in grain money.

It was a dreary morning on September 7, 1876, as four of the gang members rode in to case the town. They had breakfast, and then returned to the others where final plans were laid out. That afternoon the group eased back into Northfield. Frank James, Charlie Pitts and Bob Younger rode directly across the square in the center of town and dismounted in front of the bank. They were to have waited at that position until Cole Younger and Clell Miller arrived from a different direction. As they spotted Younger and Miller coming down Division Street, the trio decided to enter the bank. Jesse James, Jim Younger and Bill Stiles remained near the bridge toward the opposite corner of the square.

Inside the bank, the trio drew their guns on the teller, A. E. Bunker; the assistant bookkeeper, F. J. Wilcox; and the head bookkeeper, Joseph L. Heywood, who was at the moment substituting for the absent cashier. Heywood advised the bandits that the vault had a time-lock and couldn't be opened. It was a ploy. The door was closed but the combination had not been spun. If the bandits would have turned the handle, the vault door would have opened.

Meanwhile, Miller walked back and forth outside the bank and aroused the suspicion of the hardware store proprietor, J. S. Allen. When Allen approached the bank he was ordered away by Miller. As Allen fled, he shouted a warning to the townspeople. Henry Wheeler, a medical student home on vacation, heard Allen and began hollering as well. Cole Younger fired a warning shot into the air which was a prearranged signal for Jesse and the others waiting near the bridge. They galloped toward the bank yelling at bystanders to get inside. A Swedish fellow named Nicholas Gustavson did not understand English and was shot down. He would die later. The citizens of Northfield were ready to fight. Another

Northfield, Minnesota, as it looked a few years before the attempted robbery by the James-Younger gang. Beyond the bridge lies the town square. The First National Bank (the building with arches) can be seen to the right of the square. *Wild Horse Collection.*

hardware store proprietor, A. R. Manning, fired his rifle at Charlie Pitts. The shot missed Pitts, but killed his horse. Manning then wounded Cole Younger with a slug in his thigh. He then spotted Stiles and squeezed off another shot. It struck Bill Stiles in the heart and he died instantly. Henry Wheeler had found a rifle which he carried upstairs to a second-floor window in the Dampier House, a hotel. Wheeler's first shot missed Jim Younger. His second struck Clell Miller. Miller dropped dead. Another shot from Wheeler's rifle hit Bob Younger in the right elbow as he dashed from the bank. A. E. Bunker had earlier fled from the bank taking a slug in the shoulder from the revolver of Charlie Pitts. Frank James was the last of the outlaws to exit from the bank. Before he did so, he shot Joseph Heywood in the head. Heywood slumped over, dead. Cole doubled back to pick up brother Bob, and the outlaws thundered out of town.

The telegraph operator at Northfield immediately wired other communities in the vicinity. Several posses were formed. Governor John Pillsbury offered a $1,000 reward for each of the bandits. The wounds suffered by the Youngers impeded the flight of the outlaws. In five days they traveled less than fifty miles (80 kilometers). Frustrated by their progress, Jesse decided that the group should split up. He reasoned that he and Frank could move rapidly and possibly draw the posse away from the others. Seven days after the attempted robbery, Frank and Jesse James headed toward South Dakota.

It wasn't long before the Youngers and Charlie Pitts were spotted near the Watonwan River several miles from Madelia. Posse members were able to trap the fugitives in a thicket alongside the river. Bob Younger had the worst wounds so he loaded while the others fired at the posse. Suddenly Charlie Pitts fell dead after taking a slug near his heart. The posse poured a barrage of lead at the Youngers. Jim was hit in the mouth. A slug destroyed Cole's gun, and another grazed his head. Bob staggered out of the woods attempting to surrender when he was shot again, this time in the chest. The posse was ordered to hold their fire. The Younger brothers surrendered.

It was fortunate for the Youngers that they were not hanged, for the people of Minnesota seemed to have no respect for the body of a dead outlaw. Charlie Pitts' body was sold to a doctor who bleached the bones and used the skeleton in his medical practice. Henry Wheeler, the medical student that killed Bill Stiles, was allowed to place his victim in a pickling box, and then transport it back to medical school for purposes of dissection. A promoter embalmed the body of Clell Miller, and then displayed it from town to town for all curious people willing to pay a fee. Miller's family was eventually able to retrieve his body with a court order.

Considering the course of events, the Youngers received excellent treatment. They were taken to a hotel in Madelia where their wounds were treated and where they were allowed to sleep. During subsequent interviews, Cole cleverly solicited compassion by telling of the murder of his father and the burning of the family homestead. According to a reporter for the Pioneer Press (of St. Paul), Cole stated: "We tried a desperate game and lost ... and we will abide by the consequences."

When they were well enough to travel, the Youngers were transported by rail to Faribault where they were jailed in separate cells. People flocked to Faribault from throughout the state in order to parade through the jailhouse and view the famed outlaws. Cole discussed the unfortunate circumstances of their lives with all who would listen. After spending a month in the Faribault jail, the Younger brothers finally appeared in court. Realizing that they would not be hanged, the trio pleaded guilty to the murders of J. L. Heywood and Nicholas Gustavson,

Cole Younger, shortly after his capture following the ill-fated raid at Northfield, Minnesota. *Minnesota Historical Society.*

to injuring A. E. Bunker, and to the attempted robbery of the First National Bank of Northfield. Each was sentenced to life imprisonment in the Minnesota State Penitentiary at Stillwater. The Youngers were model prisoners. Cole compared the discipline necessary in a prison environment to that of the discipline required in military service.

Following the disastrous raid at Northfield, Jesse and Frank James moved their families to Tennessee where they assumed new identities. Jesse and Zee became J. D. and Josie Howard, while Frank and Annie took the names of B. J. and Fannie Woodson. While residing on the outskirts of Nashville, Annie gave birth to a son. After losing twins, Zee presented Jesse with a daughter. The Howards and Woodsons farmed, attended church, and blended right in with the community. Frank (B. J. Woodson) seemed to enjoy a peaceful life of farming, but Jesse grew restless. It had been three years since the fiasco at Northfield.

During the night of October 8, 1879, Jesse and his new gang held up a train on the Chicago and Alton Railroad at Glendale, Missouri. Riding with Jesse were Wood Hite, Ed Miller (brother of Clell), Dick Liddil, Bill Ryan, and a fellow named Tucker Bassham, whom Ryan had brought along and vouched for. The group had neither the intelligence nor expertise of the old gang. The express car yielded an undetermined amount of cash–estimated at between five and ten thousand dollars–which as before was carted off in a grain sack. The robbery put Jesse James back on the front page of newspapers across the country.

Several months later, Tucker Bassham was arrested after he openly boasted of being a member of the James gang. Bassham confessed to his part in the heist, and was imprisoned. The following year, Bill Ryan joined Jesse on another job. Together, they held up a stagecoach at Mammoth Cave, Kentucky. Frank, who had declined to participate in the two previous jobs, was finally persuaded to join his brother. He rode with the gang as they robbed a government paymaster at Muscle Shoals, Alabama.

Loose talk also got Bill Ryan into trouble, and he was arrested as well. Bassham received a pardon for testifying against Ryan. It was believed that no member of Jesse James' gang could be convicted in Jackson County, Missouri. Times had changed, however, and the jury brought back a verdict of guilty against Bill Ryan for his part in the train robbery at Glendale. Following Ryan's arrest, Jesse moved his family back to Missouri.

Jesse, Frank, and their men struck again on July 15, 1881. That evening, gang members boarded the Chicago, Rock Island & Pacific train during its stops at both Cameron and Winston, Missouri. Shortly after the train departed from Winston, the bandits made their move. The engineer was forced to bring the train to a stop. The outlaws emptied the safe in the express car of nearly $10,000. The conductor, William Westfall, was shot to death by Jesse during the robbery. It is believed that Jesse knew him as the conductor who had brought the Pinkerton agents to Liberty, the night of the explosion at the Samuel house. A passenger, Frank McMillan, was also fatally injured during the shooting. Following the train robbery at Winston, the price on the heads of Jesse and Frank James was raised to $10,000 each.

Anticipating that a certain train on the Chicago and Alton Railroad would be carrying a rich purse of $100,000, the gang plotted its strategy. On September 7, 1881, Jesse and Frank James, accompanied by Dick Liddil, Wood and Clarence Hite, and Charles Ford, stopped the train with a large pile of rocks on the track at a place called Blue Cut. Jesse was furious when the safe yielded only a few thousand dollars. Either his information was wrong or they had stopped the wrong train. While fleecing the passengers of their cash, Jesse announced that the next time a reward was offered, he would burn the entire train.

The $10,000 reward on Jesse's head seemed to bother him more and more. He became suspicious of his own men. When Ed Miller advised Jesse that he wanted to call it quits, speculation is that Jesse took Miller into the country for a ride. It was Miller's last ride.

On November 5, 1881, Jesse moved his family from Kansas City to St Joseph, Missouri, into a house on a hill that commanded a long view in all directions. In St. Joseph, Jesse assumed the name of Thomas Howard.

Things continued to unravel for Jesse James. During a quarrel over Charles Ford's sister, Dick Liddil killed Wood Hite. Wood's brother, Clarence, was arrested in connection with the Winston robbery. He was tried, found guilty, and received a sentence of twenty-five years in prison. Meanwhile, Dick Liddil feared that Jesse would seek revenge for Wood Hite's death, and he turned himself in to the Clay County sheriff, offering testimony in turn for leniency.

Charles Ford had been hiding out at Jesse James' home in St. Joseph. Charles' younger brother Bob joined them to discuss a possible robbery of the Platte City, Nebraska bank. Following breakfast on April 3, 1882, the trio adjourned to the parlor to relax. With his gun belt lying on a daybed nearby, Jesse stepped on to a chair to straighten a picture that was hanging crooked. While Jesse's back was turned, Bob Ford drew his revolver. Jesse heard the click of Ford's hammer and turned his head, but it was too late. Ford's bullet crashed into Jesse's left temple, and the famed outlaw fell dead.

Later that year, Frank James surrendered to Missouri Governor Thomas T. Crittenden. While jailed at Independence, two of the charges against him were dropped. The following year he stood trial at Gallatin for the murder of Frank McMillan who was killed during the Winston robbery. The trial which was held before capacity crowds at the Gallatin Opera House was quite a spectacle. After eight days of ebb and flow, the jury acquitted Frank James. In April of 1884, Frank was tried in Huntsville, Alabama on robbery charges. Witnesses corroborated the defendant's testimony that he had been in Nashville, Tennessee at the time of the robbery. Once again, Frank was acquitted. Two days before Frank James was due to stand trial (on February 23, 1885) in Otterville, charges against him were dismissed after the main witness for the prosecution had died. With no further charges against him, Frank James became a free man for the first time in twenty years.

The Younger brothers had been led to believe that they might be eligible for parole after serving ten years of their sentence. The

Following his capture in 1876, Bob Younger spent thirteen years in the Minnesota State Penitentiary at Stillwater before dying from tuberculosis. *Minnesota Historical Society.*

possibility gave them hope. They worked diligently at their prison jobs. Cole worked in the library for several years, and then became a hospital trustee. Jim was a postal clerk before he assumed Cole's old position in the library. Bob worked binding medical books before he became an accounting clerk. There was a substantial lobbying effort, which included the support of many leading citizens and politicians in both Minnesota and Missouri, for the release of the Younger brothers. In 1889, lobbyists met with Governor William R. Merriam of Minnesota. After the Younger parole advocates made their speeches, the governor declared, "I cannot pardon these men. My duty to the state and my personal prejudice against them make it impossible."

Cole Younger would openly respond to any reporter's questions. He was often asked about the James brothers. He once stated, "Frank was a thinker, Jesse the doer." In speaking of Jesse, Cole indicated that "he could execute plans well and effectively." When discussing the gang, Cole reflected that they never rode very far after a robbery because they knew every nook and cranny in an area and it was always easy to outwit a posse. He also said that they never hid in caves and rarely used bedrolls, because that would be a giveaway that they slept outdoors. Cole further indicated that the gang nearly always slept and ate at the homes of farmers, usually giving the woman of the house a $5.00 gold piece as a token of thanks.

Bob Younger's health had been failing for some time. He was eventually moved from his cell to confinement in the prison hospital. On September 16, 1889, after serving thirteen years, Bob Younger died of consumption (tuberculosis).

After spending nearly twenty-five years in prison, Cole and Jim Younger received paroles. The terms of their parole was signed by Governor S. R. Van Sant on July 10, 1901. Cole and Jim left the confines of the Minnesota State Penitentiary a few days later, and entered the business world as tombstone salesmen for a granite company in Stillwater. They each received salaries of sixty dollars per month. The brothers looked forward to the day when they would have the parole
period behind them and could return home to Missouri.

During the next year both Cole and Jim worked several different jobs. They had trouble finding their niche. Jim became very despondent and committed suicide on Sunday, October 19, 1902, in his room at the Reardon Hotel, in St. Paul. Cole realized that Jim had not adjusted well since his release from prison. Following Jim's demise, Cole indicated

The farmhouse at Kearney, Missouri, served as a refuge for the James brothers through most of their outlaw years. *Wild Horse Collection.*

that Jim had been "acting queerly for months" and that he might have been "temporarily insane."

On February 4, 1903, the Board of Pardons granted Cole Younger a conditional pardon which would allow him to return to his home state of Missouri. A large crowd and much fanfare greeted Cole as he stepped off the train at Lee's Summit. During the ensuing months, Cole finished writing his book, *Cole Younger, By Himself,* an interesting, but rather unauthentic compilation of war stories. Cole Younger and old friend Frank James discussed the possibility of going into business together. In a way they did. Although they had no financial interest in the project, Cole and Frank joined a wild west show and allowed their names to be used as headliners. They traveled with *The James-Younger Wild West Show* as salaried employees for several months.

Frank James died at the family farm at Kearney, Missouri, on February 18, 1915. One year and three days later, on February 21, 1916, Cole Younger passed away at Lee's Summit, Missouri.

The exploits of Jesse and Frank James, Cole, Jim and Bob Younger, and their associates, collectively known as the James-Younger gang have been glorified and glamorized over the years. They have been portrayed as persecuted Confederate veterans who were driven to the outlaw way of life. In some accounts, Jesse has mythically emerged as a hero who robbed from the rich to give to the poor. There is little truth in such foolishness. Such stories were propagandized by the press, and also by the James brothers themselves and their mother Zerelda, somewhat as self-justification for their deeds, or misdeeds. Through their exploits, for whatever reason, the James brothers and the Younger brothers became legendary in their own lifetime. Today, the legend continues.

For over a century some question had existed as to whether or not the body buried at Mount Olivet Cemetery (near Kearney, Missouri) was really Jesse James. On July 17, 1995, the body was exhumed for investigation. Professor James Starrs, a forensic scientist at George Washington University, led the project to resolve the longstanding doubts regarding the authenticity of the outlaw's body. DNA analysis on both his remains and blood samples of direct descendants has virtually confirmed that the man who had been shot to death on April 3, 1882, was indeed Jesse James.

John Henry "Doc" Holliday, the gunfighting and gambling dentist. *Denver Public Library, Western History Department.*

Chapter Two
Doc Holliday and the Earp Brothers

When speaking of Doc Holliday, Bat Masterson once said that he "had a mean disposition and an ungovernable temper, was hot-headed and impetuous and much given to both drinking and quarreling. He was very much disliked, and under the influence of liquor was a most dangerous man." Doc was especially dangerous after he realized that he was dying from consumption (later to be known as tuberculosis). He became fearless. Once he knew that his days were numbered, he really didn't care whether or not his misery might be ended by another gunfighter. Masterson also indicated that, "Doc Holliday was afraid of nothing on earth." Wyatt Earp stated that Doc was "the nerviest, fastest, deadliest man with a six-gun I ever saw."

John Henry "Doc" Holliday was born in Griffin, Georgia on October 14, 1851. Doc was from an affluent family. His father was an officer in the Confederate Army, and later became a lawyer. John Henry had a formal education, and officially became "Doc" when he received his Doctor of Dental Surgery degree (DDS) in 1872. In 1873, Holliday was diagnosed as having consumption. The prognosis was that he probably had only a few months to live. With the assumption that a dry climate might prolong his life, Doc headed west.

When he arrived in Dallas, Texas, Doc hung out his shingle and began to practice dentistry. He also took up another profession—gambling—and began drinking heavily. Doc's dental practice floundered, possibly because of his coughing spells and drinking habit. For whatever reason, he gambled more. He dealt faro and played poker.

On New Years Day of 1875, Holliday was involved in a harmless shoot-out at a local saloon. He, and a bar owner named Charles W. Austin, traded several shots without either man drawing blood. It is possible that too much celebrating might have clouded their vision. Following the incident, Holliday was encouraged to leave town, which he did.

Doc Holliday found another stopping point about 150 miles (240 kilometers) further west at Ft. Griffin, Texas. There he obtained a job running a faro table at a saloon and brothel. Two weeks later he was indicted, along with several other employees, following a raid on the establishment. Holliday left Ft. Griffin, but he would return a couple of years later. In 1876, in nearby Jacksboro, Doc Holliday killed a soldier of the Sixth Cavalry. Suddenly the U.S. Army was after him. Doc cut a trail to Colorado.

Using the alias of Tom Mackey, Doc began dealing faro in Denver, at a place called the Babbit House. A story is told about an encounter between Holliday and a fellow named Bud Ryan. Following heated words, Ryan attempted to draw his revolver but was too late. Doc was quicker. He unsheathed his knife and severely wounded Ryan.

Holliday wasted no time putting Denver behind him and headed to the gold fields of Deadwood. It is believed that Holliday first met Wyatt Earp while in Dakota Territory. Doc and Wyatt would remain friends until Holliday's death.

By early 1878, Doc Holliday was back in Ft. Griffin. Sometime during that year he met "Big-nose Kate." Kate was born Mary Katherine Haroney on November 7, 1850, in Budapest, Hungary. She was one of nine children sired by her father, Dr. Michael Haroney. Mary Katherine became a foster child in Iowa following the deaths of her parents in 1866. The following year she fled from her foster home. Kate had a child, fathered by Silas Melvin, whom she may or may not have married. The child became ill and died in infancy. Kate, variously using the last name of Fisher or Elder, became a prostitute, moving from one frontier community to another. Doc and Kate both worked at John Shanssey's saloon in Ft. Griffin. They were very close romantically. Although she didn't give up her profession, Kate became Doc's mistress. They were virtually inseparable for several years.

According to legend, Kate saved Doc's neck in early May of 1878. While at his poker table one day in Ft. Griffin, Doc was involved in a dispute with Ed Bailey. After warning Bailey not to turn over the discards, the obviously irritated Holliday raked in a pot without showing his cards. Bailey reached for his revolver, but Doc's knife was much faster. Bailey dropped to the floor, dead. Doc was convinced that he had killed Bailey in self-defense, but the town was not. There was no jail in Ft. Griffin, so Holliday was "jailed" at the hotel, where he was kept under guard. Meanwhile, Bailey's friends began to incite a lynch mob, and things did not look good for Doc. "Big-nose" Kate set fire to a shed that was attached to the rear of the hotel. As citizens of Ft. Griffin scrambled to set up a water brigade, Kate ordered Doc's guard, at gunpoint, to release his prisoner. The guard obliged, and Kate and Doc fled the scene. The degree of truth in the Ft. Griffin story is a matter for speculation.

Upon their arrival in Dodge City, Kansas, Doc ran an advertisement in the *Dodge City Times* (on June 8, 1878) announcing the availability of his dental services: "DENTISTRY. J. H. Holliday, Dentist, very respectfully offers his professional services to the citizens of Dodge City and surrounding country during the summer. Office at Room No. 24, Dodge House. Where satisfaction is not given money will be refunded." When Doc and Kate registered at the Dodge House, which was owned by George B. "Deacon" Cox, they did so as Mr. and Mrs. J. H. Holliday. No evidence has ever been uncovered to indicate that they were legally married.

Dodge City was a bustling cow town. Its saloons were crowded with Texas drovers. The success (or lack thereof) of Doc's dental practice is uncertain. Regardless, Dodge City was perfect for Doc and Kate. He was clever with a deck of cards, and she had plenty of customers for her usual trade.

According to legend, Doc Holliday bailed Wyatt Earp out of a serious predicament in Dodge City. Wyatt faced the drawn revolvers of two Texans who taunted him to draw while several of their cohorts looked on. Wyatt knew that to draw would be suicide. Doc arrived on the scene with his famed sawed-off shotgun. It could have blown a couple of Texans into oblivion. The Texans backed down, and Wyatt Earp was forever grateful to Doc Holliday.

Doc Holliday's 21-inch pacifier was a Belgian made double-barrel shotgun. The barrels were cut to a mere 12 inches in length. A five-foot leather shoulder strap could be threaded through a brass ring affixed to the barrel rib permitting the weapon to be slung from the shoulder and easily hidden beneath a duster. The lock plate carried the stamp "Meteor Belgium." The weapon, which was sometimes called a "whipit," held two 10-guage loads. Probably because the weapon was so terrifying, history records no incidents of anybody being shot with it.

Doc and Kate had a bumpy relationship. While they obviously loved each other, they were heavy drinkers and fought like cats. Occasionally they would separate. Usually they were back together again before anyone noticed. They moved with regularity from one boomtown to another—normally when Doc was in some kind of hot water.

Kate and Doc arrived at Trinidad, Colorado, in early 1879. Their stay was abbreviated when Doc pumped two slugs into a gambler who called himself Kid Colton.

Shortly thereafter, the couple traveled to Las Vegas, New Mexico. Doc set up a gaming table in a saloon on Centre Street in East Las Vegas. One of the saloon girls was the mistress of a former army scout named Mike Gordon. At dusk on July 19, 1879, Gordon demanded that his girlfriend quit her job. When she refused, he stood in the street and poured lead at the front of the building. An "unidentified" man stepped through the saloon door, and shot down Mike Gordon. The former army scout died the following morning. Some historians believe that Doc Holliday was the shooter, but there seems to be no proof to substantiate the claim. On the following day, Doc and a new partner, Jordan J. Webb, contracted with a carpenter for the construction of a one-story saloon at the cost of $372.50.

For the second time since his arrival in Las Vegas, New Mexico, Holliday was indicted for keeping a gaming table. On August 12, 1879, he posted bail in the amount of $200. On the following day, Doc was charged with carrying a deadly weapon for which he was required to post bail in the amount of $100.

Doc Holliday and Wyatt Earp had become close friends. When Wyatt arrived in Las Vegas in mid-October of 1879, he told Doc about the new silver camp at Tombstone, Arizona. Doc always liked the activity in a thriving boomtown, so it didn't take much persuasion on the part of

Doc Holliday and the Earp Brothers

Wyatt to convince Doc that Arizona Territory was the place to be.

In November, Doc and Kate, Wyatt and Mattie Earp, and the James Earp family arrived at the home of Virgil and Allie Earp in Prescott, Arizona. While in Prescott, Doc found a faro game to his liking and decided to remain in town when the clan headed on to Tombstone.

After winning a tidy sum in Prescott, Doc chose to tend to some unfinished business in Las Vegas before reuniting with the Earps. He still had two unsettled charges pending in the district court, as well as an outstanding debt to W. G. Ward, the carpenter that constructed Doc's saloon. After receiving full payment from Holliday, Ward recorded a satisfaction of the lien he held on the property. The old charges against Doc Holliday were dropped, and he was refunded the bail money ($300) that he had previously posted for both cases.

With his debts settled, Holliday walked into a saloon on the town plaza. There he ran into Charlie White, a bartender with whom he had an altercation two years earlier in Dodge City. When White saw Holliday he started shooting. Doc drew and fired a slug that knocked White to the floor. Charlie White, whose wound was superficial, left town immediately.

When Doc returned to Prescott, his turbulent romance with Kate Elder took a turn for the worse. They agreed that a separation would be appropriate, and Kate left for Globe, Arizona. Holliday moved in with

Steely-nerved Wyatt Earp boasted his way to fame. Compared to many, he wasn't much of a gunfighter. *Denver Public Library, Western History Department.*

John J. Gosper and Richard E. Elliot. Gosper was secretary of state for the Arizona Territory, and Elliot was a mine owner. Doc settled back in at the faro tables and he began to prosper once again.

Doc Holliday traveled to Tombstone in September of 1880. The Earp brothers had been there for nine months and were established in their new jobs. Wyatt was working as an express messenger, or shotgun, for Wells Fargo. Virgil was a Deputy U. S. Marshal. The lavish Oriental Saloon of Milt E. Joyce became a regular hangout for Holliday and the Earps. Wyatt had purchased a 25 percent interest in the Oriental's gaming concession.

On October 11, 1880, a fellow named Johnny Tyler attempted to stir up trouble at the Oriental. When Tyler and Holliday squared off they were both immediately disarmed by Milt Joyce and others. Joyce confiscated their firearms. Doc exited the saloon, and then returned a few minutes later brandishing another pistol. Joyce struck Holliday with a gun barrel, and then wrestled him to the floor. During the tussle several shots were fired. Milt Joyce received a slug through his left hand, while one of his partners, William C. Parker, was shot in the left foot. Milt Joyce filed charges against Holliday for assault with intent to kill. When Joyce was unable to appear in court due to the severity of his wound, the charges against Doc were reduced to assault and battery. Holliday paid a fine of $20 plus court costs.

On March 15, 1881, one of J. D. Kinnear's stagecoaches was held up near Drew's Station, in the vicinity of Contention City. During the robbery attempt, Eli "Bud" Philpot, a Kinnear employee, and passenger Peter Roerig were killed. When Luther King later confessed that he had held the horses during the holdup, he named as one of his accomplices, Billy Leonard, a friend of Doc Holliday. King also named Jim Crane and Harry "The Kid" Head as participants. Strangely, King was allowed to walk out the back door of Sheriff John Behan's office and "escape" to freedom. A rumor (supposedly instigated by Tom and Frank McLaury) quickly circulated that Doc Holliday was involved in the holdup. The fabrication may have been a ploy to divert suspicion from Ike Clanton, Frank Stillwell and Pete "Spence" Spencer, friends of the McLaurys.

Sheriff Behan was a close personal friend of Milt Joyce, who had grown to hate Doc Holliday. Behan had an increasing dislike for Wyatt Earp, Doc's best friend. Behan was infatuated with pretty Josephine Marcus, who in turn had eyes for Wyatt Earp. Antagonism grew. Again, on April 13, 1881, Milt Joyce filed charges against Doc Holliday.

Evidently Joyce had called Holliday a stage robber, and Doc responded with a fight and threats against Joyce's life. This time Doc paid court costs and the charges were dismissed.

In May, Doc Holliday was indicted in connection with the Kinnear stagecoach holdup. After several continuances the case was dropped.

Kate Elder traveled from Globe to Tombstone in order to celebrate the Fourth of July with Doc. As was the case so often in the past, Doc and Kate had a spat. Kate walked out on Doc and proceeded to go on a drinking spree. With the encouragement of Milt Joyce and John Behan, she became very intoxicated. Before the night was over, Behan had persuaded Kate Elder to sign an affidavit stating that Doc had told her he had committed the two murders at Drew's Station. The following day, Sheriff Behan arrested Doc Holliday for murder. Once Kate had sobered up she realized her stupidity and withdrew her statement. For lack of evidence against Holliday, the murder charges were dismissed.

Billy Leonard, who had been Doc's friend in Las Vegas, New Mexico, and Harry "The Kid" Head were killed during a June gunfight in New Mexico. With Head and Leonard dead, and Luther King having disappeared, it became more important to catch Jim Crane. The Earps believed that a confession from Crane might free Doc Holliday from the allegations against him.

Indications are that Wyatt, Morgan and Warren Earp, along with Doc Holliday, were part of a posse that attacked Jim Crane and six other cowboys in, or near, Guadalupe Canyon which is close to the Mexican border. A bloody gunfight left five of the cowboys dead. Those who were killed were Jim Crane, Newman Haynes "Old Man" Clanton (Ike's father), Charles "Bud" Snow, Dixie Gray and William Lang. Billy Byers was wounded, and Harry Ernshaw escaped. It is believed that both Doc Holliday and Warren Earp suffered leg injuries during the shoot-out.

Many factors led to the animosity between the Clanton faction and Holliday and the Earps. It has been suggested that earlier Wyatt and the Clantons were cohorts in some cattle rustling escapades, and that their dislike for each other originated then. There seems to be no proof to substantiate this theory, but it is a possibility. Before his Tombstone days, Wyatt Earp was in and out of trouble. He was arrested for horse stealing, arrested for fighting, reprimanded for neglecting to turn in fines he had collected from prostitutes while a policeman in Wichita, and was run out of Las Vegas, New Mexico, for attempting to work a swindle with "Mysterious" Dave Mather.

Mrs. Virgil Earp indicated that the Earp family was outraged following a late-night rendezvous between James Earp's sixteen-year-old stepdaughter, Hattie Earp, and one of the McLaury brothers. It has also been suggested that some of the animosity might be traced back to an old gambling quarrel.

Doc and Kate resolved some of their problems, and then attended a fiesta together in Tucson. While sitting at a faro table one evening, Doc was approached by Morgan Earp who had been looking for him. Morgan advised Doc that trouble was brewing in Tombstone, and that the Earps sure could use his help. Kate and Doc accompanied Morgan back to Tombstone the following day. It was Tuesday, October 25, 1881. After checking in at the boardinghouse of Camillus S. Fly, Doc left Kate and headed to the Alhambra Saloon for a little faro and refreshment. Later that night, he went to A. D. Walsh's Can Can Lunch and Eating Counter in order to dine. At Walsh's place, which was located inside the Alhambra, Doc spied Ike Clanton. The two entered into a heated quarrel. Marshal Virgil Earp arrived and quickly ended the dispute. Doc returned to his boardinghouse. Ike Clanton and Tom McLaury had arrived at Tombstone earlier in the day in a wagon to pick up supplies. Ike found a late-night poker game and played cards and drank until after dawn. Without sleep, and quite intoxicated, Ike Clanton strutted about town boasting of his intention to kill Doc Holliday.

At approximately 11 a.m., October 26, 1881, Virgil Earp encountered Ike Clanton walking down Fourth Street with a Winchester rifle, and a revolver. Earp arrested Clanton for carrying firearms. Ike paid a fine and was released.

Shortly thereafter, Wyatt Earp approached Tom McLaury, who had been a participant in the poker game with Ike Clanton until daybreak. When Earp taunted McLaury and he refused to fight, Wyatt struck the cowboy's face with the barrel of his revolver.

Before noon, Billy Clanton and Frank McLaury rode into town. When Frank McLaury left his mount on the boardwalk and entered a store, Wyatt grabbed the horse by the bit. Frank emerged from the store and the two had angry words. Earp demanded that McLaury keep the animal off the sidewalk because it was a violation of a city ordinance.

As matters began to boil, Sheriff John Behan approached the Earps in a futile attempt to get them to lay down their arms.

With his guns back in his possession, Ike Clanton arrived at C. S. Fly's boardinghouse at about 1:30 p.m. looking for Holliday. Mollie

Fly intercepted Clanton and turned him away. Mollie alerted Kate that Ike was looking for Doc. Doc Holliday dressed, exited the building, and then walked through the block to the corner of Fourth and Allen Streets where he met Virgil, Wyatt and Morgan Earp. Doc was deputized by Virgil. The four men walked down Fourth Street, and then up Fremont Street toward Fly's place where they knew Ike Clanton was waiting.

Ike Clanton, Billy Clanton, Billy Claiborne, Frank McLaury and Tom McLaury were gathered in a narrow vacant lot between to C. S. Fly's Gallery (a photography studio) and the Harwood House (behind the O. K. Corral). They obviously were not expecting an all-out fight. Tom McLaury had checked his gun and gun belt with saloonkeeper Andy Mehan, and was unarmed. There were reports that Ike Clanton was also unarmed, although that seems unlikely. Billy Claiborne had just arrived at the vacant lot. When he saw Holliday and the Earps round the corner, he fled. Ike Clanton also scampered to safety. Doc Holliday was carrying a shotgun that had been handed to him by Virgil Earp. He also carried a revolver in his belt. All of the participants, with the exception of Tom McLaury, were armed.

The shooting commenced. A slug from Morgan's revolver hit Billy Clanton's right wrist. Wyatt shot Frank McLaury in the stomach. Tom McLaury had been standing behind his horse which shied when the first shots were fired exposing McLaury to a shotgun blast from Doc Holliday. Shooting with his left hand, Billy Clanton put a slug into the leg of Virgil Earp. Although badly wounded, Frank McLaury continued to fire. One of his shots nicked Doc Holliday in the hip. Holliday tossed his shotgun away and drew his pistol. Either he or Morgan Earp shot Frank McLaury through the neck. Morgan Earp was wounded in the shoulder by another slug from the gun of Billy Clanton. Clanton was then dropped by the gunfire of either Wyatt or Morgan. Billy Clanton and the McLaury brothers were dead. Doc Holliday, Virgil Earp and Morgan Earp were wounded.

History records the gunfight at the O. K. Corral as one of the most famous in Old West history. Although Holliday and the Earps entered the conflict (with badges) on the "side of the law," there will always be debate as to whether or not they were justified in their actions.

On November 29, 1881, Justice Wells Spicer ruled that the Earps and Holliday were discharging their official duty and therefore could not be convicted of any crime. Ike Clanton and his friends were enraged at Spicer's decision. Death threats against Holliday and the Earps were widespread. For safety purposes, Doc sent Kate back to Globe. Holliday and the Earps moved into Billicke's Cosmopolitan Hotel, a building that would offer them more security.

On the evening of December 28, 1881, at approximately 11:30 p.m., Virgil Earp exited the Oriental Saloon, and was struck with a shotgun blast as he crossed Fifth Street. Buckshot pierced his back and left arm. He was carried to nearby hotel where a doctor went to work on him. His arm was saved, but the wound left him permanently disabled.

On Saturday night, March 18, 1882, Morgan and Wyatt Earp were enjoying a game of pool at Campbell and Hatch's Billiard Parlor on Allen Street when shots rang out from the rear door. One slug passed through Morgan's stomach and shattered his spinal column. With Wyatt, Virgil, Warren, James, and the Earp women at his side, Morgan Earp died within the hour.

The following day, Marietta Spencer stated that she believed her husband, Pete, and Frank Stillwell (with the assistance of others) had killed Morgan Earp.

Following Morgan Earp's death, it was agreed that Virgil and his wife should leave Tombstone, because he would be easy prey for another attack. On March 20, 1882, Wyatt and Warren Earp, Doc Holliday, Sherman McMasters and "Turkey Creek" Jack Johnson were at the Tucson railroad depot with Mr. and Mrs. Virgil Earp and Morgan Earp's casket, when Frank Stilwell was spotted. Wyatt and Warren Earp, Holliday, McMasters and Johnson all gave chase. Frank Stilwell was gunned down at close range alongside the railroad tracks. He had a bad powder burn on one hand as if he had grabbed the barrel of a shotgun.

After returning to Tombstone, the Earp party set out in search of other members of the Clanton bunch. Late morning, on March 22, 1882, they rode to Pete Spencer's place. They were unaware that "Spence" was sitting in the Tombstone jail along with Indian Charley, a gambler named Freis, and other suspects in the death of Morgan Earp. At Spencer's place the group found Florentino Cruz, another suspect. Cruz was assassinated in much the same way that Stilwell had been.

There wasn't much sentiment in Tombstone for the actions of Doc and the Earps. Sheriff John Behan deputized a large posse which included the likes of Johnny Ringo and Ike Clanton to pursue the killers of Stilwell and Cruz.

With the heat on, Doc, Wyatt, Warren and the others made their way to Trinidad, Colorado, where they spent a few days with old friend

City Marshal Bat Masterson. At this point the group decided to split up in case they were being tailed. Wyatt and Warren went to Gunnison, and Doc headed to Pueblo and then on to Denver.

While in Denver, Doc Holliday was "arrested" by a bounty hunter, Perry Mallen, who was posing as a sheriff from Los Angeles. It marked the beginning of a legal (or not so legal) entanglement for Holliday. Through some clever manipulating, Bat Masterson was able to help Doc out of his jam. Also, because of Masterson's assistance, the courts in Colorado had a much higher opinion of Holliday than did those in Arizona.

Doc pushed on to Leadville in July of 1882. Silver mining had already peaked and the economy was beginning to decline. Doc Holliday's health worsened. After several bouts with pneumonia, Doc's tubercular coughing fits became more prevalent and he lost a considerable amount of weight. Holliday's dependence on alcohol increased. The more he drank the less effective he was at the faro tables.

While working in Leadville, Doc was determined not to violate the city ordinance that prohibited the carrying of firearms. One evening in July of 1884, while dealing faro at Hyman's Saloon, Doc was called upon to draw by Johnny Tyler and several of his cohorts. Tyler was the troublemaker that caused the fight between Holliday and Milt Joyce at the Oriental Saloon in Tombstone nearly four years earlier. When Doc advised Tyler that he had no gun, they harassed and insulted him.

Doc Holliday had borrowed five dollars from Billy Allen, a part-time policeman who had been a friend of Ike Clanton in Tombstone. Allen may have made the loan knowing that Doc might have trouble repaying it. Doc was not doing well and had little money. When the debt became due, Doc tried to buy more time. Allen issued an ultimatum to Doc that the debt must be paid by noon Tuesday, or else. Doc had really been down on his luck and when noon on Tuesday arrived he didn't have the money to pay Billy Allen. Doc heard that Allen was armed, and that he would be coming to Hyman's to pay Doc a visit. To avoid being arrested for carrying a gun, Doc had his revolver hidden beneath the bar. He then took a position from which he could quickly reach his weapon. When Billy Allen entered the saloon, his hand was in his pocket. Under the assumption that Allen had a pistol concealed, Doc grasped his revolver and fired—twice. The first slug hit Allen in the arm, and the second missed altogether. The bartender grabbed Doc and his weapon. Holliday was arrested and jailed. He was released on bail when friends posted his bond. Doc was in and out of court for seven months before the case was resolved by a verdict of "not guilty."

Historians have questioned Doc's motive for borrowing the five dollars from Billy Allen. Some assume that if Doc really needed it he could have borrowed the five dollars from a friend, without being confronted with a deadline for repayment. The theory has merit. It is very possible that he simply wanted a confrontation with Billy Allen and that the loan would be a good way to precipitate some trouble. Furthermore, if he had really wanted to repay the loan he could have borrowed the money from one of the friends who later posted his bond.

Doc's tuberculosis continued to worsen. He believed that hot sulfur springs might help curtail the progression of his illness. Doc traveled to Glenwood Springs, Colorado, in May of 1887. He had sent for Kate Elder who arrived shortly thereafter. The couple established residence at the Hotel Glenwood. Kate depleted her monetary savings in order to pay expenses when Doc became incapable of working. She remained with Doc through his final days. After being bedridden for two months, John Henry Holliday died on November 8, 1887. A tombstone in Linwood Cemetery reads, "DOC HOLLIDAY, 1852-1887, HE DIED IN BED."

After deserting Mattie in 1882, Wyatt married Josephine Marcus in San Francisco. Wyatt called her "Josie." Mattie became a prostitute and eventually committed suicide in 1888. Josie and Wyatt traveled from mining camp to mining camp as saloon owners or prospectors. Wyatt Berry Stapp Earp died in Los Angeles, California, on January 13, 1929, at the age of eighty.

Bodies of Dalton gang members are propped against the wall of John J. Kloehr's livery stable following the Coffeyville raid. From left to right are Bill Powers (alias Tim Evans), Bob Dalton, Grat Dalton, and Dick Broadwell. *Archives & Manuscripts Division of the Oklahoma Historical Society.*

Chapter Three
Coffeyville: Last Raid of the Dalton Gang

At different times in the past, the Dalton brothers had discussed the possibility of doing one last job and then calling it quits. This time they were serious. The heat was on the Dalton gang, especially from the railroad. Train robberies were becoming too dangerous. Bob Dalton discussed his plans as his brothers Emmett and Grat listened intently. It was Bob's idea to rob two banks simultaneously—something that had never been done before. Coffeyville, Kansas, was their target. They knew Coffeyville well, for they had previously lived there. It would be "easy" Bob indicated, as he outlined their agenda. They agreed that it would be their last robbery. They would leave Coffeyville with the loot and ride to the Osage Hills, where they were certain they could elude any posse that might follow them. From there they would head to the Cherokee Strip where their black friend, Amos Burton, would be waiting with a covered wagon full of provisions and ammunition. They would change into overalls in order to look like farmers, tie their horses to the rear of the wagon, and cover the money, saddles and guns inside. From there they would head northwest to Seattle, where they would board separate boats for South America. The plan was set. They were sure it would work. Actually, they were right about one thing. It would be their last job.

Five men headed toward Coffeyville. As they passed near Kingfisher, Oklahoma, the Dalton brothers considered stopping there to see their mother. But they only thought about it and rode on. Bob, Emmett and Grat Dalton, Bill Powers and Dick Broadwell made camp several miles south of Coffeyville on California Creek. While in camp, Bob Dalton went over every detail again and again to make sure there would be no mistakes. The night before the raid, the group rode in along Onion Creek to a point just over a mile from Coffeyville where they rested until morning.

The Dalton gang's targets were Coffeyville's two banks. The C. M. Condon & Company Bank occupied a triangular tract of land on the north side of the Plaza, an open area in the center of town. Directly east of the Condon & Company, across Union Street, was the front entrance of the First National Bank. It was situated in the middle of a block of stores that ran between Eighth Street and Ninth Street.

Previously, at one of the Coffeyville town meetings, the citizens had decided that should ever an emergency arise that threatened the townspeople or their property, that firearms would be made immediately available at the town's two hardware stores. The Isham Brothers' Hardware was adjacent to, and on the south side of the First National Bank. The other hardware store, A. P. Boswell & Company, was situated across the Plaza.

On the morning of October 5, 1892, the Dalton gang rode into Coffeyville from the west side. They traveled east on Maple until they reached Eighth Street. They had planned to hitch their horses at the corner of Eighth and Walnut Streets, but a crew of laborers was working on Eighth Street and it was badly torn up. Making a quick change of plans, they rode into the alley that paralleled Eighth and Ninth Streets and ran west from the north side of the Plaza. It was a fateful mistake because the alley was in plain view from the entrance to Isham Brothers' hardware.

Bob and Emmett Dalton walked east from the alley, passed in front of the Condon Bank and crossed Union Street toward the First National Bank. Grat Dalton, Bill Powers and Dick Broadwell were not far behind. When the trio reached the Condon Bank, they entered. All five had revolvers in their holsters and were carrying Winchester rifles. Bob and Emmett had hardly entered the First National Bank before townsmen began running toward the hardware stores.

At the Condon Bank, Grat ordered Charles T. Carpenter, the vice-president, and Charles M. Ball, a cashier, to open the safe and fill their grain sack. Ball advised the outlaws that the safe had a time lock and couldn't be opened until 9:45. Grat responded by telling Ball that it was 9:42, and that they could wait three minutes. While Ball was stalling, people were scurrying in all directions outside, yelling "the Daltons are here." Over at the First National Bank, Bob and Emmett were having a little more success. While Emmett covered the employees and customers, Bob went behind the counter and ordered cashier Tom Ayers to fill his sack. When Ayers began dumping silver coins from the drawers, Bob Dalton told him "just the paper money!" With a sack containing $23,000 dollars, Bob and Emmett exited through the banks back door. As they stepped into the alley, they were confronted by a man named Lucius Baldwin who was waving a six-gun. Bob fired his Winchester, hitting Baldwin in the chest. It was a fatal wound. The brothers turned up the alley to Eighth Street and then ran west. As they crossed Union Street they spotted George Cubine and Charles Brown standing in the doorway to Rammel's drugstore. Seeing that Cubine had a rifle, Bob fired one shot that dropped Cubine where he stood. He was dead. Brown reached

Shattered glass at the C.M. Condon & Company Bank in Coffeyville, Kansas, following the Daltons' raid. *Kansas State Historical Society.*

for Cubine's rifle. Bob Dalton shot again and killed Brown instantly. As the two ran down Eighth Street, Bob told Emmett, "Go slow; I can whip the whole damned town!"

When Bob and Emmett arrived at the alley where their horses were hitched, they realized that the others were still in the Condon Bank. They started back up the alley to help their cohorts when the trio emerged from the bank with a sack that contained only $1,500 dollars. The five outlaws received a barrage of gunfire from the Isham Brothers' hardware store. The gang returned their fire. Cashier Tom Ayers, now at the hardware store, was wounded in the left cheek by a bullet from this exchange. Grat Dalton and Bill Powers were also wounded but continued to run.

Meanwhile, Coffeyville's city marshal, Charles T. Connelly had cut through a vacant lot from Ninth Street and arrived at the alley. As he did so, he looked west and failed to see Grat Dalton in the opposite direction. Grat dropped the marshal with a fatal shot.

Bullets continued to fly from the hardware store into the alley. Bob Dalton spied a gunman in a store window and turned to fire a shot. In doing so, he stepped out into the alley too far, and caught a rifle slug that sent him reeling. While on the ground, Bob spotted livery stable owner John J. Kloehr behind a fence. Bob fired at Kloehr, but missed. Somehow Bob Dalton was able to get to his feet, but as he started to stagger along a wall Kloehr dropped him with a slug in the chest. Kloehr then saw Grat Dalton struggling to reach his horse and put a bullet through his neck. Meanwhile, Bill Powers who had taken a slug earlier was never able to reach his horse. He lay dying in the alley. Dick Broadwell and Emmett Dalton were both wounded and bleeding, but they were able to mount their horses. Broadwell was hit twice more as he rode off. Emmett saw his brother Bob leaning against a rock and turned back to help him. When he did so, he was blasted from his saddle by a load of buckshot from the shotgun of Carey Seamen, a barber. When he reached the edge of town, Dick Broadwell toppled from his horse. He was dead. Bob and Grat were also dead.

It was over. In addition to the aforementioned casualties, Coffeyville citizens Charley Gump and T. A. Reynolds had also been wounded.

With the assistance of town physicians, Emmett Dalton survived. Of the gang members that participated in the raid, he was the only one who did. Emmett was charged with two counts of murder and one count of robbery. He was sentenced to life in prison.

Although he knew nothing about the robbery plans, Amos Burton followed through as he was instructed. He waited with a wagon and provisions at the Cherokee Strip but the Dalton bunch never showed up.

After serving fifteen years and twenty-eight days, Emmett was pardoned by Governor Edward W. Hoch. Emmett Dalton married a girlfriend from his outlaw days and embarked on a successful and honest career in the business world.

There were many heroes in Coffeyville. Besides those previously mentioned, credit should be given to those men who applied continuous heat on the outlaws from inside the Isham Brothers' hardware store. Henry H. Isham, the store owner, was assisted by Charles Smith, Lewis Dietz and a fellow named Anderson. Isham, Smith and Anderson each had a Winchester, while Dietz used a revolver. On that October morning at Coffeyville, the Dalton gang blazed its way into history in one of the most famous gunfights to ever occur in the Old West.

The Tewksbury homestead (photographed shortly after the Pleasant Valley War). John Tewksbury and William Jacobs were shot to death at this location on September 2, 1887. *Arizona Historical Society.*

Chapter Four
The Pleasant Valley War

In the Tonto Basin of Arizona lie the lush pastures of Pleasant Valley, scene of the bloody Graham-Tewksbury feud. The conflict between the Grahams (a clan of Iowa natives) and the Tewksburys (who were partially of Indian blood) had its roots in cattle, but was nurtured by greed, prejudice, hatred and revenge. Some historians have indicated that the Graham-Tewksbury feud was a battle between cattlemen and sheep men. That is only partially true. Violence was initiated (in February 1887) in an incident between range riders and sheepherders, but the trouble had started much earlier. Basically, the feud began as a conflict between cattle rustlers. It was a game of who could get away with the most. They stole cattle and they stole horses, usually under the cover of darkness. They would hide the stock until the new brands healed, at which time the animals were driven to market in Mexico, and elsewhere. The rustlers were predominately a clique of friends who rode for area ranches. Cherry Creek loosely became a dividing line. Thieves from the west of Cherry Creek stole from ranches to the east, and vice-versa. As hostilities heated up, the factions became more defined and territorial guidelines more evident. For the most part, the territory west of Cherry

Creek belonged to the Graham faction, while that to the east became Tewksbury country.

Roughly a mile and a half separated the Graham and Tewksbury ranches. At one time the two families got along fine. In fact, they were partners in a rustling operation. They would pick up strays belonging to other ranchers, divide the stock, and apply their own brands. Evidently, the bitterness precipitated in 1883 following an incident in which the Grahams allegedly branded some stolen stock without advising the Tewksburys. There were many factors, however, that led to the heightening of animosities.

The Blevins clan would become an integral part of the feud. Mart Blevins, and four of his sons (John, Charles, Hampton and Sam), established a small ranch near the headwaters of Canyon Creek in 1884. The Blevins would align with the Grahams. When Andy Cooper, brother of the Blevins boys, arrived in Pleasant Valley, the Grahams gained an unscrupulous ally. Andy was wanted by the law in both Texas and Oklahoma. Some of Andy's friends (also of questionable character) hired on with the huge Hash Knife outfit. Several Hash Knife cowboys became players in the Graham-Tewksbury feud.

The Hash Knife outfit (officially the Aztec Land and Cattle Company) owned a massive tract of land above the Mogollon Rim, north of Pleasant Valley. Their estimated 60,000 head of cattle often grazed in the Tonto Basin. The Hash Knife outfit never became directly involved in the Pleasant Valley War, but some of their cowboys did. John Paine was an excessive drinker who was always ready for a fight. Tom Tucker (who later would become a lawman) seemed to have a nose for trouble. Tom Pickett was accustomed to danger, having ridden with Billy the Kid in the Lincoln County War. Other Hash Knife toughs became involved in Pleasant Valley "activities" as well.

During late 1885, 1886, and much of 1887, rustling in Arizona Territory had reached enormous proportions. Stolen stock from southern Arizona would be driven north to the canyons around Tonto Basin. Brands were "doctored" before the animals were taken to various northern markets. On their return trip, the rustlers would gather a new herd and drive them to Tonto Basin before they were eventually moved on to market places further south. The stock was usually horses for they could be moved rapidly.

Many people believed that Andy Cooper and his Blevins family, Paine, Tucker and Pickett were the heart of the rustling operation. Because they were identifiable friends of the Graham family, the Grahams also became the object of accusations. And so it was, when the Tewksburys had horses stolen, they immediately pointed their fingers at the Grahams. Though no evidence indicated they were involved in the horse stealing ring, the Grahams were implicated for two reasons. They had done some rustling of their own in the past, and they associated with known horse thieves.

The Daggs brothers (of Flagstaff) owned a large herd of sheep which had grazed on open land north of the Mogollon Rim prior to its purchase as a part of extensive acreage acquired by the Hash Knife outfit. The Hash Knife was intent upon driving sheepherders from their vast new holdings. In February 1887, P.P. Daggs ordered his sheepherders to move the flock south, over the Mogollon Rim and into Pleasant Valley. As the sheepherders neared the pass which led over the Mogollon Rim they were ambushed. One of Daggs' herders (a Basque from Spain) was shot to death and then beheaded. Many of the sheep were driven over a sheer cliff to their death. William Jacobs and two fellow sheepherders, both Indian, moved the remaining sheep down to the Tewksbury ranch where they sought refuge. In much the same manner that the Grahams were drawn into the worsening hostilities, so now were the Tewksburys. Five months later, Mart Blevins (father of the five brothers) rode out to retrieve some strays that had wandered from their grazing area. He never returned. The Blevins and their Hash Knife friends made an exhausting search for the old man, but to no avail. Their assumption was that he had been killed. Naturally, they accused the Tewksburys.

On the 9th of August, a confrontation occurred at the Newton ranch. Jim Tewksbury, Ed Tewksbury, Jim Roberts and Joseph Boyer were inside Newton's cabin when Hampton Blevins, John Paine, Tom Tucker, Bob Gillespie and Bob Carrington rode up to the front door. Paine asked Jim Tewksbury (who had stepped to the front door) if they could come in. Tewksbury advised him that Newton's cabin wasn't a boarding house. There are conflicting reports as to who fired the first shot, but suddenly gunfire erupted in both directions. Slugs hit Hampton Blevins and John Paine. Both toppled dead from their horses. One shot hit Tucker in the chest, another nicked one of his ears. He managed to spur his mount and get away. Gillespie and Carrington each received superficial wounds. They whirled their horses and scampered away in another direction. None of the four gunmen inside the cabin were hurt. The carcasses of two horses lay beside the bodies of Blevins and Paine.

When Tucker wasn't seen for two days Bob Gillespie rode out and found him. Having lost much blood, Tucker had been too weak to return home on his own. He had struggled to the cabin of Bob Sigsby where he had taken refuge. Tom Tucker would later recover.

James D. Houck was a newly appointed deputy sheriff of Apache County (where Commodore Perry Owens was sheriff). Houck was also a brother-in-law of the Basque sheepherder who was slain and decapitated
near the pass over Mogollon Rim. He was, therefore, sympathetic to the Tewksbury cause. On the evening of August 17, 1887, Jim Houck (who was carrying a warrant for the arrest of John Graham) encountered eighteen-year-old Billy Graham who was returning home from a dance. At the sight of each other, both men drew and fired several rounds. Graham was wounded. He booted his mount and raced toward home. Billy Graham died two days later.

By now, the battle was full-blown. There were no lawmen in Tonto Basin, and none arrived until the first of September. Sheriff William Mulvenon (of Yavapai County) and a small posse rode in, surveyed the situation, and then departed without making any arrests.

A story, which cannot be substantiated, claimed that the Grahams offered a bounty for the death of any Tewksbury. One evening a sniper was spotted by Jim and Ed Tewksbury. Jim fired a volley which seriously wounded the attacker, who was left to bleed to death.

Faced with increasing danger, John Blevins relocated, with his wife, mother, and youngest brother to the town of Holbrook (about 75 miles or 121 kilometers away). Andy Cooper and his brother, Charles Blevins, remained in Pleasant Valley.

At dawn, on September 2, 1887, Andy Cooper and several cohorts waited in seclusion outside the Tewksbury cabin. John Tewksbury and William Jacobs emerged from within and began to gather up some horses. A barrage of gunfire dropped the two in their tracks. They were both killed instantly. The gunmen held the cabin in siege throughout the day, as hogs (it is said) chewed on the bodies of Tewksbury and Jacobs. After nightfall, those who had been pinned down in the cabin were able to slip away under the cover of darkness. The following day, Andy Cooper set out for John Blevins' house at Holbrook in order to lay low for awhile.

Many lawmen on the western frontier had a reputation for being excellent marksmen. Those towns where the law was upheld by peace officers of such repute were often avoided by outlaws. This was the case at Navajo Springs in Apache County, Arizona. The citizens there had a no-nonsense sheriff named Commodore Perry Owens.

Owens, who was named for Oliver Perry, naval hero of the War of 1812, was born and raised in Tennessee. While still a teenager, he left home and worked his way west as a cowboy. He was employed by a railroad contractor when he was attacked by a band of renegade Indians intent on rustling a herd of horses. With a display of fine marksmanship, Owens shot and killed two of the rustlers. Amazed by his accuracy, the other Indians whirled their horses around and made a dash to safety. This incident gained him the reputation of being a deadly shot. It was also the catalyst that thrust him into his position as sheriff of Apache County. Perry Owens was an imposing sight. His gun belt holstered a Colt .45 peacemaker along with cartridges for both the Colt and the two Winchester rifles riding in scabbards on his mount. Sheriff Owens had a warrant for the arrest of Andy Cooper.

Alongside the Puerco River, approximately forty miles (64 kilometers) west of Navajo Springs, lay the cow town of Holbrook. It was the home of John Blevins, his wife Eva, and the widowed mother of Andy Cooper and the Blevins boys. Owens decided to ride over to Holbrook

Commodore Perry Owens was a crack marksman who wasted very few bullets. *Arizona Historical Society.*

Thomas Graham, a principal figure in the Pleasant Valley War, was killed in 1892. *Arizona Historical Society.*

to question Mrs. Blevins as to the whereabouts of her son. Anticipating no trouble, the sheriff rode alone. It was September 4, 1887. As he arrived at the house, on Joy Nevin Avenue, he tied up his horse, and then routinely withdrew one of his two Winchesters which he carried as he approached the front porch. The gunfight that erupted was incredible.

After being allowed to enter the house by Eva, Owens spotted Andy Cooper, with pistol in hand, peering from behind a door. Both men fired. Cooper collapsed where he stood. He was dead. John Blevins fired at the sheriff from behind another door. Owens shot Blevins through the right shoulder. He also went down. Owens looked for cover and dashed out and around the side of the house. As he did he met Mose Roberts, a brother-in-law who had accompanied Cooper on his ride from Pleasant Valley. Roberts had emerged from the rear of the house with a six-shooter in hand. Owens' rifle barked again, and Roberts fell dead. As Sam Houston Blevins, youngest of the three brothers, ran on to the front porch brandishing a revolver, the sheriff shot him through the heart.

In a matter of seconds, Perry Owens had killed three men and wounded another in rapid succession. John Blevins was taken into custody and jailed at St. Johns. The two Blevins women were left weeping at the house in Holbrook.

Perry Owens never participated in another gunfight. Nobody

dared to take him on. He had achieved the reputation of being one of the most deadly marksmen anywhere. Following his tenure as sheriff, Owens worked as a railroad detective on the Santa Fe, and then as a Wells Fargo express messenger.

Prior to dawn on September 17, 1887, the Grahams attacked a party of Tewksbury men while most were still asleep in their bedrolls. The Tewksbury group had been camping near the trail homeward from Holbrook when they were besieged. Miraculously, the Tewksburys were unhurt and quickly returned the Grahams' fire injuring Harry Middleton and Joe Ellenwood. Middleton was taken to the Graham ranch where he died from his wounds.

Upon the suggestion of Governor C. Meyer Zulick, Sheriff William Mulvenon raised a large posse--one which was capable of fighting both the Grahams and Tewksburys if necessary in order to end the Pleasant Valley War. On the 9th of September, Mulvenon left Prescott and headed to Payson where he met Deputy Sheriff John W. Francis who had arrived from Flagstaff with several lawmen. Also joining the posse were Jim Houck (the deputy sheriff who shot Billy Graham) and George Newton, both Tewksbury partisans. Houck and Newton were influential in convincing Mulvenon to round up the Grahams first.

Perkin's store (a stone building once used for protection against Apaches) was located near both the Graham ranch and the cabin of Al Rose (a Graham supporter). Shortly before dawn on the 21st of September, the posse took occupancy of the store and an unfinished stone building nearby. While most of the lawmen remained behind the walls, six others rode around the vicinity. Mulvenon's ploy was intended to draw some of Graham's men out to investigate who the strangers were. The decoy partially worked. John Graham and Charles Blevins cautiously rode toward Perkin's store, circled it, and then rode over to the unfinished building. Mulvenon sprang from hiding and ordered the two to raise their hands. Graham and Blevins whirled their horses and drew their guns. It was a mistake. Both men were blown from their saddles by a barrage of lead from the posse's weapons. Blevins died instantly. The posse left John Graham to die and headed toward the Graham ranch in hopes of arresting his brother Tom. At Graham's place Mulvenon found badly injured Joe Underwood, his wife, their two small children, and Miguel Apocada, a Mexican hand. Apocada was arrested. Tom Graham had managed to elude the trap. Shortly thereafter, the posse rode to Al Rose's cabin. He gave up without a fight.

George Newton left the posse a day earlier and rode to the Tewksbury ranch. He convinced Mulvenon that the Tewksbury clan would surrender peacefully. When the posse arrived Newton was waiting with six others. Ed and Jim Tewksbury, Jim Roberts, George Wagner, Jake Lauffer and Joe Boyer turned themselves in, as did George Newton. With their nine prisoners the posse left for Prescott.

As the cast of characters died, so did the Graham-Tewksbury feud. Jim Tewksbury died (in 1888) from tuberculosis. Cool-headed Thomas Graham was murdered in 1892 virtually ending the Pleasant Valley War. Ed Tewksbury was tried for Graham's murder, but was acquitted. He would later become a lawman at Globe, Arizona.

This photograph of Andy Cooper is believed to have been taken earlier in 1887, the year he was shot and killed by Sheriff Perry Owens. *Holbrook Senior Center.*

Gambler Luke Short carried his six-shooter in a leather lined pants pocket. *Kansas State Historical Society.*

Chapter Five
Jim Courtright and Luke Short

Timothy Isaiah Courtright was born in the year 1845 at Abraham Lincoln's hometown, Springfield, Illinois. He was one of six children raised in a strict farming family. Courtright left home when he was fifteen and worked his way to Iowa. At the age of sixteen, he enlisted in an Iowa regiment of the Union Army, and fought under General John "Blackjack" Logan during the Civil War. Somehow, about this time, Tim became Jim, and the lad who wore his hair long was dubbed "Longhaired Jim".

General Logan took a special interest in Courtright, possibly because of his accurate marksmanship. Jim was Logan's most trusted scout, and the two cultivated a friendship which would last long after the war was over.

After the Confederate States surrendered, Courtright was stationed in Missouri with another Union scout, Wild Bill Hickok. Longhaired Jim was then transferred to Little Rock, Arkansas, where he met the love of his life, Sarah Elizabeth (Betty) Weeks. Betty, a mature fourteen-year-old, and Jim were married in 1866 following a short courtship. Jim trained Betty in the art of firearms, and she became an excellent marksman, as well. For a while the couple performed a shooting act with a touring Wild West show.

On April 5, 1876, Jim Courtright was appointed city marshal of Fort Worth, Texas. Longhaired Jim (whose long hair was now gone) performed his duties well as an officer of the law, but became too involved in the political scene. He backed the wrong party and it cost him his position as marshal.

Following a friend's recommendation, Courtright accepted a position as security guard for the American Mining Company in the booming new silver camp at Lake Valley, New Mexico. One night while Jim was on duty, two Mexican outlaws attempted to rob a shipment of ore. It was their last mistake. In the gunfight which ensued, both bandits were slain by the accurate rifle shots of Jim Courtright.

Before long, the mines played out and the population of Lake Valley dwindled. In need of employment once again, Jim contacted his old friend and former commanding officer General John Logan who owned a cattle ranch near Silver City, New Mexico. Logan's ranch had been plagued by cattle rustlers and unwanted nesters (squatters), so the timing was perfect to employ Courtright's keen marksmanship. Jim was hired by Logan as a ranch foreman.

One afternoon in 1883, Jim Courtright and Jim McIntire rode out to the shack of two French squatters, to see if they had responded to a previous order to get off the property. The Frenchmen had ignored the warning. McIntire (who was also a former city marshal) and Courtright shot and killed the nesters. Throughout the vicinity an outcry arose over the slayings. Courtright and McIntire decided to flee the area. Longhaired Jim headed back to Fort Worth where he assumed he would be safe. Meanwhile, warrants had been issued in New Mexico for the arrest of both Jims on the charge of murder. The following year, Courtright was surprised when (on October 18, 1884) he was placed under arrest by a relentless New Mexico lawman, John Richmond, and two Texas Rangers.

On the day after Courtright's arrest, officers escorted him to a nearby restaurant for a meal. A mob entered the restaurant and closed in around Courtright's table. During the confusion, he dropped a napkin, leaned over to pick it up and somehow came up with two revolvers which he quickly pointed at the lawmen. The officers had no choice but to back away and watch Courtright escape.

Over a period of time, the folks around Silver City, New Mexico, had virtually forgotten about the deaths of the two Frenchmen. Eventually, both McIntire and Courtright returned to Silver City and turned themselves in. By then, the outraged nesters had moved on, and the influence of General Logan on the townspeople led to rapid acquittals for each.

Once again Jim returned to Fort Worth where he established the T.I.C. Commercial Detective Agency, with Jim McIntire as a partner. The agency primarily operated a protection racket. T.I.C. (the initials of Courtright's given name) "protected" gambling joints and gamblers in return for a monthly fee. One gambler who refused to participate in Courtright's shakedown was cool and dapper Luke Short of Dodge City fame.

Luke Lamar Short was born in Mississippi, in 1854. His family moved to Texas when Luke was only two-years-old. As a teenager he worked as a drover to trail cattle herds to the Kansas railheads. Seeking a more lucrative existence, he headed to Nebraska and began peddling bootleg whiskey to the Sioux Indians. His business thrived until he was arrested by the U. S. Army. Shortly thereafter, Luke headed to the silver camp at Leadville, Colorado. There he operated as a professional gambler. It was a trade he would practice for the rest of his life. Eventually, he showed up in Dodge City, Kansas, where he purchased the gaming concession at the Long Branch Saloon. During his time in Dodge City, Short became fast friends with Bat Masterson and Wyatt Earp. Later he traveled to Tombstone, Arizona, where he dealt faro at the Oriental Saloon. Nearly twelve years after he first arrived in Dodge City, Luke Short returned with money in his pocket. He purchased the Long Branch Saloon which he operated for about four years, before moving on to Ft. Worth, Texas. There, Luke and his partner, Jake Johnson, owned the gaming concession at the White Elephant Saloon.

Evidently, the T.I.C. Commercial Detective Agency had sent Luke Short a threatening note. Short and his friend Bat Masterson set out to find Courtright. When they did, the ensuing confrontation didn't last long. As heated words were exchanged, Short reached inside his coat. Believing that Short was going for his gun, the fast and usually deadly Courtright drew and squeezed his trigger. His revolver didn't discharge. The delay gave Short (who carried his revolver in a specially tailored

Jim Courtright was a deadly marksman. He once killed four men in two gunfights. *Wild Horse Collection.*

leather-lined pocket) time to draw and fire. By fate, or luck, Short's first bullet struck the cylinder of Courtright's revolver making it useless. Short emptied his pistol, with three slugs hitting Courtright in the right shoulder, right thumb and heart. Officer J.J. Fulford arrived at the scene immediately to find his friend lying on his back. Courtright mumbled his last words, "Ful, they've got me."

The crowd that quickly gathered was astonished. Jim Courtright was fast and accurate, and seemingly invincible in a gunfight. People were amazed that Luke Short (who carried his revolver in a pocket) could come out victorious against such a formidable foe. Luke Short was lucky. It is believed that when Courtright first squeezed his trigger the hammer caught on his watch chain. That, and the fact that Short's first bullet struck the cylinder of Courtright's revolver, made this a most bizarre gunfight.

The gunfight precipitated much controversy. Some say it wasn't the watch chain which prevented Courtright's pistol from discharging—and that the cylinder had actually jammed. This seems unlikely as Courtright would have kept his weapons in fine working condition. Others believe that Short's first shot hit Courtright's thumb making him unable to cock his hammer. The general consensus is that Courtright won the draw, and that his weapon misfired.

Longhaired Jim Courtright was buried at Pioneer's Rest Cemetery. His body was later moved to the Oakwood Cemetery at Fort Worth. After Jim's death, Betty Courtright moved to California.

Luke Short was never convicted in the slaying of Jim Courtright. On December 23, 1890, Short was wounded in a gunfight following an argument with another gambler named Charles Wright. Wright ambushed Short with a shotgun blast from behind. Some of the buckshot hit Luke's left leg. Short returned fire with one of his bullets striking Wright's wrist before he was able to scamper to safety. Later, Short suffered from edema (or dropsy), and his health worsened. Luke went to the mineral spa at Geuda Springs, Kansas, for therapy. While there, Luke Short died on September 8, 1893. His remains also lie in the Oakwood Cemetery at Ft. Worth.

The Courtright-Short gunfight, that occurred on February 8, 1887, may be the most famous confrontation between two such formidable and celebrated individuals in the annals of Old West history.

This photo of Chris Evans was taken at the jail in Visalia after he had lost an eye and had both arms wounded during the battle at Stone Corral. *Tulare County Library.*

Chapter Six
Terror in the San Joaquin Valley

The first of a series of train robberies on Southern Pacific's line through the San Joaquin Valley in California occurred on the night of February 22, 1889. As engineer, Pete Boelenger, eased his train out of Pixley (headed toward Alila), two masked bandits climbed aboard the tender. Once the train disappeared from the view of Pixley, Boelenger was ordered to bring it to a halt. The engineer and fireman were led at gunpoint back to the Wells Fargo express car where messenger, J.R. Kelly, was given the order to open up. When the express messenger refused to respond, the masked men set off a charge of dynamite beneath the rail car.

Meanwhile passenger Ed Bentley, a deputy sheriff from Modesto, and three Southern Pacific employees had stepped to the ground and were inching their way toward the Wells Fargo car. They were spotted by the robbers, however, who cut loose with their shotguns. Bentley and a fellow named Gabert were seriously wounded. The other Southern

Pacific employees scampered to safety.

Even though his car was partially destroyed, J.R. Kelly stood his ground. When the bandits threatened to kill Boelenger and the fireman, Kelly relinquished and threw out the strongbox. The masked men grabbed the box and vanished into the night.

A carbon copy of the Pixley job occurred on January 20, 1890. Once again, the target was a Wells Fargo express car on the Southern Pacific Railroad. Under the cover of darkness, two masked robbers boarded the tender, as the train departed from the station at Goshen. About two miles south of town, the engineer, S.R. DePue, was ordered to stop the train. As before, the engineer and fireman were escorted to the Wells Fargo express car. This time the messenger offered no resistance and tossed down the strongbox (which purportedly contained $20,000). At that moment, a man climbed from beneath the rail car. One of the bandits shot him in the back. He was a hobo who had been riding in the framework below the car's platform.

Another Southern Pacific train was stopped outside the town of Alila, on February 6, 1891. Once again, the method was similar. Two masked men apparently swung up behind the tender as the train pulled away from the station at Alila (later to be renamed Earlimart). The engineer and fireman were marched back to the express car, and the messenger was ordered to open up. The bandits encountered stubborn Wells Fargo messenger, C.C. Haswell, who flatly refused to cooperate. The masked men fired a volley of shots into the side of the rail car. Haswell returned their fire. During the exchange of gunshots, the fireman was shot in the stomach. The frustrated bandits fled empty handed.

Haswell was charged with firing the shot that struck the fireman, a fellow named Radcliff. During his trial, Haswell testified that the bullet came from the gun of a third would-be robber who was located on the other side of the train. Haswell was acquitted.

Southern Pacific detective, Will Smith, was certain that the Dalton brothers (Bob, Grat and Emmett) were responsible for the Alila job, and possibly the others. Smith easily convinced others that he was correct, and they set out in search of the Daltons. Bob, Grat and Emmett had been visiting their brother Bill, who resided at Paso Robles in San Luis Obispo County. It was the first place Will Smith would look, but he wouldn't find the brothers. Grat Dalton was later arrested and convicted in connection with the Alila train robbery. Grat escaped from jail, and his conviction was ultimately overturned.

Years later, following the demise of Bob and Grat Dalton (in the famous gunfight at Coffeyville, Kansas), Emmett reflected on their days in California. According to Emmett, the pursuit by Will Smith, more than any other factor, led to the formation of the Dalton Gang. He indicated that even though they were innocent, they were suddenly running from the law.

Christopher Evans and John Sontag were most likely involved in the train robberies at Pixley, Goshen and Alila. John Sontag and his cohort Chris Evans would later become the target of one of the largest manhunts in California history.

John Sontag worked a mining claim which was located near the farm and home of Chris Evans, not far from Visalia. Evans became friends with the Sontags. At what point George Sontag began riding the outlaw trail with John and Chris is a matter for speculation. It is probable that George joined the others after the Alila job, because he lived in Minnesota as of May 1891. Of the train robberies that followed, George would later confess (while at Folsom Prison) to participation in a robbery at Collis Station. He further indicated that John and Chris worked alone during each of the other robberies.

On September 3, 1891, an attempted robbery of a Southern Pacific train occurred near Ceres. The procedure was nearly a duplicate of earlier heists. Two masked men evidently climbed aboard the tender as the train eased away from town. As before, the engineer was ordered to stop the train once the community was out of sight. After the locomotive drew to a halt, the engineer and fireman were marched back to the express car. There they confronted a faithful and reluctant Wells Fargo messenger, U.W. Reed, who refused to cooperate. With one charge of dynamite the masked men blew a hole in the rolling door. As they prepared another charge, however, they were fired upon by two railroad detectives who had dropped to the ground from a passenger car. The bandits fired back, then wisely aborted their effort and fled to safety. During the exchange of gunfire, a slug struck one of the detectives, Len Harris, in the neck.

A connecting spur ran west from the main Southern Pacific line to Collis Station (later to be renamed Kerman). It was the scene of another train robbery on August 3, 1892. At nearly midnight, two robbers slipped aboard the tender as the train (bound for Fresno) pulled away from Collis Station. This time the scenario was a little different. The engineer and fireman, Al Phipps and Will Lewis, were forced to step down from the locomotive. In an attempt to disable the engine, one of the cylinders was dynamited. Six more charges of dynamite destroyed part of the express car. There were more bandits this time—possibly four. The robbers may have known that the express car would yield a substantial amount of silver coins, for they brought a wagon. Phipps and Lewis were compelled to carry the sacks of silver to the wagon. The dynamite blasts had awakened some threshers who were camped in a nearby field. Realizing a robbery was in progress, they begin to fire randomly at the moonlit figures alongside the train. The bandits quickly made their escape into the darkness, leaving three unopened safes untouched.

Five very similar robberies had occurred on the Southern Pacific Railroad line through the San Joaquin Valley. Apparently there was no evidence connecting the Sontag brothers or Chris Evans (or for that matter anyone else) to the thefts. Things, however, would begin to come unglued for the trio. Suspicion grew when it was realized that neither John nor Chris had been at Visalia the night of the robbery. George babbled that he had been a passenger on the train, and gave a firsthand account of the holdup. Chris, on the other hand, in response to questioning, advised that George and John had spent the night at his farm. There were too many contradictions. Finding George Sontag, Will Smith escorted him to the sheriff's office for questioning. While George was detained, Smith and Deputy Sheriff Witty hopped into a wagon and rode out to Evans' farm. Smith and Witty entered the farmhouse and were

The farmhouse of Chris Evans was the scene of two shoot-outs. Evans and John Sontag escaped after both incidents. *Tulare County Library.*

talking with Evans' teen-aged daughter when suddenly they were confronted by John Sontag and Evans whose weapons were leveled at the lawmen. Smith and Witty bolted through the front door. As they did, Smith drew, whirled and fired at Evans. His shot missed. Sontag, who was holding a shotgun, fired and hit Smith. Another shot dropped Witty. The badly injured officers watched as Evans and Sontag unhitched their buggy and escaped. When word reached town of the incident, Deputy Sheriff Overell charged George Sontag with robbery, and jailed him.

On a hunch, Overell and two deputies (Beaver and Hill) decided to stake-out Evans' farm in case the fugitives returned. Their hunch was right. Evans and Sontag returned prior to dawn. The deputies spotted two shadowy figures and ordered them to surrender. Gunfire erupted and almost immediately a slug hit Beaver. He collapsed and would later die. Once again, the outlaws escaped.

The death of Oscar Beaver and a reward of $10,000 (offered by the Southern Pacific Railroad) were all the catalysts needed to launch a huge manhunt. During a search of Evans' farm, the stolen coins from the Collis Station robbery were recovered. George Sontag was subsequently convicted and sentenced to life imprisonment.

A month later, at a place called Sampson Flat, a posse stopped at the cabin of Jim Young. At that moment, a recluse named Mainwaring walked from the cabin to fetch a bucket of water. As the deputies carelessly approached him, Sontag and Evans opened fire from the cabin.

Jim Young's cabin was a temporary hideout for Chris Evans and John Sontag. The outlaws killed two lawmen at this location. *Tulare County Library.*

Deputy U. S. Marshal Vic Wilson and Deputy Sheriff Andy McGinnis were dropped in their tracks. Wilson was dead, and McGinnis seriously wounded. He would soon die, as well. As the posse retreated to find cover, the fugitives fled into a wooded area. Nearby, authorities later found a small fortress which had been constructed by Evans and Sontag. Through its narrow openings, the duo could have possibly held off a small army.

Throughout the cold winter, Evans and Sontag moved from one sympathizer's cabin to another. Somehow they were able to remain in continuous contact with Molly Evans (Chris's wife), who would see that they always had plenty of food and supplies. When weather permitted, a posse would target cabins in remote locations. Lawmen found people to be very tight-lipped, possibly out of fear of reprisal. A fellow named Black was found shot to death at his cabin. It was rumored that he had been an informant against Evans and Sontag.

On April 29, 1893, just outside the community of Badger, the Visalia stagecoach was stopped by Chris Evans and John Sontag. They had heard that their nemesis, Will Smith, would be on board. He was not. Had be been, it might have been his last ride.

In the Tulare County foothills at a place known as Stone Corral, was the isolated and abandoned Bacon cabin. After bedding down their horses on Saturday evening, June 10, 1893, a posse consisting of U. S. Marshal George Gard; Deputy Sheriffs Hi Rapelji, and Fred Jackson; and Tom Burns, a detective, adjourned to the cabin for the night. As Jackson gazed from a window, out into the twilight, he spotted two men walking toward the cabin. As they grew nearer, Jackson realized that it was Sontag and Evans. Jackson leveled his weapon and fired. His slug tore into the left arm of Evans. The two fugitives dove for cover behind a straw pile. It offered very little protection from the lawmen's bullets. Sontag was hit—then hit again. Buckshot from a shotgun blast tore into Evans' right eye, putting it out. Anxious to end the fray before nightfall, Jackson ventured from the cabin and moved toward the straw pile. An outlaw's bullet smashed Jackson's ankle and he hit the ground writhing in pain. Later, his leg would require amputation. The siege finally ended as darkness set in.

At dawn, the lawmen spread out and cautiously approached the straw pile. They found John Sontag lying there badly wounded and unconscious. Evans was gone. Sontag was taken into custody and moved to Visalia. He died three days later.

On the following day, Chris Evans was found nearly seven miles (11 kilometers) from the scene of the gunfight, at the cabin of Lige Perkins in Wilcox Canyon. Evans was weak from the loss of blood, and offered no resistance to Sheriff William Hall.

It was nearly two months before Evans was strong enough to be tried at Fresno. In a surprise development at the trial, George Sontag appeared as a witness for the prosecution. Sontag was on crutches. He was recovering from a wound received during an attempted prison break at Folsom. Chris Evans was convicted. While he awaited sentencing at the Fresno County jail, he engineered a daring escape. Ed Morrell was a waiter at the restaurant which the county had hired to provide food for the prisoners. It was Morrell's task to carry meals into the jailhouse. The waiter had a crush on Eva Evans (Chris's daughter) and he also admired the outlaw, so he was easily drawn into the scheme to spring Evans loose. On the evening of the escape (December 3, 1893), Morrell carried Evans' tray to his cell, as usual. Morrell slipped a gun to Evans, and then drew one of his own. The two apprehended the jailer, Ben Scott, and used him as a shield as they stepped through the front door. As Morrell untethered two waiting horses, the city marshal, John D. Morgan, suddenly appeared on the scene. Gunshots were fired and Morgan took a slug in his side. The shots frightened the horses, causing them to bolt and run. Without their mounts, Evans and Morrell raced through an alley to the next block where they commandeered a one-horse cart belonging to newsboy, Benny Cochran. Within moments they had disappeared from sight and were on their way to the foothills.

Once again Evans escaped to the area known as Sampson Flat, and its hundreds of acres of high mountain valleys in the foothills of the Sierra Nevada Mountains. It was a place where he and John Sontag had often taken refuge. This time he had a different cohort. Evans had many friends who would risk their own well-being to shelter the fugitives. Occasionally he and Morrell would travel down to Visalia and slip into Evans' house to visit family.

On February 19, 1894, the fugitives were spotted by a deputy who had been posted near the farm. He rode into town to report his findings. Soon, the farmhouse was surrounded by thirty heavily armed men. Evans and Morrell surrendered without a fight.

Chris Evans was sentenced to life imprisonment at Folsom Penitentiary. Ed Morrell was convicted of horse theft and also received a life sentence. After serving fourteen years Morrell's sentence was commuted, and he was released. Within days, George Sontag walked out of Folsom a free man. For several years the daughters of Chris Evans petitioned the Governor for their father's release. Evans, who had grown quite ill, was finally set free on May 1, 1911. Within weeks Chris Evans was dead.

John Sontag lies wounded and unconscious in a pile of straw and manure at Stone Corral. Three of the four posse members that captured him are: Deputy Sheriff Hi Rapelji (second from left), Detective Tom Burns (fourth from right) and U. S. Marshal George Gard (third from right). The fourth member of the posse, Deputy Sheriff Fred Jackson, was wounded and is not in the photograph. *Fresno Historical Society Archives.*

John Wesley Hardin in 1871 at the age of 18. When this photograph was taken in Abilene, Hardin was already a seasoned gunfighter. *Kansas State Historical Society.*

Chapter Seven
John Wesley Hardin: Deadly Son of a Preacher

John Wesley Hardin was born in Bonham, Texas, on May 26, 1853, and named for the founder of the Methodist faith. Wes, as he was usually called, was the son of Mary Elizabeth Hardin and James Hardin, a circuit preacher of the same denomination. Wes and his father were very similar in many ways, but totally different in others. Both were intelligent, and had a thirst for knowledge. Each taught school for a while, and during some point in their lives they both practiced law. But there the similarities ended. While his father spread the word of God, Wes Hardin became one of the most dangerous of all western gunmen.

In two separate incidents, during November of 1868, fifteen-year-old Wes Hardin killed his first four men. While visiting his uncle's farm near Moscow in eastern Texas, Hardin got into a scuffle with a former slave named Mage. After Mage got his nose bloodied, he threatened Wes. The following day, as he was riding back to the farm, Hardin was accosted by Mage who was carrying a big stick. The former slave seized the bridle of Wes' horse. Hardin drew his revolver and shot the black man three times. Mage died within days. Wes headed home to tell his father about the incident. Fearing carpetbagger justice, the elder Hardin suggested that Wes lay low for a while. He traveled northeast to a friend's farm, believed to be near Sumner, to hide out. While he was there, he received word from his brother Joseph that Union soldiers were in the vicinity looking for him. He knew that if the soldiers headed toward the farm, they would need to slow down at a nearby creek crossing, so he set up camp there and waited. Before long three bluecoats approached. Hardin ambushed the soldiers as they crossed the creek, killing two with blasts from his double-barrel shotgun. The other soldier drew, and returned fire grazing Hardin's left arm. By then, Wes had drawn his revolver and gunned down the third soldier.

The Hardins had relatives and friends throughout central Texas who were glad to shelter the fugitive from "Yankee avengers." So, Wes fled south to Navarro County where he stayed with relatives and worked for a short time as a school teacher, and then as a cowhand. Wes then ventured further south, and trouble followed him. One evening, Hardin was approached by a fellow whom he had beaten badly in a card game earlier in the day. The poor loser fired a shot at Hardin. It was the last thing he ever did, as Hardin dropped him with a slug in the head, and another in the chest. Within days, Wes Hardin shot down an employee of a circus troupe following a quarrel. He then fled to another uncle's farm, near Brenham, where he would lay low for a few months.

Not wanting to stay in any one place too long, Hardin decided to head for Louisiana. Before he reached the state line, he was arrested by a deputy sheriff near the town of Marshall. He was charged with a murder that had occurred in Waco, which he had not committed. While captive in the small jailhouse at Marshall, Hardin somehow obtained a Colt revolver, which he kept hidden. A Captain Stokes, of the newly organized and short-lived Texas State Police, and a guard named Jim Smolly, were assigned the duty of transporting Hardin from Marshall to Waco for trial. During their trip west, Stokes left Smolly to guard Hardin while he went to a nearby farmhouse to find some fodder for the horses. It was the advantage Hardin was looking for. He produced the revolver that he had kept hidden and mortally wounded Smolly. He quickly mounted and fled the scene before Stokes returned.

Wes Hardin headed to Gonzales County and the cattle ranch of his cousins, the Clements, south of the town of Smiley. There he worked as a cowpoke and found safety for a while. A cattle drive carried him to Abilene, Kansas, during the summer of 1871, where he dispatched a fellow named Charles Cougar, following a quarrel.

The very next day, Wes Hardin joined a manhunt for a Mexican named Juan Bideno. Wes was joined by Hugh Anderson, Jim Rodgers, and John Cohron, whose brother Bill had been killed by Bideno two days earlier. The group tracked the Mexican to the settlement of Bluff City, about five miles (8 kilometers) north of the Oklahoma state line, where they found him eating at a café. As Hardin walked in, with the others behind him, Wes shot Bideno through the head at close range.

During his brief stay in Kansas, John Wesley Hardin was supposedly befriended by Wild Bill Hickok, who was city marshal of Abilene at the time. Upon completion of their business, Hardin and the other cowhands returned to Texas and the Clements' cattle ranch. He hadn't been back long when he heard that two members of the Texas State Police were asking questions about him in Smiley. Hardin, apparently intent on a fight, sought the duo out. He approached them as they were eating crackers at the general store. According to the popular version of the story, Wes asked the policemen who they were looking for. After they responded, he asked if they would recognize Hardin when they saw him. One of the officers replied that they had never seen him. "Well," said Hardin, "you see him now!" As he spoke he drew and fatally shot Green Parramore in the head. His second shot hit John Lackey in the mouth and he reeled backwards. Lackey was able to scramble out the front door and run for cover. Cautiously, Hardin exited through the rear door and rounded the building only to find that Lackey had disappeared. Unbeknownst to Hardin, the policeman had fled to nearby Round Lake where he submerged himself. The cold water helped curtail the bleeding, and Lackey survived.

Hoping to settle down one day, Wes Hardin married his longtime sweetheart, Jane Bowen. Wes once said of her, "She was as true to me as the magnet of steel." During their marriage, Jane gave birth to three children, two daughters and a son. When he was traveling Hardin had been known to ride a long distance to see Jane. On one occasion, he covered about a hundred miles (62 kilometers) in six hours. Commenting about the trip, in his own words, Hardin said, "…ruined a good horse worth $50 doing so. The sight of my wife recompensed me for the loss of old Bob."

During the year 1872, Wes Hardin was involved in shootings in Sabine, Trinity, and Angelina counties. He was wounded twice, and was also captured. Mannen Clements broke Hardin out of jail in October of that year. Clements slipped a file to Wes, with which he cut the bars. Mannen then returned and pulled Hardin through the opening with his lariat. Wes then joined his cousins in the Sutton-Taylor feud. They fought for the Taylor clan. The Taylors and Clements were related by marriage. In one incident, Hardin and Jim Taylor were confronted by Jack Helm who fought for the Sutton faction. He was accompanied by six cohorts. Hardin raised his shotgun and blasted Helm in the chest. After he collapsed, Taylor fired several rounds into the dying man's head. When the action started, Helm's cohorts quickly scampered away.

Comanche, Texas, was the scene of the killing for which John Wesley Hardin was eventually convicted and imprisoned. It was May 26, 1874 (Hardin's twenty-first birthday) and the town was festive with people who had gathered for horse races. Wes had won a substantial amount of money on the races, but his day was dampened when he learned that Charles Webb, deputy sheriff of nearby Brown County was in town with the intention of killing Hardin. Webb found Hardin at Jack Wright's Saloon. Hardin invited Webb to the bar for a drink As Webb stepped toward the bar, he drew his revolver and fired. Hardin was alert and jumped to one side and the deputy's shot only grazed him. Wes fired, and his bullet hit Webb in the head. The deputy sheriff collapsed on the barroom floor. He was dead. Wes, his cousin Bill Dixon, and Jim Taylor, who had accompanied him to the bar, all fled. Not able to find Wes and his companions, an enraged mob from Brown County sought out Wes's brother, Joseph Hardin, and cousins Joe and Bud Dixon, and then lynched them all. John Wesley Hardin had a $4,000 price on his head, and he felt the heat. Wes and his wife Jane left the state.

For three years in Florida and Alabama, Wes remained anonymous under the alias of J. H. Swain, Jr. during which time he brokered cattle and horses and dabbled in other businesses. The Texas Rangers finally discovered his whereabouts, and cornered Hardin while he was on a business trip in Pensacola, Florida. While Hardin's train sat at the depot, John Armstrong and other Texas Rangers stormed both ends of the smoking car where Wes was relaxing with friends. Hardin reached for a concealed revolver, but as he drew the weapon caught on his suspenders. Jim Mann, who was sitting beside Wes, drew his pistol and fired at Armstrong. As the bullet sailed harmlessly through the ranger's hat, Armstrong put a fatal shot into Mann's chest. Armstrong then slugged Hardin with the barrel of his revolver and took the fugitive into custody. Hardin was tried in Austin, Texas, and was found guilty of second-degree murder for the slaying of Deputy Sheriff Charles Webb. John Wesley Hardin was sentenced to a term of twenty-five years in the penitentiary at Huntsville.

Wes Hardin spent his years in prison constructively. He studied law. After serving fifteen years, Hardin was released in February of 1894, and pardoned the following month. His wife Jane had died two years earlier. Wes went to Gonzales where he opened a law practice and lived for a while with his children. He soon moved his law practice to Junction and then on to El Paso. It was during this time that he penned his autobiography, *The Life of John Wesley Hardin as Written by Himself.* While residing in Junction, Wes married a young girl named Callie Lewis. Within hours after their vows were exchanged, Callie packed up and left him. The despondent Wes Hardin relocated to Kerr County where he stayed briefly before moving on to El Paso.

Wes Hardin reopened his law practice in his room on the second floor of the Herndon Lodging House. Actually, it was a case that brought Hardin to El Paso in the first place. His services had been procured by notorious gunman "Deacon" Jim Miller, who earlier had married Sallie Clements, daughter of Mannen. Hardin was hired by Miller to prosecute a man who had tried to kill him. Wes didn't have many other clients, however, and business was slow. He spent many hours at either the Acme Saloon or whoring around with Helen Buelah Morose, a former prostitute and wife of rustler Martin Morose. Speculation has it that Wes Hardin and John Selman, city constable, conspired to kill Martin Morose. Morose's death would benefit both. Selman would be rid of a nemesis, and an obstacle would be eliminated in Hardin's romance with Buelah Morose. At any rate, Martin Morose turned up dead. According to rumor, he had a large sum of money in his possession when he was slain, and furthermore that Hardin grabbed the money and failed to split it with Selman. Whether this was just a rumor or whether this precipitated Selman's actions of August 19, 1895, we may never know.

On that date, during the evening, Wes Hardin was in the Acme Saloon, rolling dice on the bar top with an acquaintance. John Selman entered the saloon and began shooting—at Hardin's back. Wes Hardin never had a chance to draw. As his lifeless body crumpled to the floor Selman continued to shoot until he was restrained by his son, John Selman, Jr., and Chief Jeff Milton, both members of the El Paso police force.

The incident was so clouded by conflicting testimony that a hung jury was the result. A retrial was scheduled, but John Selman was gunned down by Deputy U. S. Marshal, George Scarborough, before the case came to court.

There were other explanations as to Selman's motive in the Acme Saloon slaying of Hardin. Some say he was simply after the acclaim for disposing of such a famed gunfighter as John Wesley Hardin, and adding another notch to a list that already included a Deputy U. S. Marshal, Bass Outlaw, among others.

John Wesley Hardin was probably involved in more gunfights than anyone else on the western frontier. No one will ever know just how many men he actually killed. He claimed to have disposed of forty-four, but then again, he was known to blow a little smoke. Only about twenty-five percent of those are verifiable through county records and documents, but then again, in those days, many deaths went unrecorded. Regardless of the count, Wes Hardin, the deadly son of a preacher, was one of the most dangerous gunfighters of all.

Billy the Kid (Henry McCarty, William H. Bonney, or Kid Antrim) as photographed outside Beaver Smith's Saloon, at Fort Sumner, in about 1879. This is the only authentic photograph of Billy in existence. *Western History Collections, University of Oklahoma Library.*

Chapter Eight
Billy the Kid and the Lincoln County War

At the First Presbyterian Church at Santa Fe, New Mexico, on March 1, 1873, wedding vows were exchanged between William Henry Harrison Antrim and Catherine McCarty. Among the witnesses were Catherine's two sons, Joseph (who was called Josie), and Henry (who was probably thirteen-years-old). The record of this civil ceremony is among the earliest documentation we have as to the life of Henry McCarty (otherwise known at various times as Henry Antrim, William Antrim, Kid Antrim, William H. Bonney, Billy the Kid, or simply the Kid). Henry was most likely the son of Michael McCarty, Catherine's former husband. Following Michael's death (in New York), Catherine moved west with her sons. Henry's early years are shrouded in mystery, but he was destined to become legendary.

Shortly after the wedding, the Antrims moved to Silver City, New Mexico, where William prospected and Catherine took in boarders to supplement their income. Catherine died of tuberculosis on September 16, 1874, just a year and a half after their wedding. Henry was, as his teacher and others later indicated, a helpful child who was no more of a problem than any other boy his age. He was a jovial lad as well, who always had a good sense of humor.

The Kid's first scrape with the law resulted from a petty theft of clothes from Charlie Sun, a Chinese laundryman. He was locked up in the Silver City jail. The Kid couldn't stand the idea of being confined, and after only two nights behind bars escaped by wiggling through a chimney. Kid Antrim fled to Arizona Territory where he spent much of the next two years as a cowhand, rustler, thief, and part-time gambler. Twice he was arrested for larceny, but the guardhouse at Camp Grant couldn't hold him, and twice he escaped. Why he didn't flee the area is a question for speculation, but he remained in the vicinity to get into even bigger trouble—murder.

On August 17, 1877, at George Adkins' Saloon in Bonita, near Camp Grant, the Kid scuffled with an Irishman named Frank Cahill. "Windy" Cahill, a local blacksmith, had picked on Antrim before, but this time the Kid decided that enough was enough. He drew and shot Cahill through the stomach, mortally wounding him. This time Antrim fled the scene. He headed back to New Mexico Territory, where he continued to run stolen horses, this time for John W. Kinney, who was known as "King of the Rustlers." It is presumably at this time that the Kid first met, and then joined up with Jessie Evans and the Boys, the gang of rustlers that operated out of Kinney's ranch outside La Mesilla. They were so brash that they had been known to sell cattle before they were ever rustled. Evans and the Boys ran rampant through southeastern New Mexico, and as they were feared by most, nobody attempted to stop them. That is, until newspaperman Col. Albert J. Fountain founded the *Mesilla Valley Independent*, in which he lambasted the Boys. He offered the Boys twelve ropes and twelve cottonwood trees if room could not be found for them in the county jail. On behalf of the Boys, Evans sent word to Fountain that they planned to kill him on sight. When Governor S. B. Axtell was telegraphed for help, he responded. In short order things became too hot for Jessie Evans and the Boys in Dona Ana County. They decided on a change of scenery and headed to Lincoln County, New Mexico. Whether the Kid accompanied the Boys to Lincoln County, or not, is uncertain. The Kid and Jessie Evans both resurfaced there, ultimately with opposing factions in what was to become known as the Lincoln County War.

The "House" was located at the western end of Lincoln's only street. It was the largest civilian structure in Lincoln County, and headquarters for L. G. Murphy & Company. It was also a store, a saloon, a bunkhouse, and even a Masonic Hall. Lawrence Gustave Murphy and James Joseph Dolan were a shrewd and powerful partnership. Dolan was so close to Murphy that many people mistakenly thought him to be an adopted son. Through the House they held a virtual monopoly over Lincoln County's trade. Most of the juicy government contracts for supplying beef to Indian reservations and military posts were controlled by the House, as well. Murphy and Dolan were aided in this effort by cohort John Henry Riley. The financial power of the House regulated much of the cattle flow in the region, and it also held the reins to the sheriff's office.

With the flip of a coin, we see the other side. The large cattle ranchers believed that merchants, with little experience in raising cattle, should have no control over government contracts, and that the beef suppliers should be able to deal directly with the government. John Henry Tunstall, or the "Englishman" as he was often called, had an ambition to pocket half of every dollar spent in Lincoln County. He presumed that with his cattle ranch, a store to compete effectively with the House, a bank from which he would make loans to all of the small ranchers (making them all indebted to him), one of his pawns as Indian agent, and the genius of his attorney Alexander Anderson McSween, he could realize his ambition. Though not as rich, McSween (called Mac by his friends) was equally ambitious. He wanted position and money, and was spurred toward that end by his wife, Susan E. McSween. Cattle baron, John Simpson Chisum, was fighting his own battle, but would soon join the Tunstall-McSween faction.

The Kid signed on with John Tunstall as a hand, and as a gun. By now he was using the name of William H. Bonney, or Billy. Billy the Kid was to be very loyal to Tunstall, and would be involved in the Lincoln County War through its duration.

Jimmy Dolan and John Riley assumed command of the House as L. G. Murphy became terminally ill. Accusations and litigation were followed by more accusations and more litigation. Tensions grew as the hatred between Dolan and Riley on one side, and Tunstall and McSween on the other heightened.

On the morning of February 18, 1878, Jimmy Dolan helped select a posse which was instructed to head off John Tunstall, return him and his party to Lincoln, and furthermore to confiscate some of Tunstall's horses as payment for an outstanding debt. Accompanying the posse were Jessie Evans, Tom Hill and Frank Baker, who were members of the Boys. While descending into a canyon leading to the Ruidoso Valley, Tunstall and his men encountered a flock of turkeys. John Tunstall remained with the horses while the others scattered out over a distance of several hundred yards (or meters) in pursuit of the flock. Suddenly, a few members of the posse appeared near Tunstall, and he spurred his mount to ride forward to talk with them. As he neared, Buck Morton shot Tunstall in the chest. A second shot from the revolver of Tom Hill crashed into Tunstall's skull, He was dead.

Following John Tunstall's murder, many sympathizers gathered at McSween's house. Another large group consisting of Dolan, Riley,

Lawrence Gustave Murphy (right) and James Joseph Dolan (left) controlled much of the economy in Lincoln County. *Lincoln County Heritage Trust.*

Sheriff William Brady, and members of the posse assembled at the House (now officially J. J. Dolan & Company).

Realizing that Sheriff Brady would not arrest Tunstall's killers, McSween had the Kid and Dick Brewer (Tunstall's foreman) furnish sworn affidavits in the presence of Justice of the Peace Wilson. Town Constable Atanacio Martinez, armed with warrants that had been issued by Wilson, deputized William Bonney and Frank Waite. The trio proceeded to the House in order to arrest those men named in the warrants. At Dolan's place, the three encountered Sheriff Brady and a large party of gunmen. They were bolstered by troops from nearby Fort Stanton. Not only did Brady refuse to allow Martinez to make any arrests, but he took the constable, Bonney and Waite into custody and marched them to the jailhouse. Martinez was only detained, but Bonney and Waite remained in jail for twenty-four hours. To add to the humiliation, Brady confiscated the Kid's rifle. There never had been any question about the Kid's allegiance to the Tunstall-McSween faction, but this ncident unleashed a new fury and defiance.

The factions aligned. The small farmers of the Ruidoso and Hondo valleys and the Hispanics to whom Tunstall had extended credit aligned themselves with McSween, as did cattle baron John Chisum, for a while. The ranchers from the Seven Rivers area had already been involved in the Pecos War against Chisum, so they naturally allied themselves with Dolan and Riley. Others siding with the House included District Attorney, 3rd Judicial District at Las Cruces, William L. Rynerson, U. S. District Attorney Thomas B. Catron, Sheriff William Brady and his deputies, the Democratic political machine known as "The Santa Fe Ring," and John Kinney, the "King of the Rustlers."

Still holding warrants for the arrest of Tunstall's killers, and realizing that the only way justice would be served would be to serve it themselves, certain members of the McSween faction formed a heavily armed vigilante group. They called themselves the "Regulators." The group included Dick Brewer, who was named their leader, William Bonney, John Middleton, Fred Waite, Josiah "Doc" Scurlock, Charlie Bowdre, Frank MacNab, Henry Brown, Jim "Big Jim" French, and Sam Smith. Bent on vengeance, and suspecting that the killers were holed up at Jim Dolan's cattle camp over on the Pecos, the Regulators headed southeast. The group sighted five men near the Rio Penasco. Two of the men peeled off, but the Regulators chased the other three. One of the three went down when his horse gave out. The group ignored him because the remaining two men were Buck Morton and Frank Baker. The fugitives eventually surrendered. Over strong objections from the Kid, Brewer agreed to take the duo back to Lincoln. The posse stopped at Chisum's ranch and picked up a hand named William H. McCloskey. As the group rode toward Lincoln, Morton reached over and snatched McCloskey's revolver from its holster, and then fired at him point blank, fatally wounding the ranch hand. Morton and Baker wheeled their horses in an attempt to flee. The Regulators opened fire and gunned them down. Buck Morton's back had nine bullet holes in it, which either indicated excellent marksmanship on the part of the Regulators, or simply an assassination by the posse knowing that Sheriff Brady would have turned them loose upon their arrival in Lincoln.

Three weeks later, on April 1, 1878, at approximately 9:30 a.m., Sheriff Brady emerged from his office with four deputies—Billy Mathews, George Hindman, George Peppin, and John "Jack" Long (a.k.a. Frank Rivers). They walked down the street in the direction of Alexander McSween's place. As they headed east, they were unaware of the impending danger. Prior to dawn, six Regulators had slipped into the corral adjacent to Tunstall's store, and had drilled gun ports in the corral wall. The firing squad consisted of Frank MacNab, Big Jim French, Henry Brown, John Middleton, Fred Waite, and Billy the Kid. Their rifles were ready. As the sheriff and his deputies passed the corral gate, the Regulators opened fire. Sheriff Brady was killed instantly, being hit in the head, back, and side. George Hindman staggered a few steps, and then collapsed. He would also die. Jack Long also took a slug, but he was able to scamper to safety, as did Mathews and Peppin. They took cover and returned the Regulators' fire. A bystander, John Wilson, was wounded by a stray bullet as he worked in his garden to the south. Big Jim French and Billy the Kid ran through the corral gate to Brady's fallen body, either to grab a warrant that they presumed he might have had on him, or to fetch the Kid's rifle (confiscated earlier) that Brady was carrying. Billy Mathews fired from across the street and his slug nicked the Kid, and then hit French in the thigh as the duo scurried back into the corral. The Regulators figured a way to hide Jim French as he was too hurt to ride. The others mounted, and then bolted from the corral gate and charged toward the east end of town amid a volley of gunfire. John Middleton reined-up and briefly returned the deputies' fire, scattering them once again. He then followed the others out of town.

The Regulators had heard that some of the men for whom they were looking were laying low on the Mescalero Apache Indian Reservation, and they decided to flush them out. This time the riders included Dick Brewer, Billy Bonney, Frank MacNab, John Middleton, Charlie Bowdre, Fred Waite, Henry Brown, Doc Scurlock, George and Frank Coe, John Scroggins Ignacio Gonzales, Steve Stephens, and Big Jim French, who was now feeling well enough to ride. The first night out, they camped on the Rinconada. The following morning (April 6th) they rode to Blazer's Mill, about two miles from Mescalero. Blazer's Mill was a small settlement that had blossomed around the sawmill of former dentist, Doc Blazer. The Regulators put their horses in the corral, and then went into Doc's house for a meal. Blazer's corral was enclosed by a fence constructed of planks from the sawmill, thereby hiding the horses inside. Had the horses been visible, Andrew L. "Buckshot" Roberts certainly wouldn't have wandered in. Roberts rode with the posse that killed John Tunstall. Frank Coe had finished eating first, and went outside where he saw Roberts approaching the house. Coe greeted Roberts, and then the two sat down on the porch to chat. Frank Coe informed "Buckshot" Roberts that the Regulators had a warrant for his arrest. Roberts cocked his rifle as it lay in his lap. Realizing that Roberts was outside, Bowdre, Bonney, and George Coe slipped out to help. Suddenly, Bowdre popped around the corner of the house with his revolver in hand and ordered Roberts to get his hands in the air. Roberts comment was, "Not much Mary Ann," and the two fired simultaneously. Bowdre's bullet hit Roberts in the stomach, while Roberts' slug nicked Bowdre's gun belt, and then hit George Coe in the hand. A second shot hit John Middleton, who was now nearby, in the chest. Badly injured, Roberts stumbled back through a doorway and into Doc Blazer's office—and temporary safety. Spotting Blazer's hunting rifle, a Springfield .45-.60, he latched on to the weapon and quickly loaded it with shells that lay nearby. Flattening himself on the floor, Roberts drew a bead through the partially opened doorway. When a head popped up from behind a log pile, Roberts fired. The shot hit Dick Brewer in the eye, and he fell dead.

Having lost their leader, the discouraged Regulators loaded the two injured men into a wagon and headed toward Fort Stanton for medical assistance. "Buckshot" Roberts died the following afternoon. He, and Richard M. "Dick" Brewer, are buried side-by-side at Blazer's Mill.

On the 18th of April, the Grand Jury completed its deliberations on a string of territorial cases. In the murder of John Tunstall, they found indictments against Jessie Evans, George Davis, Frank Rivers (a.k.a. John

Long), and Miguel Seguro (Manuel Segovia). James J, Dolan and Jacob (Billy) Mathews were named as accessories. In the murders of Sheriff William Brady and George Hindman, the jury brought in indictments against William Bonney, John Middleton, Fred Waite, and Henry Brown. Many of the Regulators were indicted in the killing of Andrew Roberts, including Charles Bowdre (who fired the fatal shot), Bonney (this time under the name of Henry Antrim, alias "Kid"), Middleton, Waite, and Brown, among others. James J. Dolan and John H. Riley were indicted for cattle theft. They were asked to leave the county, and they obliged. They would, however, be heard from again. Furthermore, Alexander McSween was exonerated of charges against him. McSween had won a battle, but not the war. The worst was yet to come.

Frank MacNab, now leader of the Regulators, publicly stated that it was time to clean up the rest of the murderers and rustlers in the Seven Rivers area. The Seven Rivers bunch beat MacNab to the punch. A posse of about thirty-five men mounted up and headed for Lincoln. George Peppin, Robert and John Beckwith, Marion Turner, Billy Mathews, Tom Green, and Jack Long were among the group that included many men from the posse that had murdered John Tunstall. On the evening of April 29th, Frank MacNab left Lincoln accompanied by Frank Coe and his partner Ab Saunders. The trio headed toward Coe's farm on the Hondo River. The Seven Rivers bunch spotted the three as they stopped to water their horses. The posse cut loose with a barrage of bullets. MacNab was killed, Saunders wounded, and Coe was allowed to surrender. Under the cover of darkness, the posse filtered into Lincoln. Shooting broke out about 9:00 a.m. on April 30th. The siege continued throughout the day, until it was interrupted by troops from Fort Stanton who "escorted" seventeen posse members back to the garrison.

The Regulators, with Doc Scurlock now in command, raided the Dolan-Riley cattle camp at Black River on May 14th. Their purpose was to retrieve horses stolen from the Tunstall ranch and others that were the property of Saunders and MacNab. As Scurlock, Bonney, and the others swept in, they killed Manuel Segovia (another member of the posse that killed John Tunstall), Billy Wier, and a teenage boy.

Although Jimmy Dolan was in "exile," he was still active in the Lincoln County War. Making use of his influential friends, who in turn made use of their influential friends, Dolan had John Copeland (a McSween puppet) removed from his post as sheriff of Lincoln County. Law required a new sheriff to post bond as tax collector. With all the commotion in Lincoln County, Copeland had failed to do so. Governor Axtell issued a proclamation that removed Copeland and appointed in his place, George W. Peppin, formerly one of Sheriff Brady's deputies, and a friend of the House. Whichever faction controlled the sheriff's office had "right" on its side, at least for the time being. On the other side, of course, were the "villains" and "assassins." Dolan had put the wheels into motion for a showdown, and it was now up to Peppin to follow through. Peppin appointed John "Jack" Long, Marion Turner, Buck Powell, and José Chavez y Baca to serve as deputies. He also began to recruit a posse to serve several outstanding warrants against the Regulators. Alexander McSween fled his home and took refuge with the Regulators, a group which was now growing with the addition of several Hispanics. They avoided near skirmishes with two separate posses, and stayed on the move. They would not be elusive too long, however.

July 14, 1878, was a quiet Sunday in Lincoln. Much of the posse was out of town, down in the San Patricio area. Jimmy Dolan was back in town, and was at the Wortley Hotel. He was accompanied by George Peppin and about five others. Jack Long, Billy Mathews, and five cohorts occupied the Torreon (Lincoln's defense tower). They were taken completely by surprise when a large group of riders thundered into town, led by Alexander McSween, William Bonney, and Doc Scurlock. Each was heavily armed. Once in town, the Regulators scattered. McSween, Bonney, Jim French, and ten other men went straight to, and occupied McSween's house. Scurlock, Bowdre, Middleton, and another ten men took over Isaac Ellis' store and house. Henry Brown, George Coe, and Sam Smith manned the Tunstall store. Martin Chaves and a sizable group of Hispanics occupied the José Mantano store. The Regulators barricaded windows, drilled holes for gun ports, and settled in for a long siege.

Having been summoned by a rider, Buck Powell led the posse back into Lincoln. They arrived that evening. Dolan's forces were further bolstered on Monday when John Kinney rode in with a group that included some of his ranch hands and Jessie Evans and the Boys. Most of the Seven Rivers bunch arrived as well. By now, both forces numbered close to fifty each.

Sporadic shooting occurred Monday, Tuesday, and Wednesday, through each day and even after dark. Daniel Huff died on Monday. He was hastily buried, and the cause of his death is unknown. On Wednesday, one of Dolan's men, Charlie Crawford, was picked of on a hillside nine-hundred yards (over 800 meters) away by a buffalo gun. He wriggled in agony until Fort Stanton soldiers moved him later in the day. Crawford was to die a week later. W. H. Johnson and two other members of the Dolan faction were wounded. That night, Ben Ellis was shot in the neck while tending to his horses. Thursday brought another day a sporadic shooting.

One month earlier, Congress passed the *Posse Comitatus Act*, which prohibited military use of Federal troops in any civil action, unless approved by the President of the United States. Colonel Nathan A. Dudley, commanding officer at Fort Stanton, had his hands tied. Though he tried to disguise the fact, he was openly more sympathetic to the Dolan cause than that of McSween. Thursday evening, Dudley called his officers together to discuss the Lincoln situation. They supported his decision to "place soldiers in the town of Lincoln for the preservation of the lives of the women and children." On Friday morning, July 19, 1878, he led one company of cavalry into Lincoln. The detachment set up camp directly opposite the Mantano store and house.

The McSween group had occupied the most strategic locations in town. The diversion and cease fire created by the arrival of the detachment gave Dolan's men an advantage. They were able to move in closer around the McSween house. With a howitzer trained on their front door, Martin Chaves decided to abandon the Montaño store. He moved his men to the Ellis house. Not knowing what Dudley's intentions might be, the McSween camp grew uneasy. When Peppin realized that Chaves and the Hispanics had moved down to the Ellis house, he took a group of men and advanced in that direction. Suddenly, a large throng of riders bolted from Ellis' corral with their guns blazing. The riders included Scurlock, Bowdre, Middleton, Chaves, and all the men who had been at both the Montaño's and Ellis' places. Several injuries were inflicted on both sides as this band of Regulators rode out of town.

Some of men in Peppin's posse gained access to an outside wall of the McSween house and they began to pile kindling against the building. Gunfire, which erupted from the hill north of town, attempted to drive the posse back. Scurlock, Bowdre, Chaves, and the others had moved to this new vantage point. When the cavalry trained their howitzer on the hillside, the Regulators disappeared.

Meanwhile, McSween's house had been set on fire by Jack Long and a fellow known only as Dummy. Henry Brown, George Coe, and Sam Smith, who were now in the grain warehouse behind the Tunstall store, opened fire on Long and Dummy as they retreated from the burning house. In what may have been the only humorous incident during the Lincoln County War, the two dove into the outhouse and submerged themselves below ground level to avoid the gunfire. Elizabeth Shield, Susan McSween's pregnant sister, ran out and extinguished the flames. The house, however, was torched again, and this time the fire took hold. Gunfire increased, to and from the slowly burning house. Eventually, a temporary cease fire was called in order that Susan McSween, Elizabeth Shield, and the children could be evacuated. The blaze illuminated the sky as darkness fell. As the heat intensified, Alexander McSween sat disconsolately. He was out of ideas.

Billy the Kid outlined a plan. He would take a few men and dash toward the Tunstall store creating a diversion that would allow the others to run for the back gate, from which they could escape to the river. By now there was no time for options. With their guns blazing, Billy the Kid, Big Jim French, José Chaves y Chaves, Tom O'Folliard, and Harvey Morris darted through the doorway and raced toward the store. Morris was immediately felled by a slug. He died in his tracks. The others were met by gunfire coming from one corner of the Tunstall store, so they changed their direction and sprinted toward the river where they escaped to safety. Meanwhile, Robert Beckwith was at the wrong place at the wrong time. He had approached McSween's back door with a warrant urging him to surrender. Gunfire erupted again as McSween and the others attempted to run. Robert Beckwith was shot down, as was Alexander McSween who fell on top of him. Francisco Zamora and Vicente Romero made it to the chicken house before they also were killed. Yginio Salazar was gunned down near the rear gate, and left for dead. He would later crawl nearly a half-mile to safety. Ignacio Gonzales was shot in the arm, but he reached the river and safety. Florencio Chaves and José Maria Sanchez escaped as well. Henry Brown, George Coe, and Sam Smith, who had been occupying the grain warehouse behind the Tunstall store, were also able to flee. The troops from Fort Stanton had done little more than to watch the confrontation, but their mere presence aided in the defeat of the McSween faction. The battle was over, but the war with Billy the Kid was not.

Following two more deaths in separate incidents, turmoil again mounted in Lincoln County. John Selman (who would later shoot John Wesley Hardin—in the back) and his brother Tom joined forces with John Kinney, Jessie Evans, Jake Owens, and many other members of the old George Peppin posse. The gang was sometimes called "Selman's Scouts." On the 18th of August, they raided the Feliz ranch (once the Tunstall ranch) and stole about two-hundred head of cattle. The Regulators answered. Bonney, Bowdre, Scurlock, Middleton, and the others were joined by ten new men, bringing their band to about thirty-six in number. On the 6th of September, they rode to the Fritz ranch, a Dolan-Riley stronghold, and proceeded to "rustle" back one-hundred-fifty head of cattle and fifteen horses.

President Rutherford B. Hayes gave all law breakers fair warning when he announced that beginning on October 13, 1878, the U. S. Army would again be permitted to furnish troops to support civil authorities. A marked decrease in lawlessness, and a semblance of civil order began to take place.

The Regulators began to break up. John Middleton, Henry Brown, Fred Waite, Frank and George Coe, and others abandoned their outlaw ways, at least for the time being, and departed in various directions to presumably earn an honest living. The others followed Billy the Kid.

A potentially dangerous parley occurred at Lincoln on February 18, 1879, ironically exactly one year after the killing of John Tunstall. Billy the Kid, Doc Scurlock, Tom O'Folliard, George Bowers, and José Salazar met with Jessie Evans, Jimmy Dolan, Billy Mathews, Billy Campbell, and Edgar Walz. Throwing this bunch together was like a powder keg waiting for someone to light the fuse. Incredibly, they agreed to a truce. Furthermore, they assented to aid each other in resisting arrests and never to give evidence against the other in any prosecution. Anyone who broke the pact was to be killed on sight. Following the parley, they all got drunk together. While heading down the street later that evening, the group encountered Houston Chapman, Susan McSween's lawyer. Billy Campbell, who was one of Dolan's men, shot and killed Chapman at point blank range. Campbell proclaimed that he had "promised my God and General Dudley" that he would kill Chapman, and now he had done it. In the confusion that followed, the Kid and Tom O'Folliard slipped out of town and headed for San Patricio.

Billy the Kid grew tired of running. He decided to write to the new territorial governor, Lew Wallace, in an effort to make a "deal." Bonney agreed to testify as a witness to the Chapman murder if Governor Wallace would grant him amnesty. Bonney further requested a meeting with the governor to discuss the matter. Governor Wallace, who was presently penning his classic novel *Ben Hur*, was intrigued by the idea and scheduled a secret meeting at the residence of old Squire Wilson the evening of March 15, 1879. The meeting materialized. The Kid walked in with a Winchester in one hand and a revolver in the other. The governor's plan was simple. Bonney would submit to arrest and would remain in jail until the Grand Jury convened. After he identified the murderers of Chapman, he would receive a pardon and be free to go. Bonney had good intentions and followed through with his part of the bargain. Wallace did not. District Attorney Rynerson saw to it that the Kid remained behind bars. Following the Grand Jury, the Kid waited twenty days for Wallace to come through before he took matters into his own hands. Billy the Kid and Tom O'Folliard (who had surrendered with him) easily escaped and headed toward Fort Sumner.

While drinking in Bob Hargrove's saloon at Fort Sumner, on January 10, 1880, the Kid was tipped off that a fellow standing by the bar, named Joe Grant, intended to kill him. Bonney, in his ever-smiling way, approached Grant and began admiring his pearl-handled revolver. The Kid then innocently asked if he could examine it. Grant obliged. While doing so, Billy noticed that there were only three cartridges in the cylinder, so before handing it back, he rotated the cylinder so that it would fire next on an empty chamber. Within a short time, Grant challenged the Kid. He thrust his six-gun toward Bonney's face and pulled the trigger. As the weapon clicked, the Kid fired a round into Grant's head. He died instantly. One story that surfaced indicated that the dead man was a bounty hunter. That is unlikely, because at this time Billy the Kid had no price on his head.

Surrounded by some of the original Regulators, the Kid went back to rustling cattle and horses. His gang took on a new look with the addition of many toughs like the scoundrel Dave Rudabaugh, Las Vegas killer John Webb, and Texas hard case Joe Cook. They thieved at will, and nobody dared to stop them. Nobody, that is, until Pat Garrett came along.

Pat Garrett was a saloonkeeper, small rancher, and former buffalo hunter with nerves of steel. During the summer of 1880, Garrett was appointed deputy sheriff of Lincoln County. He was then convinced to run for the office of sheriff, in the fall election. Garrett had strong support and was easily elected. Prior to assuming his new office, Garrett was appointed U. S. Deputy Marshal, a position that would allow him to cross county lines. The Kid was a frequent customer at Beaver Smith's

Saloon in Fort Sumner, where Garrett had worked as bartender, and they knew each other well. Pat Garrett was determined to do well at his new position, which meant bringing in Billy the Kid, dead or alive. The new sheriff laid trap after trap, and came close, but continued to come up empty. On December 19, 1880, near the outskirts of Fort Sumner, the Kid and Tom O'Folliard were riding at the front of the gang. They were trailed by Dave Rudabaugh, Tom Pickett, Charlie Bowdre, and Billy Wilson, when (whether by instinct, or not) Billy the Kid wheeled his horse around and rode to the back of the pack to get some chewing tobacco from Billy Wilson. At that moment they were confronted by the posse of Pat Garrett. O'Folliard went for his gun, as the posse shot him down. The Kid and the others all escaped. Tom O'Folliard, who was probably Billy the Kid's closest friend, died within the hour. Garrett and his men turned their attention to tracking the Kid.

The Kid and his followers weren't able to disguise their trail through the snow. Four days later, at Stinking Springs, Garrett's posse cornered the fugitives in a dilapidated rock house that was once used as a forage station. The building had one door, and no windows or other openings. As it was about 2:00 a.m., Garrett decided to wait until daybreak. At dawn, Charlie Bowdre emerged from the building with a nose bag to feed his horse. Pat Garrett ordered him to throw up his hands, but Bowdre quickly drew two pistols and exchanged shots as three bullets crashed into his body. He staggered, and then dropped dead. His cohorts reached out and were able to pull two of the horses into the house. They intended to saddle them, and then ride through the doorway with their six-shooters blazing. As they pulled the third horse, Garrett shot it down and it blocked the doorway making an escape virtually impossible. The Kid laughed and joked inside as if he didn't have a worry in the world. Later in the day, the outlaws surrendered.

At La Mesilla, on April 13, 1881, Judge Warren H. Bristol pronounced sentence on William Bonney. The judge declared that the defendant shall be confined to prison in Lincoln County until May 13, 1881, at which time he shall "be hanged by the neck until his body be dead." As Bonney was chained in preparation for the one-hundred and fifty mile journey (just over 240 kilometers) to Lincoln, newspaper reporters indicated that the Kid looked quite cheerful.

Under heavy guard, Billy the Kid arrived back in Lincoln on April 21, 1881. He was incarcerated in the county courthouse (the old Murphy-Dolan store). The Kid was kept in leg and arm shackles, chained to the floor, and was guarded twenty-four hours a day. On the 28th of April, Deputy Robert Olinger led the other prisoners over to the Wortley Hotel for dinner. Deputy J. W. Bell remained at the courthouse to guard the Kid. While the others were away, Bonney told Bell that he needed to use the outhouse. Bell agreed to escort Billy outside, and he did. Upon their return to the courthouse, the Kid slipped his small hands out of the cuffs, produced a six-gun and shot Bell to death. Where the gun came from is a matter for speculation. Bonney could have grabbed Bell's revolver, and then again, one could have been planted for him in the privy. Alerted as to the commotion, Robert Olinger left his prisoners in front of the hotel, and dashed across the street. As he neared the courthouse, Billy called out from an upstairs window, "Hello Bob." As Olinger looked up, the Kid blasted him with both barrels of a shotgun. Thirty-six buckshot entered his body. Billy the Kid then armed himself with two pistols and a Winchester rifle, stepped out on to the porch, and in his usually jovial manner announced that he was "master, not only of the courthouse, but also of the town." The Kid worked on his shackles for about an hour before he was able to free one leg. Lincoln was paralyzed. Nobody raised one finger to stop him. With a blanket roll, a few supplies, and an arsenal of weapons, Billy the Kid leisurely mounted a pony and rode out of town to the west. He stopped at Yginio Salazar's house where Yginio helped him remove the shackles, and then furnished him a good horse. Though already famous, the escape from Lincoln made Billy the Kid legendary. Stories of his daring escapades rolled off the presses everywhere.

 Under the circumstances, most fugitives would have traveled great distances to get as far away from Lincoln as possible. Not Billy the Kid, however, for he found a certain security amongst his circle of friends in the New Mexico Territory which he knew so well. In response to a rumor that the Kid was in the Fort Sumner area, Pat Garrett, Thomas McKinney, and John W. Poe headed in that direction. When they arrived, Garrett decided to stop and see an old friend, Pete Maxwell, whom he assumed might know the whereabouts of the Kid. The sun had already set, and Maxwell had retired early to his bedroom in the southeastern corner of the house. It was a warm evening on July 14, 1881, and Maxwell left his outside door wide open for circulation. While the others waited out front, Garrett stepped into the darkened bedroom to awaken Maxwell. Garrett sat on the edge of the bed as the two talked.

 Meanwhile, the Kid, who was staying at a nearby house, had just returned from a rendezvous in a nearby peach orchard with Celsa Gutierrez, a Mexican girl that the Kid would occasionally "meet." Bonney was hungry, and he decided to cut a steak from a side of beef hanging in Pete Maxwell's smokehouse. The Kid spotted the men waiting out front, and wondering who they were, went to the doorway and spoke to Maxwell, "Pedro, quien sonos estos hombres afuera?" Maxwell whispered to Garrett, "That's him!" Garrett drew his gun and fired, and then leaped to the floor as he fired again. The second shot wasn't necessary as the first had hit its target right above the heart. Billy the Kid died instantly. He uttered no other word, nor did he know who killed him.

Three sheriffs of Lincoln County. Seated are Pat Garrett (at left), and John W. Poe. Standing between them is James Brent. *Wild Horse Collection.*

Newton, Kansas as it looked during the autumn of 1872.
Kansas State Historical Society.

Chapter Nine
Shootout at the Tuttle Dance Hall

Newton, Kansas, became a convenient shipping point for Texas cattle when the Santa Fe Railroad arrived in 1871. No longer would cowboys need to drive their beef fifty miles to the nearest railroad in Abilene. Newton prospered overnight, with the construction of new stockyards, saloons and dance halls. With cattlemen and railroad construction workers mixed together, it was a wild and rowdy place.

The Tuttle Dance Hall was situated in a sleazy section of town surrounded by cribs where prostitutes peddled their wares. The establishment was owned and operated by a fellow named Perry Tuttle. It was the place where a skinny lad named Jim Riley blazed his way to western notoriety.

The frail Riley, who was subject to coughing fits, was a friend of tough Mike McCluskie, a railroad foreman and part-time night policeman. Several days earlier McCluskie had gunned down a gambler using the alias of Bill Bailey (his real name was William Wilson). Hugh Anderson, a friend of Bailey, vowed revenge. Believing matters would cool down, McCluskie left town for a few days but he couldn't resist the fun of a Saturday night in Newton and he headed back into town.

The time was about 1:00 a.m. in the morning, on August 20, 1871, when Hugh Anderson and four friends walked through the front door of the Tuttle Dance Hall. McCluskie was sitting at a faro table with other railroad men. Also sitting at the table was Jim Riley. As Anderson approached the faro table he drew and shot McCluskie through the neck. McCluskie was able to get off a couple of stray shots as he collapsed. Anderson shot McCluskie two more times for good measure. When the shooting started, Riley jumped up and moved away from the table. Meanwhile, Anderson's friends had opened fire, as well. Jim Martin took a slug in the throat, and Patrick Lee was shot in the stomach. A fellow named Hickey was dropped by a bullet in the leg. Martin staggered through the front door and would die in the street. What then happened is one of the most amazing displays of marksmanship, in a short reaction time, ever recorded.

With a six-shooter in his hand, Jim Riley calmly closed and locked the saloon door. His gun barked with deadly authority. With quick consecutive shots he dropped the entire group of cowboys. He killed Billy Garrett with bullets in the shoulder and chest. He shot Henry Kearnes in the chest and Kearnes would die. Another Riley bullet hit Jim Wilkerson in the nose and he was seriously wounded. Hugh Anderson was hit twice in the leg, and an unnamed cowboy also took a slug in the leg. Six bullets—seven hits. Some say, one or two of the leg hits could have been caused by McCluskie as he collapsed to the floor. At any rate, Riley was unscathed and the feat was incredible.

Mike McCluskie died the following morning after he had requested that authorities notify his mother in St. Louis. Martin, Garrett and Kearnes were also dead. Anderson, Hickey, Wilkerson and the unnamed cowboy were all injured. The gunfight that is also known as Newton's General Massacre had claimed nine casualties—four dead and five wounded.

Should Jim Riley have wanted to bask in his glory, he possibly could have become a real legend. He chose to disappear that night after the gunfight, never to be seen or heard from again.

Nearly two years later, at Medicine Lodge, Kansas, Hugh Anderson was challenged to a duel to the death by Mike McCluskie's brother Arthur, who was known as Art. The fight was fair. With their backs turned to each other, both walked until they heard a shot, at which time they whirled and fired. Their first shots missed, and they charged toward each other and then connected. McCluskie shot Anderson in the arm, and Anderson shot McCluskie in the mouth. Both men were on the ground. Anderson put two more slugs into McCluskie. Just when it looked like McCluskie was finished, he raised his head and shot Anderson in the abdomen. McCluskie and Anderson crawled toward each other as they drew their knives. Anderson stabbed McCluskie in the neck as McCluskie buried his knife into Anderson's side. With guns and knives Art McCluskie and Hugh Anderson had shot each other and stabbed each other until both men lay side by side—dead.

[Authors note: It is generally believed that Riley's first name was Jim, although there is no proof to substantiate the belief. It is also presumed that the frail lad had consumption (tuberculosis). He obviously was fearless, possibly because he knew he would die soon anyway.]

The Ransom Saloon at Ingalls was frequented by the Doolin Gang.
Archives & Manuscripts of the Oklahoma Historical Society.

Chapter Ten
Raid on the Doolin Gang at Ingalls

Bill Doolin, George "Bitter Creek" Newcomb and Charles Pierce were all members of the Dalton gang. Bob Dalton had decided not to include the trio in their ill-fated last raid at Coffeyville, Kansas. Following the Daltons' decimation, Bill Doolin organized a new gang. In addition to Bitter Creek Newcomb and Charley Pierce, other gang members (at one time or another) included Bill Dalton (who, although a brother of Bob, Grat and Emmett, never rode with the Daltons), George "Red Buck" Weightman (sometimes spelled Waightman), William "Little Bill" Raidler, Bob Grounds, William "Tulsa Jack" Blake, "Little" Dick West, Dan "Dynamite Dick" Clifton (who had several aliases), "Arkansas" Tom Jones (whose real name was Roy Daugherty), Alf Sohn, and Oliver "Ol" Yantis. The gang was variously known as the Doolin gang, Doolin's Wild Bunch, the "Oklahombres," and the Doolin-Dalton gang.

Lawlessness thrived on the Oklahoma frontier, and the Doolin gang was feared by many. Doolin, Yantis and Newcomb (who courted Yantis' sister) robbed the Ford County Bank at Spearville, Kansas, on November 1, 1891. In their haste to stuff their sack full of bank notes, they left a substantial sum behind. Four weeks later, Ol Yantis was identified near Stillwater, Oklahoma, and was shot to death by C.

M. "Chalk" Beeson, Thomas J. Hueston and George Cox. Though the robbery at Spearville was but one of many, it led to the first fatality of a gang member.

Led by the efforts of U. S. Marshal E. D. Nix, a formidable task force was organized to fight crime on the Oklahoma plains. Passage of the *Organic Act* gave the marshal authority to deputize local law enforcement officers as federal deputy marshals, thereby allowing them to cross borders in pursuit of fugitives. It also put additional heat on outlaw gangs such as Doolin's bunch—already the primary objective of territorial crime fighters.

The Doolin gang often hid out near the tiny Oklahoma town of Ingalls. Occasionally, the band would drift into town and head for the Ransom Saloon. One such day was September 1, 1893. The law had been tipped off that the gang might be headed for Ingalls. A posse was organized that included Jim Masterson, Thomas J. Hueston, Dick Speed, Lafayette "Lafe" Shadley, W. C. Roberts, John W. Hixon, Henry Keller, M. A. Janson, George Cox, J. S. Burke, Ike Steel, Red Lucas and H. A. "Hi" Thompson. They also headed toward town. Seven of the outlaws preceded the posse into Ingalls. When they arrived at about 10:00 a.m., Arkansas Tom Jones, who was ill, went straight to the unfinished second-floor of the O. K. Hotel to lie down. Doolin, Dalton, Blake, Clifton and Weightman left their mounts at the livery and then stepped next door to the Ransom Saloon. They ordered drinks and then settled in for a game of poker. Newcomb lingered on the street.

Almost immediately the lawmen began to filter into town one by one. Newcomb became suspicious. Ingalls was small, and there usually weren't too many people moving about. He rode to the door of Ransom's to caution the others. When Arkansas Tom looked out from the upstairs hotel window, he also became suspicious and reached for his rifle.

One of the lawmen, Dick Speed, inquired of a youth as to who the man on the horse was across the street. Everybody in town knew the Doolin bunch, and the boy replied, "Why that's Bitter Creek!" Seeing Speed raise his rifle, Newcomb pulled his Winchester from its scabbard. Speed triggered a shot that hit the magazine of Newcomb's weapon. He was able to return one shot, but then his rifle jammed. Jones threw open a window and began to fire. His first bullet hit Speed in the shoulder. The second dropped him in the dust. Dick Speed was dead. Newcomb spurred his horse and raced out of town, as bullets flew harmlessly by him.

The lawmen closed in on the saloon, with a barrage of bullets.

Jones climbed a ladder to the attic where he knocked a hole in the hotel roof. From his new vantage point he picked off another lawman, Tom Heuston, who collapsed to the ground with two slugs in his body. During the hail of bullets that flew in each direction, a boy, and a horse were killed, and four bystanders were wounded. One of those, N. A. Walker, was shot in the abdomen and would die several days later. Inside the saloon, Ransom was nicked, and his bartender Neil Murray was wounded by two slugs.

Bill Doolin sprang out of Ransom's side door and dashed to the livery (that was located just south of the saloon). From there he provided cover for Dalton and Weightman as they scampered across. The three continued to fire as Clifton and Blake scurried to the livery. They quickly bridled their horses.

Simultaneously, with their six-guns blazing, the outlaws galloped out of both of the stable doors. Doolin and Clifton exited from the rear, as Dalton, Blake and Weightman rode out through the front doors. They whirled their horses and headed for a nearby draw. John Hixon shot Bill Dalton's horse out from under him. Dalton hit the ground running. The outlaws were slowed by a wire fence, which Dalton quickly cut. As he did, lawman Lafe Shadley crawled too close. Bill Dalton shot him three times. The bullet holes were so close together that they could have been covered by one hand. Doolin (or possibly Blake) doubled back to pick up Dalton, who leaped up behind him, and they scurried to safety. After the other fugitives had fled, lawmen surrounded the hotel. Arkansas Tom held out for nearly an hour, before Jim Masterson threatened to blow him away with two sticks of dynamite. Jones tossed out his Winchester and surrendered. The siege was over.

The seriously injured Shadley and Hueston were taken to Stillwater, along with the body of Speed. By the following day, they had both died. The youth who was killed was named Dell Simmons. Frank Briggs, a teen-ager, received a shoulder wound. The only member of the gang to definitely have been injured was Bitter Creek Newcomb who received a gash in his leg when the magazine on his Winchester was shattered. There is speculation that Clifton may have received a neck wound, as well. In addition to the two horses there were nine or ten casualties (five dead, four or five wounded).

Arkansas Tom Jones (Roy Daugherty) received a fifty year sentence, but was paroled in 1910. Upon his release he returned to robbing banks until he was killed in 1924. Other gang members had already met their demise. Bill Dalton left the Doolin gang to form his own outfit. Shortly thereafter he was killed by a posse at the home of his wife and two children in 1894, near Ardmore, Oklahoma. Tulsa Jack Blake died in 1895 during another attack by a posse on the Doolin gang near Dover, Oklahoma. A bullet struck Blake's cartridge belt causing a shell to explode that killed him. The other gang members all safely escaped. The Doolin gang operated for about a year and a half after the raid at Ingalls. The gang broke up in April of 1895. Bitter Creek Newcomb and Charley Pierce were gunned down (for a reward) by the Dunn brothers at the Dunn ranch on the Cimarron River in Oklahoma in 1895. Red Buck Weightman was shot to death at a hideout in Arapaho, Oklahoma in 1896. On a moonlit night, Bill Doolin was shotgunned by lawmen Heck Thomas and Bill Dunn (one of the Dunn brothers that killed Newcomb and Pierce) in 1896 while leading his horse near his father-in-law's house just outside of Lawson, Oklahoma. There were twenty-one holes in Bill Doolin's dead body. Dynamite Dick Clifton was shot and killed by deputy marshals the following year near Checotah, Oklahoma.

The plaza at Marysville from a lithograph printed in the Marysville City Directory of 1858-1859. *Yuba County Library.*

Chapter Eleven
Hanging Bell

When Dr. Thomas Hodges gave up the medical profession to follow a career in outlawry he assumed the alias of Tom Bell. His new occupation was short-lived—as was Tom Bell.

The adventuresome Hodges, who grew up in Tennessee, headed west to participate in the Mexican War as a medical orderly. After the war, he returned to Tennessee and settled into a practice in medicine. Following the discovery of gold in California, Hodges' free spirit prevailed, and he joined thousands of others who were driven by the dream of riches. Prospectors swarmed over the hills in search of the mother lode. Only a few struck it rich. Thomas Hodges was not one of those. Unable to find much success in the gold fields, Hodges had other ideas of how to become wealthy. He turned to thievery. That also proved to be an unsuccessful profession and he quickly landed in jail. There Tom Bell (as he was now calling himself) met Bill Gristy (who's real name was Bill White). Gristy was a scoundrel who was rough on the edges, but a seasoned thief (something Bell was not). On the other hand, Tom Bell had intelligence, an attribute that was lacking in Gristy. The two seemingly complemented each other. Neither Bell nor Gristy was imprisoned for very long. They, and a few other prisoners, escaped when a gate was mysteriously left unlocked one night in May of 1855.

Tom Bell and Bill Gristy organized a gang. The gang, which was active through much of 1856, had high expectations but low realizations. Their lack of success was due in large part to poor planning. On one occasion, the gang accosted a wagon driver who had just delivered a load of beer in Nevada City, California. The driver, who was carrying his payment of $300, drew his revolver in an effort to defend himself. A gunfight erupted in which the driver was wounded. Gristy grabbed the $300, and the robbers sped away. The incident near Nevada City was typical of the capers (or attempted capers) of the gang. The loot from their petty endeavors didn't amount to much.

On another occasion, near Oroville, Bell and Gristy chased a horseman whom they were attempting to rob. Bill Gristy shot the rider in a leg and he stopped. After relieving the man of $200, Tom Bell made use of his medical expertise. He bound the man's wound and helped him into the wagon of a passing teamster whom they also robbed.

A salesman named Rosenthal was accosted by Tom Bell and a few gang members on a road near Auburn. Rosenthal was robbed of $1,250, and then left tied to a tree about one hundred yards from the road. When his body was discovered it had been partially devoured by wild animals.

On August 11, 1856, Tom Bell's gang attempted to rob the Wells Fargo stage between Marysville and Camptonville. The coach was carrying a shipment of gold. The outlaws hid in an area along Dry Creek and awaited the vehicle. As the stagecoach approached, they rode out from behind their cover and ordered the driver to halt. Wells Fargo express messenger, Bill Dobson, fired a blast from his shotgun. Passengers also opened fire on the outlaws, as driver John Gear whipped his horses. A blazing gun battle and chase ensued. One of the bandits was shot from his saddle. A passenger was killed and two others wounded, as was John Gear who was able to outdistance the outlaws and abort the robbery.

When a man was killed on the western frontier it was one thing, but when a lady was shot to death citizens became enraged. The passenger who was killed was a Mrs. Tilghman, wife of a Marysville barbershop owner. A large posse set out highly intent on finding the outlaws.

The Mountaineer House was a travel stop near Auburn operated by a rogue named Jack Phillips. Phillips was known to shelter and feed many a fugitive passing through. An informer led law enforcement officers to a tent bunkhouse on Phillips' property where Bill Gristy and other outlaws were hiding out following the robbery of a pack train in the Trinity Mountains. The officers burst into the tent with guns blazing. One load of buckshot instantly killed a bandit named Walker (who's real name was George Skinner). Another blast hit gang member Pete Ansara in the leg. Two of the robbers threw up their hands and surrendered. Gristy dashed from the tent, leaped on his horse, and rode away. He would be tracked and captured.

The authorities promised Gristy leniency if he would advise them as to the whereabouts of Tom Bell. Bill Gristy ratted on Bell, but was jailed anyhow. Bell and other gang members were located near a place called the Franklin House. As the posse closed in, gunfire was exchanged. Gang member Ned Conner was gunned down, but Bell and a cohort named Tex Owen managed to elude the lawmen.

Tom Bell was ultimately captured by a posse near the Merced River on October 4, 1856. He was allowed to write letters to his mother and mistress, Elizabeth Hood, before vigilante justice prevailed. Thomas Hodges (Tom Bell) was promised that his letters would be mailed, before he squirmed at the end of a rope until he strangled.

This photograph of Mysterious Dave Mather was taken shortly after his appointment as assistant city marshal of Dodge City in 1883. *Boot Hill Museum.*

Chapter Twelve
Mysterious Dave Mather

At one time or another, Dave Mather rode on both sides of the law. He was soft spoken, cunning, had a wicked demeanor and, for the most part, kept his thoughts to himself. These traits created a certain aura, which most likely led to his nickname, "Mysterious Dave".

David Mather was born in Connecticut on August 10, 1851. He, and his younger brother Josiah, drifted west when the latter was still a teenager. For a while Dave and Josiah rode with a band of rustlers in Arkansas. After parting ways with Josiah, Dave surfaced in many different places during the next several years. Mather accepted a position as a peace officer in Las Vegas, New Mexico. The job was offered to Mather even though his closest associates were gamblers and fairly shady characters. Mather, himself, was allegedly under suspicion for participation in a couple of robberies. While serving the law at Las Vegas, Mather was involved in two shooting incidents. On one occasion (November 20, 1879), after rounding up several drunken and rowdy soldiers to carry them to jail, one of the enlisted men attempted to flee. Mather fired several shots, one of which nicked the soldier, who promptly surrendered. On January 25, 1880, a railroad foreman, Joseph Castello, attempted to break up a quarrel between two of his workers. The commotion quickly drew a crowd. Castello and one of his henchmen unholstered their pistols and advised the gathering to back away—that it was none of their business. As Mather arrived on the scene, Castello aimed his handgun at the police officer and ordered him to stop. Mather's response was deadly. He drew and fired. Castello dropped where he stood. The slug penetrated his lung and stomach, and he would succumb eight hours later. Dr. Russell Bayly remained with the victim during that time in order to make his period of dying as comfortable as possible.

Soon after the Castello incident, Mysterious Dave moved on to Dodge City, Kansas. About a month later, Mather, Charlie Bassett, and two others headed to the Gunnison area of Colorado to try their luck in the gold fields. Following a jail break in Las Vegas, New Mexico (November 1880), the newspaper charged that among those who assisted in the escape were Dave Rudabaugh and Mysterious Dave. Fourteen months later (January 1882), Mather was arrested in Fort Worth, Texas, for stealing a gold chain and ring (in Dallas) which belonged to a black woman of questionable character named Georgia Morgan. Morgan, who claimed to have been intimate with Mysterious Dave, followed him to Fort Worth intent on revenge. She was carrying a pistol and large butcher knife. Georgia Morgan was also arrested, fined $8.25, and was allowed to return to Dallas. Apparently the charge against Mather was dropped as nothing further materialized regarding this incident.

About June 1, 1883, Mysterious Dave Mather was appointed assistant marshal of Dodge City at a salary of $75 per month. The city council raised his pay to $125 on the 6th of July, to which the Ford County Globe responded, "Dodge City pays her marshal $150 per month and the assistant marshal $125 per month. Besides this, each of them is entitled to kill a cowboy or two each season." In addition to assisting City Marshal Jack Bridges, Mather served concurrently as a deputy under Sheriff Patrick F. Sughrue. On April 7, 1884, George M. Hoover was elected mayor of Dodge City. Hoover appointed William M. Tilghman as new City Marshal, and Thomas C. Nixon to replace Mather as assistant marshal. The appointment did not affect Mysterious Dave's position as deputy sheriff which he continued to hold.

A strong resentment grew between Dave Mather and Tom Nixon. Mysterious Dave and David Black were proprietors of the Opera House Saloon, an establishment which they planned to turn into a dance hall. Tom Nixon and Brick Bond owned the Lady Gay Saloon which was partially a dance hall. On May 22, 1884, the city council passed legislation making it unlawful for anyone to maintain a dance hall ". . . or any other place where lewd women and men congregate for the purpose of dancing or otherwise." Mather was prohibited from converting his establishment into a dance hall, while for some reason dancing continued at Nixon's Lady Gay. Not only did Nixon have Mather's old job but the latter was certain that Nixon was behind some of the problems that the Opera House was experiencing. Some say that a woman was responsible for much of the friction between the two peace officers, but that is only conjecture.

The feud heightened on the evening of July 18, 1884, when Nixon fired a shot at Mather who was standing in the doorway of his saloon. It was a close call for Mysterious Dave who suffered powder burns from the shot. Sheriff Sughrue disarmed Tom Nixon and escorted him to jail. He was charged with assault with intent to kill, and then released on $800 bond.

At approximately 10 p.m. on the 21st of July, Mysterious Dave descended the stairs from his saloon and spied Nixon standing near the corner. Mather called out to Nixon as he approached him, "Tom!" As Nixon turned, Mather's Colt .42 barked four times. "Oh, I'm killed," gasped Nixon as the slugs slammed into his body. He had been hit in the chest, left side, and twice in the right side. Tom Nixon died instantly. Following the murder trial, which lasted three days, the jury deliberated for only twenty-seven minutes before acquitting Mysterious Dave Mather.

Dodge City's Junction Saloon was a busy spot on the evening of May 10, 1885. Mysterious Dave, his brother Josiah, and Sheriff Pat Sughrue were among those present. Dave was playing cards with a fellow named Dave Barnes. A dispute arose when Mather raked in a pot which Barnes claimed was his. Almost immediately shots flew in several directions. One slug passed through Mysterious Dave's hat creasing his skull. It was believed to have been fired by Barnes. Josiah Mather fired several shots from behind the bar. Dave Barnes slumped to the floor—dead. Intent on joining the melee, Barnes' brother John started to draw. Sheriff Sughrue grabbed his arm and wrestled the gun from his grasp. Following the shooting, in which two innocent bystanders were also injured, Sheriff Sughrue arrested Josiah and Dave Mather. The sheriff later stated, "Dave Mather had a gun on when I arrested him but it was loaded and no empty shells were in it." The Mather brothers were each allowed to post a $3,000 bond. They failed to appear in court, their bonds were forfeited, and apparently that was the end of the Dave Barnes matter.

Three months later Dave Mather was appointed City Marshal of New Kiowa, Kansas. In keeping with his name, Mysterious Dave disappeared the following year, never to be heard from again.

This photograph of early Lampasas, Texas, shows the scene of a gunfight that occurred on June 7, 1877, between the feuding Horrell and Higgins factions. Looking west down Third Street, its intersection with Live Oak Street is at right and the public square at left.
Keystone Square Museum and the Lampasas County Historical Commission.

Chapter Thirteen
Feuds of the Horrell Clan

Trouble followed the Arkansas-born, Texas-bred Horrells wherever they went. Much of it was of their own making. "The Horrell War" occurred in Lincoln County, New Mexico, in late 1873 and early 1874. Basically it was a conflict between Tejanos (Texans) and Hispanics. "The Horrell-Higgins Feud" which occurred in Lampasas County, Texas, culminated in 1877. Both were bloody affairs.

Between 1839 and 1857 the marriage of Samuel and Elizabeth Horrell produced eight children: William, John, Samuel, Jr., James Martin "Mart", Thomas, Benjamin, Merritt, and Sarah. They were a tough bunch. The Horrell family moved from Caddo Gap, Arkansas, to a ranch near Lampasas, Texas, in about 1857. Eleven years later they packed up their belongings and set out for California with a thousand head of cattle. When they reached Las Cruces, New Mexico, they sold their herd. The oldest son, John (William is believed to have perished during the Civil War), gathered the drovers to pay them their final wages. In a dispute over the amount of his wages, a cowpoke named Early Hubbard killed John Horrell. The family decided to stay in the vicinity, at least for a while. About three months later Sam, Sr., met his demise at the hands of Apaches near the San Agustin Pass in the San Andres Mountains. Soon thereafter the Horrells pulled up stakes and returned to the Lampasas,

Texas area.

John, Mart and Ben had married three sisters. Children were born to each of the couples. Tom also married but had no offspring. Merritt, the youngest son, remained a bachelor and lived with Mart and his family. The brothers raised cattle in the area along Little Lucy Creek. They were a no-nonsense bunch, and each of the boys was very skillful with firearms. The Horrells were well liked and had many friends.

State Police Chief, F. L. Britton notified Governor Edmund Davis that action was necessary to bring a large gang of rustlers to justice and listed four of the Horrell brothers among sixteen names in his report. Shortly thereafter, two Horrell friends, G. W. and Mark Short were involved in an altercation during which G. W. Short shot the sheriff. When a posse attempted to arrest the Shorts, Ben, Tom and Mart Horrell, accompanied by a number of their cohorts, intervened with guns drawn. The posse had no alternative but to watch in vain as the Shorts rode to safety.

A law enacted in 1871 to "Regulate the Keeping and Bearing of Deadly Weapons" specifically excluded Lampasas County. The Short brothers' incident was the catalyst which prompted Governor Davis to extend the law to include Lampasas County. F. L. Britton sent seven policemen, under the command of Captain Thomas G. Williams, to

Mart Horrell was wounded in a shootout with police at Jerry Scott's Matador Saloon. *Sarah Harrison Cobb.*

Lampasas in order to enforce the new provisions.

Bill Bowen, a fugitive from the law, had fled to Lampasas months earlier to seek refuge with his in-laws, the Horrells. On March 14, 1873, Sam, Mart and Tom Horrell were having drinks at Jerry Scott's Matador Saloon with several cowboys including Bowen when they were confronted by members of the State Police. Captain Tom Williams and the other policemen had seen Bowen go into the saloon and decided to investigate. After entering the building, they tried to arrest Bowen for wearing a revolver. When Williams approached him and attempted to grab his pistol, gunfire erupted. Captain Williams and Officer T. M. Daniels were killed instantly. The lifeless body of Officer Wesley Cherry crumbled to the ground just outside the door. Another policeman, Andrew Melville, was shot in the street. He staggered into a hotel but would soon die. Three other officers were able to flee. Mart Horrell was injured in the exchange of gunfire. He was taken to his mother's home to recuperate. Within a few days a posse of policemen, headed by Britton, arrived at Elizabeth's home and arrested Mart. They also arrested Allen Whitecraft, Jim Jenkins, Jerry Scott and James Grizell. None of the others could be found. The five prisoners were jailed at Austin. Horrell and Scott were then transferred to Georgetown. Artemisa Horrell was allowed to remain with her husband, Mart, to nurse his wound.

Once Artemisa thought that Mart was capable of riding she notified his brothers. On the 2nd of May a mob of about thirty-five men rode into Georgetown in a show of force. While most of the men were shooting at random in order to keep townspeople at bay, Bill Bowen smashed in the jailhouse door with a sledgehammer. The prisoners were freed, and the mob rode off into the night. A. S. Fisher, a local attorney, was wounded by a bullet during the jailbreak.

The Horrells decided that it was time to pack up and leave Texas in search of greener pastures. After selling most of their cattle to local businessmen, the clan assembled its wagons and headed west.

In late September of 1873, the Horrells settled along the Ruidoso River, in Lincoln County, New Mexico. They probably could have picked a better spot. There had been several incidents which created friction between Hispanics and Anglos in the vicinity. In the eyes of Ruidoso Valley Hispanics, Tejanos (Texans) were as bad as Anglos could be. The feud which unfolded over the next few months was predominately between Texans and Hispanics. It is commonly referred to as "The Horrell War."

The first bloody conflict occurred on the night of December 1, 1873. Sheriff Jacob L. Gylam, a Texan, was called Jack by the Anglos and Jackicito by the Hispanics. David C. Warner was another Texan who had moved to the valley. They both liked their liquor. So did Tom and Ben Horrell and their buddy Zachariah Crumpton. Having had too much to drink, the group decided to "shoot up" the streets of Lincoln. They were raising quite a ruckus when Constable Juan Martín approached and asked them to surrender their guns. Gylam insulted his fellow law officer and told the group to ignore him. The hell-raisers then headed toward a brothel, shooting their revolvers into the air as they walked down the street. Martin rounded up a mob of fellow Mexicans that included Seferino Trujillo and Juan Patrón. When Martin and his men arrived at the brothel they knocked on two doors of adjoining rooms which were occupied by Tom Horrell and Dave Warner. One or the other shot and killed Martin. Warner was shot to death in the return of fire. When the gunfight started, Ben Horrell and Jack Gylam ran from the brothel. They were chased down the street and cornered by the mob. The Hispanics then riddled both men with much lead. In his report to the Adjutant General, Major John Mason, commandant at Fort Stanton, wrote that "the Texans were murdered in cold blood, one at least (Ben Horrell, just 20 years old) while on his knees badly wounded, had surrendered and begged for mercy, was inhumanly murdered by having been pierced by nine balls his body then taken and thrown across the creek near the town." None of the bodies were removed until the following day. Gylam's body was found with thirteen slugs in it. During the night someone had cut off one of Ben Horrell's fingers in order to steal his gold ring. Prior to daybreak, someone had carved a cross on the forehead of Juan Martín.

Three days later two Mexicans were found dead in a pasture at the Horrell Ranch. The following day, the 5th of December, newly appointed Sheriff Alexander H. "Ham" Mills led a large posse to the Horrell homestead and demanded they surrender. The Horrells refused. Shots were fired by both parties sporadically throughout the day. No one was injured. Ham Mills and his posse returned to Lincoln early that evening, without prisoners.

On the 20th of December, a Saturday night, the Horrells and their friends rode into Lincoln. They went straight to a house where a Mexican wedding dance was in progress. The Anglos poured a barrage of lead into the house before riding off into the darkness. They left behind four dead and three wounded. Killed were Isidro Patrón (Juan's father), Isidro

Padilla, Mario Balazan and José Candelaria. Wounded were Balazan's nephew and two women, Apolonia Garcia and Pilar Candelaria.

On January 7, 1874, Governor Marsh Giddings posted rewards of $100 each for Zach Crumpton, Jerry Scott and three Horrell brothers (actually there were four). This act "officially" made them fugitives from the law. It also gave anybody the right to bring them in. Six days later L. G. Murphy, J. J. Dolan, William Brady and José Montaño organized a vigilance committee for the purpose of eliminating the Horrells once and for all.

Realizing that their time in New Mexico was limited, the Horrells sold nearly 1,100 head of cattle, a few horses and oxen for the sum of $9,802.50. On the next day (January 20) Sherff Mills and a large posse of Hispanics surrounded the Horrell ranch. That night, under the cover of darkness, the Horrells slipped away and moved down river to the Casey ranch. One day later, Ben Turner (brother-in-law of the deceased Ben Horrell) and a boy named Edward "Little" Hart made their way to the house of a Hispanic in order to procure some corn. Ben Turner was ambushed and slain.

Realizing that the Horrells had abandoned their ranch, J. J. Dolan and a group of opportunists rode to the site. After pilfering the Horrell house they "confiscated" crops and other items which they hauled back to Lincoln.

Incensed by the course of events, the Horrells decided it was their turn to reciprocate. They sent word to Lincoln that they were heading to town for a "reckoning" with L. G. Murphy, J. J. Dolan, Steve Stanley, Ham Mills, Juan Patrón, Juan Gonzales, Bill Warnick and Joe Haskins. Most of the men in the Horrell clan departed for Lincoln on Friday, January 30th. They were armed to the teeth. At Picacho, C. W. King, Edward "Little" Hart and Tom Kennan detoured to the Haskins' homestead. When Joe opened the door, they shot him dead as his horrified Hispanic wife watched.

At some point on the road to Lincoln, the Texans decided to abandon their plan, possibly because they had foolhardily given their opponents advanced warning of their coming. They chose to raise a little more havoc and then head to Texas. The Horrells decided to raid the ranches of some of their enemies and steal their horses before departing from New Mexico.

With the wagons full of their women and children (escorted by Merritt Horrell and a few other men) safely out of the area on a southerly route, the rest of the men turned east along the Rio Hondo. They pillaged the ranches of Ham Mills and his half-brother Steve Stanley. They stole whatever horses they could gather and rode hard down river toward Missouri Plaza (Missouri Bottom). When they reached the settlement of Roswell, the Horrells raided the ranches of Van C. Smith and Aaron O. Wilburn driving off all of their horses. The band then turned south along the Pecos River.

Along the trail, the Horrells encountered the wagons of five Hispanic teamsters who were freighting corn to the South Spring River ranch of John Chisum. The Horrell bunch assassinated all five Mexicans Pablo Romero, Juan Silva, Severiano Apadaca, Severiano Aguilar and Reymundo Aguilar.

The next target of the Horrell gang was the ranch of Hugh Beckwith at Seven Rivers. Beckwith, like Ham Mills and Steve Stanley, was married to a Hispanic woman. A few miles north of the ranch, the group encountered Robert Beckwith (Hugh's oldest son) from whom they stole a horse, saddle and gun. Shortly thereafter, they ripped down a corral fence and drove off Hugh Beckwith's horses.

Meanwhile, Aaron Wilburn and Van C. Smith had rounded up a posse which began tracking the horse thieves to the south. Wilburn and Smith were both known to be excellent marksmen. Van C. Smith was a former sheriff of Yavapai County, Arizona, and later would become a deputy sheriff under John Behan at Tombstone, Arizona. They recruited additional riders at Seven Rivers. Eventually the Horrells' trail turned west toward El Paso. Realizing that the Horrells would probably sell the stolen stock in El Paso or Mexico, the posse hastened its pace.

At some point, the horse thieves joined up with Merritt Horrell and the wagons carrying the women and children. This slowed their movement toward El Paso. Smith, Wilburn and the posse spotted the Horrell clan at a place called Hueco Tanks, about 30 miles east of El Paso. Once they were within shooting distance, the posse rained lead on the Horrell band. Zach Crumpton was killed instantly. Three other members of the clan were wounded. Fearing for the safety of the women and children, the Horrells waved a white flag in order to negotiate with the posse. Smith and Wilburn agreed that if the Horrells would return their horses, their caravan could proceed without further harm. Smith and Wilburn cut out their horses, and then headed north. At this point, it seems as though the Horrell band turned back to the east in the direction of Fort Davis.

Further down the road, the Horrells encountered a tribe of

Apaches. The clan drew their wagons together as a defensive precaution. The party of Indians remained at a distance and only observed. While this was happening one of the wounded men died (a fellow named Steele or Still). The Horrells buried him, and then built a fire over his grave so the Apaches wouldn't discover it. Eventually the Indians moved on without incident. After they did, the Horrells also left.

The clan headed back to Lampasas County. "The Horrell War" in New Mexico was over, but problems between Anglos and Hispanics would continue. Later (for the murders which occurred at the Mexican wedding dance), the Grand Jury would hand down indictments against Sam and Merritt Horrell, Jerry Scott, Zach Crumpton (who was deceased), Robert Honeycutt, James Wilson, Edward Hart, C. W. King, Thomas Bowen (Bill Bowen), Captain James Randlett, Robert Casey and others. An attempt was made to prosecute Randlett and Casey. Randlett obtained a change of venue to Socorro County, where his case was thrown out of court. Charges were eventually dropped against Casey, and warrants were never served on any of the others.

The Horrell party arrived in Lampasas County determined to keep the peace. Almost immediately, however, there was an altercation with the sheriff and his posse. Merritt Horrell and Jerry Scott were wounded during the conflict about which the newspaper later reported that "no shots were fired by the Horrell party." Merritt Horrell and Bill Bowen agreed to stand trial for the death of Captain Tom Williams and the other members of the State Police. When the case was finally heard in October of 1876, both men were acquitted. The Horrells were making an effort to lead a peaceful life, for a change. Their passiveness would not last for long, however.

Although the feud between the Horrells and Higgins actually began in 1877, its roots go back four years earlier. The Higgins family first established a ranch in Lampasas County in 1857, about the same time the Horrells did. They were neighbors, and originally they were friends. Several incidents turned the friendship into a bloody feud. John Calhoun Pinckney Higgins, usually known as "Pink", was incensed in 1873 when the Horrells killed one of his in-laws, the aforementioned State Police Captain Tom Williams. While riding line one day, Pink Higgins heard a distant shot. He decided to ride out and investigate. He found Zeke Terrell butchering a cow with a Higgins brand. Pink Higgins unsheathed his rifle and killed Terrell on the spot. According to legend, Higgins stuffed Terrell's body inside the disemboweled cow, then notified authorities where they could find the occurrence of a miracle, a cow giving birth to a man. Zeke Terrell had been a Horrell employee. Ike Lantier was a former Quantrill raider who cowpoked for the Horrells. While watering his horse one day, he was startled by an approaching rider and drew his revolver. Pink Higgins, who had already drawn his weapon, fired a slug into Lantier's midsection and killed him instantly. On more than one occasion, Higgins accused the Horrells of tampering with his cattle. Tom Horrell was riding through the brush one day when he met Higgins, his henchman Bill Wren and brother-in-law Bob Mitchell. Quick tempered Pink Higgins cursed Horrell and threatened to kill him. According to the story told, the cool-headed Tom Horrell eased back in his saddle and said something like, "Well, three against one wouldn't be much credit to you." Higgins and his cohorts turned and rode off without further confrontation.

January 22, 1877, was a cold day. Merritt Horrell was standing in front of a fire in the back of Jerry Scott's saloon, and was unaware that Pink Higgins had entered the building. Higgins shot Horrell twice, and after he crumpled to the floor Higgins shot him two more times. Merritt Horrell was dead. He never had a chance to draw or return fire. On the following day a posse of Texas Rangers brought four of Higgins' men into Lampasas for questioning, but Pink Higgins could not be found.

While en route to the Lampasas courthouse on the morning of March 26, 1877, Tom and Mart Horrell were ambushed about five miles outside of town by Higgins men. Tom was knocked from his saddle as a slug ripped into his hip. Mart received a superficial neck wound but was able to valiantly drive off the attackers. Mart helped Tom reach the Tinnins homestead, nearby, and then hastened into town to report the incident.

About a month later, Pink Higgins and Bob Mitchell decided that they had been dodging the law long enough and surrendered to authorities. Both were allowed to post bond and return home.

There was another bloody occurrence about the first of June. At daybreak one morning, two of Higgins' cowboys stepped out of a line shack where they had bunked for the night. As they did so, they were shot down by a barrage of rifle fire. One of the men was killed instantly, while the other would live three more days. It is believed that Tom and Mart Horrell and Bill Bowen were responsible for the incident.

Another confrontation took place at the intersection of Third Street and Live Oak Street in Lampasas on the morning of June 7,

1877. Frank Mitchell and his father, Mack, were loading flour at the store of Yates and Brown on Third Street at about 10:00 a.m. Several members of the Horrell bunch had congregated near the well at Public Square adjacent to Live Oak Street. The group included Tom, Mart and Sam Horrell, Jim "Buck" Waldrup and Bob McBee. John Dixon and Rufus Overstreet of the Horrell faction were nearby at the home of Dixon's mother. When Pink Higgins, Bob Mitchell, Bill Wren and Ben Terry rode south on Live Oak Street they were spotted by the men at Public Square. The Higgins men also saw the Horrells. Shooting started immediately as everybody scattered for shelter.

Bill Wren took a slug in one hip but managed to drag himself up a flight of stairs to a second-story window from where he had a better vantage point. Pink Higgins spurred his mount and rode away to recruit help. Frank Mitchell, who was Bob's younger brother, opened fire on the Horrells from the front door of Yates and Brown. One of his shots dropped Buck Waldrup (who would die the following day). Mart Horrell returned the fire and killed Frank Mitchell where he stood.

Sporadic shooting continued for over an hour. At approximately 11:30 a.m. Pink Higgins returned with reinforcements. The men of both factions fortified themselves and nothing much happened after that.

John Pinckney Higgins was a cattleman who earned a reputation as being a tough, unyielding individual. *Center for American History, University of Texas at Austin (W. P. Webb Papers).*

Early in the afternoon, impartial citizens were able to talk both parties into a cease fire.

The following month, fourteen Higgins riders raided the Horrell ranch. The Higgins men took positions surrounding the ranch house and bunkhouse from where they poured rifle fire at the Horrells. The Horrell brothers and their men fought back with a vengeance. After a two-day siege, the Higgins' ammunition began to run low. They departed leaving two Horrell men with minor wounds.

On the 25th of July, Carson Graham departed from the Higgins ranch and headed toward Lampasas to purchase supplies. He was ambushed on the road. Beside his body the Horrell brand had been etched into the dirt.

Major John B. Jones, who was commander of the Texas Rangers' Frontier Battalion, rode into Lampasas County with a detachment of reinforcements for the already present Rangers. Jones was determined to end the feud between the Horrells and Higgins one way or another. He exercised the first part of his plan by arresting five members of the Horrell faction. They were kept under guard at the Ranger camp in order to protect them from the Higgins bunch. Jones then arrested Higgins, Mitchell and Wren and put them under heavy guard at a separate location. This method would allow Major Jones to negotiate with each party without them having to come face to face with each other. His plan was successful. Both parties signed letters of truce. The first letter was dated July 30, 1877, and was signed by the Horrell brothers:

Lampasas Texas
July 30th 1877

Messrs Pink Higgins Robert Mitchell and William Wren.
Gentlemen:

    From this standpoint, looking back over the past with its terrible experiences both to ourselves and to you, and to the suffering which has been entailed upon both of our families and our friends by the quarrel in which we have been involved with its repeated fatal consequences, and looking to a termination of the same, and a peaceful, honorable and happy adjustment of our difficulties which shall leave both ourselves and you, all our self respect and sense of unimpaired honor, we have determined to take the initiatory in a move for reconciliation. Therefore

Tom Horrell, a man of calm demeanor, and his wife, Mattie Ann, a proud but boastful woman. *Sarah Harrison Cobb.*

we present this paper in which we hold ourselves in honor bound to lay down our arms and to end the strife in which we have been engaged against you and exert our utmost efforts to entirely eradicate all enmity from the minds of our friends who have taken sides with us in the feud hereinbefore alluded to.

And we promise furthermore to abstain from insulting or injuring you and your friends, to bury the bitter past forever, and join with you as good citizens in undoing the evil which has resulted from our quarrel, and to leave nothing undone which we can effect to bring about a complete consummation of the purpose to which we have herein committed ourselves.
PROVIDED: -

That you shall on your part take upon yourselves a similar obligation as respects our friends and us, and shall address a paper to us with your signatures thereon, such a paper as this which we freely offer you. Hoping that this may bring about the happy result which it aims at we remain

                        Yours Respectfully,
                        Thos. L. Horrell
                        S. W. Horrell
                        C. M. Horrell

Witness
Jno B. Jones
Maj. Frontier Battalion

Major Jones delivered the Horrell letter to Higgins, Mitchell and Wren. They responded with their letter of August 2, 1877:

Lampasas Texas
Aug 2nd 1877

Messrs Mart. Tom and Sam Horrell
Gentlemen

Your favor dated the 30th of July was handed to us by Maj. Jones. We have carefully noted its contents and approve most sincerely the spirit of the communication. It would be difficult for us to express in words the mental disturbance to ourselves which the said quarrel with its fatal consequences, alluded to in your letter occasioned. And now with passions cooled we look back with you sorrowfully to the past, and promise with you to commence at once and instantly the task of repairing the injuries resulting from the difficulty as far as our power extends to do. Certainly we will make every effort to restore good feeling with those who armed themselves in our quarrel, and on our part we lay down our weapons with the honest purpose to regard the feud which has existed between you and us as a by gone thing to be remembered only to bewail. Furthermore as you say we will abstain from offering insult or injury to you or yours and will seek to bring all of our friends to a complete conformity with the agreement herein expressed by us.

As we hope for future peace and happiness for ourselves and for those who look to us for guidance and protection and as we desire to take position as good law abiding citizens and preservers of peace and order we subscribe ourselves

Respectfully &c
J.P. Higgins
R.A. Mitchell
W.R. Wren

Witness
Jno B. Jones
Maj. Frontier Battalion

Both factions were ready for peace. Each was sick and tired of the death, destruction, fear and mental anguish associated with the feud. Rarely is a truce between feudists adhered to, but this one was.

Pink Higgins remained in Lampasas until the turn of the century when he moved his ranching operation to the vicinity of Spur, Texas. He was responsible for a couple of other killings (which had nothing to do

Major John B. Jones successfully negotiated a truce between the hostile factions in the Horrell-Higgins Feud. Jones, who was commander of the Texas Rangers' Frontier Battalion, also helped establish peace in the Hoodoo War at Mason. *Texas State Library & Archives Commission.*

Pink Higgins and some of his men. Back row (Left to Right), Powell Woods, Unknown, Buck Allen and A.T. Mitchell. Front row, Felix Castello, Jess Standard, Bob Mitchell and Pink Higgins. *Center for American History, University of Texas at Austin (W.P. Webb Papers).*

with the Horrells) before he died of a heart attack at age 66.

Tom and Mart Horrell were arrested for the May 28, 1878, murder of storekeeper J. F. Vaughan, thirty miles west of Waco. The two brothers were locked up in the jailhouse at Meridian on the 8th of September to await trial. On the night of December 15th, a large mob of masked men rode to the jailhouse, whisked past the jailer and with a volley of gunfire assassinated Tom and Mart Horrell in their cells. Many people thought that the Horrells were innocent of Vaughan's murder, but the brothers never had a chance to prove it in court.

Sam was the only remaining Horrell brother. In 1880 he moved back to New Mexico where he raised his six children. Sam Horrell died in California on August 8, 1936.

Mission Dolores was the scene of a duel on January 12, 1851, between Will Hicks Graham and William Walker. *San Francisco History Center.*

Chapter Fourteen
Will Hicks Graham, Duelist

The discovery of gold at Sutter's Mill, on the American River in California, caused the greatest gold rush in North American history. San Francisco, which had been a community of less than 1,000 residents, quickly became overcrowded with fortune hunters from all over the world. A city began to grow which eventually became the trading and finance center of northern California.

Among the thousands who flocked to San Francisco with visions of wealth was Will Hicks Graham. The Philadelphia native arrived in June of 1850, one month before his 21st birthday. The lad obtained employment at the offices of Probate Judge R. N. Morrison. Graham, and several other clerks, began to study law under the tutelage of the elderly judge.

The holiday season for Judge Morrison was dampened by the harsh criticism of San Francisco Herald editor William Walker, who severely blasted Morrison's decisions in an estate battle which received much publicity. All of Judge Morrison's clerks agreed that Walker's attacks were highly unwarranted, and decided that a measure of vindication was necessary. Will Hicks Graham was accorded the task of avenging his mentor's honor. With shades of knight-errantry, Graham (on behalf of Judge Morrison) challenged William Walker to a duel.

The encounter occurred on January 12, 1851, at Mission

Dolores with many prominent citizens in attendance. According to the terms of the duel, the adversaries would be armed with identical Colt revolvers. They would face each other at a distance of ten paces, and would then advance a step after each shot was fired. The contestants had five balls in their chambers, and the duel would end when one of the participants was hit. Once the two squared off, the skirmish was over quickly. Graham's first ball pierced only cloth, but his second struck Walker in the thigh. The duel was over. Graham faced charges of engaging in an unlawful duel and aggravated assault. He was eventually acquitted of the charges. Walker eventually recovered from his wound. Many years later, the feisty newspaperman would meet his demise in front of a Honduras firing squad.

The economic growth of San Francisco was matched by its political and social turbulence. Unprosecuted crime reached such heights that citizens finally responded by taking matters into their own hands. In June of 1851, the Vigilance Committee was organized with about 200 members, one of which was Will Hicks Graham. Within a month, nearly 35 "undesirables" were rounded up by the committee. Each of the "accused" received a "trial" and a sentence. Four men were hanged to death by the Vigilance Committee, while about thirty others were banished from the territory.

Portsmouth Square was the site of the first duel between Will Hicks Graham and George Frank Lemon. The Belle Union (in the background) was perhaps San Francisco's most notorious sin spot. It was a gathering place for gamblers, painted ladies and customers willing to part with their wages. *San Francisco History Center.*

During the time that Graham was involved with the Vigilance Committee, he also became entangled in a love triangle. Will had been courting Anne Hughes, a girl that had been introduced to him by a city official named George Frank Lemon. When Will discovered that Lemon was having an affair with Anne he became incensed. One afternoon Graham approached Lemon while the latter was drinking with friends at the Oriental Hotel. Graham tossed a glass of water in the city official's face, and then tendered an invitation to a gunfight. When the next day passed and Lemon had failed to respond to the challenge, Graham had a notice printed (July 1, 1851) in two of San Francisco's daily newspapers. He accused Lemon of being a "... scoundrel, villain, liar and poltroon," and further declared that he was "... out of the pale of gentlemen's society." Furthermore, Graham posted a notice at Portsmouth Square. This time Lemon responded.

At daybreak, Graham and Lemon each entered Portsmouth Square with their own circle of friends. As he walked toward Lemon, Will Graham shouted, "Draw and defend yourself." When the shooting started Graham backpedalled, then stumbled over the bottom step of the Union Hotel. Lemon seized the opportunity and charged his opponent. George Lemon fired a ball which tore through Graham's mouth. Friends immediately stepped in to separate the antagonists.

Will Graham's pride had been hurt by Anne's affair with Lemon. It was further tarnished by the wound he suffered at Portsmouth Square. Determined to end the ordeal once and for all, Graham challenged Lemon to a formal duel, complete with seconds and prearranged rules. Lemon obliged. This time the confrontation occurred at Benicia. Following the exchange of several shots, Lemon took a slug in his ribcage, thereby ending the duel. The fight at Benicia was the last encounter between Graham and Lemon. Despite everything that had occurred, Will Graham and Anne Hughes were united in matrimony. The ghost of the relationships past was hard to ignore, however, and the couple had a rocky marriage.

Will Hicks Graham continued his study of law and soon became a practicing attorney. He dabbled in politics for several years without much success. His reputation for violence probably prevented him from successfully attaining nomination for any office. Graham held an appointed office as Deputy State Sealer of Weights and Measures for a few years. Following the divorce of Will and Anne, Graham moved his law practice to the booming mining camps along the California-Nevada line. He tried cases from Aurora, Nevada through the Excelsior Mountains and eventually into the Owens River basin of California.

Will Graham's first encounter with roughneck A. J. "Yank" McGuire occurred at Aurora when the two exchanged harsh words. Several months later, the disdain was rekindled when McGuire testified against one of Graham's clients during a trial at the mining camp of Montgomery. During a break between sessions, the two confronted each other inside a local saloon. Hatred showed in their eyes as both men drew and commenced firing. Graham was a little quicker, but shots flew in both directions. One of Will Graham's slugs hit McGuire flush in the chest. He managed to discharge two or three more shots before collapsing on the floor. An innocent bystander caught a stray slug and was killed. Graham received a superficial wound on an arm from one of McGuire's shots. Yank McGuire survived but was later convicted of murdering an unarmed man who refused to drink with him.

Will was small in stature, but made up for it in his aggressiveness. He was never known to back down from any confrontation. Whether in the courtroom or during a gunfight, Will Hicks Graham truly had a fighting spirit. He died at the Lafayette Hotel in Los Angeles on October 16, 1866, and probably carried that fighting spirit to his grave.

Thomas Edward "Black Jack" Ketchum and his band of outlaws operated during the 1890s in New Mexico, Texas and Arizona. *Union County Historical Society.*

Chapter Fifteen
The Black Jack Ketchum Gang

Green B. Ketchum and Temperance Katherine Wydick were married in 1847 in Christian County, Illinois. By 1850 they had settled along the San Saba River at a place known as China Creek Community, in San Saba County, Texas. Green and Temperance were members of the Cumberland Presbyterian Church. Among their eight children (three of which died in infancy) were two brothers who would become notorious outlaws—Samuel W. and Thomas Edward Ketchum. Through much of their twenties, the brothers worked as ranch hands for cattle outfits in Texas and New Mexico. At some point, the duo decided to pursue what they assumed would be a more plentiful profession—that of robbing banks, stagecoaches and trains. It may have been more lucrative, for a while, but in the end it would be their undoing.

Whether Thomas "Black Jack" Ketchum and his brother, Sam, ever actually rode with Butch Cassidy's Wild Bunch is a matter for speculation, though some members of the Wild Bunch rode with the Ketchums. Will Carver was a member of the Wild Bunch before, and after, joining forces with Black Jack Ketchum. William Ellsworth "Elzy" (or Elza) Lay participated in his last robbery while riding with the Ketchums. The most ruthless member of Cassidy's gang, Harvey Logan (Kid Curry), and "Deaf" Charley Hanks might have joined up with Lay and the Ketchums in late June 1899. After fatally shooting Sheriff Joe Hazen earlier in the month, Logan probably fled Wyoming, headed south, and could have joined up with the others. During their exploits in New Mexico, the group was generally known as the Ketchum Gang.

Tom Ketchum probably got his nickname as the result of a confusion of identities. Will Christian, who was nicknamed, "Black Jack" and his brother, Bob (who used the alias of Tom Anderson), were responsible for a series of robberies in 1896. Christian, who resembled Tom Ketchum, was killed in April of 1897 in Graham County, Arizona. The dead man was originally identified as Thomas Ketchum. Some of Ketchum's earlier crimes were actually attributed to Christian. When Will Christian's activities ceased due to his death, Tom Ketchum somehow inherited the sobriquet of "Black Jack."

Black Jack Ketchum and his band operated during the mid and late 1890's, predominately in New Mexico, Texas and Arizona. Black Jack Ketchum was an able marksman and was generally considered to be the gang's leader. Either he, or his brother, Sam, usually masterminded the robberies. Neither was very astute at planning a caper. Many jobs were bungled due to poor preparation.

Samuel W. Ketchum helped mastermind many of the gang's robberies. *Union County Historical Society.*

On May 14, 1897, three men robbed a train as it pulled out of the station at Lozier near the eastern boundary of Terrell County, Texas. Tom Ketchum and Will Carver climbed aboard the locomotive with drawn revolvers and commanded George Freese, the engineer, to stop the train. Dave Atkins cut the telegraph wire from the station before meeting the others at the express car with a supply of dynamite. The robbers blew two safes open, loaded three sacks with their loot, then departed on horseback. Wells Fargo later admitted that their loss from the Lozier robbery amounted to about $42,000.

On the 3rd of September, four bandits halted the Texas Flyer near Folsom, New Mexico. After being clubbed to the floor of the express car by Sam Ketchum, Charles Drew, the express messenger, obliged the robbers by unlocking one of two safes. The other safe was blown open on the third attempt with a substantial charge of dynamite. The Folsom robbery yielded approximately $3,000.

About the first of December in 1897, a rumor was circulating that a train would be held up near the Arizona-New Mexico line within a few days. The railroads moved swiftly by adding additional armed guards to all express cars. On December 9, 1897, the Texas Flyer was again the target of the Ketchum gang. The robber band consisted of Tom and Sam Ketchum, Will Carver, Dave Atkins and Ed Bullion (who used the alias of Ed Cullen). New gang member, Ed Bullion, was a brother of Will Carver's sweetheart Laura Bullion. When the train stopped at the station near Steins Pass the outlaws seized the engineer. The express car doors rolled open. Inside the darkened car, Charles Adair (the express messenger), C. H. Jennings and Eugene Thacker leveled their shotguns in anticipation of trouble. When the bandits called out to the express messenger, their answer was a shotgun blast and then another. As the other outlaws scampered for cover, Bullion remained too close to the express car. A blast from the shotgun of C. H. Jennings struck Bullion in the forehead. He was killed instantly. The other four all received superficial wounds before they were able to mount their horses and escape. The proceeds from the raid were minimal (a bag of U. S. mail taken from the Postmaster just prior to the bungled train robbery), and the outlaws got nothing from the express car.

A huge manhunt ensued, which included such formidable peace officers as John E. Thacker, Jeff Milton and George Scarborough. Within days, the posse had arrested six suspects, including one who had a recent bullet wound. None of the six were involved in the robbery at Steins

Pass, but they had great difficulty attempting to prove their innocence. Ultimately, three of the men were erroneously convicted of mail theft, and were sentenced to terms at the New Mexico Territorial Prison.

On the night of April 28, 1898, the Ketchums, Will Carver and Dave Atkins struck the Southern Pacific train No. 20 as it departed from the station at Comstock. The method was similar to previous robberies. At gunpoint, two of the bandits forced the engineer to stop the train. The express car was uncoupled and isolated from the rest of the train. Dynamite was used to blow the safe which was subsequently cleaned out. Satisfied that there was no more loot, the bandits escaped into the darkness. The size of their take was undetermined.

The Texas & Pacific Railway was the next target of the Ketchum Gang. Striking at night, as they usually did, the outlaws brought the train to a standstill about five miles outside of Stanton near the crossing at Mustang Creek. The robbery, which occurred on July 1, 1898, was spectacular. The dynamite used on two safes blew the entire express car into splinters. The proceeds from the Stanton robbery were estimated to be as much as $50,000.

During the spring of 1899 there was much friction between Tom Ketchum and the other members of the gang. Tom would have sudden mood changes which often elevated into displays of uncontrollable rage. Dave Atkins was the first gang member to quit. Eventually, Sam Ketchum and Will Carver also grew tired of Tom's tantrums. Sam and Will also parted company, and then headed across part of New Mexico to Turkey Canyon to meet Elzy Lay who had agreed to ride with the gang.

Shortly after 10 p.m. on July 11, 1899, the gang raided a Colorado and Southern train near Folsom, New Mexico. The participants included Sam Ketchum, Will Carver and Elzy Lay. Bruce "Red" Weaver or Harvey Logan may also have been involved. Realizing that a holdup was in progress, the express messenger cleaned out the small safe, hid the contents under some gunny sacks, and relocked the safe. The bandits rolled open the express car door, lit their explosives, and blew open both safes. Although the small safe was empty, the larger one furnished the outlaws with a fine payday.

Before long, the C & S train arrived at Trinidad, Colorado, with its whistle wide open. Sheriff Edward Farr (of Huerfano County) and Deputy U.S. Marshal W.H. Love organized a posse and set out for Folsom in order to pick up the robbers' tracks. The trail led along Turkey Creek and into rocky Turkey Canyon (New Mexico), which would quickly become a bloodbath.

As the posse drew near, a rifle shot dropped Deputy Tom Smith, killing him instantly. Gunfire immediately erupted from both sides. The posse outnumbered the outlaws, but the latter had better vantage points from which to shoot, somewhat equalizing the fight. Sheriff Farr collapsed dead in his tracks when a slug crashed into his skull. Elzy Lay was shot in the shoulder and the side. The wounds were not serious, but he was losing blood. A bullet from Sam Ketchum's rifle pierced the lung of Deputy U.S. Marshal Love. He would soon die. Two more deputies were wounded before Sam Ketchum's shoulder was shattered by a rifle slug. In the darkness of night the bandits escaped. The badly wounded Sam Ketchum didn't get far, however. Knowing that his situation was hopeless he urged the others to ride on—and they did. Ketchum was discovered the next day, arrested, and taken to Trinidad. Doctors amputated his arm, but gangrene had set in. Sam Ketchum died on the 24th of July.

On August 15, 1899, in response to a tip, lawmen crashed through the door of Elzy Lay's hideout near Carlsbad, New Mexico. Lay, who was not wearing his revolver, staged a furious fist fight before he was subdued and arrested. He was sentenced to life imprisonment in the New Mexico Territorial Prison. Later (January 10, 1906), Elzy Lay received a pardon for helping to quell a prison riot.

One day after the arrest of Lay, Black Jack Ketchum attempted

William Ellsworth "Elzy" Lay, prisoner #1348 in the New Mexico Territorial Prison. Lay rode with both the Ketchum Gang and Butch Cassidy's Wild Bunch during his outlaw days. *New Mexico Sstate Records Center and Archives.*

a train robbery single-handedly. Whether, or not, he was taking out his frustration over his brother's death is uncertain but the attempt was badly bungled. Ketchum shot, and wounded, the express messenger. Then he exchanged gunfire with Frank Harrington, the conductor. Each shot the other. Black Jack's right arm had been peppered by a load of buckshot. Ketchum jumped from the train and escaped into the brush. The following day he was found propped against a tree near the railroad tracks. Ketchum lost his arm to amputation, as his brother had a month earlier.

Thomas "Black Jack" Ketchum was tried and sentenced to be hanged. On Friday, April 26, 1901, Ketchum jauntily ascended the gallows at Clayton, New Mexico, for his execution. After the hood was affixed, and the noose placed around his neck, Black Jack exclaimed, "Let her rip!" The man who had participated in several bungled robberies would now have his own hanging bungled. Because of a miscalculation in the length of the hangman's rope, the drop was too long. The trap doors opened, his body plunged downward, and he was decapitated.

Earlier in the day, Ketchum had dictated a letter to President William McKinley advising him that three inmates at the New Mexico Territorial Prison were not guilty (as charged) in the 1897 robbery at Steins Pass, Arizona. He further informed the president that the job was done by Dave Atkins, Ed Bullion, Will Carver, Sam Ketchum, Bronco Bill (who was implicated but did not participate) and himself, and furthermore that his attorney had a list of the articles stolen and where they could be retrieved.

Thomas "Black Jack" Ketchum was hanged at Clayton, New Mexico, on the morning of April 26, 1901. Moments after this photograph was taken, Ketchum dropped through the trapdoors and was decapitated. *Union County Historical Society.*

This is a sketch of the Julesburg stagecoach station. It replaced the original stage station which was burned by Indians. *Denver Public Library, Western History Department.*

Chapter Sixteen
Jack Slade and the Julesburg Vendetta

In 1829, Joseph Alfred "Jack" Slade was born in Carlyle, Illinois, a community in which his father had been one of the town founders. Jack Slade joined the army at age 18 and headed west. He would become one of the most ornery characters on the western frontier.

The incidents which made Jack Slade legendary occurred during his tenure with the Overland Stage Company. Overland, it seems, had a ruthless and undependable stationmaster whom they desired to replace. Jules Beni ran the stage station at Julesburg, Colorado. The station was unprofitable as horses and supplies continued to disappear. Slade accepted the position and set out for Julesburg with Jules' discharge papers in his possession.

After his replacement by Slade, Beni remained in the area, and a deep resentment grew between the two. The animosity culminated at Julesburg, in 1858, when Jules Beni sought out Jack Slade and gunned him down. The former stationmaster emptied his pistol, then grabbed his shotgun and fired a blast into Slade's already wounded body. Certain that Slade was dying, Beni turned and departed.

Miraculously, Slade recovered. He had been hit by 13 slugs, several of which remained inside his body. Eventually he was strong enough to resume his duties as stationmaster.

Slade, who became known as Captain Jack, drove his workers hard to maximize efficiency. Coaches ran on schedule. The station at Julesburg became profitable for the Overland Stage Company. Jack Slade had gained a reputation for being a tough hombre—one who most certainly could defy death.

Following the shooting, Jules Beni fled the immediate area. But word filtered back to Jack that he was still in the territory, and furthermore, that he was boasting that he was going to finish Slade off once and for all. Captain Jack knew that he could not afford to have Jules catch him during another unsuspecting moment. So, Slade sent his men out to find the former stationmaster, with a bounty if they could capture him alive. Soon Slade received word that Beni had been captured at another relay station. Jack Slade saddled up and rode hard, with retaliation on his mind. When he arrived he found Jules tied to a corral fence post. According to legend, Slade shot Jules Beni several times in order to watch him die a slow death. Legend also has it that Slade sliced both ears off the corpse, and then carried one around with him for many months.

As time passed, whiskey affected Jack Slade more and more. When drunk he would become reckless and obnoxious. His circle of friends remained loyal to him regardless of the circumstances. His wife, Virginia, stood by him through thick and thin. Numerous stories of shootings, beatings, stabbings and hangings are attributed to Jack Slade. He had become a menace to society.

Overland transferred Slade across the territory to a new stage station which he named Virginia Dale in honor of his wife. Slade's reputation followed him, and the violence continued. Eventually he became so intolerable to the Overland Stage Company that they fired him. Shortly thereafter Slade was involved in a shooting in Wyoming. When a warrant was issued for his arrest, Jack and Virginia fled to the gold fields of Montana.

Rich placer gold had just been discovered at Alder Gulch, and Virginia City was a booming new mining town when the Slades arrived in 1863. Rather than chase the mother lode, however, Captain Jack decided to establish a freighting business. Slade borrowed heavily to set up his new enterprise, and although it looked like he was making a substantial amount of money, he was deeply in debt. When he was sober, Jack Slade was a benevolent and charming individual. He attracted a new group of friends who seemed to follow him, even through his frequent spells of intoxication.

The Montana gold camps were virtually lawless, largely because of the infamous sheriff, Henry Plummer. Plummer ran his operation from Skinner's Saloon in nearby Bannack. Although it was unknown to the citizens of Bannack, he was the leader of a large band of outlaws. Plummer knew when gold shipments departed, and upon which stagecoaches payrolls were due. A tip to his gang was usually followed by a robbery or hijacking. Business owners and gold miners finally had their fill of ineffective law enforcement and took matters into their own hands. On December 23, 1863, a band of vigilantes was organized. The assemblage was large, heavily armed, and would be effective. Jack Slade's freight wagons had been a target of Plummer's band, so he rode with the vigilantes.

When the vigilantes captured gang member Red Yeager in early January, he confessed to several crimes and informed the group that Henry Plummer was his leader. Hopeful of saving his own neck, Yeager passed along the names of each of his cohorts. It was all the vigilantes would need. Yeager was hanged anyway. By February 3, 1864, eighteen other members of the gang, including Henry Plummer, had been hanged or shot to death. The vigilantes with whom Jack Slade rode would soon bring about his own demise.

It wasn't unusual for drunks to raise a ruckus in a booming gold camp. When the ruckus resulted in destruction of property and beatings and insults of innocent citizens, it was a detriment to society. Such was the case with Jack Slade. He and his friends would gallop down the street firing their six-shooters into the air, or would ride their horses into a store or saloon intent upon destroying supplies within. Jack Slade had become a major detriment to the community. When sober Slade would pay restitution for his dastardly deeds, but warning after warning regarding his conduct went unheeded.

The Vigilance Committee, realizing that enough was enough, ruled that Slade should die. On March 10, 1864, a weeping and begging Jack Slade was hanged from a beam supported by two gate posts just outside Virginia City. When word reached Virginia Slade as to what was happening she rode into town at breakneck speed. She was too late. The body had already been moved to the Virginia Hotel, where it was laid out. The shrill cries of Virginia Slade attested to her love for Jack.

Twenty-five of the Arizona Rangers' legendary "twenty-six men" at Morenci in 1903. *Arizona Historical Society.*

Chapter Seventeen
The Arizona Rangers

In 1901 the Arizona legislature passed into law a bill which created the semisecret Arizona Rangers. The company of fourteen men was organized "for the pursuit and arrest of criminals in the mountain fastness and frontier regions." The law enforcement unit was to consist of one captain (at a salary of $120 per month), one sergeant (who would be paid $75 per month) and twelve privates (each to receive pay of $55 per month). Throughout its brief history the Arizona Rangers was a controversial organization. Despite the criticism it received, however, the Rangers were usually an effective law enforcement agency. Its lawmen were able to cross county boundaries when chasing criminals and they could provide local support when needed. The Rangers helped maintain the international border between Mexico and Arizona, chased rustlers, and even dealt with such ordinary offenses as disorderly conduct and drunkenness.

In reference to the Rangers, Territorial Governor Alexander Brodie advised (in his report to the Secretary of the Interior for the fiscal year ending June 30, 1904), "They are used as peace officers, preserving law and order wherever they may be in the Territory. The force is composed of fearless men, trained in riding, roping, trailing, and shooting. The very best men to be found are enlisted, and they come for the most part from the interior parts of the Territory, where they can be detailed for important work with assurances of success owing to their knowledge of the country."

During its brief existence, the Arizona Rangers had three captains. Each of them left his mark. The first was Burton Mossman. By age twenty the tough but intelligent cowboy had become a ranch foreman. In December 1897, at age thirty, Mossman became superintendent of the huge Hash Knife outfit. The Hash Knife owned over a million acres of ranch land, with more than 50,000 head of cattle. Additionally, they controlled nearly another million acres of railroad property. The ranch had been plagued by rustlers, so Mossman declared war on them. He was not only effective in catching rustlers "in the act," but he would often take the offensive and go after those he suspected. In 1898 Mossman was appointed deputy sheriff of Navajo County. When the Arizona Rangers were created, his qualifications were perfect to be their first captain. A tough and persistent lawman that was excellent with firearms, intelligent, and able to supervise many men, were just the traits the Rangers needed for a leader.

"Cap," as he became known, was fearless in his pursuit of outlaws throughout the Arizona Territory. Once, while tracking a bandit named Salivaras, Mossman descended a trail into an appropriately named Paradise Valley. Realizing that he was being followed, Salivaras took cover and ambushed Mossman. A slug nicked the captain's right leg. Mossman returned a shot with his rifle before leaping from his horse. No further shots came from the outlaw's position. Cap cautiously inched his way toward the outlaw. He found Salivaras dead. Mossman's only shot had split the bandit's skull.

Dayton Graham, Mossman's hand-picked sergeant, was directly responsible for the demise of gang leader and deadly killer, Bill Smith. A few months earlier, after robbing a Union Pacific train in Utah, the Bill Smith gang hid out along the Black River in Arizona. A posse, which included three Arizona Rangers, tracked the gang to their hideout. When the gang was asked to surrender, a gun fight broke out. After leaving one Ranger dead, and another critically wounded, the gang rode off into the night, and then headed to Mexico. The incident at Black River put Bill Smith and his gang on the Arizona Ranger's most wanted list. One evening Smith doubled back across the border into Douglas. A local merchant asked Douglas peace officer, Tom Vaughn, to check out a suspicious-looking customer at his saloon. Ranger Dayton Graham accompanied Vaughn as they approached the man (which neither knew to be Bill Smith). Without warning, Smith drew and dropped both men with consecutive shots. Vaughn took a slug in the neck while Graham was hit in the chest and arm. Again, the elusive Smith escaped into the darkness. Graham did not know who had shot him, but he would not forget the assailant's face. In fact, Sgt. Graham was obsessed with the face of the man who had shot him. Regardless of what town he was in, Dayton Graham would walk into every saloon hoping to see that face once again. One night he did. Bill Smith was sitting at a monte table when he glanced up to see Graham approaching. Smith went for his gun, but it was too late. Dayton Graham shot Bill Smith in the head, and twice in the stomach. When the coat was removed from Smith's corpse, steel hacksaw blades were discovered sewn into the lining. He would never need them.

Augustine Chacón was an outlaw and murderer who was widely sought by Arizona authorities. In 1897 Chacón was sentenced to hang for the murder of a Morenci store keeper named Becker. While awaiting the gallows at Solomonville, Chacón was permitted to receive a prayer book from his girlfriend to "comfort him during his final days." Two days before the scheduled hanging, Chacón's jail cell was found empty. The thick cover of the prayer book had contained hacksaw blades.

For the most part, Chacón would hide out in Mexico where he committed no crimes, and therefore was not a wanted man. Chacón, however, was a real nemesis to the citizens of southern Arizona Territory where he would raid at will. He had become a significant thorn in the side of Burton Mossman. The captain knew that Mexican authorities would not extradite Chacón, for he had no criminal record in his homeland. Mossman concocted a plan to lure him across the border. Mossman decided to make a deal with Burt Alvord, a former lawman now wanted by the Arizona Rangers. Alvord and Chacón had previously spent time in jail together and knew each other well. Mossman offered Alvord a pardon if he could entice Chacón into Arizona Territory on the pretense of a lucrative horse stealing deal. While this scenario was developing, President Theodore Roosevelt had appointed a new territorial governor, Alexander O. Brodie. Knowing that he would soon be replaced as captain of the Arizona Rangers, Mossman obtained a commission as Deputy U. S. Marshal in order to follow through on the Chacón matter. Alvord and Chacón headed north. The ploy had worked. At some point during their trip the two were intercepted by Burton Mossman and Billy Stiles, Alvord's henchman. Chacón was put into irons, and then taken to Solomonville where he was hanged on November 23, 1902.

On September 1, 1902, Thomas H. Rynning replaced Burton Mossman as captain of the Arizona Rangers. Rynning was an orphan who drifted west as a teenager. He rode with the U.S. Cavalry during the final campaign against Geronimo, was a member of Buffalo Bill's Wild West Show, and participated in the Spanish-American War as one of Teddy Roosevelt's Rough Riders. Like Mossman, Tom Rynning (also a crack shot) led by example. He side-stepped no one and when necessary, he simply let his gun do the talking.

The legendary "twenty-six men" were the result of Rynning's reorganization of the Arizona Rangers. The new structure provided for one captain (to be salaried $175 per month), one lieutenant (to be paid $130 each month), four sergeants (each to receive $110 a month), and twenty privates (whose pay would be $100 per month each). Captain Rynning had greater cooperation with the Mexican authorities then did his predecessor. This led to a higher degree of prosecution of those seeking refuge across the border. Rynning reported (in 1904) that his Rangers averaged an amazing total of 10,140 miles per month in the saddle.

Ranger Webb dashed into the Cowboy Saloon at Douglas after hearing a gunshot within. He was immediately confronted at gun point by the saloon keeper. Webb responded by pumping two slugs into the man's body, killing him instantly. Tom Rynning and two other Rangers had been nearby. As they entered the saloon, one of the Rangers was shot in the chest by a gambler. Rynning dropped the gambler with a shot that entered his arm and side. The gunfight was over. The toll was one dead and two wounded.

When Mexican miners began a rebellion (principally against their American engineers) at the remote mining community of La Cananea, Sonora, in 1906, the Mexican Army requested help. Captain Rynning led a force of about three hundred men (which included a few Rangers) across the border where they were dispatched by train into the Cananea Mountains. While his volunteers battled the Mexican miners, Rynning went to the community hospital to check on casualties. As he did, he was fired upon by three Mexicans. Rynning shouldered his rifle and returned their fire. His shots wounded all three miners who scampered to safety. The siege ended and Rynning returned to Arizona to face growing criticism against the Rangers and their activities.

In 1907, Henry Cornwall Wheeler succeeded Thomas Rynning to become the third, and last, captain of the Arizona Rangers. The native of

Jacksonville, Florida, was also a superior marksman who had come up through the ranks of the Rangers. He always performed well in the line of duty.

On the night of October 22, 1904, while serving as a sergeant in the Rangers, Wheeler foiled a robbery at the Palace Saloon in Tucson. A fellow named Bostwick lined all of the customers against the wall at gunpoint while an associate patrolled the street. Realizing that something was wrong, Wheeler charged through the front entrance. He was shot at from two directions—by Bostwick and by his confederate who was across the street. Wheeler, who was unscathed, shot Bostwick in the head and chest. The would-be robber dropped dead. His associate fled the scene.

H.C. Wheeler had a run in with a miner at the railroad depot at Benson on February 28, 1907. Evidently, the miner, J.A. Tracy, had been infatuated by the attractive lady companion of D.W. Silverton. Following several heated words, Tracy pulled his revolver and threatened Silverton. Wheeler, who was nearby, drew his pistol and ordered Tracy to drop his. Tracy responded by firing two shots which hit Wheeler in the thigh and foot. Wheeler emptied his pistol at Tracy. Four slugs connected and the antagonist would later die.

The voice of opposition to the Rangers continued to grow through 1907 and 1908. They were accused of interfering in local affairs without just cause. They often raised the ire of local law enforcement officers. Several times they involved themselves in labor disputes when many people thought they should not have. They were often accused of overstepping their authority for one reason or another.

Critical publicity heightened in 1908 following the repercussions of the Jeff Kidder incident. Seasoned gunman Jeff Kidder, of the Arizona Rangers, was wounded in a gunfight with Mexican policemen south of the border. He was jailed at Naco, without medical treatment and left to die. The Rangers were accused of crossing the border on a revenge mission.

Following much political infighting, the Arizona Rangers were abolished in 1909. The legend of the "twenty-six men" lives on. They were a small but effective force.

Wild Bill Hickok had difficulty holding employment, partly because of his crude demeanor. *Wild Horse Collection.*

Chapter Eighteen
Wild Bill and the Naked Bull

Of all the law enforcement officers on the western frontier, Wild Bill Hickok is one of the most legendary. His life has been so romanticized through colorful publicity, books and the motion picture industry (along with a receptive audience ready to digest it) that it is sometimes difficult to isolate reality from legend. Someone once said that Hickok never killed a man except in self defense, or in the line of official duty. There may be a little truth to the statement if one considers that "in the line of duty" includes the use of a gun, from behind a badge, as a means of authority even when it was totally unwarranted.

James Butler Hickok was tall in stature, had blue eyes and light hair, and at times was a natty dresser. He was proficient in the use of firearms, had a no-nonsense attitude, and was obviously courageous, although he rarely gave his opponent much chance in a gunfight. Many of his girlfriends were whores, and he frequented brothels and gambling dens. At the poker tables he often supplemented his modest income as a peace officer. Toward the end of his life, he was arrested several times for vagrancy. His sobriquet "Wild Bill" suited him fine, for he was definitely rough on the edges. Hickok had a problem holding any job very long. In fact, the position from which he gained most of his fame, as City Marshal of Abilene, Kansas, he held for only a short time. Hickok was hired in April of 1871, at $150 per month plus a percentage of fines. He was discharged by the end of the year. In an era when many peace officers operated behind a badge, at times, and ran from it at other times, Wild Bill Hickok was unwavering. He always believed in law, order, and justice, and did his part to uphold it. But, he did it his way.

Hickok was a capable marksman before he ever ventured west to Kansas as an eighteen-year-old. His first position as an officer of the law was as constable of Monticello Township, Johnson County, Kansas. He was elected to that position in 1856, at age nineteen. Following that job, he worked as a stagecoach driver on the Santa Fe Trail. While employed as a wagon master for Russell, Majors & Waddell, Hickok was attacked by a cinnamon bear at Raton Pass. He killed the bear, but in doing so was severely injured. While recuperating, he was transferred to Rock Creek Station on the Oregon Trail in Nebraska, where he became engaged in a bloody gunfight. The stage depot at Rock Creek was operated by Horace Wellman, his common-law wife, and a helper named Doc Brink. Trouble brewed between the station staff and the McCanles family who lived directly across the creek, but owned the property on which the station was located. Not only was Dave McCanles having problems collecting his lease payments from Russell, Majors & Waddell, but Hickok was sneaking around with McCanles' live-in mistress and common-law wife Sarah Shull. McCanles insisted on calling Hickok "Duck Bill," among other things, which infuriated Wild Bill. The matter came to a head on July 12, 1861, when Dave McCanles called out to Hickok, "Come out and fight fair." Hickok refused to come outside, so McCanles opened the door and stepped in. Wild Bill who was waiting with his pistol drawn, shot Dave McCanles in the chest. After hearing the yelling and a gun shot, McCanles' cousin James Woods, a ranch employee James Gordon, and McCanles' twelve-year-old son Monroe, all dashed toward the stage station. As Woods approached the kitchen door, Hickok opened fire once more. He wounded Woods twice and nicked Gordon, and they both turned to flee. Doc Brink fired a blast from his shotgun and killed

Gordon. Horace Wellman caught the injured Woods and hacked him to death with a hoe. Dave McCanles passed his last breath cradled in the arms of his son.

Following the Civil War, during which he served the Union forces, Hickok worked as a gambler in Springfield, Missouri. At the town plaza, on July 21, 1865, Wild Bill squared off against Dave Tutt, a former friend, and scout for the Union, who had defected to join the Confederate Army. The two had been squabbling for days. Once again, it was a dispute over a female. The object of their affections was a girl named Susanna Moore. The conflict had reached a boiling point the prior evening when Hickok and Tutt threatened each other during a card game at the Lyon House. As a large crowd watched, the two confronted each other at a considerable distance. Tutt fired first, but missed. Wild Bill took careful aim, steadied his pistol with his left hand, and then squeezed off a shot. His slug hit Tutt in the chest, and he fell face first into the dust. He was dead.

Wild Bill Hickok was elected sheriff of Ellis County, Kansas, in August of 1869. Hays City, the county seat, was a rowdy frontier town. During his tenure, Hickok used his gun often, the necessity of which has often been questioned. On August 24th, Hickok fatally gunned down John Mulrey, a drunken cavalryman who refused to be arrested. On the 27th of September, a group of intoxicated teamsters were creating a ruckus inside one of the saloons. When Hickok arrived, he mortally shot one of the leaders, Samuel Strawhim through the head. The action was unwarranted, but it stopped the trouble. In November, during his bid for re-election, Hickok was defeated by his own deputy, Peter Lanihan. A brawl occurred at Drum's Saloon on July 17, 1870, when Hickok, who was drunk, got into it with Seventh Cavalry troopers who also had too much to drink. When the troopers threw Hickok to the floor, he drew his revolver and commenced firing. One soldier, John Kile, was killed. Another was severely wounded.

On April 15, 1871, Wild Bill Hickok was hired as city marshal of the busy cattle town of Abilene. It was there that he became involved in his most famous shootout. Respected gunman Ben Thompson and a fellow Texas gambler Phil Coe built a very popular brew house called the Bull's Head Saloon. Coe and Thompson promoted it by hanging a rather obscene sign in front of the structure. A certain part of the bull's anatomy was greatly exaggerated. At the request of town officials, Hickok instructed Coe and Thompson to alter their sign. When the two declined to do so, Hickok sent a painter to coat out the bull's masculinity. When the paint dried, all of the genitals were still distinctively pronounced. The incident caused much bitterness between Hickok and the saloon owners.

Some citizens thought that a showdown might occur between Ben Thompson and Hickok, but it never came to pass. The Bull's Head prospered so well that Thompson sent to Texas for his wife and boy. When Ben met them in Kansas City, their buggy flipped crushing his wife's arm and his son's foot. Ben's leg was broken, as well. Shortly thereafter, Thompson sold his interest in the Bull's Head and took his family back to Texas.

Before long, Coe also sold his interest in the Bull's Head, but the bitterness between he and Hickok continued. Actually, it heightened when Jessie Hazell became Coe's mistress. Hickok was infuriated because he had earlier taken a shine to Jessie.

Their disagreements came to a climax on October 5, 1871. Some old Texas friends of Coe had just driven their herd into Abilene. They decided to drink up the town for "old time's sake." Wild Bill even bought them a round, but in doing so he warned them against disturbing the peace. At approximately 9:00 p.m., Hickok heard a gunshot and responded immediately. Coe and a couple of Texans had their six-guns unholstered. As Hickok approached, Coe told him that he had shot a dog. Hickok drew, but Coe already had his revolver in hand and got off the first shot, which hit Hickok's coat doing no damage. Hickok quickly put two slugs in Coe's stomach. When policeman Mike Williams dashed on the scene to help Hickok, Wild Bill whirled and shot Williams twice in the head, killing him instantly. Obviously, Hickok was apprehensive about being surrounded by hostile cowboys, and acted too hastily. Hickok's eyesight was failing, possibly as a result of gonorrhea, and that may have been a factor in the accidental shooting. A very distraught Wild Bill paid Williams' funeral expenses. Coe died an agonizing death three days later. Two months later, Wild Bill Hickok was discharged from his post as city marshal of Abilene.

Through his entire life Hickok never did spend much time in any one place. He traveled briefly with Buffalo Bill Cody's "Wild West Show," but spent most of the next five years "drifting." Wild Bill married Agnes Lake whom he had met while she traveled with a circus. He left her two weeks later to head to the boomtown of Deadwood, Dakota Territory. On August 2, 1876, inside Saloon No. 10, Hickok sat with his back to the door, with a poker hand that included a queen and two pairs, aces and eights. John "Broken Nose Jack" McCall approached Hickok from the rear and shot him in the back of the head. Later, before he was hanged, McCall was asked why he didn't go around and shoot him from the front, like a man. McCall's answer was, "I didn't want to commit suicide."

Clay Allison recuperates after shooting himself in the foot. The wound occurred as the former Confederate soldier attempted to stampede U.S. Army mules near Cimarron, New Mexico in 1870. *Bill H.Hubbs, Barney Hubbs Colleection.*

Chapter Nineteen
Bad, Bad Clay Allison

Trouble often followed Clay Allison, but he seemed to thrive on it. Though normally an easy-going individual, he was known to be quick tempered and impulsive on occasion. Because of these traits, and some questionable deeds, history has depicted Robert Clay Allison as rather violent. In one incident, after a mob lynched an accused murderer in Cimarron, New Mexico, Allison supposedly decapitated him and displayed his head on a pole in a local saloon. Following another vigilante-style lynching, Allison allegedly tied the rope end opposite the noose to his saddle horn and dragged the corpse over rocks. Two days later, Clay Allison gunned down a friend of the lynching victim.

Legend has it that during a cattle drive in Wyoming, Allison developed a severe toothache and visited a Cheyenne dentist. After the dentist accidently broke off one of his teeth, the enraged Allison forcibly extracted one of the dentist's front teeth.

On December 21, 1876, Clay Allison and his brother John had

stopped in Las Animas, Colorado during a trip from their home in Texas. The brothers were enjoying the revelry at the Olympic Dance Hall, but had entirely too much to drink. When they were approached by Charles Faber, a deputy sheriff, who asked them to check their guns, they simply ignored him. The Allisons loved the dance hall girls, and they enjoyed dancing, but sometimes carried matters to the extreme. The more they drank, the more belligerent they became. Before long they were trampling the feet of other couples on the dance floor.

Incensed by the course of events, Charles Faber lined up two deputies and returned to the Olympic Dance Hall. Faber had a double-barrel shotgun in hand. As Faber entered the building, John Allison was still on the dance floor. Clay was leaning against the bar with his back to the door. Someone hollered, "Look out!" John whirled to see what was happening. Faber thought John Allison was going for his gun and shot him in the chest and shoulder with a barrel of buckshot.

Clay drew and fired four quick shots at Faber. One pierced his chest, and the deputy sheriff fell dead on the floor. As Faber collapsed, the other barrel of his shotgun discharged striking John again. This time he was hit in the leg. Clay stepped to the entrance and fired several more shots at the other two deputies as they fled into the dark. Clay then dragged Faber's body over to his bleeding brother assuring him that vengeance was done. Clay Allison turned himself in, but was later released from custody. John eventually recovered from the buckshot wounds.

The incident was Clay Allison's last gunfight. A few years later, he married the sister of John's wife, and sired two daughters, the second whom he never saw. During his wife's second pregnancy, Clay Allison fractured his skull when he fell beneath a wagon near Pecos, Texas. He died almost immediately.

After killing two employees at the Medicine Valley Bank, the four would-be robbers were apprehended. The prisoners, who would not live out the night, are (at center from left to right) John Wesley, Henry Brown (city marshal at Caldwell), William "Billy" Smith, and Ben Wheeler (deputy city marshal at Caldwell) whose real name was Ben Robinson. *Kansas State Historical Society.*

Chapter Twenty
Misfortune at Medicine Lodge

Earlier, during the Lincoln County War in New Mexico, Henry Newton Brown fought beside Billy the Kid as members of the Regulators, who were allied with the Alexander McSween faction during that bloody conflict. Brown was a cattle rustler, thief, and fine marksman. Some people found him to be a bit strange. He neither drank, nor smoked, nor gambled—unusual traits for a tough guy on the western frontier. After leaving New Mexico, Brown moved on to Texas where he found work as a cowpoke, deputy sheriff of Oldham County, and later as deputy constable of Tascosa. It is during this time spent in Texas, that Brown first met Ben Wheeler (who's real name was Ben Robertson).

Later, when Henry Brown became city marshal of Caldwell, Kansas, he sent for Wheeler who by then was living in Indianola, Nebraska, having deserted his first wife and four children in Texas. Wheeler deserted his second wife and child in Nebraska and proceeded to Caldwell where Brown swore him in as a deputy.

Henry Brown, a quiet man who always wore a kerchief around his neck cowboy-style, did a fine job of maintaining law and order in Caldwell. The appreciative citizens once gave him a new Winchester rifle with an engraved plate showing their appreciation for his "valuable services to the citizens of Caldwell, Kansas." On March 26, 1884, Brown married a local girl, Maude Levagood. Slightly over a month later, he would make her a widow.

Using the excuse that they were leaving to hunt for a murderer that was rumored to be in the vicinity, Brown and Wheeler rode west. Shortly thereafter, they were joined by John Wesley and William "Billy" Smith. The four men headed toward Medicine Lodge. A city marshal's pay was pittance, and Brown needed more money to support his new bride. In fact, the Browns had just purchased a new house.

It was a dreary, rainy morning on April 30, 1884, when the four men reined up in front of the Medicine Valley Bank. Billy Smith remained with the horses as the other three entered the bank. E. Wylie Payne, the bank's president, was formerly a tough cowpuncher who had taken a lot of hard knocks en route to making his money. When the trio thrust their six-guns at him and demanded that he fill their sack, his reaction was to reach for his revolver. It was his last mistake, for they shot him down in cold blood. The bandits immediately turned to the cashier, George Geppert, and shot him twice, as well. Before Geppert died, he staggered to the bank vault and locked it. The empty-handed trio dashed from the bank, leaped on their mounts, and the four men raced out of town. A posse quickly gathered and was in hot pursuit. Brown, Wheeler, Wesley, and Smith rode toward the Gypsums, a rugged region of low-lying hills. None of the group was familiar with the area, and they galloped straight into a box canyon with no outlet. The posse approached and had them trapped. It was simply a matter of waiting them out, and before long the fugitives chose to surrender. The bandits were returned to Medicine Lodge and locked up in jail.

Henry Brown concocted a story to "explain" the attempted robbery. He stated that Payne had planned the whole affair in order to hide a shortage in bank funds. Brown further indicated that he thought he had been double-crossed when Payne went for his gun, and for that reason, the bank employees were shot. Naturally, town officials realized the story was preposterous. Later that same afternoon, Brown penned a letter to his new bride, which stated, "…it was all for you, my sweet wife, and for the love I have for you. ...if a mob does not kill us, we will come out all right [sic] after a while. ...good-bye my darling wife. H. N. Brown."

At approximately 9:00 p.m., an angry mob of citizens stormed the jailhouse. As the prisoners were pulled outside, Brown was able to wrestle free and tried to make a dash for it. He was immediately cut down by a load of buckshot, and died instantly. Wheeler's vest was set on fire by a gun flash. He also bolted from the crowd, but bullets quickly wounded him, and he fell. Wheeler, Wesley, and Smith were dragged to a large elm tree where nooses were looped about their necks and they were hanged.

When word reached Caldwell, its townspeople were in shock. They couldn't believe that their faithful marshal had been involved in such an escapade. The *Journal* indicated that Henry Brown and Ben Wheeler "had made two as good officers as the city has ever had."

Front Street, looking west from Railroad Avenue (now Central), in 1897. *Boot Hill Museum.*

Chapter Twenty-One
Dodge City: Frontier Cow Town

    Fort Dodge, Kansas, was established as a military post in April of 1865 to protect wagon trains and travelers on the Santa Fe Trail. The fort also served as a base for soldiers participating in the Indian wars to the south. Just west of the military compound, the community of Dodge City began to emerge. By the time the Atchison, Topeka & Santa Fe Railway arrived in September of 1872, Dodge City had become a substantial trade and supply center. Nearly two-thirds of the early population consisted of buffalo hunters, who slaughtered the large herds roaming the prairie. Initially, tanners would pay up to $4.00 per buffalo hide. As the supply exceeded the demand, the price per hide fell to just over a dollar.

    Lawlessness ran rampant during the earliest years, as there was no local law enforcement. The mixture of buffalo hunters, railroad workers, soldiers, gamblers, traders, and drifters, were the ingredients for a rowdy and boisterous town. Legend has it that in 1872 two men had a gunfight in which one was killed. The murderer was nowhere to be found, and the dead man's identity was unknown. His body was wrapped in a blanket and buried with his boots on. Boot Hill, the most famous cemetery in western lore, was born. It was the burial ground for drifters, the unknown, and the penniless. Others were interred in the post cemetery at Fort Dodge.

By 1875 Dodge City had become a foremost railhead for the Texas cattle industry. During that year alone, a quarter million head of cattle were processed through Dodge City holding pens. The influx of Texans created problems for the community. Many were former Confederate soldiers who didn't mix well with the troops from Fort Dodge. The cattle drives that occurred between June and September bolstered the summer population of town immensely. Saloons, gambling dens, dance halls, and brothels did a booming business. In 1876, there were nineteen businesses licensed to sell liquor. The population that year was 1,200, but it would double within the next two years.

Following its incorporation in November of 1875, Dodge City enacted ordinances to regulate firearms within the community. A city marshal was appointed in order to enforce the new laws. It was immediately apparent that "flexibility" was a necessity. Front Street paralleled both sides of the railroad track, which was called the deadline. Most of the respectable businesses were located north of the deadline, where possession of weapons was thoroughly discouraged. On the other hand, little effort was made to enforce any gun controls on the south side where most of the gambling joints and brothels were located. Prostitution was "illegal," but not prohibited. Ordinances governing the brothels and cribs were simply a means of bringing additional monies into the city treasury. At one time, "justice" must have been an embarrassment to many hard working citizens, whether it took place outside or inside the courtroom. It is said that on one occasion a judge declared, "Any person caught throwing turnips, cigar stumps, beets, or old quids of tobacco at this court will be immediately arraigned before this bar of justice." It is also said that the description "red light district" originated in Dodge City, from railroad employees leaving their lanterns in front of the brothels.

Many notable gunfighters left their mark on Dodge City during the early years. The list included men such as, Jim, Ed, and Bat Masterson, Wyatt Earp, Luke Short, Doc Holliday, Clay Allison, Ben and Billy Thompson, Fred Singer, Charlie Bassett, Bill Tilghman, and "Mysterious" Dave Mather.

In 1876, soon after he was kicked off the police force and run out of Wichita for failing to turn in fines he had collected from prostitutes, Wyatt Earp became a policeman in Dodge City. During that year, Wyatt was badly beaten up in a fist fight by a cowboy named Red Sweeney.

The fisticuffs were over the affections of a dance hall girl. Earp went to Texas, where he roamed around for a while before returning to Dodge City in 1878, at which time he assumed the position of assistant marshal.

On April 9, 1878, just five months after his appointment as city marshal, Ed Masterson (brother of Jim and Bat) disarmed a rowdy cowboy, Jack Wagner, in order to calm a disturbance at the Lady Gay Dance Hall and Saloon. Masterson handed the revolver to A. M. Walker, Wagner's boss. As soon as Masterson and his deputy, Nat Haywood, turned their backs and left the building, Walker returned Wagner's six-gun. The two cowboys then charged out on to the street in pursuit of the lawmen. As Wagner neared Masterson with his gun drawn, the marshal grabbed the weapon in an effort to disarm him once more. Walker drew and attempted to shoot Haywood point blank, but his revolver misfired. As the others grappled, Wagner's pistol discharged sending a slug through Masterson's stomach. The marshal drew and rapidly fired four shots. One tore into Wagner's abdomen, while the other three struck Walker. Ed Masterson, with his apparel on fire from the flash of Wagner's revolver, walked through the plaza, across the deadline, and into a saloon. He died about thirty minutes later. Jack Wagner died the following day. A. M. Walker eventually recovered from his wounds. Ed Masterson wasn't the only lawman killed in Dodge City that year. U. S. Deputy Marshal Harry T. McCarty succumbed to a similar fate.

The famed Long Branch Saloon was the scene of a notable shootout. "Cockeyed" Frank Loving was a professional gambler who had been attracted to the high-stakes poker games in Dodge City. Levi Richardson worked for a freighting outfit. Loving and Richardson had been quarreling for days over a woman. The dispute came to a boiling point on the evening of April 5, 1879, as the two exchanged heated words. Richardson snarled, "You wouldn't fight." Loving angrily responded, "You try me and see!" Both men went for their six-shooters. Loving's revolver misfired, as Richardson wildly got off the first shot. As Loving ducked behind a stove, the two exchanged lead. One shot nicked Loving's hand but he continued to shoot. Richardson was struck once, twice and a third time as he reeled backward, and then collapsed dead on the floor.

Jim Masterson (the most active gunfighter of the brothers) and A. J. Peacock were partners in the Lady Gay Dance Hall and Saloon. Masterson detested a bartender named Al Updegraff, whom Peacock had hired. A quarrel ensued between Masterson and the others in which all three men drew their guns. Following a few wild shots the confrontation was quickly broken up. Masterson was in a quandary, as hostilities continued between him and his partner. He decided that he could use some help and telegraphed his brother Bat, who was in Tombstone. Shortly after he arrived in Dodge City (April 16, 1881), Bat spotted Peacock and Updegraff crossing the street. From a fair distance he called out to them, "I have come a thousand miles to settle this—now fight." The three drew as they darted for cover, and opened fire. Suddenly shots came from a nearby saloon. Updegraff took a slug in the chest that was probably fired by either Jim Masterson or Charlie Ronan. A bystander, James Anderson, was also wounded. Brandishing shotguns, Sheriff Fred Singer and Mayor A. B. Webster, took advantage of a lull in the shooting and stormed into the plaza putting a halt to the shooting. Updegraff survived the incident, and Bat Masterson was fined for "discharging a pistol upon the streets."

Luke Short, a part-owner in the Long Branch Saloon, became embroiled in a "saloon war" with reform minded Dodge City officials. Following the arrest of three female Long Branch employees on April 30, 1883, Short became involved in a gunfight with L. C. Hartman, a policeman. The two were unhurt after exchanging shots before disappearing into the darkness. Following the incident, Luke Short was run out of town by city officials. Short recruited an army of assorted gunslingers that included his friends, Wyatt Earp and Bat Masterson, in an effort to offset the political power of Mayor Deger. Suddenly, the city was like a powder keg waiting to explode. Short's group, the self-proclaimed "Dodge City Peace Commission," and city officials reached a détente before serious trouble broke out. Short was allowed to settle his financial affairs, as well as his differences with the city. Luke Short and his friend, W. H. Harris, were able to sell their interests in the Long Branch Saloon, after which Short moved on to Fort Worth, Texas.

"Mysterious" Dave Mather was at different times a horse thief, stagecoach robber, and officer of the law. He was also known to be a petty thief, who once stole a gold ring and chain from a black woman prior to his appointment as assistant city marshal of Dodge City. In 1884, Mather sustained a grudge against Tom Nixon who had replaced him as assistant city marshal. Nixon, who took a shot at Mather and missed, was arrested, but released on $800 bail. Three days later Mather spotted Nixon and shot him four times (see the chapter on Mysterious Dave

Mather). At the murder trial, Dave Mather was acquitted. Less than a year later, while playing cards at the Junction Saloon, a fellow named Dave Barnes jumped up from the poker table with gun in hand, accusing Mather of raking in a pot that wasn't his. Barnes fired a shot that went through Mather's hat. Josiah Mather, Dave's brother, fired several shots from behind the bar. Dave Barnes slumped to the floor. He was dead. After the Mather brothers each posted a $3,000 bond, which they forfeited, the Dave Barnes matter became history.

Boot Hill had already disappeared by 1880. Fort Dodge was closed as a military compound in 1882. When the cattle drives from Texas stopped following the summer of 1885, Dodge City, Kansas, settled into a peaceful mode.

Bat Masterson's reputation greatly exceeded his activity with a gun. *Denver Public Library, Western History Department.*

Sam Bass, who robbed banks, trains and stagecoaches met his demise at Round Rock, Texas. *Denver Public Library, Western History Department.*

Chapter Twenty-Two
Shootout at Round Rock

In late 1877 Samuel Bass rode out of Nebraska heading for Texas with money in his saddlebags, but he no longer had a gang. On the 18th of September, at Big Springs, Nebraska, the Sam Bass gang had recorded one of the most profitable train robberies in Old West history. The haul, which exceeded $60,000, was masterminded by one of the gang, Joel Collins. A week later Collins and gang members James Berry and Bill Heffridge were shot down, with the authorities retrieving $25,000. Bass returned to the Denton, Texas area where he had lived from 1870 to 1876.

Sam Bass began looking for new gang members. In Denton, he convinced old acquaintance Frank Jackson to ride with him. Jackson was a tinsmith who had gunned down a notorious horse thief a year earlier. In Dallas, early in 1878, he recruited Seaborn Barnes. Like Jackson, Seab Barnes was highly trusted by Bass, and both were loyal to him. Jim Murphy, who had a small ranch outside of Denton, decided to join the group. The freshly minted twenty-dollar gold pieces from the Big Springs heist that Bass was spreading around certainly didn't do anything to hurt his recruiting effort.

During the spring of 1878, the Sam Bass gang recorded four train robberies in the Dallas area. The robbers netted very little loot (just $150 from the Mesquite job). The holdups, however, precipitated a massive manhunt. On June 13, 1878, while camping at Salt Creek, in Wise County, the gang was surprised by a posse that was led by Texas Ranger Captain June Peak. Gang member Arkansas Johnson was shot and killed. The others shot their way to safety and escaped on foot. Subsequently, they were able to steal some horses and headed to Denton County.

Jim Murphy began to feel the heat. He wanted out. He figured that if he simply left the gang, he would still be a wanted man, so he decided to cut a deal with the Texas Rangers. The Rangers agreed that robbery charges against Murphy would be dismissed if he would tip them off prior to the gang's next job. The opportunity came shortly thereafter at Round Rock, Texas.

On July 19, 1878, Sam Bass, Frank Jackson, Seab Barnes, and Jim Murphy rode into Round Rock. Murphy had already betrayed his companions, so the Texas Rangers, the local law enforcement officers, and the citizens of Round Rock were expecting trouble. Exactly when they were expecting it seems to be an unanswered question. There is speculation that the group arrived on the 19th only to case the bank, not to rob it. They may or may not have intended to rob the bank that day. Murphy dropped off at a store on the edge of town in order to avoid any trouble. Obviously, the plan was for him to reconnect with the others in town, if the robbery was scheduled to happen that day.

Regardless, Bass, Barnes, and Jackson tied up their horses on Lampasas Street adjacent to the alley that led to May Street. They walked about one and a half blocks to Koppel's Store, which was located on the corner of Main and Mays. In doing so, they passed Deputy Sheriff Moore who thought they might be carrying guns, which would have been a violation of the local ordinance. Moore, in turn, notified Deputy Sheriff A. W. Grimes and they also headed to Koppel's Store. Moore waited outside, and Grimes entered. Neither of the lawmen recognized the outlaws.

Grimes approached Bass and asked him if he was carrying any hardware. Bass whirled, drew, and fired. Grimes reeled backwards and dropped dead near the store entrance. As the group fled the store, they exchanged shots with Moore. The deputy sheriff took a bullet in the chest, but continued to shoot. One of his slugs hit Bass' right hand, near his ring finger. The gang ran for their horses.

Texas Ranger Dick Ware was at the barber shop, lying back in a chair with his face lathered awaiting a shave (one sign that they were not expecting trouble at the time). He charged out on to Main Street and gave pursuit, as did other lawmen. In the alley behind Highsmith's Livery Stable, near where the horses were tied, Seab Barnes was hit in the head by one of Ware's bullets and died instantly.

As Sam Bass neared his horse, he was hit again. The bullet entered near his spine, and exited beside his naval. He went down. His loyal cohort, Frank Jackson, while returning enough fire to hold their pursuers at bay, managed to help Bass up into his saddle.

The two rode north, and then west, to a densely wooded area about three miles from town. Bass had become too weak to continue. Jackson hastily bound his friend's wounds, and at the insistence of Bass, rode on alone.

The following morning, the badly bleeding Bass crawled from the woods to a railroad construction site nearby, where he received water from section hands. The posse picked him up there and returned him to Round Rock. He was thoroughly interrogated but refused to say anything about his gang. Bass did say that he thought Dick Ware had fired the shot that downed him, although records indicate that the shot was actually fired by Texas Ranger George Harrell. Sam Bass died the following day, July 21, 1878, on his twenty-seventh birthday. He, Seaborn Barnes, and A. W. Grimes were all buried in the Round Rock Cemetery, on the street later to be named Sam Bass Road, just west of the Chisholm Trail.

Jim Murphy got his deal. All charges against him for robbery were dismissed. Murphy returned to Denton. Fearing reprisals against himself or his family, they moved from his ranch to a house on East McKinney Street, which he felt would be safer. Murphy became very despondent, and a year later took his own life by swallowing atropine.

Evidently, Frank Jackson changed his identity and may have opted for a more peaceful life. The day he rode out of Round Rock, he did so into permanent anonymity.

Bannack, Montana, in the 1860s. *Montana Historical Society.*

Chapter Twenty-Three
Henry Plummer, Renegade Sheriff

A large band of renegades called the Innocents terrorized the gold mining industry in southwest Montana during the early 1860s. Their leader was lawman Amos Henry Plummer, who had left a trail of trouble and blood from the gold fields of California to the boomtowns of Montana. In 1852, as a nineteen-year-old, Plummer was appointed marshal of Nevada City, California. A few years later, he was sentenced to ten years in prison at San Quentin for killing the husband of a woman with whom he was having an affair. It was at San Quentin that Henry Plummer met Cyrus Skinner, whom he would connect with again in Bannack, Montana. Plummer only served six months, and was released in 1859. On October 27, 1861 he killed a fellow named William Riley at a house of ill-repute. Plummer was incarcerated, but escaped. Following several robberies, and possibly two more murders, Plummer wound up in the mining camp of Lewiston, Idaho. Unknown to the townspeople of Lewiston, Plummer led a gang of highwaymen. When a posse of vigilantes was organized to rid the area of lawbreakers, Plummer volunteered his services. Shortly thereafter, he had a vigilante leader killed in order to disrupt the pursuit of their prey.

Thousands of eager prospectors flocked to Montana when a gold strike was made at Grasshopper Creek in June of 1862. The boomtown of Bannack (initially called Bannack City) had blossomed before the winter set in. Among the earliest arrivals into the vicinity were Cyrus Skinner and Henry Plummer and his renegades. Skinner built a saloon at nearby Yankee Flats, and then moved it to Bannack. The rowdy gold camp needed law enforcement, so former law officer Henry Plummer was appointed to the post of sheriff. He immediately hired three of his comrades, Jack Gallagher, Buck Stinson, and Ned Ray, as deputies. Town fathers insisted that Plummer also deputize D. H. Dillingham, another new Bannack citizen. After serving for about a month, Dillingham turned up dead. He had learned too much, and was shot down by Stinson and two other gang members named Hayes (sometimes spelled Haze) Lyons and Charley Forbes. The killers were arrested, tried, and then turned loose. Plummer and his deputies infiltrated every group and club in town, except for the Masons.

Amos Henry Plummer married Electa Bryan. After three months of marriage, Electa permanently departed for her parent's home in Cedar Rapids, Iowa.

Henry Plummer ran his operation from Skinner's Saloon, where he supplemented his sheriff's pay at the faro tables. Skinner was not only a saloon keeper, but he was one of Plummer's road agents, as well. His saloon was "headquarters" for the gang. In his position as the chief law enforcement officer, Plummer knew upon which stagecoaches payrolls were due, and also the ones which were departing with "plentiful" strongboxes. If the take was substantial, the Innocents would schedule a raid. Often the coaches were "marked" in order to identify them to his road agents.

Rich placer gold was discovered in 1863 at Alder Gulch, and the mining town of Virginia City sprang to life. Plummer's domain as sheriff was increased to include Virginia City. His band of outlaws also turned its attention to that locale. Thousands of dollars in gold shipments were hijacked. Miners who worked hard each day for a few nuggets or a little gold were often robbed. Some who resisted were shot.

Law enforcement throughout the gold camps of southwestern Montana was obviously ineffective. The time had come to do something about it. Through the efforts of men like Colonel Wilbur Fisk Sanders, Captain James Williams, John Fetherstun, Neil Howie, John X. Beidler, Paris Pfouts, John Lott, and Nathaniel Langford, a large group of vigilantes was formed on December 23, 1863. They were backed by the "Incorporators," the business interests in the vicinity. The Montana

Vigilantes were many, heavily armed, and a force to be reckoned with.

The first strike against the Innocents actually occurred two days earlier when a posse of twenty-four men chased and captured George Ives. Ives, one of Plummer's henchmen, was quickly tried for the robbery and brutal murder of a Dutchman named Nicholas Thiebalt. A noose was placed around his neck, and he was jerked to eternity. Plummer and his deputies were not present to intervene.

When Henry Plummer quarreled with a confederate, Jack Cleveland, at Goodrich's Saloon at Bannack, the argument turned to gunfire. Plummer's accuracy prevailed and Cleveland was shot down. During the hours before he died, Cleveland told Hank Crawford, a local butcher, all about the Innocents and their secret leader, Henry Plummer. When Crawford started to spread the word as to what he had heard, Plummer realized it was time to rid the town of one butcher. With his shotgun in hand, Plummer confronted Crawford. As he did, the two were spotted by Frank Ray, a friend of Crawford's, who realized what was happening and fired at Plummer. The ball shattered Plummer's right arm, ending the trouble. Crawford decided that Bannack had become too dangerous, and he fled town. By now, however, the Vigilantes knew what they needed to know. They were ready to unleash their own reign of terror.

Many members of the Vigilantes worked at the nearby gold mines. The frozen ground during the early weeks of January 1864 made it an ideal time for a roundup. Among the earliest to have their necks stretched were Erastus "Red" Yeager and G. W. Brown. After the Vigilantes unanimously voted to hang the two road agents, Yeager confessed as to his own guilt. Furthermore, he confirmed that Plummer was their leader; that Bill Bunton was second in command; and that the others were George Ives (already deceased), Stephen Marshland, Dutch John Wagner, Alec Carter, Sam Bunton, Cyrus Skinner, Whiskey Bill Graves, George Shears, Johnny Cooper, Buck Stinson, Ned Ray, Mexican Frank (last name unknown), Robert "Bob" Zachary, Frank Parrish (sometimes spelled Parish), Boone Helm, "Club Foot" George Lane, Hayes Lyons, Bill Hunter, George Lowry, Billy Page, Doc Howard, Jem Romaine, Billy Terwilliger, and Gad Moore. There were so many that he even left out a few. He further advised that all were clean-shaven except for their moustaches, and that each member of the band wore a neckerchief, which was tied with a "sailor's" knot. Their password was "I am Innocent," from whence came the name of the gang. Yeager then passed along the details of many crimes, and named the perpetrators. He and Brown were then hanged in a grove near a place called Lorraine's Ranch.

On the 10th of January, Henry Plummer answered a knock on his front door, whereupon he was immediately seized by the Vigilantes. Plummer offered no resistance, possibly due to the fact that his revolver was inoperative. The Vigilantes had already grabbed Buck Stinson and Ned Ray. The trio was dragged to a crude gallows that Plummer himself had helped to construct many months before. The sheriff declared to God that he was too wicked to die. There was no trial. There was no vote. The three were hanged. As ice began to gather on the corpses, they were cut down by Bannack citizens. Before the bodies could be buried, there would be more deaths. Two Vigilantes entered the cabin of Joe Pizanthia, otherwise known as the "Greaser." Pizanthia, who was not a gang member, opened fire. One slug struck Smith Ball in the hip, and another shattered the chest of George Copley, and he would soon die. Within seconds, the Vigilantes emptied their guns into Pizanthia, tearing his body to shreds. Afterward, they cremated his corpse. Before the day was over they had also hanged Dutch John Wagner.

Four days later, at Virginia City, five more gang members, Boone Helm, Frank Parrish, "Club Foot" George Lane, Jack Gallagher, and Hayes Lyons dangled from ropes. Helm was a tough and violent individual. After the noose was placed around his neck, he barked, "Kick away, old fellow; I'll be in Hell with you in a minute." A few of the Innocents fled the area. Those who didn't were foolish. Immediately thereafter, Stephen Marshland, Bill Bunton, Alec Carter, Johnny Cooper, Bob Zachary, George Shears, and Whiskey Bill Graves were captured and executed. Cyrus Skinner was tracked down and hanged in Hellgate (Missoula) on January 25, 1864. Bill Hunter was able to escape to the Gallatin River area, where a blizzard drove him take refuge in a cabin. There he was captured and hanged on February 3rd of the same year. Hunter was the last of Henry Plummer's gang to meet his maker at the hands of the Vigilantes. The Vigilantes were effective, as lawlessness was minimized. Once again, gold shipments left with confidence high that they would reach their destinations.

Trouble followed Billy Brooks. This photograph of the sometimes good-sometimes bad guy is unauthenticated. *Boot Hill Museum.*

Chapter Twenty-Four
Bully Brooks

Some called him Bully—some called him Billy. He was also one of several men who were dubbed "Buffalo Bill." His given name was William L. Brooks. He was reportedly born in Ohio, about 1849, though virtually nothing is known about his youth. Brooks was a gunfighter who operated on both sides of the law.

William Brooks surfaced at Wichita, Kansas, in 1870. He was a tough guy in a tough town. When he first became newsworthy he had already established a reputation as an adept buffalo hunter, a gunfighter, and a no-nonsense individual with a lot of grit. Brooks always looked prepared to go to battle. He wore a pearl-handled Colt revolver, and usually carried a Winchester.

Brooks was employed for nearly two years as a stagecoach driver. For several months he ran the route between Wichita and Newton, a blossoming cow town. Newton was a wild place that badly needed law enforcement. William Brooks was hired as Newton's first town marshal, a job he would not hold for long.

On June 9, 1872, two Texas cowboys, Joe Miller and James Hunt, were raising a ruckus at E.T. "Red" Beard's dancehall. Somebody sent for Marshal Brooks, and he quickly responded. The marshal escorted the Texans to the edge of town, where Miller whirled and opened fire. Three slugs hit Brooks. The gritty marshal then chased the pair for ten miles before returning to Newton to have his wounds dressed. In reporting the incident Wichita's *Eagle* stated: "One shot passed through his right breast, and the other two were in his limbs. . . . Bill has sand enough to beat the hour-glass that tries to run him out."

The episode may have been a catalyst for Brooks to seek greener pastures elsewhere, as just two months later he was employed as a policeman at Ellsworth. Shortly thereafter he moved on to Dodge City.

The *Eagle* reported another shooting which occurred on December 23, 1872, " . . . at Dodge City on Monday night of last week, between 'Bully' Brooks, ex-marshal of Newton, and Mr. Brown, yard master at the former place, which resulted in the death of Brown. Three shots were fired by each party. Brown's first shot wounded Brooks, whose third shot killed Brown and wounded one of his assistants. Brooks is a desperate character, and has before, in desperate encounters, killed his man." Evidently, a prostitute named Jessie was sweet on Brooks, and then dumped him for Brown, which was obviously the cause of their quarrel. It was later reported that Brown did not die, but that he was nursed back to health by Jessie.

Just five days later (on the 28th of December) saloonkeeper Matthew Sullivan was shot to death at his place of business. The slug, which killed him instantly, came from a gun pointed through an open window. *The Kansas Daily Commonwealth* (Topeka) reflected on the killing: "It is supposed that the unknown assassin was a character in those parts called Bully Brooks, but nothing definite is known concerning the affair, or what led to it."

Brooks, who was once again driving stages for his old employer, seemed to attract trouble like a magnet. For some reason, Brooks had really upset an acquaintance, buffalo hunter Kirk Jordan. On the 4th of March in 1873, as Brooks walked down a Dodge City street, he looked up in time to see a buffalo gun leveled at him. By instinct (sensing that there was no time to draw) he dove behind two water barrels. A slug from Jordan's rifle smashed through both barrels and lodged in one of the iron hoops. The assailant quickly ducked between two buildings and out of harm's way. The following day Jordan and Brooks were seen shaking hands, evidently resolving their differences.

Bully Brooks' employer, the Southwestern Stage Company, was vying for a mail contract (on the route from Caldwell to Fort Sill) which was held by their competitor, Vail & Company. The route was so important to Southwestern Stage that they decided to prevent Vail & Company from fulfilling their agreement at all costs. Southwestern offered Bully Brooks and several others a large bonus if they could sabotage the mail run. The most effective way to do so, they figured, was to steal all of the Vail & Company mules. They set out to do so.

Vail & Company had stock located at Caldwell, Skeleton Creek, Kingfisher and Stinking Creek. The rustlers effectively stole the mules located at Caldwell and Skeleton Creek. The raiding party that went to Kingfisher was attacked by Indians, and one of the rustlers, Bill Watkins, was killed and scalped. The thieves were so blatant and obvious in their actions that it wasn't long before everyone knew what was going on. A posse of one hundred and fifty men gathered at Wellington. The group, that was headed by Sheriff John G. Davis, was heavily armed and intent upon bringing an immediate end to the thievery. On July 28, 1874, Bully Brooks was cornered at a hideout near Caldwell. After a stand-off which lasted several hours, he surrendered to the posse. He, and two other suspects, Charley Smith and L.B. Hasbrouck, were jailed at Wellington.

At nearly midnight on the 29th, a large mob disarmed the guards, then dragged Brooks, Smith and Hasbrouck from the jailhouse. On the following morning their lifeless bodies could be seen hanging from a tree near the bridge at Slate Creek.

Daniel Riley "Dee" Harkey and his bride, Sophie New, on the occasion of their wedding in August of 1886. *Myrtle Fritschy.*

Chapter Twenty-Five
Dee Harkey: Guts and Grit

D. R. "Dee" Harkey became an officer of the law in 1882 at the age of sixteen. He wore a badge until 1911. Harkey was not quick on the draw, nor was he more than an adequate marksman, but he was long on guts. Also, he was either very lucky or he had a guardian angel for he was shot at many times. Dee Harkey had a great deal of compassion for other people. Few lawmen on the western frontier would ever give a man who had attempted to murder him a second chance. Dee could not shoot a man once he had "the drop" on him. Nevertheless, he was a highly effective lawman, even though he did things his own way.

Dee Harkey was born at Richland Springs, Texas, on March 27, 1866. One of thirteen children, he was orphaned when he was three years old. Dee was virtually raised by his oldest brother Joe (who was seventeen years old at the time of their parents' death). Joe was elected sheriff of San Saba County, Texas, in 1880. Two years later, Dee was sworn in as one of his deputies.

The first man that Dee Harkey ever arrested was one of the most hardened killers in the Old West, "Deacon" Jim Miller. In a San Saba saloon one night, Miller, Bill White and the three Renfro brothers had been raising a ruckus. When White struck a fellow who was currently on jury duty, the sheriff was beckoned. Within minutes, Joe and Dee Harkey burst through the lattice saloon door. Dee thrust his revolver in Miller's face. Deacon Jim raised his hands and said, "My God kid, don't kill me!" Dee took his gun. At the same time, Joe Harkey had disarmed White. The Renfro brothers were commanded to drop their gun belts, and they did. The Harkeys then marched the five down to the San Saba jailhouse and locked them up. All five were released the following day.

Joe Harkey had been advised by U.S. Marshal Gozlin, of San Antonio, to be on the alert for two bandits who had robbed a stagecoach near Mason. According to Gozlin, one of the men was tall and the other was shorter and heavyset. He further advised that there had been a $1,000 bill among the loot. Joe Harkey was informed that he would receive a $500 reward should he be able to arrest these robbers. It wasn't long before two men matching the bandits' description rode into San Saba. Joe recognized them as being former Indian fighters named Pitts and Yeager.

Dee was asked by Joe to shadow the suspects because he was young and they wouldn't pay much attention to him. Dee Harkey followed Pitts and Yeager to the bank where he saw them change a $1,000 bill. Before long, the robbers mounted up and rode out of San Saba. Joe and Dee trailed them at a distance. Pitts and Yeager rode east about 45 miles to the town of Lampasas. From there they turned to the southwest and headed to Llano. They were generally heading back toward the location of the stagecoach robbery. Joe Harkey decided to confront them in Llano. Pitts and Yeager had stopped at a blacksmith shop to have their horses shod. On the pretext of having their own horses shod, Joe and Dee were able to get close to the bandits, at which time the Harkeys drew in unison and arrested the fugitives. Joe Harkey received his $500 reward plus another $500 for delivering the bandits to Marshal Gozlin at the Lometa railroad depot. Joe had made a nice bonus on Pitts and Yeager, while his little brother gained valuable experience as a lawman.

Gozlin, Pitts and Yeager never reached San Antonio alive. When the Santa Fe train arrived into Austin, the wives of Pitts and Yeager and the mother of one of the wives were allowed to board the train and accompany the fugitives to San Antonio. Unknown to Gozlin they had smuggled weapons aboard. When the train was about seven miles south of Austin, Gozlin was shot in the back of the head. He died instantly.

Gozlin's deputy and a conductor who quickly armed himself opened fire on Pitts and Yeager. During the exchange of fire the mother was shot through the stomach by the deputy. One of the fugitives was killed and the other wounded so badly that he would die shortly thereafter. Joe Harkey had warned Gozlin that Pitts and Yeager would kill him if they had a chance. Gozlin was careless, and Harkey was right.

Dee Harkey was shot at often during the many years he wore a badge, but he was only hit once, and it was by a girl. Harkey was quite fond of Mary Quinn who lived at Richland Springs. He escorted her to several dances and other events. When Joe Harkey instructed Dee to arrest Mary's father for stealing two mules, duty prevailed over emotion. As Dee attempted to make the arrest, Mary appeared with a cocked revolver. "Dee, that's my father and I'm going to protect him," she stated, then pulled the trigger. The bullet was deflected by a silver watch in Dee's vest pocket causing nothing more than a superficial wound. Dee Harkey never made the arrest. It was soon discovered that Quinn was an escaped convict wanted for murder. Shortly thereafter he killed the sheriff of Coleman County and was gunned down by several deputies.

On August 4, 1886, Dee Harkey married Sophie New, a young teenager who lived in Bee County, Texas. They were able to obtain a marriage license over the objections of Sophie's mother who tried to block the marriage because of her daughter's adolescence. Dee turned in his badge and rented a farm at Torro Creek (in Bee County) from a fellow named George Young. One day Young accused Harkey of abusing a steer he had sold him. It was the beginning of some bad blood between the two. Young attempted to badger Harkey into a fight, but the latter would have none of it. The landlord then turned some of his horses out in Harkey's cornfield where they destroyed part of his crop. George Young was plowing his garden of sweet potatoes when Harkey approached him to discuss the damage to his corn. Both men were carrying knives. Heated words quickly turned into a fight, and each man pulled his knife. Young, the larger of the two men, threw Harkey to the ground and cut him several times. Finally, while Young was on top of him, Harkey thrust his blade into his foe's back. Young leaped to his feet and ran toward his house while yelling at his wife to bring his shotgun. Once inside his house, George Young collapsed and died. Dee Harkey was arrested, charged with murder, and spent twenty-one days in jail before bond could be posted. When the case came to trial he was acquitted.

In 1890, Dee Harkey moved to Eddy, New Mexico (later to be

renamed Carlsbad). He worked as a grocery clerk and then as a butcher. Before long, Harkey received an appointment as a deputy U.S. marshal. His instructions were to clean up Eddy County. Phoenix, just south of the community of Eddy, was a mecca of saloons, dance halls, gamblers and prostitutes. Furthermore, the condition existed because most of the county officials were saloon owners or pawns of those men who controlled the vice in Eddy County. The sheriff, Dave Kemp, was a partner in the largest gambling hall in Phoenix. His primary concern was to protect the interests of the saloon owners. Gambling was licensed in the territory and was a legitimate business, but the extensive rings of prostitution were not. Dee Harkey made this problem his number one priority.

The saloon owners built rows of little shacks (or cribs as they were commonly called) where their prostitutes could live and peddle their wares. The girls would work in the dance halls until about midnight, and then escort their partners to the cribs for further entertainment. Late one night, Harkey and two deputies raided several of the cribs. They hit the cribs one at a time, and did so quietly so no one would realize what was happening. Sixteen couples were arrested and whisked off to a train bound for the Socorro jailhouse. Nobody knew what had happened until the following day. Saloon owners were incensed. Threats against Harkey's life were commonplace. That night, Harkey and his deputies struck again. Sixteen more couples were hurried away to the train, and

Looking north on Canyon Street in Eddy, New Mexico, in 1893. Six years later the community was renamed Carlsbad. *Southwestern New Mexico Historical Society of Carlsbad.*

subsequently the jail at Socorro. The county officials were Republicans who previously had no opposition. Dee Harkey and other solid citizens organized the Democratic Party in Eddy County. A primary election was held in order to nominate a ticket to oppose the Republicans. On the day of the general election, Democrats swept the Republicans out of office. Gradually, the undesirable elements began to pull out of Phoenix and head for greener pastures.

One evening during the spring of 1895 a gunfight broke out in Phoenix, between a group of about fifteen Mexicans and an equal number of Anglos. The Mexicans were led by Tranquellano Estabo, who was handy with a gun. The Anglos, were from Eddy, and were led by Walter Paddleford. When words erupted into gunfire, Estabo's bunch dove to the ground behind the railroad tracks. The fellows from Eddy scrambled for cover behind several barrels which were filled with empty beer bottles. When Dee Harkey rode onto the scene, three Mexicans had been killed and one wounded, while one Anglo had also been slain.

As lead flew in both directions, Harkey approached and ordered both factions to cease fire. The Mexicans stopped firing, then so did the Anglos. Harkey walked between both groups, and then approached the Anglos. Paddleford stepped forward. He tore his shirt open and pointed to his bare chest, advising Harkey to shoot him there. He exclaimed, "My dad was a war horse and I was his papoose, and you are afraid to shoot me." Harkey simply snatched the Winchester from Paddleford's hand, and then marched the whole bunch off to jail.

Harkey would have further confrontations with both Paddleford and Estabo. Paddleford jumped bail and headed to Mexico. Harkey tracked Paddleford to Sonora, Mexico, where he arrested him again. Armed with a writ which assured them safe passage out of Mexico, Harkey and his prisoner returned to Eddy County. Once again, Paddleford was allowed to post bail. He jumped bail again and disappeared. No further effort was ever made to bring Walter Paddleford to trial. During the summer of 1895, Tranquellano Estabo killed a fellow gambler during a quarrel at Phoenix. When Dee Harkey attempted to arrest Estabo, the Mexican shot at him then rode out of town at breakneck speed. Harkey chased the fugitive on horseback for three miles before catching up with him. Estabo pleaded, "Don't kill me! Don't kill me!" Harkey escorted Estabo to the Eddy County jail and locked him up.

Before he escaped from the penitentiary in Texas, Jim Nite had been serving a life sentence for killing a cashier during a bank robbery.

Nite fled from Texas to New Mexico where he formed a new outlaw gang. They were a ruthless bunch that robbed and killed as they moved about the territory. After the gang rustled some horses in Eddy County, Dee Harkey and three deputies set out to track them down. Whereas the outlaws had plenty of fresh horses and could simply swap saddles from one to another, the posse had to stop on the second day. They shod their horses using felt from a hat as a liner. It allowed the horses to continue. On the third day, Harkey encountered a goat herder who told him that five men had stolen all his food, guns and ammunition the night before. Dee knew he was on the right track. Two days later, the lawmen arrived at a ranch house that Nite had robbed of all the supplies he needed. The lawmen picked up fresh horses and continued their chase.

Harkey flagged down a Rock Island Railroad train in order to procure water for their horses. It was discovered that Nite had held up the train one day earlier. At this point, a fellow named Tom Tucker joined the posse. He was a former Hash Knife cowboy who participated in the Pleasant Valley War in Arizona. At daybreak the following morning, the lawmen stumbled onto the fugitives while they were still in camp. Harkey's men were able to scatter the outlaws' horses before an all out gun battle erupted.

Harkey was pinned on a knoll between his deputies (who were above and behind him) and the outlaws below. He knew he could not move from his position without being hit. So, he unmercifully rained lead on Nite and his men. With their horses gone and a hail of bullets dropping from above the outlaws quickly surrendered. The ordeal was over.

Jim Nite was returned to the penitentiary in Texas to finish serving his life sentence. His four confederates escaped from jail and headed in different directions. Will Morrow was captured in Montana. Dan Johnson was caught in Arizona. The two were returned to New Mexico where they were tried and convicted. The other fugitives made good their escape.

When Dee Harkey retired from service as a lawman he remained in Eddy County as a successful rancher.

Judge Isaac Charles Parker was feared as "the hanging judge" when in actuality he was quite fair. *Fort Smith National Historic Site.*

Chapter Twenty-Six
Fort Smith and Indian Territory

In 1830, President Andrew Jackson used his executive power, and ignored two United States Supreme Court decisions that were won by the Cherokee Indians, to mandate that Indians spread across the southeastern states be relocated west of the Mississippi River. When they were finally relocated, in 1838 and 1839, it was to the newly established Indian Territory, the area that is present day Oklahoma. The Cherokee Indians were the first to be "rounded up." Many of them hid out in the hills of North Carolina and Tennessee to avoid being moved west. Those relocated in the so-called Indian Removal were followed by the Chickasaw, Choctaw, Creek and Seminole. Known as the "Five Civilized Tribes," they were moved to Indian Territory with great difficulty, a lack of food, limited medical assistance, and death for many, along the route that would later be called the "Trail of Tears."

At Tahlequah in the Indian Territory in 1843, representatives of sixteen tribes and U.S government officials held an historic meeting for the purpose of establishing laws for the territory and creating amicable relations between the tribes which had been forced westward and those already living there. The United States government recognized the Five Civilized Tribes as self-governing nations within their own allotted lands. Each tribe had its own laws, courts, and law enforcement. Their police, called the "Lighthorse," were only allowed jurisdiction over their tribe members, and had no power over Caucasian invaders. Although whites were supposedly "prohibited" in Indian Territory by the U. S. government, except by special license, the restriction was generally ignored. It became an ideal place for white fugitives to hide out. Before long there were criminals scattered throughout Indian Territory, and the Lighthorse couldn't touch them.

Following the Civil War, Texas drovers cut wide paths through Indian Territory driving their cattle to the Kansas railheads. Overland mail routes required that stage stations be constructed across Indian land. Eventually, ribbons of track were laid by the railroad companies and that meant new depots. The lack of law enforcement brought an influx of undesirables into and through the area. Gunfighters, gamblers, prostitutes, whiskey peddlers, thieves, drifters, and other undesirables produced an unprecedented increase in criminal violence.

The federal judge and federal marshal for the Western District of Arkansas were originally located in Van Buren. They were responsible for law enforcement in 30 Arkansas counties and their jurisdiction supposedly included the vast area of Indian Territory, commonly called the "Nations." In 1871, a step was taken in the right direction, when their offices were moved to Fort Smith, Arkansas, just 100 yards (91 meters) from the eastern edge of Indian Territory. The appointment of Judge Isaac Charles Parker, by President Ulysses S. Grant in 1875, as the federal judge at Fort Smith, was a great stride toward improving law and order in Indian Territory. As a member of the House Committee on Indian Affairs, Parker had become extremely concerned with the plight of the Indian. Certain that he could make a difference, Parker personally requested the Fort Smith post. Because of the number of men that Judge Parker sentenced to the gallows, he became known as "the hanging judge." In actuality, the most feared court in the west was one of the fairest. During a span that exceeded twenty years, Isaac Parker tried approximately 13,000 major criminal cases. Parker pronounced 172 death sentences, of which only 88 were carried out. About 4,000 defendants were acquitted (over 30% of those tried). An accused individual facing

George Maledon was a perfectionist with his ropes and technique. He dropped the trapdoor for many convicted men. *Fort Smith National Historic Site.*

trial probably stood as great a chance of being released in Judge Parker's court as any in history.

George Maledon was a Deputy U. S. Marshal who had accepted the additional position as hangman just prior to the arrival of Isaac Parker into Fort Smith. Of the 88 men that actually dropped through a trap door, George Maledon hanged 87 of them. He excused himself from one execution because the condemned man had been a fellow Union soldier. The gallows at Fort Smith was designed to allow twelve men to hang at one time. No more than six men were ever hanged simultaneously. Five were executed together on more than one occasion. Hangings at Fort Smith were quite a spectacle as hundreds of people usually attended the show. The hangman received $100 for each individual executed, less expenses which sometimes included the burial of unclaimed bodies.

Indian Territory had the greatest concentration of badmen in the West. Isaac Parker and his force of many deputy U. S. marshals became "the law" in Indian Territory. The cleanup began. During Isaac Parker's two decades on the bench, 65 of his lawmen would die while attempting to bring law and order within their jurisdiction, an average of over three per year. Whiskey running was big business in Indian Territory, and it became a major target for federal marshals. More often than not, arrests made by U. S. marshals were for running whiskey. Often they would "collect" a dozen men before taking them to jail at Fort Smith.

Matters were not always easy for the lawmen from Fort Smith, however. Possibly their most difficult task was the capture of the elusive Cherokee, Ned Christie. Christie would become a much hunted man.

Ned's Father, Watt Christie, operated a popular blacksmith shop and was probably the best gunsmith in the Goingsnake District. As a young boy, Ned worked in his father's shop. By the age of ten, Ned Christie had become a proficient gunsmith and was considered one of the finest marksmen in the Indian Territory.

An event occurred during Ned Christie's childhood that would impact his life. In the Goingsnake District, the area that is now Adair County, Oklahoma, an organization was founded to actively oppose acculturation into "white" society. In the Cherokee language, the word *Keetoowah* means traditional full-blooded Cherokee. The organization was named the Keetoowah Society. As U.S government policy changed toward the Indians in the late 1860s, the Keetoowah Society tended to become more of an underground movement. Their members became

Cherokee Indian, Ned Christie, a gunsmith and gunfighter. *Archives and Manuscripts Division of the Oklahoma Historical Society.*

known as the Nighthawk Keetoowahs.

In 1885, Ned Christie was elected by the Goingsnake District as their representative in the Cherokee Senate. He had become a popular member of the Cherokee Nation. Christie was also a Nighthawk Keetoowah.

Near Tahlequah, on May 4, 1885, Christie and his companion John Parris had left a secluded cabin, a bawdy house, and were crossing a foot bridge at Spring Branch. As they did so they were confronted by Deputy U. S. Marshal Dan Maples, who was in the vicinity to arrest an outlaw named Bill Pigeon. The two Indians, who were both drunk, turned and ran. When the deputy commenced shooting, Christie whirled and returned the fire, mortally wounding Maples, who tumbled into the stream. Parris, who was soon apprehended, stated that Christie had killed Maples. A few days later, lawman Joe Bowers, armed with warrant, rode out to Christie's cabin to arrest him for the killing of Maples. Christie opened fired, wounding Bowers in the leg and the deputy high-tailed it home.

Lawman John Fields of the Lighthorse was determined to talk Christie into surrendering, and he ventured out to Christie's cabin to do so. With his rifle in hand, Ned Christie emerged from his cabin and commenced firing. Fields wheeled his mount, taking a slug in the neck as he dashed to safety. It was the last time anybody tried to apprehend Ned Christie without help. A few months later when a posse approached his place it was also met by accurate gunfire and eventually had to retreat with three wounded lawmen. It would be more that three years before another attempt was made to capture Ned Christie.

Isaac Charles Parker, had recruited noted Deputy U. S. Marshal Heck Thomas to help him improve conditions in the Indian country. In 1889, Thomas rode out of Fort Smith headed toward Tahlequah. He was accompanied by fellow officers, Isbel, Rusk, and Salmon. At daybreak, they worked their way toward Christie's cabin. Sensing danger, Christie's dogs suddenly began barking. Awakened, Christie began firing from his sleeping loft, behind a gable. One of his shots drilled L.P Isbel in the shoulder. The lawmen set fire to the cabin in order to flush the fugitive. As the fire began to rage, Christie's wife and son dashed out a door and headed for a wooded area. As they ran, his son was wounded twice by the lawmen's gunfire. Moments later, Christie burst from the inferno in a dead run. A bullet from the six-gun of Heck Thomas caught Christie in the face. It crushed his nose and put out his right eye, but he kept on running and made good his escape.

Whereas most outlaws would have stayed on the run continually fleeing from their pursuers, Ned Christie wished to remain near Tahlequah. So, he built a log fort on a high rim above Rabbit Trap Canyon. The two-story structure with massive walls that were two logs thick became known as Ned's Fort Mountain. The fortification was first tested in 1891 by Deputy Dave Rusk (who had accompanied Heck Thomas during the raid on Christie's cabin two years earlier) and a posse of Indians. When they attacked, Christie and a few Keetoowah cohorts unleashed a deadly barrage on fire, wounding four of the invaders. The posse turned tail and retreated. It is said that Rusk approached the fort on two other occasions, only to be driven back by a volley of bullets. Later, when Dave Rusk's general store at Oakes, north of Tahlequah, was burned, the conflagration was attributed to Christie and the Nighthawk Keetoowahs. As time passed, Ned Christie became engaged in more hostile acts. He no longer had broad support from the Cherokee Nation and began loosing the loyalty of many fellow Keetoowahs.

The next assault at Ned's Fort Mountain occurred on October 11, 1892. A posse, consisting of Charley Copeland, Milo Creekmore, and others, crept toward Christie's stronghold. A hail of bullets flew from the fortress and two lawmen were wounded. The group planned another method of attack. They seized Christie's wagon which was located nearby, loaded is with brush, set it afire, then rolled it toward the fortress. The blazing wagon veered, stopped, and never reached its mark. After tossing several sticks of dynamite which did no damage, the frustrated posse retreated.

For over seven years the law had failed to capture Ned Christie. He was now high on the most wanted list, and a "successful" invasion at Ned's Fort Mountain had become a priority. Three weeks after the last failed attack, Deputy U. S. Marshal Paden Tolbert led a posse to Christie's fortification. They carried a cannon (a three-pounder) which they were certain would penetrate Christie's log walls. Prior to dawn, on November 2nd, the group took their positions and awaited daybreak. As light peeked over the canyon, one of Christie's companions, Arch Wolf, emerged from the fort. The Indian was a wanted fugitive, and Tolbert yelled at him to surrender. Wolf leaped back inside and gunfire commenced. During a lull in the shooting, a temporary cease-fire was called in order that three women and a young boy could flee to safety. Time and again the posse touched off the cannon's fuse, but the cannonballs did no

Deputy U.S. Marshal Heck Thomas shot out Ned Christie's right eye, but failed to apprehend him
Archives & Manuscripts Division of the Oklahoma Historical Society.

damage to the building's façade. The siege remained a stalemate throughout the day and into the evening. The attackers then decided to use the charred remains of Christie's wagon to construct a rolling breastwork as close to the fort as possible. They tossed sticks of dynamite at the base of the fort's wall, and made a beeline for cover. The ensuing explosion set the stronghold on fire. With the fort ablaze, Christie and Wolf had no choice except to run for cover. Arch Wolf sprinted to safety (only to be apprehended later and imprisoned). While dashing through the heavy smoke, Christie almost ran over posse member Wess Bowman. Christie got off a quick shot which only singed Bowman's face. He whirled and fired at the fleeing Indian. The slug hit Christie behind the ear and he sprawled on his face. He was dead. As somewhat of an exclamation point for the futile and frustrating years of being unable to apprehend the fugitive, young Sam Maples stepped up and emptied his six-shooter into Christie's carcass. Sam was the son of Deputy U. S. Marshal Dan Maples, whom Christie allegedly had shot down at the footbridge spanning Spring Branch in 1885—the incident that started all the trouble.

One person who was a thorn in the side of Judge Parker was a woman, Belle Starr. Belle, whose maiden name was Myra Maybelle Shirley, was able to live in Indian Territory because she was married to a Cherokee named Sam Starr, who also was in and out of trouble.

Their farm, located on the Canadian River, was always a welcome haven for outlaws, and many stayed there on different occasions. Belle Starr was intelligent, clever, well-cultured, and flamboyant. She was also a friend and fence for rustlers and bootleggers. She was destined to appear before
Judge Parker several times. Prior to 1882, each time she appeared in court, Judge Parker was compelled to free her for lack of evidence. Finally, she and Sam were caught red-handed stealing a neighbor's horses. For a change, there was evidence. Sam was sentenced to one year, and Belle was sentenced to two consecutive six-month terms at a rehabilitation center in Detroit, Michigan. They were released after serving nine months because of good behavior. Following the shooting death of Sam Starr, Belle had an affair with a fellow named Blue Duck. When Judge Parker sentenced him to be hanged for murdering a farmer, Belle hired a team of excellent attorneys, and sent them to Washington to appeal to President Grover Cleveland. It helped, as Cleveland commuted the sentence to life in prison. When Eddie Reed, Belle's son by her first marriage, was convicted for stealing horses, he was sentenced to seven years in prison by Judge Parker. Once more, Belle sent her lawyers to Washington to see the President. To the chagrin of Isaac Parker they returned with a full pardon for Eddie Reed.

Isaac Parker soon had the limits of his jurisdiction reduced by Congress. In 1889, his effort to protect the Indians ended when the territory was opened for homesteading. The size of the Indian reservations was reduced, and in 1890 the Oklahoma Territory was established. The new entity had its own government, court system, and law enforcement.

Jim Masterson, most deadly of the famed brothers. *Wild Horse Collection.*

Chapter Twenty-Seven
Battle for the Gray County Seat

Two noted gunmen, former city Marshals of Dodge City, Kansas, Jim Masterson and Bill Tilghman were involved in the famous "Battle for the Gray County Seat" at Cimarron, Kansas. Factions from the towns of Ingalls and Cimarron had been squabbling for some time for the right to be county seat. Cimarron, eighteen miles west of Dodge City, had a population of about 1,500. Ingalls, with a population of only two hundred, was situated six miles west of Cimarron. Although smaller, Ingalls was supported by multimillionaire Asa T. Soule, who had made his fortune from a concoction called "Hop Bitters." Soule wanted Ingalls to be the county seat and he freely spent much money toward this goal. He promised the residents of Montezuma and Hess a railroad from Dodge City if they would vote solidly for Ingalls as county seat. Soule also promised a sugar mill to the township of Ensign. Cimarron also attempted to "buy" votes by offering the township of Foote $10,000 which they backed with a bond. It was later determined that the bond was a forgery, and the township received nothing. The election was held on Monday, October 31, 1887, amid accusations on both sides of ballot box stuffing and other fraudulent activities. Ingalls won by majority of 236 votes. The county records were moved to Ingalls on February 21, 1888. When A.T Riley of Cimarron was appointed County Clerk pro tem, the records were retuned to Cimarron where they were housed at the temporary courthouse, located on the second floor of the building at 115 S. Main Street.

When new elections were held for the county clerk's office (Thursday, November 1888), an Ingalls man, Newt F. Watson, defeated the clerk from Cimarron. When he demanded that the county records be moved to Ingalls, the protest came to a boil. When the town of Cimarron refused to relinquish the county records, Ingalls (and Asa Soule) decided to take them by force. They organized a raiding party which included several Dodge City gunmen.

Among them was Jim Masterson who was a more active gunfighter than his brother Bat. Years later, Dodge City resident George Bolds (a former Gray County official) reflected on Jim Masterson: "I can still shut my eyes and see him walking down the street, six-shooter

Drew and Will Evans fought for the Cimarron faction during the battle for the Gray County seat. *City of Cimarron.*

under his coat, hat tilted to one side, a cigar in the corner of his mouth and his face as an impassive as an Indian's. I maintain he was the most deadly man with a gun outside Harvey Logan, the executioner for the Wild Bunch in Wyoming. If Jim Masterson had ever met Logan, or that buck-toothed Billy the Kid, my chips would have been on Jim." Bill Tilghman was also a highly respected gunman. As marshal he served Dodge City well, behind a unique badge made from two twenty-dollar gold pieces. He would later become a state senator in Oklahoma. Among the other hired guns from Dodge City were Fred Singer, Neil Brown, and Ben Daniels.

Newly elected Sheriff J. H. Reynolds (an Ingalls man) did not participate with the raiding party because he was recuperating from wounds received during a chase of rustlers. Newt Watson was accompanied by the gunmen and others, including the aforementioned George Bolds. The raiding party, all of whom were deputized, numbered ten.

The raid occurred Saturday, January 12, 1889. At approximately 11:30 a.m., the Ingalls group arrived by wagon at the temporary courthouse in Cimarron. A few of the men ascended the stairs where they found A. T. Riley at work. At gunpoint, they demanded the county records. Riley had no choice but to oblige them. Word of the raid spread quickly around Cimarron. No sooner had the county books been loaded into a wagon, when Cimarron townspeople opened fire on the group near the wagon. The Ingalls men returned their fire, as they managed to climb into the wagon. With Charlie Reicheldeffer at the reins, and the county records in their possession, they dashed out of town leaving four of their cohorts trapped on the second floor of the courthouse. Four members of the Ingalls' faction were injured as bullets flew in many directions. Bill Tilghman was nicked in one leg. George Bolds, who took two slugs, one in the head and one in a leg, was more seriously injured, as were Ed Brooks and Charlie Reicheldeffer.

In addition to the injuries to the Ingalls men, J. W. English of the Cimarron faction had been shot in the head. He was dead. Two Cimarron men incurring serious injuries were Ed Fairhurst and Jack Bliss. Another, a fellow named Harrington, received a superficial gash. Altogether there were eight casualties—one dead and seven wounded.

The four men trapped inside continued to shoot from the second floor windows. A few members of the Cimarron group worked their way into the lower story of the building and fired shots up through the floor at the remaining Ingalls men. Trapped were Jim Masterson, Fred Singer, Billy Allensworth, and Newt Watson. They climbed on top of desks, filing cabinets, and a safe to avoid being hit. The siege lasted for six hours.

After receiving a telegram from the mayor of Cimarron, Sheriff Reynolds pulled his injured body out of bed and rode into Cimarron in order to escort the men back to Ingalls and safety.

A story is told that the Cimarron forces agreed to the end of the siege following the receipt of a telegram from Bat Masterson. Supposedly, he informed them that if his brother and the others were not allowed to leave town, he would "come in with enough men to blow Cimarron off the face of Kansas." There seems to be no truth to this story.

At any rate, the county records remained at Ingalls until Cimarron won them back in the election of February 1893, after which they were returned to Cimarron for good. Today, Cimarron remains the county seat of Gray County.

Chauncey Dewey was the central figure in the Dewey-Berry feud. *Kansas State Historical Society.*

Chapter Twenty-Eight
The Dewey-Berry Feud

Cheyenne County, in the northwestern corner of Kansas, was the scene of a bloody encounter on June 3, 1903. The gunfight which occurred that afternoon was the culmination of several years of strained relationships. The vendetta would continue in the courtroom for many years thereafter. The fight, which had its roots in land and cattle, was known as the Dewey-Berry Feud.

Following the great Chicago fire of 1871, C. P. and A. P. Dewey became extremely wealthy through real estate speculations. The brothers reinvested their fortune in mortgages and consequently became richer. Northwestern Kansas land, which previously had little value, came into demand in 1885 causing real estate values to jump considerably. The Dewey brothers offered loans of from $700 to $1000 on quarter sections which they would hold as security. The land boom dissipated and the economy became rough in 1887. The Deweys foreclosed on several thousand acres of land, predominately in Cheyenne, Rawlins, Sherman, Thomas and Decatur Counties.

As the cattle business flourished during the late 1890s, C. P. Dewey became more interested in investing in Kansas. The interests of A. P. Dewey lay elsewhere, so the brothers divided their holdings and went their separate ways. During a period of financial depression between 1893 and 1897, settlers found it difficult to pay taxes on their land. C. P. Dewey cut a deal with several counties whereby they would accept a payment of approximately fifty percent for the taxes due. Dewey would pay the taxes and take tax deeds (or tax liens) on those specific properties. Basically he worked every angle he could to obtain property at the "right" price.

C. P. Dewey established a cattle ranch in the southwestern corner of Rawlins County. Its land extended into Thomas, Sherman and Cheyenne Counties. He dubbed it Oak Ranch. Its 40,000 acres were approximately half of his Kansas holdings. The ambitious Dewey wanted Oak Ranch to become the largest in the state of Kansas. Dewey, who continued to make his home in Chicago, placed his son, Chauncey, in charge of Oak Ranch. C. P. Dewey invested in other areas of Kansas, as well. He purchased a large tract of land in Riley County where he constructed a lakefront resort. Manhattan Beach, on Eureka Lake, was located near the town of Manhattan.

Chauncey Dewey was refined, well educated and had all the polish of an eastern gentleman. He was straight forward, looked a man right in the eye when he talked to him, and was well liked by his employees. The cowboys at Oak Ranch appreciated Chauncey because he "led by example." He had the culture of an Easterner, but also the horsemanship, marksmanship and ranch savvy of a Westerner. Chauncey, who was in his early 20s when he operated Oak Ranch, was ambitious like his father, but he often took less than desirable means to achieve an end.

Dewey obtained title to as much land as possible. He not only fenced his property but ran miles and miles of wire across open range virtually boxing in many small landowners. This enraged the settlers because they couldn't keep cattle without the use of grazing land. Dewey claimed that the fences were designed to keep his cattle out of settlers' crops.

Furthermore, Chauncey Dewey continued to purchase more land. When settlers refused to sell, they would often become isolated when Dewey purchased all of the land surrounding them. By 1901 the situation had become very tense. Believing that a fight was inevitable, settlers armed themselves to the teeth. So too did Dewey's riders.

The settlers were led by a family named Berry. Their resentment toward C. P. and Chauncey Dewey originated years earlier when the Deweys foreclosed on the Berry homestead which had a past-due mortgage. When the Berrys refused to move, Dewey took out a court order for their eviction, which was carried out by the sheriff. The Berrys relocated to a property which they leased in Cheyenne County, very close to the boundary of Oak Ranch.

In 1901, Daniel P. Berry was a stout, heavily-bearded man age 60. His wife, Harriett M. "Hattie" Berry would later be a thorn in the side of Chauncey Dewey. Nearby were the residences of Daniel's sons, Alpheus W., Beach D. and Burchard B. Berry. A nephew, William Roy Berry lived a short distance to the east in Rawlins County. They were a tough bunch and very determined to stand their ground against the men from Oak Ranch. The Berrys weren't without skeletons in their closets either. In 1891, Daniel, Alpheus (his eldest son) and Beach were involved in horse stealing in Colorado. Warrants were issued for the arrest of all three, with Alpheus ultimately taking the rap in order to get his father and brother off the hook. He spent several months in the Colorado state penitentiary at Cañon City.

Several altercations occurred between the Dewey and Berry factions beginning in April of 1902. One afternoon as the Berrys were sowing a section of land in barley, Chauncey Dewey and William J. McBride confronted them and advised the settlers that they were farming on Dewey property. At gunpoint Burchard Berry ordered them to leave the premises—and they did. From the courts, Chauncey Dewey obtained a restraining order to keep the Berrys off his property and away from Oak Ranch employees. Dewey had Roy Berry arrested for disturbing the peace, and he then had warrants issued against Beach and Burchard for assault. The enraged settlers decided that enough was enough. They organized a committee to confront Chauncey Dewey with their demands. On two separate occasions they sent a large contingency to Oak Ranch in an effort to do so, but both times Chauncey Dewey was out of town. On the 18th of July, 1902, nineteen armed settlers, including the Berrys, confronted Chauncey Dewey with their demands. Burchard Berry advised that if Dewey did not withdraw the warrants against the Berrys immediately that there would be retaliation. Two days later when the warrants had not been withdrawn, eleven of Dewey's thoroughbred bulls were killed, a pasture was torched, fences destroyed and several wells were trashed. On another occasion, Daniel Berry accused Dewey and his men of firing several shots through the Berry house one night. Dewey denied the allegation. Refusing to be fenced in, the Berrys would cut the wire fences and allow their cattle to roam on Dewey pastures.

Threats and counter threats were passed back and forth for several months. The situation was like a powder keg waiting for someone to light the fuse. Both factions had excellent marksmen. Not only was Chauncey a crack shot, but several of his employees were also. William J. McBride was considered the best shot at Oak Ranch. The former soldier could drop jackrabbits on the run with a rifle. Another of Dewey's marksmen was Clyde Wilson who also was a soldier and served for a while as assistant city marshal at Salina. It is said that Burchard Berry could shatter an egg thrown high into the air with either a pistol or rifle. Chauncey Dewey had sued the Berrys for unpaid rent on a quarter section of Oak Ranch land which the Berrys had been using. A judgment was issued in Dewey's favor in the amount of $35. The sheriff seized (by levy) one windmill and one water tank. Furthermore, he scheduled an auction to be held at the Berry's property on June 2, 1903, in order to dispose of these items. On the day of the sale, three Oak Ranch employees rode to the residence of Alpheus Berry to attend the proceedings. Albert Winship was accompanied by Will Day and Tom LeBow, a Dewey foreman. Burchard Berry approached the trio and ordered them to stay off Berry property. When the sheriff and auctioneer arrived, Winship was allowed to enter the premises in order to bid on the water tank which he ultimately purchased for $5. Winship was advised that he could return to pick up the tank. As he, Day and LeBow began to depart they were confronted by Burchard, Beach and Roy Berry. A heated argument ensued which included more threats. There was no fight but it was forthcoming.

Realizing that there might be trouble when they retrieved the water tank, Chauncey Dewey suggested they take a large armed force to the residence of Alpheus Berry. Ten heavily armed Oak Ranch riders headed toward the Berry place on the afternoon of June 3rd. Chauncey Dewey was accompanied by Albert Winship, William J. McBride, Clyde Wilson, Charles Wilson, Thomas O'Neill, Benjamin F. Slater, James Armentrout, Frederick Dye and Edward Tucker. Two of the men rode in a wagon while the other eight were on horseback. When they arrived at the Alpheus Berry house, McBride went to the door to ask permission to load the water tank. Daniel was dining with Viola Berry (Alpheus' wife) and her three children. Viola went to the door and gave McBride permission to load the tank. Daniel, who was reputedly unarmed, walked outside to observe. Within moments Alpheus arrived from a neighbor's house and joined his father. He was also allegedly unarmed. Dewey's men were in the process of draining the tank when Burchard, Beach and Roy Berry approached on horseback. They drew to a halt, dismounted, then tied up their horses. They turned and walked toward the tank. Gunfire suddenly erupted. Witnesses for each side later contended that the other shot first. A bullet from Chauncey Dewey's Savage rifle shattered the jaw and ear of Roy Berry. He fell to the ground. McBride fired his Winchester with deadly aim. His bullet struck Burchard Berry in the head. He was killed instantly. Daniel Berry was shot in the stomach and dropped to the ground, dead. Alpheus and Beach Berry turned to run for cover. Another bullet immediately struck Alpheus in the back of the head. He was also dead. Another bullet nicked Beach Berry in one leg as he scampered to safety. Although wounded, Roy Berry was still alive and attempted to crawl to shelter when two more bullets whistled through his felt hat. He dropped on his stomach and lay motionless feigning death. When the smoke cleared, Daniel, Alpheus and Burchard Berry were all dead. Beach Berry and his cousin Roy were wounded. A horse had also been killed by a stray bullet. After the Oak Ranch bunch departed unscathed, Roy and Beach mounted their horses and rode in separate directions. Roy headed to the home of his friend Lemuel Capron to receive assistance for his wound. Beach spurred his horse in the direction of Bird City to wire for the sheriff and coroner.

Mobs seeking vigilante justice quickly gathered at St. Francis and the Berry ranch. Beach Berry was only able to identify three of the Dewey men as having actually done the shooting—Chauncey Dewey, W. J. McBride and Clyde Wilson. Sheriff Robert McCullough and Deputy Sheriff E. B. Robertson rounded up a posse and rode to Oak Ranch on the evening of the 3rd. They received a cordial reception. Dewey agreed that he, McBride and Wilson would submit to arrest if the sheriff could guarantee them protection from the mobs. McCullough placed the trio under arrest and left them in the custody of Robertson while he rode to St. Francis to wire the Governor for additional help. Governor Bailey responded by sending the Osborne Militia (Company G, 2nd Regiment, National Guard) commanded by Captain V. E. Cunningham to assist Sheriff McCullough. A preliminary hearing was scheduled in St. Francis, a town which had no jailhouse. Word had spread that a mob planned to lynch Dewey, McBride and Wilson, and burn Oak Ranch to the ground. The presence of the Osborne Militia seemed to quell most of the harsh talk. However, eventually Sheriff McCullough and the militia (a force of 54 heavily-armed men) moved their prisoners to a temporary camp at St. Francis for the hearing which commenced on June 15th.

In a shrewd move, Dewey's attorneys filed an application for a Writ of Habeas Corpus in the Kansas Supreme Court requesting bail for their clients. A hearing was set at the state capitol in Topeka. Sheriff A. T. "Bert" Lucas left Topeka (acting as a special marshal of the state Supreme Court) en route to Cheyenne County where he would pick up the prisoners. The Osborne Militia would accompany them on their trip to Topeka. This legal action moved the accused men far from the mobs in Cheyenne County. If Dewey had sought bail in Cheyenne County, and had it granted, he might have been freed, without protection, in a dangerous and hostile environment. Bail was granted at Topeka and the accused men left for C. P. Dewey's resort at Eureka Lake to await trial. Liberty was granted under bonds of $15,000 each furnished by C. P. Dewey and two of his friends.

The much publicized trial of Chauncey Dewey, William J. McBride and Clyde Wilson for the murder of Burchard Berry opened on February 2, 1904 in the Norton County district court. After a bitterly contested trial, the jury deliberated for twenty-eight and one-half hours before returning a verdict (on March 19, 1904) of not guilty. Their decision was highly unpopular. Four days later the twelve jurors were hanged in effigy from different trees in the courthouse yard at Norton. Each of the figures, which were comprised of old clothes stuffed with hay, bore the name of a juror. An old man wandered about the streets carrying with him a hangman's noose. He claimed he was looking for a Dewey man, just any Dewey man.

C. P. Dewey's wife (who was not Chauncey's mother) sued for divorce. On June 10, 1904 C. P. Dewey died. His will was highly contested. Chauncey Dewey sold Oak Ranch, and then married the daughter of an Episcopal bishop in 1908.

The Berrys finally received some retribution from Chauncey Dewey. Following civil suits which were filed in 1905, Harriet M. Berry and William Roy Berry were awarded (in 1918) damages in the amounts of $7,140 and $1,585.35 respectfully. Dewey appealed the decrees to the Supreme Court which upheld the damages.

The Dewey-Berry feud culminated at the home of Alpheus Berry on June 3, 1903. Although the origin of these photographs is unknown, they are apparently accurate and were admitted into evidence at two trails. Daniel and Alpheus Berry were killed near the carcass of Chauncey Dewey's horse, while Roy (wounded) and Burchard (killed) were shot down beyond the sod wall. *Kansas State Historical Society.*

Colorful Black Bart, a nemesis to Wells Fargo. *Wild Horse Collection.*

Chapter Twenty-Nine
Black Bart, Poet Bandit

Wells Fargo attributes twenty-eight stagecoach robberies, or attempted robberies, to the celebrated Black Bart. How many he actually held up is speculation. He was short in stature, yet long on guts. Bart, whose real name was Charles E. Boles, hit coaches across northern California for a period exceeding eight years.

His method of operation usually followed a similar pattern. Bart would carefully select each robbery location where there was an adequate hiding place adjacent to a steep upgrade on the stage road. When the horses were struggling up the incline, and the coach was at a slow roll, he would emerge from his hiding place with a shotgun in hand. Normally, he would order the coachman to, "Throw down the box!" Bart usually wore a long linen duster and a mask fashioned from a flour sack.

Following a robbery on August 3, 1877, which occurred between Fort Ross and Duncan's Mills, Black Bart left an empty strongbox with

its waybill intact. On the waybill he scribed this poem:
> I've labored long and hard for bread,
> For honor and for riches,
> But on my corns too long you've tread,
> You fine-haired sons of b----es.
>   -Black Bart, the PO8

Naturally, there were no blanks in the poem. The hitherto unnamed outlaw now had a handle. He was a bandit who was a poet. Journalists jumped on the story with both feet. Black Bart became famous. He was glamorized, embellished, and became a feature story for many writers.

Black Bart's stagecoach robberies, or attempted robberies, according to Wells Fargo, are as follows:

July 26, 1875	4 miles from Copperopolis (bound for Milton)
December 28, 1875	10 miles from North San Juan (bound for Marysville)
June 2, 1876	5 miles from Cottonwood (bound for Yreka)
August 3, 1877	near Fort Ross (bound for Duncan's Mills)
July 25, 1878	near Berry Creek (bound for Oroville)
July 30, 1878	5 miles from LaPorte (bound for Oroville)
October 2, 1878	12 miles from Ukiah (bound for Ukiah)
October 3, 1878	10 miles from Potter Valley (bound for Ukiah)
June 21, 1879	3 miles from Forbestown (bound for Oroville)
October 25, 1879	2 miles from Bass Station (bound for Redding)
October 27, 1879	12 miles from Millville (bound for Redding)
July 22, 1880	2 miles from Henry's Station (bound for Duncan's Mills)
September 1, 1880	near Weaverville (bound for Redding)
September 16, 1880	near the Oregon state line (bound for Yreka)
November 20, 1880	near the Oregon state line (bound for Roseburg, Oregon)
August 31, 1881	9 miles from Yreka (bound for Yreka)
October 8, 1881	3 miles from Bass Station (bound for Redding)
October 11, 1881	2 miles from Round Mountain (bound for Redding)
December 15, 1881	4 miles from Dobbins (bound for Marysville)
December 27, 1881	near North San Juan (bound for Smartville)
January 26, 1882	6 miles from Cloverdale (bound for Cloverdale)
June 14, 1882	3 miles from Little Lake (bound for Ukiah)
July 13, 1882	9 miles from Strawberry Valley (bound for Oroville)
September 17, 1882	14 miles from Redding (bound for Redding)
November 24, 1882	6 miles from Cloverdale (bound for Cloverdale)
April 12, 1883	5 miles from Cloverdale (bound for Cloverdale)
June 23, 1883	4 miles from Jackson (bound for Ione)
November 3, 1883	3 miles from Copperopolis (bound for Milton)

Black Bart was a cagey bandit and a real nemesis for Jim Hume, chief of the Wells Fargo detective force. Following each robbery, a team of investigators would search the site for clues. There were never any footprints, or horse tracks, or even an indication as to where a getaway horse had been tied up. Two patterns began to emerge. When the take from one holdup was very small, a second robbery usually occurred almost immediately. Hume assumed that the bandit lived some distance away—possibly in a large city—maybe San Francisco. Also, an elderly gentleman with a big white mustache and deep gentle voice was seen in the vicinity of the robberies, sometimes before and sometimes afterwards. The description always matched. The gentleman had two front teeth missing, bright blue eyes, and was extremely polite. One lady thought he might be a preacher. Jim Hume was convinced that the old fellow was Black Bart, the phantom highwayman.

During his last robbery, November 3, 1883, near Copperopolis, Black Bart made one of his largest hauls, but left the scene amidst a hail of gunfire. He left so quickly that he would not cover his tracks as well as usual. When Ben Thorn, the astute sheriff at San Andreas, arrived at the robbery scene, he began searching for clues. Thorn surmised that if the bandit had observed the coach approaching for any distance, he must have done so from a crest on an adjacent hill. His assumption was correct. Near the hilltop, Thorn found a blanket, a belt, a case for field glasses, and two flour sacks. In one of the sacks he found a pound of sugar and a paper bag full of crackers. In the other he discovered three dirty linen cuffs and a handful of buckshot tied up in a linen handkerchief. The handkerchief was inscribed with the laundry mark, F.X.O.7.

Sheriff Thorn gave the evidence to Jim Hume. If Black Bart did live in a large city, San Francisco was the most likely spot. To assist in the investigation, Hume hired a resourceful private detective, Harry N. Morse, who had achieved renown as a relentless man hunter. He was formerly sheriff of Alameda County and a gunfighter of note. Morse was directly responsible for that part of the investigation which led to the arrest of stagecoach robber Black Bart.

There were ninety-one laundries in San Francisco in 1883. After weeks of tracing, the right laundry was found, as was the name of the customer, C. E. Bolton. It was another alias (similar to Bart's real name of Charles E. Boles) but led to the robber's arrest. Bart was transported to Calaveras County to stand trial. In a plea bargain arranged by officials of Wells Fargo, Boles (Bart) agreed to plead guilty to the November 3, 1883 robbery, and also to return the loot from that heist to Wells

Fargo. In turn, all other charges against him were dropped. He received a six-year prison term of which he served approximately five. Following his release, Black Bart retired from robbing stagecoaches.

Volney Gibson, a Jaybird, was one of the central figures in the political feud at Richmond. *Fort Bend Museum.*

Chapter Thirty
The Jaybird-Woodpecker Conflict

Richmond, Texas, was the scene of a political rivalry that ultimately turned into a blood bath. In the late 1880s the population of Fort Bend County was nearly eighty percent Black. The reins of political power were controlled by the Woodpeckers, who consisted of carpetbaggers, local Republicans (who wouldn't admit to being Republicans), and a few prominent Blacks, all of which were controlled by the Black vote. Jaybirds, on the other hand, consisted of the majority of the Caucasian population—that which one would consider to be "Southern white." Jaybirds accused Woodpeckers of much graft, which included assessing taxes based on one's political views. Much hatred grew between the two factions. The division was political, racial and social.

How the two groups got their strange names is a matter of speculation. County administrators were sometimes called Peckerwoods, which probably evolved into Woodpeckers as the term Jaybirds became popular. Presumably, the upstart Jaybirds received their title from the

Blacks because they were "uppity like a jaybird." On July 2, 1888, the Jaybirds officially launched the Young Men's Democratic Club of Fort Bend County. The club was organized "to secure a wise, impartial, economical and unselfish administration of the affairs of our county"; and furthermore to terminate the rule by "the arbitrary and selfish minority that has so long disregarded the consent of the governed." They were fighting words. The battle lines had been set.

The leader of the Jaybirds was H. H. Frost, a merchant who operated the Brahma Bull and Red Hot Bar, a general store and saloon. He was aggressive, vivacious and had guts which helped earn him the nickname "Red Hot" Frost. Though a saloonkeeper, Frost had a little religion. Carry Nation (later to gain fame as a temperance advocate), who conducted a Sunday school class, once said of him, "One poor saloonkeeper named Frost came several times and always gave a dollar." The forces behind the Woodpeckers were James Wesson Parker, a member of the State Legislature, Sheriff Jim Garvey, and Jake Blakely, a former sheriff.

Justice of the Peace, J. H. Shamblin, an active Jaybird, was shot to death at his home on the 2nd of August. The murder was committed by William Caldwell, a Black who was facing trial in Shamblin's court for cotton theft. Caldwell was tried, found guilty, and was executed by

Judge J. W. Parker was a driving force behind the Woodpeckers. *George Memorial Library.*

Ira Aten and his Texas Rangers attempted to intercede during the hostilities of August 16, 1889. Aten later became sheriff of Fort Bend County. *Fort Bend Museum.*

hanging. Although Shamblin's murderer seemingly had no political roots, Jaybirds blamed Woodpeckers for the incident.

    Several minor altercations intensified the brewing feud. On August 16, 1888, a barbecue was held in Pittsville at which several Jaybirds and Woodpeckers nearly came to blows. On the 30th of August a Black man named Jim Bearfield came into Richmond from an outlying settlement. He had been wounded in the neck and hand and his face was drawn with fear. While he was in his house, somebody shot at him through an open door. According to Bearfield, he was attacked because he knew the identity of a man who was involved in the whipping of two Blacks the previous week. Bearfield swore out a warrant against H. H. Frost. Frost retaliated by suing Bearfield for perjury. Neither case ever went to court.

    H. H. Frost locked the doors of his Red Hot Bar on the evening of September 3rd and was walking home when the still night was rattled by two shotgun blasts. Buckshot struck Frost in his right arm and

Much of the fighting occurred in front of the Fort Bend County Courthouse where several Woodpeckers had taken refuge. *Fort Bend Museum.*

destroyed his hat. Two days later a large assemblage met at the courthouse at which time it was determined that seven undesirable Blacks should be run out of town. Among those Blacks was a county commissioner, two schoolteachers and the district clerk. Following a little verbal sparring and an ultimatum, the seven reluctantly agreed to leave town.

Prior to the election of 1888 another barbecue was held. Jaybirds, Woodpeckers and those without political affiliation attended. The gathering, which was held at Duke's Station, ended in a confrontation between Volney Gibson (a Jaybird) and Kyle Terry (the Woodpecker candidate for county assessor). During his speech to the mixture of partisans, Terry referred to Ned Gibson as a "paper-collared dude." Volney Gibson, who was probably the best marksman in Fort Bend County, took offense to Terry's remark, and retorted, "Ned isn't here, but I'll represent him!" Kyle Terry accepted the challenge and leaped from the platform with his revolver already drawn. Members of the crowd grabbed him and trouble was averted—at least for the time being.

When the votes were counted, the Woodpeckers retained control of the county offices. Once again, it was the Black vote that decided the election. When invitations were mailed out for the Woodpeckers' victory celebration many were sent to Jaybirds. The Jaybirds remailed their invitations to Black prostitutes, an insult which infuriated the Woodpeckers. A few days later, Kyle Terry approached Volney Gibson regarding the invitations which had been remailed by Jaybirds. If Gibson had been armed, gunplay certainly would have occurred. The incident was followed by other encounters. Kyle Terry's distaste for the Gibsons was like a fuse waiting for fire.

On the afternoon of January 21, 1889 at Wharton, as lawyer Ned Gibson walked toward the courthouse, he was dropped in his tracks by a blast from the shotgun of Kyle Terry. Ned Gibson died immediately. Although there was no immediate retaliation, the slaying was a declaration of war to the Jaybirds.

The McFarlane house where three youths, Earle McFarlane, Dolph Peareson and Sid Peareson, manned the upstairs windows. From this vantage point Judge J. W. Parker was shot as he emerged from the courthouse. *Fort Bend Museum.*

A detachment of eight Texas Rangers, led by Sergeant Ira Aten, was dispatched to Richmond to prevent further bloodshed. Several months of relative calm passed, but the town was like a powder keg just waiting for a spark to set it off. As fate would have it, four of the Rangers had been called out of town, and another lay ill in camp when all hell broke loose on August 16, 1889.

It was early evening as Judge J. W. Parker and his nephew, W. T. Wade, rode west on a Richmond street. Volney Gibson and his brother

Guilf were riding east on the same street. As they approached each other Parker and the Gibsons drew and began shooting. Parker whirled his horse around and raced toward the courthouse. Ignoring Wade, the Gibsons gave chase. One of the slugs found its mark, hitting Parker in the back. He was able to dismount and take refuge inside the courthouse. The shots were heard by Woodpeckers, Jaybirds and others. Within moments there was a crowd in the streets. Sheriff Jim Garvey and two deputies were nearby and rushed to the aid of Parker. H. H. Frost emerged from his Brahma Bull and Red Hot Bar with a group of Jaybirds which included DeRugely Peareson, Yandell and Keane Ferris, Jeff Bryant, Charles Parnell and Will Andrus. When he heard shots, Sergeant Ira Aten and two Rangers dashed to the scene. Aten tried to intercede but was ordered away by Sheriff Garvey. Several Woodpeckers rushed to the side of Garvey who had taken up a position behind the iron fence which separated the courthouse from the street. As the Rangers looked on helplessly, bullets flew in both directions. The leaders of each faction were the primary targets. Shots dropped both Garvey and Frost. Garvey pulled himself up, fired a couple more rounds, then fell over dead. As the former sheriff, Jake Blakely, came into sight, the wounded Frost gunned him down. Blakely died instantly. Judge Parker, whose wound

Richmond, Texas, in 1892. *George Memorial Library.*

had been wrapped, emerged from the door of the courthouse. As he did, a bullet from the upstairs window of the McFarlane residence hit him in the groin. Once again, Parker struggled to safety inside the courthouse. With the leaders down, the shooting finally stopped.

As previously mentioned, Garvey and Blakely were dead. Frost would die two days later. A Black girl, Robbie Smith, had been killed by a stray bullet as the Gibsons encountered Parker (Parker and Wade were later charged in the murder). Parker would recover from his wounds. Volney Gibson, W. T. Wade, Will Andrus, Frank Schmidt and H. S. Mason also received minor injuries which would eventually mend. Following a request for the militia, Governor Ross dispatched the Houston Light Guard to Richmond as a peacekeeping force.

There were several arrests and a few lawsuits during the aftermath of the Jaybird-Woodpecker hostilities in Fort Bend County. Ira Aten became the new sheriff. Many of the Woodpeckers moved out of the area. The Jaybirds seized control of the county government, a position they would hold for many years.

The trial of Kyle Terry for the murder of Ned Gibson was set for January 21, 1890, at the courthouse in Galveston. Before ascending the steps to the criminal courtroom, Terry came face to face with Volney Gibson. Gibson drew a pistol and shot Kyle Terry in the heart. Before he could be brought to trial for killing Terry, Volney Gibson died of tuberculosis on April 9, 1891.

The community of Mason, as it looked in 1876. *Mason Historical Commission.*

Chapter Thirty-One
The Hoodoo War

Fort Mason, Texas, was officially established on July 6, 1851. It was one of many forts located on the Texas frontier to protect settlers from Indians. The site, on the bank of Comanche Creek about eight miles north of the Llano River was set just above the community of Mason which was named county seat when Mason County was established in 1858. Many German immigrants settled in the area. For the most part, they established ranches and raised cattle. They constructed solid stone buildings for permanence and protection.

Results of the 1860 census showed that Mason County had a population of 630. When votes were cast on February 23, 1861, on the issue of secession, only two votes were recorded "for" while seventy-five were cast "against." Few German settlers were slave owners, and they wanted no part of the slavery issue. When Texas seceded from the Union to join the Confederacy, the Germans in Mason County were generally despised by the non-German element as traitors. As anti-German prejudice grew, two factions emerged—the German and the Anglo. The lines between the factions were quite fuzzy. Though most Germans seemed sympathetic to the Union cause, many fought for the Confederacy. The Civil War years marked a period of many Indian atrocities in Mason County. White settlers, both German and Anglo, banded together to protect themselves from the Indians. Nevertheless, animosity between Anglos and Germans was real.

While most of the ranchers and cowboys from Mason County

were off fighting for the Confederate Army, their cattle would drift away by the thousands. Some people made a living out of rounding up strays and selling them at market. Later, when laws were passed requiring all cattle brands to be recorded, some of these same people became cattle rustlers. After the ranchers and cowboys returned from the battlefields, there became some assemblage of control over their herds. When the massive cattle drives began, they crossed the vast open range of Mason County on their way to the cow towns of Kansas. Local ranchers faced the new difficulty of preventing their cattle from joining the herds that passed through. Ranchers faced another problem during cold winters. Severe weather would often cause cattle to drift south. As they crossed the open ranges other cattle would join them. Sometimes these herds numbered in the thousands.

By 1872 Mason County ranchers had begun to string miles and miles of barbed wire fencing in an effort to control their herds. These wire fences heightened the discord which already existed between ethnic groups. Furthermore, it pitted cattleman against cattleman. In some cases, the barbed wire prevented access to water. When wire crossed the path of a herd being driven to market, cowboys would normally cut the wire rather than change direction. An increasing number of cattle rustlers in Mason County added to the amount of fence cutting, as well as the number of flared tempers.

Mason County had been divided, neighbor against neighbor, cattleman against rustler, German against Anglo, and even brother against brother. The stage was set for much violence in what was to be called the Mason County War, more popularly known as the Hoodoo War.

In late 1875, a local rancher, Tim Williamson, was arrested for rustling by Deputy Sheriff John Worley. While Worley, a lawman of German descent, was escorting Williamson to jail they encountered a large and angry mob. Williamson never had a chance to prove his innocence, nor did he ever reach the jailhouse. Without making any attempt to break up the mob, Worley stood by and watched as they shot Williamson down in cold blood. The execution raised the ire of Williamson's friends.

One such friend was Scott Cooley, who owed a lot to the Williamson family, possibly even his life. While in Kansas, at the terminus of a cattle drive, Tim Williamson met and befriended Cooley. Williamson offered Cooley employment as a hired hand in Mason County. Cooley accepted, and then accompanied the cowhands on their trip back to Texas. While working for Williamson, Cooley became seriously ill with typhoid fever. Mrs. Williamson spent many long days nursing Cooley until his health was restored. He was indebted to the Williamson family. After leaving Williamson's employment, he joined the Texas Rangers where he was a member of Captain R. C. (Rufe) Perry's Company D. Cooley had left the Rangers and was working near Menardville when he received word of Williamson's assassination. Scott Cooley packed up some supplies and rode toward Mason County heavily armed.

Cooley had several friends in the little town of Mason. He spent a few days asking questions and gathering information. Having learned what he wanted, he set out for Deputy Sheriff John Worley's place. As Cooley approached the house he spotted two men working on a windless at the well. Cooley, who did not know what Worley looked like, asked one man his name. His reply was, "Worley." It was the only identification needed. Cooley drew and shot the deputy sheriff to death. Worley's helper plunged into the well. Cooley dismounted and scalped his victim. Uncertain who the next victim might be, fear ran high through the German faction. Other friends of Tim Williamson decided to ride with Scott Cooley. He was joined by Mose and John Beard, George Gladden and John Ringgold.

Another incident occurred in Mason where mob justice prevailed. Sheriff John Clark had locked up five rustlers who had been caught while driving a herd of cattle that belonged to others. With battering rams, the mob shattered the jailhouse door, and then dragged the rustlers into the street. They marched their prisoners about a half mile down the Fredericksburg road. By the time Sheriff Clark and a few others reached the scene, the mob had scattered. Clark found a fellow named Wiggins lying on the ground dead. He had been shot through the head. Three of the rustlers were hanging from a tree limb. Two brothers named Baccus were dead. Clark cut down the third man, Turley, who was still alive. During the commotion of the lynching, the fifth rustler, Johnson, had managed to jump a fence and disappear across a plowed field.

Dan Hoerster was a prominent member of the community and a leader of the German faction. He had become a target of Scott Cooley. One day as Hoerster, Peter Jordan and a fellow named Pluenneke were riding past the Southern Hotel in Mason, a shotgun blast knocked Hoerster out of his saddle. He would die of buckshot wounds from the gun of John Beard. As Beard, Cooley and George Gladden galloped out of town, a slug from the rifle of Peter Jordan shattered Gladden's hand and the rifle he was holding.

Several days later, Sheriff Clark was inside Keller's store on the Llano River about twelve miles south of Mason. Keller and Clark spotted two men approaching the store. They were recognized as Mose Beard and George Gladden, two of Cooley's men. After Beard and Gladden dismounted, Clark and Keller opened fire from the front door. Gladden and Beard returned the fire, but with nowhere to hide they were hit by many slugs. Somehow they managed to mount one horse and ride away. Clark, Keller and another man trailed the wounded duo. Beard and Gladden were bleeding badly and had to stop. Clark and the others found them shortly. Minutes later Mose Beard died. Gladden had nine slugs in his body, and was expected to die. He was taken by wagon to his home in Loyal Valley. Gladden would eventually recover.

After regaining his strength, George Gladden shot and killed Peter Border, known as a gunman for the German faction. Gladden was captured and sentenced to 99 years imprisonment. Before long, however, he would be pardoned and released.

John Ringgold was arrested and jailed in Burnet County. Evidently, there was no evidence linking him to any of the crimes, and he was released.

Major John B. Jones was commander of the Frontier Battalion,

Formerly a member of the Texas Rangers, Scott Cooley, was a major participant in the Hoodoo War. *Mason Historical Commission.*

Texas Rangers, which was comprised of six companies that patrolled approximately four hundred miles of border. When the governor asked the Texas Rangers to intervene and shut down the trouble in Mason County, Major Jones was selected for the task. With a detachment of forty men (ten from Company D, and thirty from Company A), Jones rode to Mason. Jones launched a massive manhunt for Scott Cooley. After two weeks of searching, and no trace of Cooley, Jones realized that his men were not taking the search seriously. Most of the detachment was in sympathy with Cooley, who had ridden with Company D when he was a Texas Ranger. Reluctantly, Jones called his men together to make them an offer. He advised them that any man who was in sympathy with Scott Cooley and who did not wish to pursue him could step forward and receive an honorable discharge. About fifteen men took Jones up on his offer.

John Clark, having had his fill of violence, resigned from the office of sheriff and left Mason County. John Beard also fled the area. Some say he went to Arizona. Through the mere presence of Major Jones and the Texas Rangers, the Hoodoo War came to an end. Scott Cooley disappeared. Some say he became ill and died the following year (1876) in Blanco. Others say he lived to a ripe old age in New Mexico.

Bill Tilghman, at left, is holding a Sharps Model 1874 octagon barrel sporting rifle. Tilghman, an excellent marksman, once reportedly killed a buffalo at a measured distance of one-mile while camped with a band of Cheyennes. His hunting partner, James B. Elder, is at right. *Oklahoma Historical Society.*

Chapter Thirty-Two
Bill Tilghman, Peace Officer

One evening, during the late summer of 1871, seventeen-year-old Bill Tilghman and two companions returned to their camp after an eventful day of hunting buffalo. They discovered that their campsite, which was located alongside the Medicine Lodge River, had been pillaged by Indians. It was not an uncommon occurrence for hostile Indians from Indian Territory to venture into southwestern Kansas and cause trouble. The trio had their blankets and provisions stolen, and their dried hides had been burned. Most hunters would have packed up and moved their camp. Young Bill Tilghman, however, dared the Indians to return. He, and his cohorts, staked out their new hides to dry and then retired for the night. Before daybreak the following morning, Tilghman instructed his friends to take the horses and hunt without him. He then concealed himself near the campsite. Several hours later a lone Cheyenne rode into Tilghman's camp. After surveying the area, the Indian signaled his friends. Six more Cheyenne quickly arrived. Tilghman waited patiently until they had all dismounted and began to destroy the camp once again. He took careful aim. The first blast from his rifle killed one of the Indians instantly. The second shot dropped another in his tracks. A third Indian bit the dust as the others scrambled for their horses in an effort to escape. As the four remaining Cheyenne rode toward a nearby wooded area, Tilghman nailed another who tumbled from his horse. The other hunters were close enough to hear the shots and returned immediately to their camp. They marveled at Bill Tilghman's uncanny display of marksmanship.

William Matthew Tilghman, Jr. was born in Iowa on July 4, 1854. His family moved to Atchison, Kansas, two years later, where they established a farm. Tilghman began hunting buffalo at the tender age of sixteen. After working as an army scout for several years, Bill Tilghman established a ranch on the Arkansas River near Dodge City, Kansas. In 1877 he was appointed deputy sheriff of Ford County. Tilghman's reputation was tainted when he was arrested twice for theft in 1878. The responsibility of marriage and children soon improved his image. In 1884 Bill Tilghman was appointed city marshal of Dodge City, a position which he kept for two years. He served behind a unique badge, which had been made from a pair of twenty-dollar gold pieces and presented to him by friends.

The towns of Leoti and Coronado were vying for the seat of Wichita County. Sandwiched between these two communities was the tiny settlement of Farmer City, where Ed Prather was a saloonkeeper. Prather had been celebrating the Fourth of July (1888) festivities in Leoti with too much whiskey. He became obnoxious and started firing his gun. Bill Tilghman, who was also celebrating the holiday and his birthday, was asked to restrain Prather. He did so. Prather cursed Tilghman and returned to Farmer City. Later that evening, Tilghman entered Prather's saloon and the two exchanged heated words. Tilghman obviously went to Prather's place in order to provoke him. Prather's hand tightened around his holstered gun handle. Tilghman quickly drew his revolver and ordered Prather to remove his hand from his pistol. Prather didn't respond fast enough, and Tilghman's slug shattered the saloonkeeper's chest. Prather, who was still standing, was again told to remove his hand. Tilghman's second shot struck Prather in the head. He died instantly.

When the towns of Cimarron and Ingalls squabbled over possession of the Gray County records, Asa Soule (of Ingalls) hired several Dodge City gunmen to take them by force. Among them were two former city marshals of Dodge City, Bill Tilghman and Jim Masterson. On January 12, 1889, the raiding party, which numbered ten, arrived by wagon at the courthouse in Cimarron. As soon as the records had been loaded into the wagon, Cimarron townspeople opened fire on the group. In the midst of the battle, Tilghman and five others were able to ride the wagon out of Cimarron leaving four of their members, including Jim Masterson, trapped on the second floor of the courthouse. Four of the Ingalls men were wounded, including Bill Tilghman who received a superficial wound on one leg. J. W. English, of Cimarron, was killed during the gunfight. Three of his cohorts were also injured. Hours later, Masterson and the remaining Ingalls men were safely escorted from the courthouse. The county records remained at Ingalls until Cimarron eventually won them back in the election of 1893.

The Oklahoma District Land Rush, in 1889, attracted many people, including Bill Tilghman. After claiming a property near Guthrie, he became city marshal of Perry. In 1892 Tilghman was appointed Deputy U. S. Marshal at which time he relocated his family to Chandler, in Lincoln County.

From 1893 through 1895 Bill Doolin and his gang—sometimes known as the Oklahombres—terrorized banks and trains in Oklahoma, Kansas and Missouri. Doolin had become the center of a concentrated search, which was led by peace officers Bill Tilghman, Heck Thomas and Chris Madsen who became known as Oklahoma's "Three Guardsmen."

Bill Tilghman was a highly efficient peace officer who helped establish law and order during the early days of Oklahoma Territory. *Boot Hill Museum.*

Jennie Stevens, who was known as "Little Britches," and Cattle Annie McDougal were consorts of the Doolin gang. In 1894 Bill Tilghman and fellow lawman Steve Burke discovered the teenaged girls at a farmhouse near Pawnee, Oklahoma. While Burke restrained Cattle Annie, Tilghman chased Little Britches who fled on horseback. The spunky girl turned in her saddle and was able to fire several rifle shots at Tilghman as he pursued her. He shot her horse, spilling her to the turf. She threw dirt in his face, then scratched and bit him until he was able to subdue her.

Little Bill Raidler, one of Doolin's henchmen, was tracked by Bill Tilghman to a ranch near Elgin, Kansas, in September of 1895. When Raidler was confronted by Tilghman and two deputies, he drew his revolver. Before he could fire, a slug from Tilghman's pistol shattered his right wrist. Deputy W. C. Smith then dropped Raidler with a shotgun blast. Raidler miraculously recovered to face a prison term. Years later, Tilghman helped Raidler obtain a release and parole. Bill Raidler abandoned his outlaw ways.

In January of 1896, Tilghman tracked Bill Doolin to a health spa in Eureka Springs, Arkansas. Doolin had travelled to the health resort to seek relief for his chronic rheumatism. Bill Doolin was seated on a lounge in the bathhouse when Tilghman confronted him with his revolver drawn. Doolin had no choice but to surrender. Doolin was jailed, but managed to escape. He took refuge in New Mexico for several months, but upon returning to Oklahoma, later that year, he was shotgunned to death by a posse.

Bill Tilghman sired four children during his first marriage. His first wife died, and Tilghman eventually remarried in 1903. Three more children were born from that union. In 1910, Tilghman was elected to the state senate of Oklahoma. He resigned in 1911 to accept a position as chief of police in Oklahoma City.

After retiring from the police force, Bill Tilghman assisted the production of a movie, *The Passing of the Oklahoma Outlaws*, which was shown in theaters across the country in 1915. In August of 1924, at the age of seventy, Bill Tilghman accepted a position as city marshal of Cromwell, Oklahoma. It was a position he would hold less than three months. On November 1st, Tilghman arrested a prohibition officer named Wiley Lynn for discharging a firearm on a public street. As Lynn was being led toward the jailhouse, he unsheathed another weapon, which he fired at Tilghman. The shots were fatal. Bill Tilghman died within the hour.

In speaking of Bill Tilghman, Bat Masterson once said, "It would take a volume the size of an encyclopedia to record the many and daring exploits and adventures of this remarkable man." Bill Tilghman was probably as effective as any peace officer in the quest for law and order on the early frontiers of Kansas and Oklahoma.

North Main Street, Hays City, Kansas (now 10th Street). The building with the false front is Tommy Drum's saloon. *Ellis County Historical Society.*

Chapter Thirty-Three
Trouble in Hays City

Many towns had a cemetery known as "Boot Hill" where they buried those toughs that died a violent death at the hands of fellow ruffians, or the law. Hays, Kansas (known in the 1800s as Hays City) had one of the busiest on the frontier. Hays City blossomed in 1867 when the first mercantile store, the first hotel, the first livery stable and a few other stores were constructed. It wasn't long thereafter that bodies with their boots on began filling up space on Boot Hill. Approximately 45 men were buried in pine boxes, without ceremony, during those early years. It was an indication of just how rowdy Hays City really was.

A stone's throw from town was the military outpost, Fort Hays. In 1869, the government had accumulated more supplies than they had room to store, so they piled much of it along the newly established railroad tracks and hired two watchmen to protect the material until it could be moved. One of the watchmen was a fellow named John Hays.

One evening while Hays was guarding the supplies, three black soldiers were creating a commotion nearby. The soldiers, member of the 38th Infantry stationed at Fort Hays, were intoxicated and in bad spirits. Upon being refused admission to one of the brothels, the soldiers began to take their wrath out on others. After entering a barber shop, and damaging much of the barber's property, they returned to the street where they shot and killed the first man they saw. That man was John Hays. The following morning, the sheriff, accompanied by the barber, rode to Fort Hays and reported the incident to the military authorities. All of the troops on base were brought to attention, and the three soldiers were identified by the barber (who was also black). The sheriff took the three men into custody and returned them to Hays City, where they were locked in a cellar pending further examination. That night, the soldiers were removed from the cellar by a mob who took them to the Union Pacific railroad trestle that crossed a ravine west of town. Ropes were affixed to the soldier's necks, before they were dropped between the railroad ties. Their lifeless bodies hung beneath the trestle until the following day.

North Main Street was the scene of a bloody encounter in 1872. While attempting to break up a gunfight, Sheriff Peter Lanahan was shot in the abdomen, and disarmed by one of the participants, Charles Harris, a bartender who worked at Tommy Drum's saloon. From her brothel, Emma Bowen ran onto the street with two loaded revolvers which she gave to the wounded sheriff. Lanahan then gunned down Harris, who died instantly.

Although he was weak from his wound, Lanahan managed to enter "Old Man" Kelly's saloon where he fired several shots at another fellow who was involved in the original gunfight (the one that Lanahan attempted to break up). The shots missed and the fellow (who was also named Kelly) managed to flee the saloon.

Sheriff Lanahan had lost much blood and finally collapsed on the saloon floor he was carried to Emma Bowen's brothel where he could be comforted and assisted. Meanwhile, after fleeing the saloon, Kelly grabbed a rifle and posted himself in front of Bowen's brothel from where he proceeded to shower the house with lead wounding a bystander named May. Sheriff Lanahan held on until the following day before he died.

When the Ninth Regiment, a black cavalry unit, occupied Fort Hays in1874 there was a lot of talk about revenging the hanging deaths of the three soldiers who killed John Hays. Word filtered back into town that trouble was on its way, so the people of Hays City armed themselves in order to resist the premeditated revenge. During the melee that followed, six soldiers were killed. Their bodies were thrown into a drywell. The townspeople were victorious. There would be no further trouble with soldiers from Fort Hays.

Because of the determination of Hays City citizens that law and order should prevail, most of the disreputable characters that had remained in town to this point seemed to drift on to other locations.

Deadly killer "Deacon" Jim Miller was lynched at Ada, Oklahoma, in 1909. *Western History Collections, University of Oklahoma Library.*

Chapter Thirty-Four
Bulletproof Killer and the Pecos Grudge

James B. Miller (commonly called Jim, Deacon, or Killer Miller) was a killer for hire, whose number of victims probably equaled those of any gunfighter on the western frontier. He was an assassin who usually ambushed his prey. Miller was rarely involved in a "fair" fight.

G. A. (Bud) Frazer was a Texas Ranger and a deputy sheriff of Pecos County before his election as sheriff of Reeves County, Texas, in 1890. Miller became one of the Frazer's deputies.

An incident occurred in Reeves County which probably precipitated the bad blood between Frazer and Miller. Miller shot and killed a Mexican prisoner, then advised Frazer that he had tried to resist arrest. When the truth became known, that the prisoner had been killed because he knew that Miller had stolen a pair of mules, Bud Frazer fired him.

Miller ran against Frazer for the office of sheriff in the election of 1892, but was resoundly defeated. Shortly thereafter, Miller was appointed Pecos city marshal. The bitterness between the two grew.

Miller decided that he had had enough of Frazer and decided to assassinate him. In May 1893, Miller and two cohorts planned a scheme to stage a mock shootout at the railroad depot upon Frazer's return from a business trip. The third member of the party would shoot Frazer with a "stray" bullet from a hiding place. Somehow Frazer got wind of the plan and arrived in Pecos with two Texas Rangers.

Frazer knew that Miller would try again. But, he finally got tired of being apprehensive. On the morning of April 12, 1894, while Miller carried on a conversation in front of a Pecos hotel, Frazer approached and opened fire. His first shot hit Miller in the chest. The second struck him in his right arm as he began to draw. Miller reached around with his left hand, drew and returned the fire, but did so ineffectively as he was not left-handed. One bullet hit the ground and another struck Joe Kraus, an innocent bystander. Meanwhile, Frazer continued to fire. Three more shots hit Miller in the chest while Frazer's final shot struck him in the stomach and Miller collapsed. Thinking Miller was dead, Frazer walked off. Miller was seriously wounded, but would recover. He was wearing a steel breast plate which stopped the slugs fired at his chest.

During the election of 1894, Frazer lost his bid for re-election, and then left town. He returned to Pecos on the 26th of December to settle his affairs. In front of Zimmer's Blacksmith Shop he spied Miller and drew. The gunfight that unfolded was almost a replay of the previous one. Miller took Frazer's first slug in the right arm, once again rendering the arm useless. He drew and began to shoot with his left hand. A second bullet ripped Miller's left leg. When the third and fourth shots hit him in the chest and he continued to stand, Frazer turned and ran. Evidently nobody had told him about the steel breast plate.

The stage was set for the third and final encounter between Miller and Frazer. The event, which occurred on September 13, 1896, was no contest. Bud Frazer was seated at a poker table in a saloon at Toyah, about twenty miles southwest of Pecos. Jim Miller stepped to the saloon door, leveled his shotgun, and killed Frazer with a load of buckshot to the head.

Deacon Jim Miller killed many over the ensuing years. It came to an end in 1909, when Miller was lynched with three others in an Ada, Oklahoma livery stable for the killing of local rancher Gus Bobbitt. Miller's last request was that his hat be placed upon his head.

The TA Ranch stable building was defended by cattlemen and Texas mercenaries during the Johnson City War. *Wyoming State Museum.*

Chapter Thirty-Five
The Johnson County Invasion

    Rustlers weren't the only folks creating a nuisance for Wyoming cattle barons. The continued growth and rising expectations of small ranch owners seemingly posed an increasing threat to their control over the cattle market. Johnson County was especially a source of irritation, for there were many small ranchers in the locale.

    Hundreds of miles away, at the plush Cheyenne Club, wealthy cattlemen such as Frederick O. de Billier, his long time friend Hubert Teschemacher, Major Frank Wolcott, Fred Hesse, and William Irvine collectively contemplated an all out war against the Johnson County upstarts. The cattle barons theorized that any mere cowboy able to start a small ranch must have acquired his stock by rustling. So, they branded the Johnson County ranchers—"rustlers." Furthermore, they agreed not to hire any cowboys who owned cattle. Pressured by the big ranchers, the state legislature passed a law which ruled that unbranded stray calves found on the range were the property of the Wyoming Stock Growers Association. The association would then sell the strays to the highest bidder. The law enraged the small ranchers because it meant that they could not claim their own strays. With the proceeds, the W.S.G.A. helped finance a private police force headed by Frank M. Canton, chief cattle detective. Canton, who was formerly sheriff of Johnson County, knew its ranchers as well as its terrain.

    The outspoken Nate Champion was known to the W.S.G.A.

as "King of the Rustlers," and he was high on their "black list." On November 1, 1891, near the Powder River, Frank Canton, Joe Elliott, Tom Smith, and Fred Coates converged on a line shack where Champion and a cohort, Ross Gilbertson, were living. Champion and Gilbertson were bunked in when the gunmen kicked open the door. Nate pulled his six-shooter from his gun belt draped over a bedpost. Although grazed by a slug from one of the gunmen, Champion wounded two of the intruders. The gunmen scrambled out the door and dashed for cover. Later, Champion would again meet Canton, Smith and Elliott at the KC Ranch.

In another incident, two homesteaders along the Powder River were fatally shot from ambush. Frank Canton was the prime suspect in the slayings. Provoked by the murders, the small ranchers of Johnson County established an organization called the Northern Wyoming Farmers' and Stock Growers' Association, which defied the W.S.G.A. by announcing that they would hold a roundup and retain as their own any stray calves they found. This action served as a catalyst whereby the W.S.G.A. finalized plans for their invasion of Johnson County.

The cattle barons sent Tom C. Smith, a former Deputy U.S. Marshal from Texas, back to his home state to enlist top gunmen. He received a fee of $2,500 for recruiting G. R. Tucker, Buck Garrett, and about twenty additional hired guns. They were paid the sum of $1,000 each. The Texans gathered at Denver, and were then transported to Cheyenne aboard a special Pullman car. There they rendezvoused with a troop of detectives and dependable ranch employees headed by Frank Canton. Horses, wagons, and supplies were readied. One hundred members of the Wyoming Stock Growers Association contributed $1,000 each to finance the invasion.

On April 5, 1892, a Union Pacific train loaded with the cattlemen, Texans, horses, wagons, and supplies, rolled out of Cheyenne bound for Casper. From Casper it was a one hundred and fifty mile ride to Buffalo, which was the Johnson County seat, the planned location for the initial attack. A snowstorm and bogged down wagons slowed the trek. Later a range detective rode in with the news that a band of rustlers was staying at the KC Ranch which was located near the Hole-in-the-Wall in Johnson County. The group voted to detour to the ranch and dispose of the rustlers before heading on to Buffalo.

Nate Champion (who had run off Frank Canton and the other gunmen a few months earlier) had recently leased the KC Ranch. Canton and his men surrounded the ranch prior to daybreak on April 9, 1892. Inside the cabin were Nate Champion, Nick Ray (who was also on the W.S.G.A. black list), and two trappers, Ben Jones and Bill Walker, who were traveling through and had spent the night. At dawn, the trappers emerged from the cabin at different times. Each was quietly captured, then whisked away. When Ray stepped out into the morning air he was immediately dropped by rifle fire. Champion appeared and exchanged shots with the invaders as he dragged his badly wounded companion back into the cabin. Ray hung on for about two hours, and then expired.

Not knowing how many men were inside, Canton was hesitant to charge the cabin. Champion sporadically exchanged gunfire with the invaders, keeping them at bay. The siege lasted for several hours. At one point, Jack Flagg and his stepson passed nearby. Flagg was on horseback, while his stepson drove a supply wagon. When they were fired upon by Canton's gunmen, Flagg cut one of the wagon's team loose for his stepson, and the two raced away to safety.

Canton's men loaded Flagg's wagon with hay, set it afire, and rolled it toward the cabin. Incredibly, through the whole ordeal, Nate Champion kept a journal in which he documented the details of the attack. His last entry was, "The house is all fired. Goodbye, boys if I never see you again." He then signed the journal as Nathan D. Champion. With the journal on his body, Champion dashed from his burning cabin with his revolvers blazing. He was dropped by a volley of gunfire and died instantly. The journal was given to Chicago Herald correspondent, Sam Clover, one of two newspaper reporters who accompanied the cattle barons and their men. Champion's body was left with twenty-eight bullet wounds and an attached note which read, "Cattle thieves beware."

The invaders were careful to have had all of the telegraph wires cut leading to Buffalo. But they didn't count on the Flagg incident. From the KC Ranch, Jack Flagg and his stepson rode directly to Buffalo to warn Sheriff W. E. "Red" Angus and the citizens of Johnson County. Angus assembled a large and heavily armed posse, while riders fanned out to recruit others from throughout the county. While Sheriff Angus remained in Buffalo to help with the recruitment of reinforcements, Arapahoe Brown (who had twice been defeated in county sheriff elections) led the massive posse out to head off the invaders. Before long the posse was spotted by two of the cattle barons' outriders, who dashed back to their group with the news. During a period of confusion and indecision, Major Frank Wolcott assumed command of the cattlemen.

Realizing that the trail to Buffalo was impassible, Wolcott ordered a barbed-wire fence cut then turned his forces toward the friendly confines of the TA Ranch, located about fourteen miles from Buffalo. The ranch was nestled on an inside bend of Crazy Woman Creek. The ranch house, stable, and a couple of outbuildings were surrounded by log and barbed-wire fences, and appeared to be fairly defensible. Approximately fifty yards west of the stable, Wolcott instructed some of the men to build a small log fort from which several sharpshooters could cover the west side of the ranch. The small fortification, which was constructed on a knoll, measured about 12 by 14 feet. Breastworks were erected and trenches dug as the cattlemen worked all day, and into the night, to strengthen their defenses. As the sun rose on the morning of April the 11th, the cattlemen could see that they were surrounded. Arapahoe Brown's posse had also dug in prior to dawn, with men stationed across Crazy Woman Creek on three sides of the ranch, and across every rise to the west. They were busy constructing breastworks, as well. The Johnson County force numbered about ninety at dawn, but swelled to over three hundred as the day wore on. Shooting was mild—just enough to keep the invaders pinned down—while reinforcements continued to arrive. It also allowed them time to construct "rolling" breastworks, from the wheels of the invaders' abandoned supply wagons. Arapahoe Brown's plan was to close in on the TA buildings behind the rolling breastworks until they were close enough to lob dynamite at the buildings.

With the telegraph wires repaired on April the 12th (the second day of the siege), the Buffalo telegrapher was able to send a wire to Governor Amos Barber advising him of the invasion and requesting troops to assist in the capture of the cattle barons. Barber had known all along of the invasion plans and favored the big ranchers who helped support his campaign. He chose to do nothing until he received some word from the cattlemen. Later in the day, when he fully understood the gravity of the situation, Barber wired President Benjamin Harrison asking for assistance from the U.S. Army.

Meanwhile, the ladies of Buffalo prepared and sent wagon loads of food to the Johnson County troops, while the invaders at the TA Ranch ate potatoes. As their hopes dimmed, tensions rose, and many of the cattlemen began feuding with one another.

At daybreak, on April the 13th, the Johnson County forces put their plan into action. The rolling breastworks began to creep down the hill toward the TA buildings.

The timing couldn't have been more amazing. Within minutes of all-out war, three troops of U.S. Cavalry appeared over the rise. Colonel J. J. Vanhorn, detachment commander, announced to Sheriff Angus that they were under Presidential order to take charge of the men inside the ranch buildings and to safely escort them to jail. Major Wolcott was called out to meet with Vanhorn and Sheriff Angus. Wolcott agreed to surrender to the cavalry. The cattle barons and their men were placed under military arrest, and then led away to Fort McKinney, while hundreds of Johnson County citizens watched.

Following their defeat by Johnson County citizens, the Wyoming cattle barons and hired Texas gunfighters are shown in custody at Fort Russell. Frank Canton is seated at the extreme right, second row. Major Wolcott is standing just behind Canton's left shoulder. The photograph was taken on May 4, 1892. *Wyoming State Museum.*

The prisoners, who were charged with the murders of Nate Champion and Nick Ray, were moved to Fort Russell, at Cheyenne, where they remained for ten weeks. Insisting that the prisoners would not receive a fair trial in Buffalo, a judge ruled that the venue be changed to Cheyenne. No longer a Federal matter, the prisoners were moved once more—this time to an auditorium in Cheyenne. The same judge stipulated that Johnson County shall pay for their confinement—at a cost of $100 per day, per man. Shortly thereafter, the Johnson County Treasury went broke and the judge ordered the prisoners released without bond. Later, with prosecution hopeless, Johnson County authorities dropped the criminal charges against the invaders.

Afterwards, Major Frank Wolcott reflected on the siege at the TA Ranch. He said, "We only figured on fighting rustlers, and we were willing to take all chances of a war with them. Their ability to enlist aid amazed and stunned me. The whole country turned out to whip us, and they almost did it."

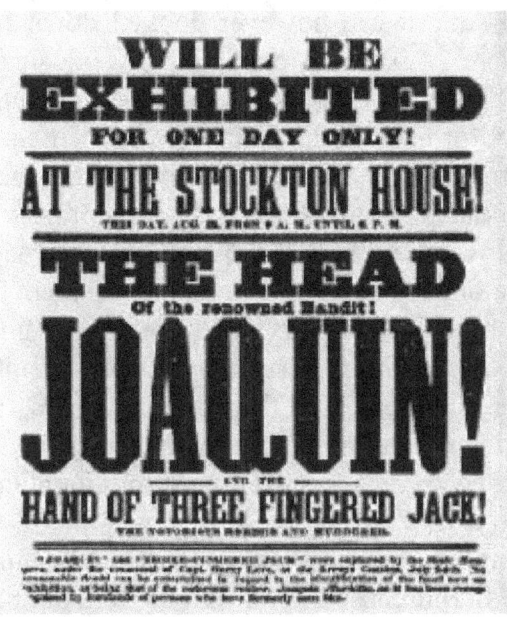

For $1.00 a curious spectator could view the head that was supposedly that of Joaquin Murreta and the hand of "Three-fingered" Jack Garcia. *Denver Public Library, Western History Department.*

Chapter Thirty-Six
Joaquin Murrieta: Bandido

Most of the facts surrounding the life of legendary Joaquin Murrieta are shrouded in mystery. For more than a century and a half, journalists and historians have attempted to separate fact from fiction when telling the story of California's first most wanted bandido. Because of his bold escapades and flare for the daring, Joaquin Murrieta has been much romanticized. To find authenticity in his story is a challenge.

Joaquin's date of birth has been stated as August 16, 1828 (which, if not accurate, is close). San Rafael de Alamito de Murrieta in the town of Trincheras, Mexico was most likely his birthplace. Joaquin Murrieta-Orozco was born the son of don Juan Murrieta and senorita Juana Orozco. He was one of ten children.

Sometime after Christmas of 1849 Joaquin left Mexico for the gold fields of California. Among many relatives and friends who accompanied him were his new bride Carmen Feliz, his brother Jesus, and possibly his close friend Joaquin Valenzuela. Following its war with Mexico, the United States promised to protect the human rights and property of Mexican citizens by negotiating the Treaty of Guadalupe Hidalgo in 1848. Anglo-Americans, however, looked down on all Hispanics, whether they were Mexican-American or Mexican immigrants, and treated them as "inferior." As more and more Mexicanos and Latinos flocked to the California gold fields, trouble intensified.

For the most part, Mexican miners staked their claims in the counties south of Sacramento. As a result, most of the violence occurred in this area. In November of 1849 an Anglo group of vigilantes attacked Mexican miners along the Calaveras River driving them from their claims. Near Stockton, Anglos passed laws which forbid foreigners from mining, and then confiscated their property which was sold at public auction. The California legislature passed the Foreign Miners Tax Law (in April of 1850) stipulating that all non-United States citizens shall pay a tax of $20 per month for the right to own a gold mining claim. This amount was later reduced to $3 per month.

At Murphy's Camp, in May of 1850, Jesus Murrieta (Joaquin's brother) supposedly purchased a mule from two Anglos. They accused him of stealing the mule, and he was lynched for his alleged misdeed. Within days of the hanging, Joaquin Murrieta was attacked by Vigilantes while working his gold claim. While unconscious (and assumed to be dead), the Anglos raped and murdered Carmen Feliz, Joaquin's wife. The events of May 1850 were the catalyst for the establishment of Murrieta's gang and its ensuing war of revenge against the Anglo-Americans in California.

Murrieta's gang was established in a military fashion, with four squadrons, each headed by a lieutenant. Joaquin Valenzuela, a veteran of the U.S.-Mexican War, was one of Murrieta's lieutenants. There were at least 62 members of the gang at one time or another, and possibly many more. An oddity is that there may have been six or more gang members named Joaquin. In addition to Murrieta and Valenzuela, the first reward posted by California Governor John Bigler was for the capture Joaquin Carillo in the amount of $1,000. Early newspaper reports attributed murders and robberies to a gang led by "Joaquin." Although he was ultimately responsible, Murietta probably did not commit nearly as many deeds as were attributed to him.

Joaquin Murrieta took out his wrath not only on Anglo-Americans but also on the multitude of Chinese miners that had settled in California. Either the Mexicans didn't like the Chinese or they considered them easy prey. Evidently the reign of terror began on January 20, 1853, when Chinese miners were robbed of their gold dust by Mexicans at two different locations. One of the Chinese miners received a knife wound. The following day, three Anglos and one Chinese miner were killed. On the 22nd of January a small posse of Anglos chased a Mexican suspected of stealing a horse near San Andreas. The Mexican led the posse into a larger group of Mexicans who in turn drove the Anglos off. An ethnic war had erupted. All of the misdeeds were blamed on "Joaquin" and his gang. Suddenly all Mexicans became suspects. Two were hanged and one was shot as all Mexicans were driven from their homes in the San Andreas area. Following more murders in early February, large posses set out to track Mexican gang members. Murrieta's men seemed to elude their trackers at every turn. Twice when cornered, gang members escaped by shooting their way to freedom. Each time Anglos and Chinese were killed or wounded. It has been estimated that by the end of February 1853, Murrieta's men had killed thirteen people and had stolen much gold dust and other valuables. Additionally, they had stolen more than 100 horses, which were probably driven to Sonora, Mexico.

In March, Murrieta was spotted in Quartzberg, near the Mexican mining camp of Hornitos, where he was believed to have taken refuge. Once again a gun battle ensued. As usual, Murrieta and his men escaped unscathed, leaving dead Anglos behind.

The California Rangers were led by a rather ruthless war veteran, Captain Harry Love. Love did not like transporting prisoners, so they usually were shot while trying to "escape." Captain Love and his rangers were saddled with the task of bringing in Joaquin Murrieta, dead or alive.

Newspapers reported various sightings of Murrieta. Often his name was spelled with just one "r." Love and the rangers followed their tips. One led to Arroyo Cantua, in the California coastal range, and then on to Murrieta's hideout, which was supposedly in a nearby canyon. Upon entering the canyon, Love and his men found a large group of men branding about 300 horses. As they were greatly outnumbered, Captain Love prudently advised the group that he was there to register names in order to collect a tax at a later date. The men obliged, and Love collected 83 names, probably all false. Love and the rangers departed intending to regroup and surprise the Mexicans. Murrieta's gang hastily rounded up most of the horses and headed toward Mexico. Captain Love and his men followed their trail south to a point where the gang evidently split up. Some of the riders continued south with the horses, while two groups headed back north. Love doubled back to follow one of the north bound trails.

On July 25, 1853, Captain Harry Love and the California Rangers tracked the group back to Arroyo Cantua. William Byrnes, the only ranger to have previously seen Joaquin Murrieta in person identified one of the Mexicanos as being Murrieta. Gunfire ensued as the Mexicans scattered. When the shooting ceased, four Mexicans lay dead. One was the man that Byrnes identified as being Murrieta. Another was the infamous "Tres Dedos" (known to Anglos as "Three-Fingered" Jack Garcia) who's real name was Manuel Garcia. Captain Love took two prisoners, both of whom would soon die. Love and his men returned to Sacramento with the head of the man identified as Murrieta and the hand of "Three-Fingered" Jack (the hand actually had three fingers and a thumb) which they provided to authorities as proof of their success.

The following month, a Mexican in Los Angeles told a newspaper reporter that Americans had attacked him and his companions at Arroyo Cantua, and that four of his compadres had been killed including Joaquin Valenzuela. A San Francisco newspaper also reported that Valenzuela, not Murrieta, had been killed. There is speculation that Murrieta was with the second group of gang members that doubled back prior to the Arroyo Cantua shootout. Furthermore, that he returned to pick up his lover, Rosa, and then proceeded to the coast where they boarded a ship for Mexico.

Captain Harry Love went on tour charging curiosity seekers $1 per person to view the head and hand, in jars, pickled in brandy. Later, other witnesses reported that Joaquin Murrieta was alive and well, living in Sonora, Mexico.

A 12-mule team in Aurora. *Wild Horse Collection.*

Chapter Thirty-Seven
Aurora: A Tough Mining Town

    Following the discovery of silver, high in the mountains of the trans-Sierra country in August of 1860, a wild but short-lived mining town blossomed. Aurora, at an elevation of 7,500 feet, was platted in early 1861. The settlement was in California until 1864 at which time it became part of Nevada. Most of the original buildings were constructed with adobe walls, covered with canvas roofs, because wood was scarce and expensive. By April, there was stagecoach service to and from Carson City. Aurora boomed throughout 1862 and 1863. By late 1864, however, the city that boasted some 5,000 residents began to decline rapidly. Prior to its waning days, Aurora was a boomtown that had many stories to tell.

    Two of the mining properties on Last Chance Hill, the Real Del Monte and the Pond were in the midst of a legal battle over claim rights. Both properties spent much money on hired guns to protect their holdings and to intimidate their opposition. John Daly, John "Three-Fingered Jack" McDowell, and some of their friends were hired by the Pond. While Daly lived in a small house with some of the friends, McDowell stayed with Nellie Sears, a prostitute. When one of Nellie's kinfolks was gunned down for allegedly stealing a horse, McDowell and Daly vowed to settle the score.

    One day while afoot on the snow-packed Esmeralda Road heading to Aurora, James Sears spied a saddled but unoccupied horse standing in front of William Johnson's way station. Obviously, because he was cold and tired from walking, Sears mounted the horse and raced away. Seeing what just happened, the owner of the horse, Louis Wedertz, asked William Johnson for help. John Rogers, one of Johnson's hired hands, saddled a horse and left in pursuit of the thief. After riding for an hour Rogers caught up with Sears. Rogers proceeded to take aim, and shot Sears out of the saddle. Sears was dead. Rogers returned to the way station with the horse thief's body draped over Wedertz' horse. James Sears was not only kin to Nellie, McDowell's woman, but also a friend of John Daly. It wasn't long before Daly paid a visit to Johnson's way station in search of Rogers. William Johnson refused to give Daly any information as to Rogers' whereabouts. Daly fumed, and then departed, evidently carrying a new grudge back to Aurora, this time against William Johnson.

John Daly and his friends used bullying tactics and intimidation to assist the Pond. When Dr. E. F. Mitchell, President of the Real Del Monte, and the company attorney William Van Voorhees, learned of a plot targeting them for death, they beefed up their security and bodyguards.

John Daly was known to have killed several men. On October 24, 1863, Daly was drinking at P. J. McMahan's Del Monte Exchange with fellow Pond hired gun, George Lloyd. Two years earlier, Daly and Lloyd were involved in a bloody fist-fight with each other, when they both lived in Sacramento. Since being in Aurora, however, they would hang out together, as did most of the Pond gunmen. That night at McMahan's they must have rekindled an old grudge. Following heated words, both men drew their revolvers. Lead flew in both directions, before George Lloyd staggered and collapsed on the floor. He was dead.

In early December, John Daly gunned down a fellow killer named Joe McGee. Daly was avenging the deaths of two of his friends who had been killed by McGee.

On February 1, 1864, William Johnson drove his wagon from his way station into Aurora, to sell several bushels of potatoes. Having arranged lodged for the night, Johnson decided to spend some of the proceeds from his home-grown potatoes drinking and gambling the evening away. When one saloon closed at 2:00 a.m. on Tuesday morning, Johnson walked over to another saloon called Porters. John Daly and some of his friends were at Porters when Johnson entered the establishment. Daly was still boiling about the incident that occurred when Johnson's employee, John Rogers, killed James Sears. Seeing the state of intoxication that Johnson was in, Daly and his friends decided to add fuel to the fire, and bought Johnson many more drinks. At 4:30 a.m., Johnson staggered out of Porters and headed up Antelope Street. Four men suddenly emerged from the shadows, and attacked Johnson. William Buckley unholstered his pistol, and knocked Johnson to the ground with a blow to his head. John Daly then shot their helpless victim through the head, killing him instantly. James "Massey" Masterson and "Three Fingered Jack" McDowell looked on, but did not participate in the slaying.

When Aurorans awoke Tuesday morning to the news of the murder, most were incensed. Things had gone too far. This time an innocent man had been killed. That same afternoon, 400 town members met at the armory where they formed a vigilance committee, which they named the "Citizens' Safety Committee." John A. Palmer was elected as the group's leader.

In the past, citizens had been afraid to testify against John Daly and his friends. Suddenly, the vigilance committee gave them the courage to reveal what they knew. Several testimonies were given that incriminated Daly and his friends.

Warrants were issued for the arrest of John Daly and his cohorts. Daly, Masterson and McDowell were arrested in Aurora along with some other "friends" who had nothing to do with Johnson's murder. William Buckley fled the area. It took two posses four days to finally capture Buckley at a place called Rush Creek near Mono Lake. Buckley was returned to Aurora and jailed with the others.

The verdict of the coroner's jury that Daly, Buckley, McDowell and Masterson had murdered William Johnson was good enough for the Citizens Safety Committee. The vigilantes, who now had possession of the jail, believed that if the prisoners were allowed to go on trial, they might be freed through some loophole. So, a gallows was hastily constructed in front of the Armory and the hanging scheduled for Tuesday, February 9, 1864, at 12 noon.

A huge crowd gathered on Tuesday for the proceedings. Guards, with fixed bayonets, formed a wall around the platform. While on the scaffold, Daly and Buckley admitted to killing Johnson, further indicating that McDowell and Masterson were innocent. The pleas of innocence went unheeded.

With the prisoners' hands tied and bandages over their eyes, the nooses were affixed around their necks. They listened to a pastor's short prayer, before the trapdoor slammed open, and the four bodies dropped to their deaths.

Many other deadly incidents occurred in Aurora. During the short life of the rowdy town, no less than sixteen individuals died from gunshot or knife wounds, with another death resulting from a severe beating. Additionally, there were many confrontations where participants were wounded.

With the Real Del Monte and Pond dispute having been settled (out of court) and because of the effectiveness of the vigilantes, most of the other toughs took heed and left the Aurora area.

Isolated by a rugged mountainous terrain, and located hundreds of miles from any major city, Aurora existed only because of the wealth of silver and gold mined from its surrounding hills. There were very few women and many of them were prostitutes. With a population that was almost entirely male, liquor flowed, and gambling was the primary means of entertainment. Aurora was an extremely wild mining camp. As the riches dwindled, so did the town.

Chapter Thirty-Eight
Bodie: Reddy or Knot

Patrick Reddy was Bodie's most brilliant attorney. When one person killed another, he normally faced a couple of options. He could have his neck snapped by the knot of a hangman's noose, or he could hire Patrick Reddy to enter a plea of self-defense, which usually allowed the shooter to walk out of the courtroom a free man.

The Bodie (originally spelled Bodey) Mining District, in California, was established in 1860. Bodie mines yielded over 3 million dollars in 1880 and again in 1881, during its most productive period. By 1883, however, most of the mines had closed. Activity in the town of Bodie followed the same pattern. During its brief life, there were approximately 70 shootings which helped create a reputation as that of a "gunfighter's town." Many men died, and many more were wounded, especially during the late 70s and early 80s when Bodie was at the peak of its boom. Patrick Reddy, the slick and silver-tongued attorney, was involved in many murder cases. To be defended by Reddy, was to be defended by the best. The brilliant negotiator had a knack for swaying a trial jury.

Quick-tempered William Baker and Booker Mine employee,

James Kennedy, didn't like each other. In fact, they have been involved in a heated argument earlier in the day on July 4, 1880. That evening, while Bodie citizens lined the streets to celebrate Independence Day, the Kennedy-Baker dispute reached a climax. James Kennedy was watching the celebration from a vantage point in front of Patrick Fahey's Mono Brewery, when he noticed that William Baker was approaching from the saloon next door. As Baker walked past, Kennedy provokingly reached out and tipped Baker's hat. That was all the excuse Baker needed as he unholstered his six-shooter and shot Kennedy point blank. After a doctor removed the lead from Kennedy's stomach, the Booker Mine employee lived for two days before he died as a result of infection from the wound.

Meanwhile, William Baker was arrested and sat in the Bodie jail. When irate citizens threatened vigilante action, Baker was moved to the county jail at Bridgeport. The murder trial opened on the 24th of August with Patrick Reddy defending William Baker. Reddy stipulated that Baker had acted in self–defense because Kennedy reached for his gun first. Although witnesses for the prosecution testified otherwise, Reddy was able to create a reasonable doubt in the minds of jurors. By day four of the trial, the Jury returned from deliberation with a verdict of not guilty.

Hard-headed George Daly was superintendent of two mines located due east of the town of Bodie. Daly ran the Jupiter and Mono for a group of San Francisco investors. One day in August of 1879, Daly's foreman Joe McDonald discovered several men sinking a shaft inside the south boundary of their Jupiter claim. When Daly confronted the men, they indicated that they were digging on the Owyhee claim and not on Jupiter property. The dispute quickly escalated. Daly immediately had his property resurveyed. The surveyor confirmed that Daly was correct and that the Owyhee group was trespassing. When George Daly confronted John Goff, an owner of the Owyhee, Goff reportedly told Daly to "go to hell." A week later, when the Owyhee men were away from their shaft, Daly had his workers fill the shaft with dirt. He also had a small cabin moved to the site which he staffed with armed guards. Upon hearing what had happened, John Goff moved his heavily armed men into a nearby cabin. Sporadic rifle fire was exchanged between the two cabins for a couple of hours before nightfall.

Prior to daybreak, the Jupiter men sneaked out under cover of darkness and attacked the Owyhee cabin, catching their men by surprise.

John Goff was shot in the head, and would soon die. Tom Hamilton suffered a neck wound.

George Daly didn't have too many friends in Bodie, somewhat because of his defiant activity during a recent labor strike. Furthermore, the Owyhee owners were Bodie citizens, and John Goff had been a popular individual in the community. It was easy to see where the sentiment of the people lay. In a vigilante type of action, several hundred miners declared that George Daly would be hanged if he set foot in the town of Bodie. Anticipating trouble, Daly had already gone to Virginia City. Meanwhile, Daly and his armed guards were officially charged with murder.

Patrick Reddy and R.H. Lindsay represented George Daly and his Jupiter men in the courtroom at Bridgeport. Following three days of testimony, George Daly and his men were found to be "not guilty." Following his acquittal, Daly returned to Bodie, much to the outrage of its citizens. Once again, miners and citizens held a meeting in which they reaffirmed their resolution of banishment previously adopted. Unwilling to back down, George Daly and the Jupiter men erected a barricade around their mine and prepared to fight. The stage was set for an all-out war.

The mood in Bodie was that of a vigilance committee although none had been formally established. In an effort to defuse tensions, Patrick Reddy suggested that a committee be established to mediate the quarrel in an attempt to save lives. After hours of negotiation, a breakthrough finally occurred. The citizens group agreed to allow George Daly to return to Bodie once each month to take care of business if he and his Jupiter men would relocate outside of the Bodie Mining District. At the insistence of Patrick Reddy and other Daly friends, the Jupiter men finally conceded. George Daly and the six other men, who were directly responsible for the death of John Goff, packed up and moved from the mining district without any further trouble. Before long, they all moved on to Colorado, where Daly ran a couple of successful mining properties. In 1881, George Daly and several others were killed in New Mexico during a battle with hostile Apaches.

In June of 1880, Peter Savage entered the store of Frenchy Mace, to find his wife arguing vehemently with the store owner. Not waiting for an explanation from Mace, Savage drew his revolver and began shooting. One slug struck Mace in the back and another caused a superficial wound on his chest. Peter Savage was arrested by authorities, and jailed. A lengthy trial commenced one week later. Savage had retained the services of defense attorney Patrick Reddy, and Reddy proceeded to perform his usual magic. The trial ended with Peter Savage exonerated from all blame in the shooting of Frenchy Mace.

With the 4th of July holiday coming up the following day, the night of the 3rd found the Bodie saloons to be very, very busy. Drinking and early celebrating continued into the morning. Encouraged by the consumption of alcohol, a shooting occurred in the Parole Saloon at about 2 a.m. Sam Howarth and James Leonard were in the mist of a heated argument when bartender Tom Woodruff stepped between the men in order to break up the dispute. Howarth drew his revolver and fired a shot at Leonard over Woodruff's shoulder. The slug entered Leonard's head beneath his left eye. The initial diagnosis was that it was certain to be fatal.

The authorities arrested Sam Howarth and locked him up. He was bound over to superior court and his bail set at $1,500. Patrick Reddy posted the bail and agreed to defend Howarth.

Meanwhile, doctors located the slug in the back of Leonard's head, and were able to successfully extract it through the patients left ear. Although he lost his hearing in that ear, James Leonard miraculously recovered.

When the case finally came to trail in December of 1882, Patrick Reddy contended that Howarth acted in self-defense. One witness testified that prior to the shooting Leonard's right hand was on his pocket. That was all Patrick Reddy needed to coax the jury into a verdict of "not guilty."

When a shooter was in trouble, it was wise to hire the expertise of attorney Patrick Reddy, rather than face the possibility of having his neck snapped by the knot on a hangman's noose.

Creed Taylor, shown above, and his sons Hays and Phillip (nicknamed Doboy) were prominent figures during the early years of the Sutton-Taylor Feud. *The Center for American History, University of Texas at Austin.*

Chapter Thirty-Nine
The Sutton-Taylor Feud

Following the surrender by General Robert E. Lee at Appomatox in 1865, thousands of dejected Confederate soldiers turned toward home. The beaten and downtrodden warriors hadn't received a paycheck in ages, their clothes were torn and ragged and their feelings ran high with animosity. Their ill will was not only targeted at the Yankees who defeated them, but often at fellow Southerners who remained at home making money in cattle, cotton and slaves while they impoverished themselves in the army of the Confederacy. When the South failed to fit the mold expected by Congress, they passed the Reconstruction Acts which heightened the agony that already existed in the South. Animosity continued to run high as Federal troops supported carpetbaggers, scalawags and former slaves who were thrown into various governmental positions. In Texas, there was very little social order even after the arrival of the occupation forces. Many former Rebel soldiers set out to re-establish what they felt was rightfully theirs, and some did so with minimal regard for the law and governmental authority.

Prior to the days of barbed wire, Texas cattle roamed free on unfenced open range. Cattle often drifted far from their home range, especially during that time when most of the cowboys were away fighting the war between the states. When a maverick (an unbranded calf) had been weaned, it was fair game for the cowboy who "found" it and applied his brand. The stealing of cattle became big business. Sometimes when cattle were found with brands that were unfamiliar in the area, the finder might register the brand locally and claim ownership of the cattle. Another practice was to register the brand in a different locale, then drive the herd to market at that location. Many rustlers altered brands to make them look completely different. Counterbranding was another means of identification used by the cattle thief. He would cancel the original brand by burning an "x" or diagonal bar through it, and would then apply his own brand as if he had legally purchased the animal. Many former soldiers found rustling to be an easy means to obtain wealth.

Rustlers ran rampant while federal, state and county law enforcement officials did little to stop them. Either they were incapable of doing so or it was a matter out of their "domain." Ranchers decided to take matters into their own hands. Committees of vigilance, called Regulators, appeared in several counties. These forces were often large, heavily armed and occasionally even had the blessing of the governor. Rustlers were not the only target of the Regulators. Their "duties" often included dispensing of known outlaws and others who had been branded as "undesirables." At the top of their "most wanted" list, in the area southeast of San Antonio, were the sons of Creed Taylor, Hays and Phillip. Phillip was known by his nickname "Doboy." The boys were tough, cool-headed and excellent marksmen.

The Taylor boys were continuously in trouble. One incident occurred in an Indianola saloon while Hays Taylor was standing at the bar. A group of black soldiers entered and stepped up to the bar. When Hays advised them that he was not in the habit of drinking with blacks, shooting broke out. Hays shot two of the soldiers then quickly fled the scene. Shortly thereafter, a few miles outside of Indianola, Hays Taylor encountered another squad of black soldiers. They were convinced that he was fleeing from something and wanted him to return to Indianola with them. Taylor refused. A sergeant fired a shot which wounded Hays in one arm. Hays quickly responded by shooting the sergeant who toppled dead from his mule. As the other soldiers scattered, Taylor fled. On another occasion, in November of 1867, Hays

Taylor was reading a newspaper while sitting propped against a hitching post, just outside a Mason saloon. Doboy Taylor and several friends were inside partying. As a group of Fort Mason soldiers approached the saloon, one of the privates badgered Hays. The private popped up the brim of Hays' hat and asked him what a damned reb could find of interest in a newspaper. Hays straightened his hat and continued to read. Spurred on by Hays' passive attitude, the private grabbed the hat again and yanked it down over Taylor's eyes. Hays drew and fired as he leaped to his feet. His slug dropped the private where he stood. He was dead. As this happened, one of the Taylor bunch, possibly Ran Spencer, was emerging from the saloon. He also fired, killing a Union sergeant. Major Thompson, the commandant at Fort Mason, arrived at that moment with his pistol in hand. He ordered the boys to surrender. With his usual quickness, Hays Taylor shot Major Thompson between the eyes. One version of this story indicates that the sergeant was actually killed after the slaying of Major Thompson. Regardless, the Taylor bunch rode out of Mason leaving three dead Union soldiers behind.

Buck Taylor (whose given name was William Riley Taylor, Jr.) was a first cousin of Hays and Doboy. His father, William, was one of Creed's brothers. Buck was attending a dance one evening at the home of Joe Tumlinson, his uncle. A squad of Union soldiers approached the house unnoticed. As they stepped through the doorway, a black sergeant pointed his finger at Buck Taylor. Buck drew his revolver and fired, killing the sergeant instantly. Amid the confusion which followed, Buck Taylor escaped to safety through a back door. He was another hunted man who rode with Hays, Doboy and the others.

A substantial reward was offered for the capture of the Taylors. Two fellows named Littleton and Stannard set out to find the Taylors and claim the reward. Littleton had exclaimed, "I will do it or die." Shortly thereafter, Littleton and Stannard were found dead on a road east of San Antonio.

The leaders of two groups of Regulators were summoned to Austin in early June of 1869 to meet with the governor. Jack Helm was a rather unscrupulous individual who led a group of Regulators which had been organized by his boss, A. H. "Shanghai" Pierce, a cattle baron who operated in the area southwest of Victoria. The other leader summoned by the governor was Captain C. S. Bell, a former Union spy and army scout. Helm, Bell and their Regulators, backed by state and Union officials, unleashed a reign of terror across DeWitt County and points south. In Galveston, the *News* reported on September 23, 1869, that "...during the months of July and August they killed 21 persons and turned 10 others over to the civil authorities."

The Choates (who lived in San Patricio County) were friends of the Taylor clan, and were suspected by Jack Helm of harboring some of the Taylor gang. On August 3, 1869, the Regulators attacked the Choate homestead killing John Choate and Crockett Choate and wounding two others. One of the wounded men, F. O. Skidmore, survived after receiving seventeen wounds, possibly the result of a shotgun blast.

After creating plenty of havoc in San Patricio County, Jack Helm met C. S. Bell near Yorktown in DeWitt County where the two planned their attack on the Creed Taylor ranch which was located on the Ecleto in Karnes County. Helm and Bell were aware that Hays and Doboy Taylor were in the vicinity but that the fugitives had been camping away from the ranch each night in order to avoid capture. The Regulators put their plan into action. C. S. Bell and his men rode directly to the Taylor place while Helm and the others remained in Yorktown as a diversion. Helm's bunch would follow, in order to arrive at Creed Taylor's house sometime after dawn. It was late Saturday night when Bell surprised Creed Taylor and the women. After placing Creed and the women under guard inside their home, the Regulators hid their horses and then waited in anticipation that Hays and Doboy would arrive in the morning. They were correct in their assumption. At daybreak on the 23rd of August, Doboy and Henry Westfall approached the house on horseback. Hays and their other companions were a short distance behind them. When she heard the horses, Doboy's wife let out a bloodcurdling scream in order to warn them. Doboy and Henry spurred their mounts and raced away amid a hail of gunfire. Hays spotted Creed who had emerged from the house. Believing that his father was in danger, Hays charged the whole posse of Regulators with his gun blazing. One of his slugs hit a posse member in the head wounding him seriously before a barrage of lead took Hay's life. As Jack Helm and the other Regulators rode toward the Taylor place that Sunday morning, they received word that C. S. Bell and his group had departed in pursuit of Doboy Taylor. Doboy and his comrades were able to elude C. S. Bell.

Two weeks later, Doboy and his friends were surprised by another posse at Pennington, Texas. After one of their men was shot to death, Doboy and a fellow named Cook surrendered to the posse. Along the trail to Crockett, Taylor and Cook made a break for freedom, and successfully escaped under the cover of darkness.

Meanwhile, Creed Taylor had been taken into custody by a couple of C. S. Bell's men. Creed was escorted to Helena where he was jailed. After spending approximately one month behind bars, Taylor was released under a bond of $10,000.

The activities of Helm and Bell created such a furor in southern Texas that Jack Helm felt compelled to publicly justify his actions. He did so in a report which was published on September 23, 1869, in the *Victoria Advocate*:

> "TO THE PEOPLE OF TEXAS: As there has been so much said by the people of the State regarding my operations, and as many know not of what they speak—attributing to me motives that are false—I take this occasion of enlightening the law-abiding citizens as to what I have done, and why I did it. About the first of June I was duly summoned by the military authorities, through Captain C.S. Bell, special officer, to assist in arresting desperadoes in Texas known as the 'Taylor party.' We found this party near the rancho of Mr. Creed Taylor and attempted to arrest them. We succeeded in wounding one, Spencer by name, the other effecting an escape. I now proceeded in company with Bell to the City of Austin, where I received emphatic orders to arrest the party. On my return home I found that about forty had collected, in open defiance of the law, determined to resist the legal authorities of the State. I immediately proceeded to summon good citizens to assist me in the capture. The sheriff of DeWitt County accompanied me, myself being deputy sheriff. Both our lives had been threatened by these desperadoes, as well as the lives of all those co-operating with me for their arrest. Mr. Jacobs, the sheriff of Goliad County, had just been killed by members of this same party. Finding that I was ready and determined in action, they divided, separating in squads of from five to fifteen. I proceeded in pursuit of the strongest of these bands, commanded by Jim Bell, a noted desperado of DeWitt County. I succeeded in capturing him and more, who were afterward killed in attempting to escape from the authorities.
>
> "About this time the Peaces—the murderers of Jacobs—were arrested, but subsequently effected an escape. One Stapp

was killed in attempting to do so. The Peaces proceeded to the rancho of John Choate, in San Patricio County, stating to Choate that they were pursued by a 'vigilance committee', and that they came to him for protection. John Choate now went to the rancho of Joe Tumlinson in DeWitt County, fifty or seventy-five miles from his home, and informed Captain Tumlinson that he had left the Peace boys at his house, and that he had loaned them one hundred and fifty dollars with which to effect an escape to Galveston. Choate insisted that Tumlinson should join him; said he had a band well fortified at his house, fully able to whip Jack Helm anywhere. Choatealso averred that Helm was a d—d rascal, and had joined the Yankees for popularity, and that he could not raise over thirty men, and they only Dutch and Yankees. Tumlinson told Choate that he knew Helm to be a good man, acting under proper authority, and that he intended to co-operate with him; that he knew the Peaces to be murderers and thieves; that he had hunted them, and would do so again. Becoming convinced that Joe Tumlinson was not his man, Choate proceeded to the rancho of Creed Taylor, about fifty miles (80 kilometers) distant, where he remained about three days, when he came to the neighborhood of Yorktown, in company with four or five desperadoes, Hays Taylor among the number. Choate now sent word to Tumlinson if he did not join him he would be killed, and that the Yankees had offered twelve hundred dollars reward for him, for the supposed killing of Stapp. Tumlinson replied that if he had done anything wrong he was willing to surrender to the proper authorities of his country, but would have nothing to do with Choate or any of his gang. Choate replied that Tumlinson must risk the consequences of his folly. Choate now went by the house of Jim Bell, and took the clothing and other effects of the Peace boys to his house in San Patricio County. Here he met the Peaces, Fulcrod, the Broolans, Doughtys, Gormans, Perrys, and about forty-two others, all known desperadoes, and many having indictments against them for thieving. Choate informed them that Jack Helm would be upon them, and that they must prepare for a fight. The house was fortified and put in condition for a regular siege, having loop-holes cut on all sides, and secret passages connecting them room to room. They had one keg of powder, five hundred shot-gun cartridges, two hundred Spencer rifle cartridges, prerarations for receiving five hundred gallons of water, provisions, and all that was necessary for conducting a siege fifty days by fifty men. I had with me one hundred and twenty-five of the best citizens of the country. Arriving at Choate's a little after day, expecting to have to fight one hundred desperadoes, I immediately proceeded to carry the house by storm. I had one man killed and two wounded in the attack. Crockett and John Choate were killed, and two others wounded. Choate perfidiously attempted to shoot me after he had surrendered, and was killed by myself in defense of my life. I now made all the necessary preparation for interring the dead, which was done. And right here let me nail to the counter those lies that allege that my men disturbed any of Mrs. Choate's property or the property of anyone else. They did no such thing. I encamped in the neighborhood of San Patricio, and conferred with Captain Smith at Corpus Christi. I now proceeded to Yorktown, and sent a report to Helena. I was met at Yorktown by C.S. Bell, and disbanded my force until I could find out the whereabouts of the Taylors. Spent three days in this matter; collected my men, about twenty-five, and proceeded to the forks of the San Antonio and Guadalupe rivers, where I succeeded in arresting the Hogans, who were members of the same party. I now sent the prisoners to Helena under charge of Tom Flemming and six others. I then proceeded in pursuit of the Taylors. At Yorktown I met Bell, and detailed fifteen men to accompany him, stating to the boys that Captain Bell was a good and true man, and would lead them. I remained in camp with the remainder of my men, to attract attention while Bell could operate. The next morning I took up the line of march for Creed Taylor's, followed by one hundred men. I proceeded by a circuitous route up the Sandies, arresting all persons that I suspicioned, and cutting off all means of escape. I arrived within seven miles of the house, when I received intelligence of the fight with the Taylors. I here disbanded my men, after complimenting them for their orderly conduct, gentlemanly bearing, and devotion to the lawsof the country. Taking ten men, I proceeded to Helena, where I met Majors Crosland and Callahan, Lieutenant Thompson, and other gentlemen, who approved of all I had done.

"I and my men are ready at all times to act with the legal authorities of my country in the enforcement of law and suppression of crime. I am a citizen of DeWitt County—deputy sheriff—and am opposed to mob law; but I am ready to give my assistance to the authorities, either civil or military, to arrest thieves and desperadoes who defy the laws, either in Texas or any other part of the United States, regardless of all threats, knowing that the law-abiding citizen is my friend, and the desperado my enemy, which is the only guaranty that I desire to know that I am right. *Jack Helm.*"

In sharp contrast to the report of Jack Helm, F. O. Skidmore wrote (several years later) a very different version of the raid in San Patricio County (which is duplicated here without notation of spelling, punctuation, capitalization or other grammatical errors):

"I was at Choate's ranche, in San Patricio County, Texas, on the 3d of August, 1869. Being an intimate friend of the family, I always stopped there when passing, and convenient to do so, and that was the case on this occasion. Not anticipating any trouble, I went, the 2d of August, 1869, to his house to remain all night; when I arrived at the house Mr. Choate was not at home, but soon arrived, and told me to put out my horse and stay with him all night.

"We conversed much that night about the reports in circulation regarding the high-handed measures of Jack Helm's party. Choate informed me that he had sent off the 'Peace boys,' so that he would not get into trouble on their account; he also said that he would fight any mob, but that any authorized officer—Federal or State—could come and take him and all his effects. I can't say that I saw anything more than usual going on at the house. There were only two men on the place except negroes; there were myself and two small boys, one my brother, aged fourteen years, the other about the same age.

"Helm's party charged the house about daybreak. I awoke at the first sound, and heard them yelling 'Charge!' Immediately several of their number rushed into the house.

"Crockett Choate shot a man named Kykendall. They retired to shelter in out-houses, behind trees and the yard fence.

Mrs. Choate then appeared on the piazza, and held a parley with Helm. She informed him that Mr. Choate would surrender if he, Helm, had the authority to make the arrest.

"Helm replied that he was authorized by the highest authority in the State of Texas—orders from military headquarters. Mrs. Choate then informed him that there were three boys in the house who had stopped for the night, and that they were innocent, and for God's sake not to kill them. Helm replied, 'Tell the boys to come out, and they shall not be molested.' "When I heard that, I went out on the piazza, and spoke to those who confronted me, and I told them that I would surrender, and without a word of warning they commenced firing on me.

"I was shot seventeen times. When I returned to consciousness I was out in the yard near a tree. I crawled to it and sat up against it, and while in this position I was shot at several times; and as I sat there, I saw John Choate receive his first wound. As stated before, Helm said he had authority for his arrest; Choate came out in obedience to this demand, his wife accompanying him, and a little in advance. He raised both his hands above his head, and said, 'I surrender myself and house to the United States authority.' Choate, with the assistance of his wife, retreated to his room. The first wound was in the knee. I saw him no more alive. I was informed that they killed him outright immediately afterwards.

"When Crockett heard Mr. Choate surrender, he broke from the house with his six-shooter in his hand. He ran right past me, all the crowd following him. I then crawled away, and made my escape to a Mexican ranche about half a mile distant from Choate's house.

"About ten o'clock they pursued me there, and carried me back to the Choate house.

"When I arrived there Crockett and the old man were both laid out, dead. I begged them to take me to Mr. Terry's, but they would not. Said they wanted to watch the place. They conducted themselves in an extremely rough and boisterous manner while at the house, appropriating whatever they desired, as if they had killed a robber chieftain and had a right to appropriate his effects. They left me nothing, not even my clothing and pocket change. They stole my saddle, six-shooter, and other things of less note. I cannot say what was taken from the house. Helm talked in a braggadocio style to Dr. Downs, my attending physician.

"The house fronts south; old man Choate was in the east room; Crockett, myself, and the two boys were in the west end. Crockett fired a great many times. John Choate did not fire a gun that I could see or hear. His sole aim appeared to be to save his life. He appealed to Captain Tumlinson, as a Mason, to save him. Captain Tumlinson claimed that he was not present just then, but I saw him soon afterwards.

"Helm's party went to San Patricio from Choate's, but parties were continually lurking about the neighborhood for a week, which kept the neighborhood in a state of anxious suspense. I was six weeks confined to bed, unable to help myself at all. But, thank God, I have lived to see such things done away with.

"Crockett Choate was killed about three hundred yards from the house."

On the 23rd of November in 1869, a group of Regulators arrived at the ranch of W. B. Morris in McMullen County. There they captured Morris' son-in-law, Martin Taylor, whom they had been chasing. McMullen County had no court or jailhouse, so the Regulators set out with Taylor and Morris bound for the jail at Oakville in Live Oak County. The bullet-riddled bodies of Taylor and Morris were discovered the following day along that route.

When Edmund J. Davis took oath as governor of Texas in 1870, the here-to-fore quasi-legal Regulators no longer had the blessing of the state's highest office. It wasn't necessarily because Governor Davis was more ethical than former Governor Reynolds. He simply wanted control of the state's military forces. With the loosely-knit Texas Rangers (temporarily) disbanded, Davis was instrumental in organizing the Texas State Police, which would become a highly unpopular organization. Jack Helm was one of four captains named to the new force. Many of the officers recruited by Helm were former members of his old group of Regulators. Two of these were Jim Cox and Joe Tumlinson who were very anti-Taylor. Another of Helm's key comrades was Bill Sutton. Sutton was hated by the Taylors. Buck Taylor and a fellow named Dick Chisholm had been shot to death outside a Clinton saloon on Christmas eve in 1868 following a disagreement with Bill Sutton. Buck Taylor had just returned from driving a herd of horses to market in east Texas. Evidently, part of the herd consisted of some Sutton horses which Taylor included in the drive (for a fee). When he later found out that Sutton's horses had been stolen, Buck confronted Bill and called him a horse thief. Sutton and his compadres were never brought to trial.

Several months prior to the incident at Clinton, Bill Sutton shot and killed a suspected horse thief named Charley Taylor. The shooting occurred in Bastrop on the 25th of March. Charley Taylor may or may not have been kin to the Taylors of the area. If he was, the relationship was distant.

The DeWitt County Taylors indicated that they were not related to Charley Taylor, and possibly did so because he was a suspected horse thief. Two years earlier an incident occurred that may indicate otherwise, however. Charley Taylor shot a fellow named Polk whose wounded body was taken to the house of a Regulator, Captain John Littleton. He is the same Littleton that later set out to get Hays and Doboy Taylor stating, "I will do it or die." As previously mentioned, he and his comrade Stannard turned up dead.

Pitkin Taylor (brother of Creed) married Susan Cochran Day in

Governor Edmund J. Davis organized the highly unpopular Texas State Police. *Texas State Library & Archives Commission (Photograph of a painting by William Henry Huddle).*

the first marriage recorded in DeWitt County history. The couple had three children—a child who died at birth, Jim and Amanda. Additionally, Susan had three children from her prior marriage to Robert Day—John, Will and Betty. Amanda Taylor and Betty Day married brothers, Henry and William Kelly respectfully. They all lived in close proximity south of Cuero. Among their neighbors were Wiley and Eugene Kelly, brothers of Henry and William, as well as Susan's sons John and Will Day.

In mid-August of 1870 the Kelly brothers and their families traveled to the community of Sweet Home in Lavaca County to attend the performance of a circus. Apparently unhappy with the show, the Kellys proceeded to shoot out the lights. It was all the excuse Jack Helm and Bill Sutton needed to continue their war against the Taylor clan. Early on the 26th of August, Bill Sutton, Doc White (who had been with Sutton when Charley Taylor was killed), John Meadows and Deputy Simmons (from Hallettsville in Lavaca County) rode to the homes of Henry and William Kelly and arrested the two brothers. With the Kellys, the lawmen set out on the road to Hallettsville. Amanda Taylor took a buggy and picked up her mother-in-law Delilah Kelly, with the intent of riding with the group to Lavaca County.

In an obvious effort to lose the women, Sutton and his bunch took a "shortcut" through the brush where a wagon would be incapable of fol-

Pitkin Taylor and his wife Susan. At Pitkin's funeral their son Jim vowed to wash his "... hands in old Bill Sutton's blood". *Elizabeth Kelly Brautigam.*

lowing.

In a later statement sworn before a Justice of the Peace, Amanda Taylor told how she saw her husband and brother-in-law killed in cold blood. She indicated that she had climbed from her buggy and ascended a rise overlooking the trail through the brush which the group had taken. She stated that the posse had stopped forty or fifty yards away and that John Meadows was no longer with them. William Kelly had dismounted and was attempting to light his pipe when Bill Sutton shot him. Instantly, Doc White shot Amanda's husband, Henry, and he toppled from his horse. The court later upheld the plea of the lawmen that they had shot the prisoners while in the act of attempting to escape. There was a huge public outcry following the Kelly murders. State Senator Bolivar Pridgen of Prices Creek in DeWitt County was extremely vocal about the killings. He condemned Jack Helm and the State Police for their methods. Newspapers across the state attacked the actions of Governor Davis. He felt the heat, which eventually resulted in the dismissal of Jack Helm from the State Police. This ouster had little effect on the citizens of DeWitt County, however, as Jack Helm still held the office of sheriff.

Doboy Taylor had "disappeared" for a while. He resurfaced in Kerrville in late 1871. With Jack Helm removed from the State Police force and C. S. Bell having moved out of the vicinity, Doboy could breathe easier. He applied for a position as agent for a cattle buying firm. When the firm hired Sim Holstein for the position, Doboy became incensed. From the gate outside Holstein's hotel, Doboy called the new agent out. The conversation over the gate became bitter. According to the *San Antonio Express*, on December 13, 1871:

> "Suddenly Taylor drew his pistol and fired at Holstein but overshot him—Holstein sprang over the gate, and before Taylor could shoot again, wrested his pistol from him and felled him to the ground with it. Taylor regained his feet, but was immediately shot down a second and third time. Then Taylor ran toward his house, calling on his friends for assistance. Another shot from Holstein brought him to the ground. His friends were prevented from doing anything by the determined attitude of Holstein. Taylor . . . survived six hours and died at 11 o'clock the same night. He was sensible to the last, and spent his last hours imprecating and cursing the man he had attempted to murder."

Sim Holstein, unarmed when he approached the gate, was obviously a very tough individual.

One night (possibly September of 1872) Pitkin Taylor heard the bell of one of his oxen out in the cornfield. In his nightshirt he stepped outside to see if one of the oxen had wandered into his corn. As he did so, several shots rang out and Pitkin Taylor slumped to the ground. Pitkin, who was badly wounded, was moved to Lavaca County for safety. He lived for about six months, then died in March of 1873. According to the Taylor-Day-Kelly version of the story, Bill Sutton and four henchmen removed the bell from one of the oxen, slipped into the cornfield, and then rattled the bell with the certainty that Taylor would step outside.

Alfred Hays Day's account of Pitkin Taylor's funeral is as follows:

> "It was a grim and tragic scene. The burial plot was near the river on a shaded knoll. Around the open grave the relatives of the murdered man were assembled. Among the mourners were young Jim Taylor, son of the deceased, and five other youthful kin of the slain man. In hideous contrast to this grief-stricken group, across the river while the funeral services were being conducted Bill Sutton assembled his cut throat [sic] gang in bold mockery. With raw drink and coarse jest and wild firing of guns they celebrated the death of Pitkin Taylor while he was being lowered into the grave.
>
> "Hearing this hilarity, Jim's mother, who had borne up well under her grief, broke down and wept. If there had ever been a doubt in young Jim's mind what he should do about the slaying of his father, it was cleared up then. If ever a man was provoked into taking the law into his own hands Jim Taylor was justly provoked; if ever a man had reason to see that Justice [sic] was meted out, Jim Taylor was inspired by that reason.
>
> "Putting his arm protectingly about his mother, he vowed to her: 'Do not weep mother [sic]. I will wash my hands in old Bill Sutton's blood!' The five other youthful relatives likewise pledged themselves to the same cause."

Bill Sutton was sitting in Bank's Saloon and Billiard Parlor at Cuero one Friday night when someone attempted to take his life. Two shots were fired into the building from the outside. One of the slugs penetrated Sutton's arm and side, wounding the lawman. On another occasion, Sutton and a few comrades were riding toward Clinton when they were ambushed. One of the men was wounded in the leg, and three of their horses were slain. No one knows who participated in either attack. We do know, however, that Bill Sutton was number one on the Taylor hit list.

John Wesley Hardin was one of the most dangerous gunfighters on the western frontier. In fact, he was probably involved in more gunfights than any other individual. In his autobiography, Hardin claims to have disposed of 44 men, but then he was known to be a braggart. About 25 percent of those deaths are verifiable through county records and documents. Many deaths, however, went unrecorded in those days. By the year 1871, eighteen-year-old Wes Hardin had already gained quite a reputation. As Hardin was being transported by the State Police from Marshall to Waco to stand trial (for a murder he had not committed), he killed a guard named Jim Smolly and escaped. Wes Hardin fled to Gonzales County to seek refuge at the ranch of his cousins, the Clements, south of the town of Smiley. He worked as a cowpoke and attempted to maintain a low profile. But Wes couldn't stay out of trouble. During the following year he was involved in several shootings, was wounded twice and was also captured. Wes' cousin, Emmanuel "Mannen" Clements, broke Hardin out of the Gonzales jail (in October of 1872) by slipping a file to Wes which he used to cut the window bars. Clements then returned and pulled Hardin through the opening with his lariat.

In April of 1873 at Cuero, Wes Hardin became involved in an argument with J. B. Morgan, a deputy of Jack Helm. There is a possibility that Morgan may have attempted to arrest Hardin while he was having a drink in a local saloon. Wes walked out of the saloon with Morgan in pursuit. As Morgan drew his revolver, Hardin whirled and shot the deputy in the head. Shortly after this incident, the Taylor faction gained some valuable recruits—Wes Hardin; Mannen Clements; his brothers Gibson, Jim and Joe; and Gibson's brother-in-law George Tennelle.

Shortly thereafter, Jack Helm led a large posse to Gonzales County, and the Clement's ranch, in search of Wes Hardin. The men were away rounding up strays, but Sheriff Helm succeeded in frightening Jane Bowen Hardin, Wes' new wife, and the Clements women. Incensed by the posse's visit, Wes Hardin, Mannen Clements and George Tennelle met with Jim, John and Scrap Taylor. They decided it was time to wage all-out war on Sutton, Helm, Cox, Tumlinson and the others. They wasted no time in taking the offensive.

On the 16th of June in 1873, Bill Sutton set out for Clinton to testify in the Bank's Saloon and Billiard Parlor shooting at Cuero on the 1st of April. Sutton was still recovering from his wounds, so he rode in a buggy. He was accompanied by Doc White, John Meadows, Horace French and Ad Patterson who were on horseback. Midway between Sutton's home and Clinton the group was ambushed. Meadows took a slug in one leg and French's horse was slain. There was no further damage. Feeling the heat, William and Laura Sutton moved to Victoria to get further away from the fighting.

One day in June of 1873, Jim Cox, Joe Tumlinson, H. Ragland and Jake Cresman were returning from the courthouse at Helena in Karnes County, where Cox was under indictment and had to answer certain charges. Tumlinson, who was his neighbor, Cresman and Ragland apparently went along for the ride. When the party reached the San Antonio River Tumlinson and Ragland opted for a different crossing than Cox and Cresman. It probably saved their lives. Jim Taylor, Scrap Taylor, Alf Day and Bud Dowlearn (whose mother was formerly a Taylor by marriage) were hidden awaiting the approach of the others. Suddenly a volley of gunfire erupted. The lifeless bodies of Jim Cox and Jake Cresman toppled from their horses. It is said that there were 19 buckshot wounds in Cox's body. Tumlinson and Ragland were far enough from the shooting that they were able to flee.

During the last week of July in 1873, Wes Hardin and Jim Taylor were at a blacksmith shop in Albuquerque, Texas where Hardin was having his horse shod. Jack Helm and a few friends spotted Jim Taylor and made a beeline to the blacksmith shop. Hearing the negative tone of the approaching voices, Hardin grabbed his shotgun and fired at Sheriff Helms. The blast scored a direct hit. Jim Taylor put several slugs in Helms' head to assure that he was dead. With Hardin's shotgun aimed directly at them, Helms' cohorts refused to participate in the action.

The Taylors received word that there was a large gathering of men at Joe Tumlinson's place. Realizing that the Sutton faction might be amassing for an attack, the Taylors decided to surprise them first. The Taylors, including Wes Hardin, crept toward the Tumlinson residence at approximately 2 a.m. They intended to get close to the porch where many men were sleeping, then open fire. Tumlinson's dogs detected the Taylors, however, and began barking loudly awakening the Sutton men who quickly took cover. Sporadic fire occurred throughout the siege which began early Tuesday morning and lasted until the sheriff and a large contingency of citizens talked the feuding parties into a truce sometime after daybreak on Wednesday. It was agreed that the principal members of each faction should accompany the sheriff to Clinton where a formal truce could be drawn up and signed. Both parties agreed, and the other participants were allowed to disperse and head toward their respective homes. The following account of this event occurred in the *Gonzales Enquirer* and was reprinted in the *Houston Telegraph*:

> "It is with no little gratification that we record a cessation of hostilities between the above name beligerents. It appears from the facts as related to us by a responsible party, that on Monday night last Wesley Hardin, accompanied with some 35 or 40 men, well armed, marched to the residence of Joe Tumlinson, in DeWitt County, surrounded his house and held him in seige for two nights and one day. In the meantime Joe Tumlinson and party, numbering 15 men, and strongly fortified, managed to dispatch a courier to Clinton for the sheriff to hasten to his assistance. After summoning about 50 men the sheriff started for the 'seat of war', where he arrived on Wednesday morning and found Hardin's men formed in line of battle. A brief conference with the parties revealed the unexpected but agreeable intelligence that a compromise had been effected between Hardin and Tumlinson; in other words, a treaty of peace had been agreed upon, and the two parties were ready to proceed to Clinton, a distance of 16 miles, and sign documents to that effect. The line of march was at once taken up. Hardin's men leading the column, the Sheriff's posse following, and Tumlinson's party bringing up the rear. Arriving at Clinton, Hardin halted on one side of the town, and Tumlinson on the other, while the sheriff's men marched directly into the town. After signing the documents and having the same recorded in the Clerk's Office, both parties quietly dispersed to the intense gratification of the law-abiding and peace-loving citizens."

In the Old West, it was rare when feudists adhered to the terms of a truce. This one lasted about four months before guns were blazing again. In late December, Wiley Pridgen (brother of ex-senator Bolivar Pridgen) was gunned down by unknown assassins near the entrance to Jim Pridgen's store in Thomaston. Several accounts have been given as to who the murderers might be, but nobody knew for certain. The Taylor faction, however, was sure that Bill Sutton was involved. The Taylors cornered Bill Sutton and some of his friends at the courthouse in Clinton. Realizing that their community might quickly become a battleground, Judge Henry Clay Pleasants and several of the town's women approached the Taylors and prevailed upon them to carry their feud elsewhere. They didn't want Clinton's citizens endangered or the town shot up. The Taylors agreed to take their fight elsewhere and hit the road to Cuero. Sutton and his men followed. Sutton sent a request for help to Joe Tumlinson, and then holed up at the Gulf Hotel in Cuero. Tumlinson arrived with reinforcements and yet another siege wound up in a stalemate. Once again, both parties agreed to sign a truce—and they did. Although the newspapers voiced optimism, nobody really expected the feudists to adhere to this armistice either—and they didn't.

During the next few weeks three more men died, and another was wounded. One of the slain men was Bolivar Pridgen's ex-slave, Abraham Pickens (who had continued to work for Pridgen). Supposedly, Pickens was killed because he would not divulge Bolivar's whereabouts. Abraham's clothes were filled with rocks and his body was thrown into the river.

Word filtered through Bolivar Pridgen to Jim Taylor that Bill Sutton and his wife Laura were preparing to leave Texas via a ship departing from the port at Indianola. Joe Hardin (Wes' brother) and his cousin Alec Barrickman, both of whom were from Comanche, were visiting in DeWitt County. Wes Hardin persuaded Joe and Alec to snoop around (as they would not be recognized) to see what information they might obtain. They discovered that Bill and Laura Sutton were scheduled to depart on March 11, bound for the port at New Orleans. Jim and Bill Taylor followed the others to Indianola. Bill was a grandson of William Riley Taylor (brother of Jim's dad, Pitkin) and was therefore Jim's second cousin. Shortly after noon on the 11th of March in 1874, Bill Sutton, his friend Gabriel Slaughter and Bill's pregnant wife Laura were standing on the ship's deck waiting for the crew to cast off. Jim and Bill Taylor quickly approached. Jim Taylor shot Bill Sutton in the head and heart. Bill Taylor also fired and his slug hit Gabriel Slaughter in the head. Sutton and Slaughter were both dead as they fell at the feet of a distraught Laura Sutton. Before the Taylors fled, Jim seized Bill Sutton's ivory-handled revolver. Following this incident Laura Sutton offered a personal reward of $1,000 for the arrest of Jim Taylor (who already had a $500 bounty on his head).

The Taylors escaped to the house of Bolivar Pridgen in Thomaston, where the news was received with great joy. Pridgen had his

Bill and Laura Sutton. Following the death of Bill Sutton, his wife, Laura, offered a reward for the capture of Jim Taylor. *The Center for American History, University of Texas at Austin.*

Prior to two devastating hurricanes, the port at Indianola once rivaled Galveston. This is where Bill Sutton was shot to death by Jim Taylor. *Calhoun County Museum.*

cook prepare a lavish meal to celebrate the occasion. Jim Taylor helped Wes Hardin prepare a herd for its drive north. They decided to spend a few days in Comanche, then reunite with the drovers at some point on the trail. Bill Taylor decided to lie low in Texas. He didn't stay hidden enough, however, and was arrested by Reuben Brown, the city marshal of Cuero. Bill Taylor was transported to the jail at Galveston to await trial.

Scrap Taylor, an active participant in the feud, would often run with Alf Day and Jim Taylor. *Elizabeth Kelly Brautigam.*

While in Comanche, Wes Hardin wagered on some horse races and won heavily. It was a nice present for his twenty-first birthday. His mood turned sour, however, when he learned that Charles Webb, deputy sheriff of nearby Brown County, was in Comanche with the intention of killing Hardin and collecting the $1,800 reward on his head. Wes was at Jack Wright's Saloon when Webb found him. Hardin offered to buy Webb a drink at the bar. As Charles Webb stepped toward the bar, he drew his revolver and fired. Alertly, Hardin jumped to one side as he drew his own pistol. Webb's bullet grazed Hardin who fired. His slug ripped through the deputy's head. Although he was already dead, as he fell, Bud Dixon (Wes' cousin) and Jim Taylor also shot him. They immediately fled the scene. A large and irate mob could not find Hardin and Taylor but were successful in capturing Bud Dixon. They also rounded up Joe Hardin and Tom Dixon (neither of whom were directly involved in the killing of Sheriff Webb). The three were locked up in the Comanche jail. Several days later an angry mob dragged the trio from the jailhouse and lynched them. Joe Hardin's cousin Alec Barrickman and Ham Anderson (two of Wes' stock hands) decided to hide at the house of Bill Stone. Barrickman and Anderson were discovered by a posse and shot to death. Another posse rode to Mason County where Hardin's drovers were holding his cattle. Three or four of the cowboys escaped. Doc Brosius (Hardin's trail boss), Scrap Taylor, Kute Tuggle and Jim White were taken into custody and escorted to DeWitt County. During the night of June 20, 1874, a mob broke the prisoners out of jail. Brosius was somehow rescued by a fellow Mason during all the commotion. The others were hanged from a tree near the Clinton cemetery.

The hunt for Taylor men continued. A posse cornered George Tennelle at the residence of John Runnel in Gonzales County. When Tennelle refused to surrender, he was shot to death by the posse.

The reward for John Wesley Hardin had been raised to $4,000. He felt the heat and knew it was time to leave Texas. He sent word to Jane who met him in New Orleans, and the couple then relocated to Pollard, Escambia County, Alabama where they stayed with friends (the Whitings) and assumed the aliases of Mr. and Mrs. J. H. Swain.

By this time, Richard Coke had become governor, the State Police had been dissolved and the Texas Rangers rode once again. Citizens of DeWitt County pleaded with Governor Coke to maintain a detachment of Texas Rangers in the area as a peacekeeping force. He agreed to do so. In late July, Captain Leander H. McNelly led a force of forty Rangers into DeWitt County. McNelly was a tough individual who had an advanced case of tuberculosis (called consumption in those days), and he knew he was dying. It was probably the reason that he had no fear. McNelly's force maintained a highly visible profile and things began to settle down in the area.

Bolivar Pridgen was successful in obtaining indictments against Joe Tumlinson and 26 other men for the murder of his employee, Abraham Pickens. Joe Tumlinson died of natural causes before he could be tried. It was probably for that reason that the case against the others never came to trial.

After two postponements, Bill Taylor's trial was scheduled for September of 1875. He was transported from Galveston to the jail at

Indianola, Texas, as it looked prior to the hurricane of 1875. The view is looking down Main Street. *Texas State Library & Archives Commission.*

Indianola a few days before his case was to be heard. During the interim, a severe hurricane struck Indianola. As the Gulf surge raised the water level in Matagorda Bay, the Indianola jailhouse began to fill with water. Concerned that the prisoners (Taylor, two rustlers and a rapist) might drown, District Attorney Bill Crain released them, and the five men made their way to the second floor of the courthouse which was adjacent to the jail. That day, and the next, Bill Taylor and another prisoner named Blackburn joined in the rescue effort. Many people were saved due to the heroism of Taylor and Blackburn. After two days, the savage winds finally subsided. The death toll was large. Sheriff Fred Busch arrived on horseback (the 17th of September) and entered the courthouse to talk with the nearly 100 survivors who had found shelter there. During an unsuspecting moment, Blackburn snatched Busch's revolver from its holster. While holding the sheriff at gunpoint, Blackburn appropriated the lawman's horse. Blackburn and Bill Taylor mounted the animal and raced out of town.

Two months later to the day, City Marshal Reuben Brown was dealing Monte in the Exchange Saloon at Cuero when a few men walked in and shot him to death. Two black men at Brown's table were wounded as well. Although no charges were ever filed, it is believed that the responsible party consisted of Jim Taylor, Bill Taylor, Joe Bennett and possibly two others. The murder was obviously a retaliation for Brown's arrest of Bill Taylor following the killing of Bill Sutton. A few weeks later Bill Taylor and Joe Bennett were ambushed by unknown assailants near the town of Clinton. Bennett received a superficial wound before the pair escaped to safety.

On December 27, 1875, Jim Taylor and a large party of armed men rode into Clinton. Their purpose was uncertain, but Sheriff Weisiger was convinced that they planned to burn down the courthouse. Weisiger recruited the help of several citizens who were determined to defend the courthouse. Two members of the Taylor bunch were Tom King and his adopted brother Ed Davis. Their father, Martin King, owned the blacksmith shop and livery stable in Clinton. While most of the Taylor men remained on the outskirts of town, Jim Taylor, Mace Arnold (who was known as Winchester Smith) and J. G. Hendrix stabled their horses at King's livery. Meanwhile, Weisiger sent a boy named Charley Page to Cuero to request the assistance of Deputy Sheriff Dick Hudson. Hudson rounded up a posse of Sutton sympathizers which included Kit Hunter (a cousin of the deceased Bill Sutton).

Sheriff Weisiger advised Martin King that a posse was on its way. Weisiger stated that a fight was certain and that King's sons would be in grave danger. The sheriff told him that his sons' lives would be spared if he would agree to help the law by locking up those horses which the Taylor gang had left at his stable. Fearing for the lives of his sons, Martin King agreed to do so.

As the posse rode in, the Taylor men who were in town scampered to reach their horses only to find that they had been locked up. Jim Taylor, Winchester Smith and Hendrix dashed through Martin King's house in an effort to reach a log building situated in an orchard. Suddenly Taylor was confronted by Kit Hunter. Simultaneously, they exchanged shots. Taylor's bullet went through Hunter's hat while Hunter's slug shattered Taylor's right arm. By then, a barrage of bullets were flying at the Taylor men from different directions. Jim Taylor and Winchester Smith were killed. Hendrix was wounded and would soon die. It all happened so fast that those members of the Taylor bunch waiting on the outskirts of town were never able to help. They departed in haste. Martin King's sons were arrested and jailed.

Martin King was a marked man for betraying the Taylors. One night several months later, a volley of gunfire killed Martin King in the doorway of Dola Davis' Saloon. A slug from the gun of one of the assassins wounded Davis in the leg during the attack.

In early 1876, a posse arrived at the residence of A. J. Allen, a member of the Taylor gang. The Henderson County sheriff advised Allen that they had a warrant for his arrest. Allen refused to submit to arrest, and a fight broke out in which a deputy was killed. Allen was severely wounded and would eventually die. Another man was wounded as well.

Once again, Captain McNelly and his Texas Rangers camped in DeWitt County. Their mere presence minimized trouble.

An incident that was peripheral to the Sutton-Taylor feud occurred on the night of September 19, 1876. Dr. Philip Brassell, a civic-minded citizen, and his son George, a Taylor sympathizer, were forced from their home by a posse—and were then murdered on the road a short distance from their home. Eight posse members were arrested and jailed by the Texas Rangers. Seven members of the posse (which included Bill Cox, a son of Jim Cox) spent years in and out of courtrooms. There were indictments, trials, changes of venue, acquittals, more indictments, more trails, convictions, appeals, more acquittals, another conviction and pardon (and not necessarily in that order). Eventually, all of the accused men walked free.

Bill Taylor remained a fugitive until April 15, 1877, when he was arrested in Coleman by the Texas Rangers. Taylor was taken to the jail at Austin. In late August, he was reunited with John Wesley Hardin. Hardin had been arrested in Pensacola, Florida, on the 23rd of August and was then transported to Austin to await trial for the murder of Sheriff Charles Webb at Comanche. Hardin was found guilty and sentenced to the penitentiary at Huntsville. Bill Taylor was transferred to the jail at Galveston in order to stand trial at Indianola. Following a change of venue to the court at Texanna (which at the time was the county seat of Jackson County), Taylor was acquitted in the killing of Bill Sutton. It was a blow for the prosecution which now asked for a delay in the murder trial of Gabriel Slaughter, obviously with the hope of preparing a better case. A delay was allowed. Taylor was granted a Writ of Habeas Corpus and was able to post bail in the amount of $5,000 which was secured by Bolivar Pridgen, John Taylor, Eugene Kelly and Rice S. Flournoy. Following another continuance, the prosecuting attorney asked for a dismissal of the case. Bill Taylor was a free man.

The bloody Sutton-Taylor feud, which for years had terrorized the citizens of several Texas counties, finally came to an end.

Cullen Baker's Kentucky-style, cap and ball rifle. *Archives Division, Texas State Library*

Chapter Forty
Cullen Baker: Fugitive

Cullen Montgomery Baker became an excellent marksman when he was a teenager. At age 18, and a newlywed, Baker killed his first man. He was accused of bullying an orphan by a Cass County, Texas, farmer named Bailey. Baker went to the Bailey farm to seek him out. Bailey, who was on his front porch, fired a shot at Baker as he approached. Baker drew and returned his fire. Baker's first shot connected, and the second hit Bailey in the head. As his horror-stricken family watched, Bailey was dead before he hit the floor. Baker fled to Arkansas, leaving his bride in Texas.

Two years later Baker fatally stabbed a fellow named Wartham. Soon thereafter he traveled to Texas to fetch his wife, whom he brought back to Arkansas. Following the birth of a daughter, Baker's wife died. A couple of years later, in 1862, he remarried and then joined the Army of the Confederate States. Before long he deserted the Confederacy and was on the run again. In fact, he was still in uniform while drinking at a bar in Spanish Bluffs, Arkansas, when four Union soldiers walked in. Baker drew, shot three of the Yankees, and then fled.

Knowing that the Union army attributed the shootings to a Confederate soldier, and realizing that the Confederate army and others were looking for him, Baker decided that the safest place for him to be was in the Union army, so he joined the Federal occupation force. After a little time passed, once again he deserted, this time to join an outlaw gang.

Following the Civil War and the death of his second wife, Baker proposed to her sixteen-year-old sister. Baker's father-in-law, who had grown to detest him, indicated that it would never happen.

A fellow named Rowden owned a country store in Cass County,

Texas. Cullen Baker owed him money, and Rowden badgered him to pay his debt. On the evening of June 1, 1867, Baker showed up at the store. He shouted at Rowden to come outside. As Rowden walked through his door with a shotgun in hand, Baker filled him with lead. Rowden dropped dead.

Later that same month, at Pett's Ferry (a place named for the ferry that crossed the Sulphur River), Baker noticed that two soldiers were closely scrutinizing him. They must have recognized Baker, or realized he was a fugitive, for one of them (a sergeant) drew his pistol. Baker also drew and killed the soldier instantly. While the other soldier escaped in one direction, Baker fled in another.

Totally on the run, Cullen Baker relied more and more on robbery for his subsistence. On October 10, 1867, between Boston and Linden, in Cass County, Baker and his new gang of bandits held up a government supply wagon. The wagon was well-protected with four armed guards. When the driver reached for his pistol, Baker fired a shot and killed him. The guards exchanged a few rounds and then fled the scene.

Baker had become a braggart and heavy drinker. In an incident that occurred at Boston, Texas, during October of 1868, Baker took another life. He spotted an army captain named Kirkham and coolly sauntered up to him stating, "I'm Cullen Baker. You looking for me?" Kirkham immediately reached for his gun. Baker shot him through the head. The army captain lurched backwards and fell dead. Once again Baker escaped, but his time was soon to run out.

Thomas Orr, a handicapped school teacher whom Baker had bullied in the past, decided that enough was enough. Accompanied by Baker's second father-in-law and two others, they decided to track Baker until they found him. The group was successful. On January 6, 1869, in southeastern Arkansas, they found Baker and one of his cohorts eating lunch alongside a road. Orr and the others never gave the elusive fugitive a chance. They opened fire with a barrage of shots. Cullen Baker, his companion, and their lunch, all bit the dust.

This photograph of William Preston Longley was made just before his execution at Giddings, Texas, in 1878. *Western History Collections, University of Oklahoma Library.*

Chapter Forty-One
He'll Hang Again, and Again!

While standing on the gallows, on October 11, 1878, at Giddings, Texas, Bill Longley looked around at an audience of hundreds, and stated, "I see a good many enemies around, and mighty few friends." Moments later he dropped through the trap door, but he dropped too far. Within minutes the rope was shortened and Longley was hanged again.

Actually, Longley had been hanged before—eleven years earlier, as a teenager. He had been caught by a posse at the home of a horse thief named Tom Johnson. Johnson and Longley were hanged. Following the lynching, which occurred at the Johnson house, the posse rode off. When the two were cut down, Longley was still alive.

From the days of his youth, William Preston Longley was argumentative, quick-tempered, and a racist, who placed little value on human life—especially those of blacks. About one mile from the Longley farm, near Evergreen, Texas, fifteen-year-old Longley claimed his first victim, a black soldier who was a member of the Reconstruction troops. Longley antagonized the soldier, who was on horseback, into going for his rifle. Longley drew his pistol and fired. The ball struck the soldier's head, and he died instantly. Later that same year (1867) at Lexington, Texas, Longley and a cohort, Johnson McKowen, terrorized a street dance that was being held by a group of blacks. They rode through the festivities, firing several shots. In their wake, they left two dead and several wounded. On another occasion, the following year, three black men had "rubbed" Longley the wrong way. He followed the men to their campsite that was located outside of Evergreen. One of the men shot at Longley as he approached, but was immediately slain by a ball from Longley's pistol. The other two men quickly fled.

The Sutton-Taylor feud, near Yorktown, Texas had gotten out of hand, and Reconstruction troops had been ordered to quell the violence. While working as a cowboy on a nearby ranch, Longley rode into town one day. Mistaking him for one of the Taylor clan, soldiers accosted Longley and a sergeant instructed him to surrender. Believing that they were after him for one of his killings, Longley drew his revolver and discharged a shot at point-blank range. The sergeant toppled from his horse. He was dead. Longley spurred his mount and outraced the pursuing soldiers.

"Wild Bill" Longley briefly rode with Cullen Baker's band of outlaws. After Baker was gunned down in early 1869, Longley joined a cattle drive that was headed for the slaughterhouses in Kansas. It wasn't long before the headstrong trail boss, a fellow named Rector, and the argumentative Longley, began to quarrel. It was all the excuse that Longley needed. He shot the trail boss several times, until his body was motionless.

Bill Longley was always on the run, and while he ran violence followed him everywhere. During a fracas in a Leavenworth, Kansas saloon, he shot another soldier to death. Longley fled the scene by hopping aboard an eastbound freight train. Shortly thereafter, however, he was captured at St. Joseph, Missouri, and subsequently transported back to Kansas and Fort Leavenworth. While behind bars, Longley was able to bribe a military guard who allowed him to escape.

Next, Longley took a job at Camp Brown, Wyoming, as a teamster. Before long, he and a quartermaster named Greggory (possibly Gregory) figured a way to short change the government by miscounting mules, and then selling those that were unreported for a personal profit. Following one sale, Longley split $300 with Greggory.

When Greggory found out that the mules had actually sold for $500, he was incensed and set out to find Longley. When Greggory caught up with Longley at a corral, the alert Longley was quicker as his revolver barked once more. Greggory lived through the night and then died. Foolishly, Longley made his getaway on a mule, and was easily apprehended. While awaiting transfer from the Camp Brown guardhouse, to serve a thirty-year term at the Iowa State Penitentiary, Longley escaped.

Bill Longley took refuge with the Ute Indians, where he lay low for about a year. By now (1872), he was no longer a teenager. But his age mattered little. He continued the same pattern of murder, run, and then murder again. As he ambled his way back south, Longley mortally wounded a fellow named Charles Stuart during a card game dispute. After returning to Texas, Longley killed another black man, this time because the victim had insulted a white woman. He engaged in a bloody gunfight with a Bell County man named Bill Scrier. Scrier finally died after receiving thirteen wounds in the altercation. On another occasion, Longley armed himself with a shotgun, and then sought out a minister named Roland Lay. Lay was blown away with two blasts of bird shot.

When Bill Longley learned that his cousin, Cale Longley, had been killed by Wilson Anderson, a boyhood friend, he rode to Anderson's farm and executed him with a shotgun blast. Following his arrest in Louisiana, Longley was returned to Texas, where he was tried and sentenced to death for the Anderson murder. While awaiting the gallows at Giddings, Bill Longley wrote to a girl, stating, "Hanging is my favorite way of dying."

Bill McCarty (at left) and Fred McCarty after they were shot to death by W. Ray Simpson. *Wild Horse Collection.*

Chapter Forty-Two
Colorado Potpourri

In 1859, ten years after the California gold rush, rich strikes in Colorado brought thousands of prospectors swarming into the territory. As new discoveries were made, mining towns cropped up throughout the mountains. Initially, they popped up as tent cities. Men outnumbered woman by a margin of thirty to one, and a large percentage of the women were prostitutes. The earliest towns had sanitation problems. Much trash was thrown into the streets. Mules, horses, and cattle contributed to the refuse. Miners slept in their clothes because tent walls were thin and mountain nights were chilly. Many never bothered to bathe, especially during colder weather. Saloons were constructed in every town as they were the primary entertainment for miners after a hard days work prospecting. Some mining camps had more saloons than all other businesses combined. In places where the gold or silver strikes were most lucrative, wild and rowdy towns sprang to life. Gradually the tents were replaced by log structures constructed of squared-hewn timber. The population explosion was eventually abetted by a maze of railroads that snaked through the valleys and over the mountains bringing in more supplies and more people.

The boom towns were a melting pot of people with varying occupations and backgrounds. There were hard cases that were running from the law in other places. Most every camp had its gamblers, dance hall girls, tin stars, and con artists or swindlers. Through the late 1800s there were colorful characters of all kinds, and they generated many stories.

The ink on the Brunot Treaty was barely dry when the town site of Silverton was surveyed and platted in 1874. The agreement (with the Ute Indians) opened the area for white settlers, and they wasted no time establishing a community. The law in early Silverton had its ups and downs. The first sheriff in the vicinity was also the mail carrier. The first lawbreaker was chained to the floor of a cabin, for a jail had not yet been built. Occasionally the town's citizens took matters into their own hands.

The first gunfight of consequence occurred in October of 1878 after an argument and fistfight between Tom Milligan and Bill Connors. Connors wouldn't let the matter drop and told Milligan that he would shoot him the next time he saw him. Shortly thereafter as Milligan was walking down Greene Street (Silverton's main street), he spotted Connors in front of the Silverton Hotel. Connors saw Milligan as well. Both men drew and Milligan shot Connors in the stomach. Connors lived for three days before he died. Milligan was acquitted on the grounds of self-defense.

Following the re-election of James Cart as town marshal, Silverton's newspaper, the *LaPlata Miner* stated on April 12, 1879, "…the re-election of Mr. Cart is a guarantee of order and respect for the law the coming summer." Ironically, "the coming summer" was a bloody one.

While walking his beat one night the following month, handicapped night watchman Hiram Ward encountered the Dermody brothers, James and Pete. They had been boozing it up at the Westminster Hall. Ward and the brothers exchanged words before the latter headed home. Like most Irishmen, the Dermodys loved their whiskey, and the following night (May 27, 1879) they were at it again. This time they were at Goode's Saloon. Ward walked in and once again the trio quarreled. Ward told the brothers to go home and sleep it off. James Dermody told Ward to mind his own business. Ward pushed Dermody outside onto the street and a fight began. Dermody bit Ward and then wrestled him into the ditch. Getting the worst of the scuffle, Ward drew his revolver and shot James Dermody dead. The press called the shooting "uncalled for." Hiram Ward was found innocent. He was soon to be back in the news again.

On August 23, 1879, Harry Cleary and "Mexican Joe" became very rowdy while drinking at Brown and Cort's Saloon. James M. "Ten Die" Brown, one of the saloon's owners, escorted Cleary out the front door. Cleary turned and shot Brown. Brown was able to get off some shots, and one stray bullet hit night watchman Hiram Ward in the left shoulder. Ward, in turn, also shot Brown. More than likely it was one of Ward's bullets that penetrated Brown's heart, but Cleary was blamed for the killing, arrested, and jailed. Late that night a mob dragged Cleary from the jailhouse and lynched him behind the blacksmith shop. It was later agreed by most that if Cleary's bullet had penetrated Brown's heart, Brown would never have been able to fire off the rounds which he did. Hiram Ward was never prosecuted for any wrongdoing.

On August 24, 1881, LaPlata County Sheriff Luke Hunter arrived in Silverton with warrants for the arrest of members of the Stockton-Eskridge gang. Burt Wilkinson, Dyson Eskridge and Kid Thomas (a black man who was also known as the ""Copper Colored Kid") had been drinking at the Diamond Saloon. Sheriff Hunter recruited the help of Silverton's town marshal, D. C. "Clate" Ogsbury. As the two men walked down Greene Street, Wilkinson and Eskridge opened fire killing Ogsbury instantly. The two gang members escaped on foot. Meanwhile Kid Thomas, who apparently fired no shots, was rounding up their horses. He was apprehended near the stable and taken to jail. Once again, a mob took the law into its own hands. They dragged the black lad from jail and lynched him behind the old county building.

When Burt Wilkinson was turned in for a $2,500 reward by gang leader Ike Stockton, the mob ruled again. According to the *San Juan Herald*:

> "...a party of masked men suddenly appeared before the guards at the jail and overpowered both of them and the jailer, went into the jail and seizing Wilkinson, passed the noose about his neck and asked him if he had anything to say before his death. He replied, 'Nothing gentlemen, Adios!' He was perfectly composed to the very last, got up on a chair and assisted the vigilantes to hasten the hanging."

About a month later, Stockton was shot in Durango by Deputy Sheriff Jim Sullivan. The bullet shattered Stockton's knee. Following amputation of his leg, Stockton bled to death.

The following year, Silverton constructed a new "mob proof" jail, consisting of two steel cages placed in the center of the building. Each cage had four locks each and the outside door was solid iron with an immense 300 pound lock.

Fairplay's fateful "Tuesday Murder" occurred on April 3, 1879. The Bergh House (now the Fairplay Hotel) hired a fellow named Thomas M. Bennett to work on a drainage ditch that ran down the street in front of the hotel. John J. Hoover was upset over the progress being made on the ditch, which also passed in front of his billiard parlor. He had a drink or two and then walked into the hotel lobby where he found Bennett. Hoover uttered a few ornery words and then shot and killed Bennett. Hoover was jailed, tried, and sentenced to eight years in prison by Judge Thomas Bowen. Enraged by the light sentence, Fairplay citizens took the law into their own hands. They broke Hoover out of jail and then hanged him from the second story window of the courthouse until he was dead.

When Judge Bowen arrived at the courthouse the following morning, he found a noosed rope across his bench. Nearby, was a second rope tagged "for the district attorney." The message was well received, as both the judge and district attorney quickly left town in a cloud of dust.

In another incident, a drunken fellow named Sam Porter staggered on to the street bragging that he would kill the first man he saw. Unaware of the danger, John Carmody approached the drunk. Porter aimed, shot, and killed Carmody instantly. The citizens of Fairplay again took matters into their own hands. On the exterior wall of the jail they nailed a strut, and then tossed a noose over it. They slipped the noose around Porter's neck, and asked him if he had any last words. "Yes," he replied, "Pull!"

Fairplay's first official public hanging occurred on July 19, 1880. Cicero Simms killed John Johnson in a local barroom, after it appeared to witnesses that they were simply having an innocent spat. Johnson, who was respected and well-liked in the community, had been providing room and board for Simms. While awaiting trial for murder, Simms, who was a skinny lad, boasted that he was too light to be hanged. He was found guilty and sentenced to death by hanging. To avoid trouble during the ordeal, Simms' two brothers were temporarily locked up in jail. Eight hundred people, including many ladies, watched as Simms climbed on to the newly constructed gallows. His face was covered, and the noose placed around his neck. The trapdoor dropped and Simms hung motionless.

Simms' brothers were released from jail and they took custody of the body. According to one story, a stagecoach driver was stopped that evening by two men who had an injured companion. The driver, who was forced to take the three men to Leadville at gunpoint, later identified the injured man as Cicero Simms.

Tin Cup had the reputation of being one of the wildest towns in Colorado. During the boom years, 26 saloons and gambling houses operated night and day. Parlor girls were quick to fleece a miner of his gold dust. Shootings and drunkenness were commonplace.

Owners of the saloons "controlled" Tin Cup. In 1880 a marshal was hired to give the town the appearance of being orderly. He was informed that the first person he arrested would be his last. The second marshal was also a pawn. He did little more than round up drunks, disarm them, and then release them. By 1882 Tin Cup had become so lively that tough Harry Rivers was hired as marshal and instructed to maintain law and order. Rivers pushed his weight around, especially when he had too much to drink. Such was his undoing.

Charley LaTourette moved from Leadville to Tin Cup in 1879 and opened a saloon called The White House. Like many saloon owners, LaTourette (whose given name was Koertenius LaTourette) was a fairly tough individual himself. He was a Civil War veteran who had served in the 115th, 133rd, and 154th regiments, and following the war he was said to have killed a man who threatened him.

One night, Rivers had been drinking heavily. He saw that LaTourette was alone in the White House and decided to badger him. The marshal walked into the saloon and started hollering vile obscenities at LaTourette. Seeing that Rivers was drunk, the saloon owner ran him off. Business had been slow so LaTourette chose to lock up early and go home.

As he stepped from the boardwalk in front of his saloon and started up Main Street toward his house, which was only a block away, Rivers began to follow him. The marshal pulled out his pistol and began to fire some "close" shots past LaTourette. As Charley LaTourette neared his home, he realized that Emma, his wife, would open the front door when she heard the gate squeak, as she always did, and that she would be endangered. Before he reached the gate, LaTourette whirled, drew, and fired. Marshal Harry Rivers collapsed on the dirt street. He was dead.

Charley LaTourette was exonerated by a kangaroo court in Tin Cup, and then again by Judge Sprigg Shackleford in Gunnison. The story has been told many times with one man or the other as villain. In actually, Harry Rivers was an honest man who was a very good marshal when he was sober. Charley LaTourette was a businessman and a family man who lived at home with his wife and adopted daughter.

The year 1892 saw one of the great booms in Colorado history—at Creede. Silver strikes brought people in to the vicinity at a rate of nearly 300 per day. Speculators, miners, gamblers, and parlor girls poured into the over-crowded area. The population swelled to about 10,000, which included at one time or another such characters as Calamity Jane, Killarney Kate, Bat Masterson, and Soapy Smith. If ever there was a red-hot town, Creede was it.

The camp had a carnival-like atmosphere. Saloons and gambling halls popped up everywhere. Robert Newton "Bob" Ford, the man who killed Jesse James, wanted part of the action. With part of the reward money he received for killing James, he opened a dance hall and saloon called the Exchange. The structure was constructed of canvas over a wooden frame.

Not much is known about Ed O'Kelley (also called Ed O. Kelly or Ed Kelly). He was a native of Missouri (home state of Jesse and Frank James), and he married a relative of the notorious Younger brothers. He had acquired a reputation as being a hard case.

On June 8, 1892, Ed O'Kelley walked through the front door of Bob Ford's club, leveled his shotgun and blasted Ford. He died instantly. One of the buckshot drove a collar button into his throat. O'Kelley fled, but was arrested shortly thereafter in Pueblo. He was charged with murder and sentenced to life imprisonment. O'Kelley served only eight years, however, and was released in 1900. Four years later he was shot to death by an Oklahoma City policeman.

The best shots in the Old West were not always the notorious gunslingers. One happened to run a hardware store in Delta, Colorado. His name was W. Ray Simpson.

Tom McCarty, his brother Bill, and nephew Fred, had been casing the Farmers and Merchants Bank at Delta for several days. At

3:30 p.m. on September 7, 1893, while Fred remained with the horses behind the building, Tom and Bill entered the bank, drew, and shouted, "All hands up!" One of the cashiers yelled for help. Tom shoved a six-shooter into his ribs. While the brothers were filling a money sack, Fred ran inside to advise the others that a crowd was forming. More confusion occurred within the bank and the brothers opened fire. Andrew T. Blachly, a cashier was killed. The robbers exited through an attorney's office which was adjacent to the bank, and into the alley.

Most hardware merchants sold guns and shells, as did Ray Simpson. When he saw the commotion and heard the shots, he grabbed a rifle and shells, and loaded as he ran to his doorway. Meanwhile the McCartys mounted and rode through the alley to Third Street. When they came within sight, Ray Simpson took aim at Fred, and fired, shattering his left temple. Fred slumped in his saddle as his horse raced on. Simpson then drew a bead on Bill, and squeezed off another round. The shot knocked Bill out of his saddle and killed him instantly. Fred's body toppled from his horse a block down the street. Tom McCarty crouched low and never looked back. He headed north, then west toward Wells Gulch and points beyond.

Ray Simpson not only ended the outlaw careers of Bill and Fred McCarty, but without knowing it he may have also ended the bandit days of Tom McCarty. Tom was so shaken by the events, it is said, that he took seclusion in Montana as a sheepherder.

J. W. Hugus was one of the earliest merchants in Meeker, Colorado. His original general merchandise store was constructed with a framed false front that was painted a fresh white. Toward the rear of the store Hugus installed a cage and large safe. It became Meeker's first bank. In 1881, following a few years of prosperity, J. W. Hugus built an attractive two-story brick building into which he moved his store and bank. It was the scene of a badly bungled bank robbery on October 13, 1896. On that ill-fated day, three men rode into town with the intention of relieving the bank of all its money. It was their last ride.

George Law, a stout fellow with red hair and mustache, was the eldest. He was flanked by two men substantially younger. One was named Jim Shirley, and the other, barely old enough to carry a gun, was simply called "Kid." The trio tied their horses to a tree near the corner of the Hugus and Company building, and then ambled through the store and into the bank. With his revolver in hand, Law reached through the bars of the teller's cage frantically waving the gun at the cashier. Twice it accidently discharged. After cleaning out the vault, the robbers grabbed three hostages to shield themselves as they exited from the building. The street was empty. There was not a soul in sight. Obviously the gunshots from inside the bank had been heard by the townspeople. A man with a rifle peered from the shadows between two buildings. Jim Shirley opened fire and the man fell. The alarmed hostages wrestled free and ran. As soon as they did, well-hidden citizens opened fire on the robbers. "Kid" and Shirley were killed immediately. Law attempted to run, but he too was quickly dropped. He was badly wounded and would soon die.

The sack of money from the vault lay on the floor of the mercantile store, close to the bank door. During all of the commotion it had been totally forgotten by the bungling bandits. J. W. Hugus' money was saved. Law, Shirley, and the lad called "Kid" were laid to rest in the Meeker cemetery.

This crowd had gathered in the street five minutes after Bob Ford was shotgunned to death. *Denver Public Library, Western History Department.*

Jeff Milton foiled a train robbery attempt by the Alvod-Stiles gang. *Western History Collections, University of Oklahoma Library*

Chapter Forty-Three
The Alvord-Stiles Gang

At different times during his life, Burt Alvord rode on both sides of the badge, sometimes as an officer of the law, and other times as a fugitive on the run. As a youth, Alvord worked at the O. K. Corral in Tombstone, Arizona, where he supposedly witnessed the famous gunfight where Doc Holliday and the Earp brothers bested members of the Clanton faction. At age nineteen (in 1885), Alvord proved that he was handy with a pistol as he gunned down a fellow known as "Six-shooter Jim" in a Tombstone altercation. The following year, Alvord was hired as a deputy sheriff in Cochise County by newly elected Sheriff John Slaughter. Alvord was a congenial guy who enjoyed socializing, and he liked to drink, so he spent much time in the various saloons about town. By doing so, he rubbed elbows with a lot of tough guys and hard cases, and he seemed to have an insight as to where certain fugitives might be hiding out.

In May of 1888, Sheriff Slaughter and two deputies, Burt Alvord and Cesario Lucero tracked three Mexican train robbers into the Whetstone Mountains. The lawmen caught up with the "bandidos" at daybreak, and surprised them while they were still in their bedrolls. When the fugitives went for their guns, the officers opened fire. After one of the Mexicans was shot, the other two surrendered.

The following month, Slaughter, Alvord, and two others, tracked another group of outlaws to the Whetstone Mountains. The lawmen confronted the fugitives at dawn and another gunfight erupted. The officers, who were unscathed, killed one and wounded two of the bandits. One of the wounded men managed to escape.

Following his tenure as deputy sheriff of Cochise County, Burt Alvord spent some time in Mexico where he took part in a cattle rustling operation. Eventually, he returned to Arizona and became constable of Fairbank. His next position was that as constable of Willcox.

While constable of Willcox, Burt Alvord became more ruthless. Alvord had a dislike for cowboy Billy King. The feeling was mutual, but King tried to resolve their differences one day in a Willcox saloon by buying Alvord drinks at the bar. Alvord suggested that they step outside the back door so they could discuss the matter in private. When the two men were outside, Alvord drew his revolver and shot King in the head, dropping him where he stood.

From his position as constable of Willcox, Burt Alvord put together a gang of train robbers, known later as the Alvord-Stiles gang. Billy Stiles, his partner and main man, was hired by Alvord as a deputy constable. Stiles was shrewd and mean. William Larkin "Billy" Stiles, when just a youth, was said to have killed his father with a shotgun blast after which he fled to Mexico and remained there for several years. In addition to Alvord and Stiles, the gang included John Patterson, alias "Three-fingered" Jack Dunlap; two brothers, George and Louis Owens; Bravo Juan Yoas; Bob Brown; Matt Burts; and Bill Downing, (whose correct name may have been Jackson) who was also a deputy constable under Alvord.

The Alvord-Stiles gang was involved in several robberies. On September 9, 1899, the gang hit a Southern Pacific Railroad train near Cochise, Arizona. Bill Downing organized a posse to follow the robbers, and naturally led them on a wild-goose chase.

Whereas most train heists occurred on lonely sections of track, Alvord and Stiles masterminded one to occur in the town of Fairbank, where Alvord was previously a constable. Because they wore badges, Alvord and Stiles did not participate. For this endeavor, their gang consisted of "Three-fingered" Jack Dunlap, George Owens, Louis Owens, Bravo Juan Yoas, and Bob Brown.

Jeff Davis Milton was employed as an express messenger for Wells Fargo. He was formerly a Texas Ranger, deputy sheriff, and a range detective. He was an excellent marksman, long on guts, and had quite a reputation. It is said that when Milton was attacked by a grizzly bear, he shoved his revolver into the bear's mouth and blew out its brains. The truth of the story is speculation, but it does indicate Milton's toughness. Alvord and Stiles planned the Fairbank robbery for an evening when Milton was off-duty.

At dusk, on February 15, 1900, the outlaws waited outside of town for the incoming train to arrive. As it approached, they rode up to the depot. When the train stopped at the station, Jeff Milton stepped to the platform of the express car. He had swapped shifts with another employee. Not expecting any trouble, especially in town, he had left his pistol and shotgun inside the rail car. The gang opened fire, and one slug hit Milton's left arm. He stumbled for his shotgun as the bandits stormed the express car. Milton fired a blast. Eleven buckshot hit Dunlap in the side. Another blast caught Yoas in the buttocks. Milton then pitched the keys to the safe behind some boxes where they wouldn't be found. Moments later he passed out from his wound. The outlaws riddled the express car with rifle fire, but they were not prepared to "blow" the safe. Yoas turned and hightailed it away from the scene while the other bandits lifted the badly wounded Dunlap across his saddle, and then raced out of town as well. Because of the valor of Wells Fargo express messenger Jeff Milton, the robbery attempt was futile.

When Burt Alvord and Billy Stiles were exposed, they became fugitives of the law. They and their gang were tracked and eventually captured and taken to the jail at Tombstone. Stiles received preferential treatment when he agreed to confess, and was released as a "trustee." On April 8, 1900, Stiles asked jailer George Bravin if he could visit Alvord and the other gang members. His request was granted. As he left the cell, Billy Stiles pulled a pistol on Bravin and demanded the keys. When Bravin put up a struggle, Stiles shot him in the leg and then proceeded to release all of the prisoners.

Burton Mossman, the first captain of the newly organized Arizona Rangers, was intent on capturing outlaw and murderer Augustine Chacón. Chacón lived in Mexico where he was not wanted, but he had escaped from jail in Arizona while awaiting the hangman's noose for the murder of a Morenci storekeeper. Mossman knew that Mexican authorities would not extradite Chacón because he had no criminal record in his homeland. Burton Mossman concocted a clever plan to lure Chacón across the border. He knew that Burt Alvord had spent time in jail with Chacón and that they knew each other well. Somehow Mossman got word to Alvord and Stiles that they would receive a pardon if they could entice Chacón across the border where he could be captured. The fugitives agreed to do so. On the pretense of having a lucrative horse stealing deal, Alvord and Chacón crossed the border into Arizona where they were intercepted by Burton Mossman and Billy Stiles. Chacón was put into irons and subsequently hanged on November 23, 1902.

Alvord and Stiles wasted little time in getting back to their criminal ways and were once again wanted men. They decided to flee to Mexico where they thought they might be safer. Two Arizona Rangers pursued them into Mexico and located the outlaws at a place called Nigger Head Gap. A gunfight erupted and both Alvord and Stiles were wounded. Alvord was hit twice and ultimately surrendered. Despite taking a bullet in his arm, Stiles was able to escape.

Billy Stiles became a lawman again in Nevada. After he killed a man he was attempting to arrest (in 1908), the victim's twelve-year-old son shot and killed Stiles with two blasts from a shotgun. After spending two years in prison at Yuma, Arizona, Alvord was released. He later worked on the Panama Canal before he died in about 1910.

Tom Horn, whose gun was for hire. *Wild Horse Collection.*

Chapter Forty-Four
Tom Horn, Assassin

"Killing men is my specialty," Tom Horn once said, "I look at it as a business proposition, and I think I have a corner on the market." Horn was a cool, cold-blooded killer for hire. He was an assassin. When "employed" to dispatch a certain individual, Horn would often follow him, learn his habits, and then would complete the job, usually from ambush with a high-powered rifle. He was callous and felt no compassion for his prey. His trademark was to prop the heads of his victims up on small stones.

After receiving a whipping from his father for skipping school, fourteen-year-old Tom Horn ran away from his Missouri home. He worked his way west with jobs on the railroad, and as a stagecoach driver. In 1876, he became a civilian scout for the United States Army, a position which he kept for over a decade. During that time he was involved in the final capture of Geronimo. He then worked as a deputy sheriff for a while before joining Pinkerton as a railroad detective for the Union Pacific.

As cattle rustling activity increased across Wyoming, Horn

learned that several members of the Wyoming Stock Growers Association were looking for range detectives. In 1894, he signed on with the Swan Land and Cattle Company. Officially he was hired to break wild horses, but in reality he was hired for his gun. He subsequently worked for other cattle outfits as well. At some point in time, Horn and his employers probably realized that justice would be better served if a "guilty" party never reached the judge, as rustlers often received light sentences or were released for lack of evidence. It was during this time that Tom Horn became known as "the exterminator," for he gave his quarry little or no chance. For each assassination, Horn usually collected a fee of five or six hundred dollars.

The number of shootings that Horn was involved in is uncertain. Two occurred in Routt County, Colorado, during the year 1900. On the 8th of July, Matt Rash, known for his rustling activity, was gunned down by rifle fire after he stepped outside his cabin. With three bullets in his body, Rash crawled back inside his cabin and attempted to leave a note by dipping his finger in his own blood. When his body was found, so was an envelope upon which there were illegible markings. Later that year, on the 3rd of October, Horn returned to Routt County. This time his victim was a black rustler named Isom Dart. Again, Horn's method was the same. He ambushed Dart with his high-powered rifle during the early morning after the rustler and his companions stepped from their cabin. Isom Dart was struck down by a bullet to the head.

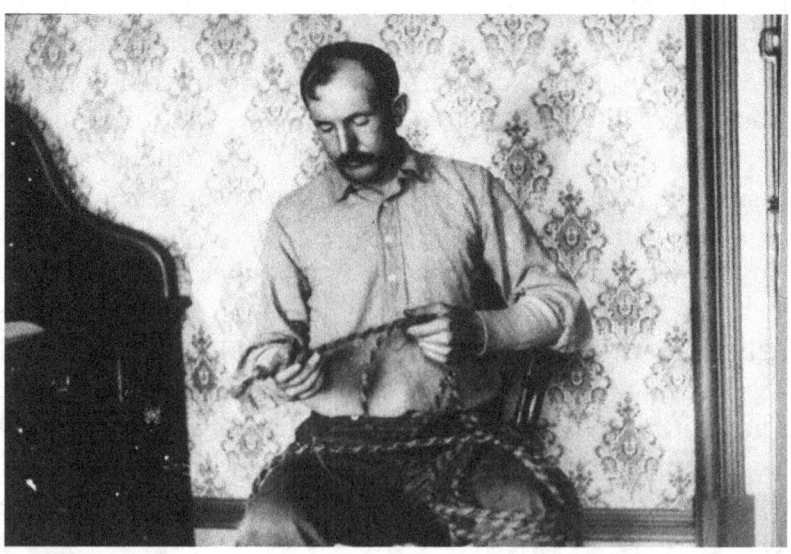

Tom Horn seems to be deep in thought as he braids a rope. *Wyoming State Museum.*

Cattle rancher John Coble, who owned a large spread near Laramie, Wyoming, hired Horn in 1901. Glendolene Kimmel, a local schoolteacher, caught Horn's eye, and the two became friends. Her family was involved in an ongoing feud with homesteader and sheepherder Kels P. Nickell. Horn decided to do away with Nickell as a favor to the Kimmels. The Nickell's farm faced the Powder River Road near Cheyenne. Horn positioned himself on a ridge where he had excellent vantage of the farm gate. Kels' fourteen-year-old son Willie hitched a team to the hay wagon and drove it toward the gate. He was wearing his father's hat and coat, and from a distance resembled the elder Nickell. When Willie stopped to open the gate, Horn shot him twice. The Nickell boy died instantly. Tom Horn was the suspected assassin, but there was no evidence upon which to prosecute him.

Several months later, an old acquaintance of Horn's, Joe LeFors, a deputy U. S. marshal, suggested that the two meet under the pretext that he knew of a "job" that Horn might be interested in. Horn traveled to LeFors' office, where the latter had plenty of liquor waiting. After several drinks, Horn began talking a little too much. When the conversation turned to the death of Willie Nickell, Horn made several incriminating statements. Unbeknownst to Horn, LeFors had a court stenographer hiding in a back room. She had taken a transcript of the entire conversation. Tom Horn was arrested and convicted based on the testimony. On a Cheyenne gallows, on November 20, 1903, he was hanged until he was dead.

Ben Thompson, when he was city marshal at Austin, Texas. *Archives Division, Texas State Library.*

Chapter Forty-Five
Vaudeville and Vengeance

Ben Thompson and John King Fisher, two of the Old West's most notorious gunfighters, met their demise on March 11, 1884, at San Antonio, Texas. Ben had nine wounds and King had thirteen. Ben Thompson supposedly participated in fourteen gunfights. John King Fisher once boasted that he had killed seven men "not counting Mexicans."

Thompson was a dapper dresser who occasionally attired himself with a long coat, stovepipe hat, and a cane. He was a gambler and former officer of the law. Fisher was a flashy dresser who often wore fringed shirts and crimson sashes. He operated on both sides of a tin star, hiding from it as a renowned rustler, or wearing it (as he was in 1884) as a deputy sheriff from Uvalde. Ben Thompson and John King Fisher were friends.

This story actually begins in 1880 when Jack Harris and Ben Thompson quarreled over a gambling incident. Harris, Joe Foster and Billy Simms were the owners of a San Antonio hot spot officially known as the Vaudeville Theatre and Gambling Saloon. For two years bitterness built between the men. Foster and Simms also were caught up in Harris' resentment for Thompson. On July 11, 1882, Ben Thompson, who was currently the Austin city marshal, entered the variety theatre. It was obvious that he intended to stir up a ruckus. When he realized that Harris was not there, he exited. Shortly thereafter, Thompson returned and lingered for a while before once again departing. As Ben walked out, Harris entered through another door. An employee advised Harris that Thompson had been "hanging around," and that he sensed trouble. Harris went straight for his shotgun. Meanwhile, Ben had stopped outside the front entrance to speak with Billy Simms, whom he had known for some time. Somebody dashed through the doorway, stating, "Jack has a gun!" As Thompson stepped back toward the front entrance he was confronted by Harris who leveled his weapon. Ben fired quickly, and missed, but his bullet ricocheted and slammed into Harris' chest. Harris turned and staggered up a flight of stairs before he collapsed. Later that night he died. Thompson surrendered to the authorities, was tried and acquitted. Although the incident occurred in San Antonio, he turned in his badge as city marshal of Austin.

In March of 1884, John King Fisher had been in Austin on official business, and wanted to see old friend Ben Thompson before he departed. After visiting several bars together, Ben decided to accompany King as far as San Antonio on King's return trip to Uvalde. A play was appearing at the Turner Hall Opera House which Ben wanted to see. King agreed that they should attend, and the friends left for San Antonio. Later that night, after the play, the two decided to party a little longer. They proceeded on to the Vaudeville Theatre and Gambling Saloon where they had a drink at the bar. The late-night variety show was about to begin upstairs so Fisher and Thompson adjourned to a private box to watch the performance. They were joined by Harris' former partners, Joe Foster and Billy Simms, and a club bouncer named Jacob Coy. Everything was fine until Thompson's conversation turned to Jack Harris' death, at which time Fisher stood, indicating that they should leave before any trouble started. When Foster began to speak, Thompson jammed his six-shooter into the saloon owner's mouth. Coy leaped forward and grabbed the cylinder. Ben withdrew his revolver. Suddenly gunfire erupted. Fisher and Thompson were shot down by a barrage of lead. King was never able to draw, and Ben who already had his pistol in hand, only fired once. Foster was shot in the leg, probably by Thompson's single shot. Joe Foster died following the amputation of his leg. It has always been suspected that the shotgun and rifle fire which felled Thompson and Fisher came from the adjacent box, and the weapons of Canada Bill, a gambler; Harry Tremaine, a vaudeville performer; and a bartender named McLaughlin. Ben Thompson and John King Fisher were too adept with their revolvers to have been massacred in such fashion by the other three occupants of their box.

Harry Tracy terrorized the Northwest until his demise in 1902. *Denver Public Library, Western History Department.*

Chapter Forty-Six
Wanted: Harry Tracy

One of the most elusive outlaws in the annals of the Old West was Harry Tracy. It wasn't that he was necessarily difficult to track for he often left a recognizable trail, but he would often elude his pursuers at the last moment as they closed in attempting to capture him. On those occasions when he was taken into custody, and jailed, the slippery Tracy would find a way to escape. No jail could hold him.

Harry Tracy, whose real name was Harry Severns, made his first jail break in 1897 following his arrest in Utah on burglary charges. He escaped with a companion, David Lant, and the two headed to Brown's Hole, Colorado to lie low. Brown's Hole, with its maze of gulches and gullies, was a popular hideout for outlaws. On March 1, 1898, a posse led by Valentine Hoy ventured into Brown's Hole. The rough terrain allowed Tracy, Lant, and a fellow bandit named Swede Johnson, to hold off the entire posse. During the gunfight that ensued, Tracy shot Valentine Hoy through the heart. The posse retreated which allowed the fugitives to escape. Tracy and Lant rode east. The posse continued its pursuit. They finally cornered the duo and forced them to surrender. Tracy and Lant were taken to the jail at Hahns Peak to await trial for the murder of Valentine Hoy.

Hahns Peak had a tough and determined sheriff named Charles Neiman. One night, Tracy and Lant tricked and overpowered Neiman and escaped leaving the badly beaten and unconscious sheriff behind. They felt certain that Neiman would be out for a long time allowing them to make good their escape. They stole two horses and rode out of Hahns Peak.

The resilient Sheriff Neiman regained consciousness and set out after the escapees. Realizing that the fugitives were not dressed for the cold weather, the sheriff was sure that they would try to hold up the Hot Sulfur Springs stagecoach. Neiman and a deputy boarded the coach in Hahns Peak with the hope that his prediction would be correct. It was. Several hours later the stage was held up. When they opened the coach door, the astonished Tracy and Lant were looking down the barrels of two shotguns. The fugitives were returned to the jailhouse. This time the outlaws decided to sleep during the days in order to spend their nights hollering, screaming, and generally making as much noise as possible in order to keep the townspeople awake. It worked. Within days they were transferred to the Pitkin County jail in Aspen. Once again they escaped after almost beating a guard to death.

David Lant disappeared. Some say he was killed by Tracy, but there seems to be no evidence to substantiate that claim. Harry Tracy fled to Oregon and seemed to abandon his criminal activity for about a year. There he married Rose Merrill and the couple lived in a small home alongside the Willamette River, near Portland. Tracy didn't settle down for long, however. Accompanied by his new cohort, Rose's brother Dave Merrill, Tracy embarked on a series of robberies in Oregon and Washington during 1900 and 1901. Merrill was captured, and in return for a light sentence, supposedly tipped off the authorities as to the whereabouts of Tracy. Harry Tracy and Dave Merrill were convicted and sentenced to the Oregon State Penitentiary at Salem.

At 7:00 a.m. on June 2, 1902, Harry Tracy and Dave Merrill staged a daring and dramatic prison break. While covered by the guns of guards Frank B. Ferrell and Frank Girard, a line of prisoners moved toward the foundry to begin the work day. Abruptly, Tracy bolted the line and grabbed two short barreled rifles from a packing crate that had apparently been smuggled into the prison. He tossed one of the rifles to Merrill, and then killed Ferrell with a single shot through his throat. Girard dashed for cover. When an inmate tried to stop Tracy from pursuing Girard, Tracy shot him in the stomach.

Merrill grabbed a ladder and sprinted toward the prison's outer wall while Tracy provided cover. Tower guard, S. R. T. Jones, momentarily exchanged fire with Tracy before he was slain by one of Tracy's bullets. Tracy wounded another guard, Duncan Ross. The convicts scaled the wall and dropped down on the outside. In hot pursuit, another guard, B. F. Tiffany, scrambled to the top of the wall where the ladder was located. Tracy spotted him and fired. Wounded, Tiffany fell outside the prison wall. Using the dying guard as a shield, Tracy and Merrill backed away from the prison into a heavily wooded area. The convicts fled to the north where they eventually crossed the Washington state line.

About the first of July, near Napavine, Washington, Mary A. Waggoner and her twelve-year-old son discovered a decomposed bullet-riddled body in a wooded area north of town. According to a coroner's ruling, the body belonged to Dave Merrill. There was speculation that Tracy had waited for the appropriate time to do away with Merrill, knowing that his brother-in-law had betrayed him prior to his arrest in Oregon. Merrill's body was returned to the Oregon State Penitentiary for burial in the prison cemetery. The coroner's ruling was refuted years later by one of Merrill's relatives who claimed that family members received letters from the fugitive during the ensuing years.

Harry Tracy became the object of a widespread manhunt. Tracy reaped havoc on his pursuers. On a drizzly afternoon, on July 3, 1902, near Bothell, he surprised a five-man posse by opening fire on them at close range. L. J. Nelson was dropped as a shot nicked his head. A news reporter, L. B. Sefret, who was along for the "scoop," was also wounded. Two more slugs hit a deputy named Raymond who died instantly. Tracy shot another deputy named Jack Williams three times, and then fled.

Later that evening, another posse led by Sheriff Edward Cudihee tracked Tracy to a residence where he had taken refuge. As the posse closed in, another gunfight erupted. Two more deputies lay dead, as the slippery Tracy once more dashed to freedom.

For two months, following his escape from the Oregon State Penitentiary, lawmen chased Tracy for nearly five hundred miles. The trail would soon end, however. While holed up in a barn at the ranch of Eugene Eddy, west of Davenport and just south of the settlement of Creston, in Lincoln County, a posse closed in on the outlaw. Tracy grabbed his rifle and dashed for cover behind a large rock in a nearby field. A continuous barrage of lead kept Tracy pinned behind the rock, which offered poor protection. He took one slug in his right leg, and then another. He was still able to hold the posse off until sundown. During the silence of the following morning, the posse cautiously moved in. Behind the rock they found Tracy's corpse. Obviously believing that his situation was hopeless, Harry Tracy had shot himself in the head.

Dallas Stoudenmire, El Paso city marshal in 1861. *Archives Division, Texas State Library.*

Chapter Forty-Seven
El Paso's Fighting Marshal

The early 1880s were turbulent years in the growing border town of El Paso, Texas. City fathers wanted to hire a lawman that would put the "fear of God" into the city's growing criminal element. They wanted a man with a widespread reputation as an expert gunman. They found him. Dallas Stoudenmire was an imposing figure who carried a brace of six-guns under his coat, in leather-lined pockets. He also carried a small snub-nosed revolver as a backup weapon. Stoudenmire had fought for the Confederate Army during the Civil War, and several years later was a Texas Ranger. On April 10, 1881, Stoudenmire was sworn in as city marshal of El Paso. Our story, however, begins a few months earlier.

Prior to the appointment of Dallas Stoudenmire, El Paso had two short-term marshals who would later participate in gunfights with Stoudenmire. Toward the end of 1880, George Campbell served for a few weeks, but received no salary. Campbell assumed that the only way he could endure would be to live off the monies he collected from arrest fees. In an effort to show town officials the importance of his position as city marshal, he persuaded some of El Paso's biggest troublemakers to shoot up the town. They riddled the houses of the mayor and an alderman with bullets. When officials found out that Campbell was behind the trouble, the Texas Rangers were called in. They found the whole matter quite humorous and refused to arrest Campbell. George Campbell was allowed to resign. A former city deputy, Bill Johnson, was appointed as interim marshal. During the months while Johnson served in this capacity, he hoped to receive a permanent commission as El Paso's city marshal. The hiring of Stoudenmire precipitated an unwarranted resentment by Johnson for the new marshal.

Four days after taking office, Stoudenmire was having lunch at the Globe Restaurant (that was owned by his brother-in-law, Doc Cummings) when he spotted trouble brewing outside on El Paso Street. Tensions had built following the recent murder of two Mexicans, and some Anglos and Mexicans were shouting harsh words at each other. Stoudenmire watched as town constable Gus Krempkau, known to be a friend of the Mexicans, was approached by George Campbell and John Hale. As they quarreled, Hale drew his pistol and shot Krempkau. With his revolvers drawn, Stoudenmire charged out the front door of the Globe Restaurant. He fired a shot at Hale that missed Hale, but accidently hit a Mexican bystander that was scrambling for cover. Stoudenmire's second shot found its mark, striking Hale in the head. Campbell, who was inebriated, had drawn his six-shooter and was waving it around shouting that it wasn't his fight. Krempkau, who was badly wounded and dying, had drawn his revolver and began firing at Campbell. One shot struck him in the wrist, another in the foot. Stoudenmire turned and shot Campbell in the stomach. The shooting stopped. Campbell died the following day, as did the Mexican bystander.

The citizens of El Paso were extremely impressed by the effectiveness of their new city marshal. Some, however, viewed Stoudenmire as a threat. They hatched a plan to dispose of the new marshal, and then enticed Bill Johnson to carry it out. He was happy to do so. Just three days after the shootout with Campbell and Hale, while walking along with his brother-in-law Doc Cummings, Stoudenmire was ambushed by Johnson who was perched high on a pile of bricks at the construction site of the State National Bank. One bullet wounded Stoudenmire in his heel. Stoudenmire and Cummings opened fire on Johnson, pumping eight slugs into his body. Johnson would die. More shots flew toward Stoudenmire from Frank Manning's Saloon. The fighting marshal whirled and charged the saloon with his six-shooters blazing. This act of daring startled the gunmen and they turned and fled. Stoudenmire was certain that the Manning brothers were responsible for the attempt on his life, but he had no proof.

The delight that city officials had for their new city marshal soon turned sour. Dallas Stoudenmire began to drink excessively. Occasionally, when he did so, he would fire his revolvers into the sky, sometimes in the middle of the night. As his alcoholism increased, so did his unfaithfulness to his wife Belle. Under pressure, Stoudenmire resigned his post. He was replaced by a former deputy, shotgun wielding Jim Gillett. Gillett, like Stoudenmire, was a former Texas Ranger and a crack marksman.

The Manning brothers, Doc, Jim, John, and Frank, were a rough bunch. They once vowed that they wouldn't shave until the South rose again. Their feud with Dallas Stoudenmire heightened following an incident in which Jim Manning and David King shot and killed Doc Cummings, after Cummings had belligerently challenged Manning to a fight. Cummings had willed the Globe Restaurant to his brother-in-law, so Stoudenmire assumed the day-to-day chore of operating the eating establishment.

The detestation between Stoudenmire and the Mannings culminated on September 18, 1882, at Frank Manning's Saloon. While Jim Manning was outside looking for his brother Frank, Dallas Stoudenmire forced a showdown with Doc Manning. As they approached each other during heated words, a bystander, J. W. Jones stepped between the two foes. As he was doing so, both men drew their revolvers. Jones was standing in the path of Stoudenmire's gun enabling Manning to get off the first shot. The bullet struck Stoudenmire in the chest and arm causing him to drop his revolver as he reeled backward. Doc Manning grabbed Stoudenmire and the two wrestled their way through the front door and onto El Paso Street. Stoudenmire was able to grasp his snub-nosed revolver, and he pumped a slug into Manning's arm. As the two men continued to grapple, Jim Manning burst on scene with his six-shooter in hand. He fired two shots, the second of which entered Stoudenmire's head behind his left ear. Dallas Stoudenmire, the man who had become a local legend, collapsed and died.

Hat Creek Stage Station in 1875. *Wyoming State Museum.*

Chapter Forty-Eight
The Deadwood Stage: Easy Prey

    Not much prospecting occurred in the Black Hills of Dakota Territory prior to 1874 because of fear of the Sioux Indians. When a rich strike was made that year in Deadwood Gulch, hundreds of gold seekers flocked to the area, and they did so in violation of the Sioux Treaty of 1868. Most arrived via the Union Pacific Railroad into Cheyenne, the nearest railhead to Deadwood. Nearly overnight, Deadwood became a busy bustling boomtown. In December of 1875, the Wyoming Territorial Legislature passed a bill that authorized the establishment of a stagecoach line between Cheyenne and Deadwood. Financiers were unwilling to invest money into such an enterprise, however, because of the existing threat of the Sioux.

    The following January, Frank Yates and his father-in-law, Captain W. H. Brown, subcontracted for the express route. The Cheyenne and Black Hills Stage, Mail and Express Line was established. Within days, F. D. Yates & Company was acquired by Gilmer & Salisbury. Immediately they ordered thirty heavy-duty Concord coaches, six-hundred well-bred horses, and one-hundred sets of stage harness. On April 3, 1876, the first three Concord coaches rolled out of Cheyenne. The Cheyenne and Black Hills Stage Company had hardly commenced business when outlaw and Indian attacks began.

"Stuttering" Brown, a Gilmer & Salisbury employee, was murdered and robbed along the Old Woman branch of the Cheyenne River. Although there were initially many Sioux raids, many people believed that his attackers were not Indian. As more prospectors pushed into the Black Hills, the Sioux attacks intensified. They ravaged freight caravans and rustled their mules. Three of Gilmer & Salisbury's stage stations between Fort Laramie and Custer City were stormed, the buildings torched and the stock stolen.

Within days, the Battle of the Little Big Horn occurred. General George Custer and 256 cavalrymen were killed by the Sioux on June 25, 1876. Following the massacre, Congress opened the Black Hills to settlement by repudiating the Sioux Treaty. Hundreds of troops were brought in to safeguard the area and to patrol the stage line which, at that time, was extended on to Deadwood. The troops were not much of a deterrent, however, as Indian and outlaw attacks continued. North of Fort Laramie, two mail carriers were found murdered and scalped. Indians were quickly blamed, but it was soon discovered that only registered mail had been stolen. It became evident that some of the crimes that had been blamed on the Sioux may have actually been committed by white men. On one occasion, a stage station between Cheyenne and Fort Laramie was attacked by a band of wild, war-painted "savages." They opened the corral and rustled the horses. Later, it was discovered that a "duplicate" key had been used to unlock the corral gate.

Stagecoach driver Johnny Slaughter was shot and killed during an attempted stage robbery two miles south of Deadwood on March 26,

The last Black Hills stagecoach prepares to leave Cheyenne on February 19, 1887. *Wyoming State Museum.*

1877. Another attempted stagecoach robbery occurred on the 1st of June, eight miles north of Hat Creek Station when a coach was halted, but the bandits were driven away by heavy gunfire from the passengers inside. Two outlaws with blackened faces hijacked a strongbox on the 14th of June twenty-five miles north of Hat Creek Station. Another strongbox was raided on the 26th of June ten miles north of the Cheyenne River. In this incident a stage driver was shot in the side, and the passengers were looted of their cash and jewelry. This robbery and others were later attributed to the Sam Bass gang when a former member, Robert McKemma, confessed to the shooting and other robberies.

Holdups became so frequent that on the 18th of July the same southbound coach was hit twice near the Cheyenne River, and the northbound was struck as well, just a few miles away. The following month, Gilmer & Salisbury began installing a new, heavier steel strongbox, with a lock that they claimed couldn't be opened in less than six days. It also proved to be vulnerable. When a stage pulled into Canyon Springs Station it was met by a barrage of gunfire. One guard was killed and another wounded, and the strongbox that supposedly couldn't be opened in less than six days was smashed open and the outlaws escaped with $27,000 in loot.

Soon after the stage line was extended on to Deadwood, competition arrived. The Western Stage Company opened a new line from Sidney, Nebraska to Deadwood, Dakota Territory. The coaches on this line were also easy prey for highwaymen. Gilmer & Salisbury soon purchased the line from Western Stage in order to eliminate competition in the Black Hills.

As much gold was being shipped from Deadwood, and the stagecoaches were an easy target for bandits, Gilmer & Salisbury knew that something had to be done to help solve the problem. They decided to build an "armored" coach. Bullet-proof steel plates lined the interior. Four gun ports were drilled through the steel which could be manned by crack riflemen, and a steel safe was bolted to the floor. The vehicle was dubbed "The Iron Clad," but was officially named the "Johnny Slaughter," in memory of the slain stage driver. The bullet-proof coach was primarily used on the Cheyenne run, but every so often it was needed on the route to Sidney.

On one occasion, $120,000 in gold bars was shipped via "The Iron Clad" to Sidney. The shipment arrived intact, but "disappeared" before it could be loaded on to a Union Pacific freight car. The armored coach had arrived too late for the gold to be transferred as scheduled to the departing eastbound train. Stage employees guarded the shipment through the night. The following morning the shipment was moved to the depot freight room to be loaded on the next train. When the time came to transfer the shipment to a railcar, it was gone. It had been taken through a hole in the floor, out a crawl space, and then loaded on to a wagon that had also disappeared. The incident occurred on March 9, 1880. "The Iron Clad" had done its part. The gold shipment had been officially signed over to the Union Pacific Railroad.

Protection from the military was minimal, and the shotgun riders of Gilmer & Salisbury could only do so much, so Black Hills gold miners decided it was time to help. They formed a posse of vigilantes to provide effective law enforcement in the area. It wasn't long before they caught three of the Canyon Springs bandits. The outlaws were lynched on the spot. As a warning to others, a sign was affixed atop their common grave:

> Here lies the body [sic] of Allen, Curry, and Hall.
> Like other thieves they had their rise, decline and fall;
> On yon pine tree they hung til [sic]dead,
> And here they found a lonely bed.
> We're bound to stop this business, or hang you to a man,
> For we've hemp and hands enough in town to swing the whole damn clan.

More hangings followed. The armored coach, and the vigilantes, certainly discouraged the highwaymen. Outlaw activity became very minimal.

Eventually, the gold rush peaked. As the placer operations tapered off, quartz mining quickly replaced it. Once railroads penetrated the area, the Deadwood Stage and others became less useful. During their heyday, however, Gilmer & Salisbury coaches logged over 5,000 miles per day from Utah to the Canadian border.

Members of the Wild Bunch at Fort Worth, Texas in 1901. Front row (left to right) Harry Longabaugh (the Sundance Kid), Ben Kilpatrick, and Robert Leroy Parker (Butch Cassidy). Back row (left to right) Will Carver and Harvey (Kid Curry) Logan. *Wyoming State Museum.*

Chapter Forty-Nine
Butch Cassidy and the Wild Bunch

In 1882, at the age of sixteen, Robert Leroy (George) Parker left home to ride with a rustler named Mike Cassidy. Parker adopted his friend's name, and used the alias of George Cassidy. How he further obtained the nickname of "Butch" is open for speculation. Some say he received the handle from Mike Cassidy, while others believe that he acquired the name while working in a Rock Springs butcher shop.

Although Butch Cassidy participated in an aborted train robbery in 1887, his first successful robbery was probably the San Miguel Valley Bank in Telluride, Colorado. Cassidy and a partner, Al Hainer, bought a ranch in Fremont County in 1890, possibly with some of the proceeds from the robbery. Cassidy, who always liked fine horses, and Hainer "appeared" to be in the ranching business. It wasn't long before two Big Horn ranchers traced some of their stolen horses to Cassidy and Hainer. The duo was arrested near Auburn, Wyoming, found to be not guilty, and released. In June of 1894, Butch Cassidy was arrested by Deputy Sheriff Robert Calverly, at Star Valley, Wyoming. Cassidy was charged with stealing sixty horses from rancher John Chapman. This time Cassidy was found guilty and sentenced to a term in the Wyoming State Penitentiary.

Although he was arrested several different times, this would be his only conviction. It was also the only time Cassidy served a prison sentence.

Upon his release in January of 1896, following a pardon by Governor William Richards, Butch Cassidy formed the notorious Wild Bunch. Among those who rode with Cassidy were Harvey Logan, known also as "Kid Curry;" Harry Longabaugh, better known as "Sundance," or "the Sundance Kid;" Elzy Lay; Ben Kilpatrick; "Flat Nose" George Curry (sometimes spelled Currie); Will Carver; Lonie Logan; Harvey Ray; Walt Punteney; and Tom O'Day.

Harvey Logan was to become one of the most wanted men in the United States. While teenagers, brothers Harvey, Lonie and Johnny Logan, accompanied by an adopted cousin Bob Lee, left their Missouri home and traveled west to become cowboys. It wasn't long before the four turned their attention to cattle rustling. For a while they rode with the rustler gang of "Flat Nose" George Curry. It was during this time that Harvey Logan acquired the sobriquet "Kid Curry."

While still a teenager, Harry Alonzo Longabaugh was convicted of stealing a horse. He was sentenced to the state penitentiary at Laramie. The "pen" was full to capacity, however, so Longabaugh served his time at the Crook County jail at Sundance, and furthermore that is why he was dubbed "the Sundance Kid." After his release, Longabaugh continued to stay in trouble. He escaped from the law following a train

Butch Cassidy during a short stint at the Wyoming State Penitentiary. *Wyoming State Museum.*

hold-up in Malta, Montana, and was a wanted man. Butch Cassidy and the Sundance Kid had met years earlier at the Hole-in-the-Wall, during Cassidy's rustling days. Sundance was eager to join Cassidy's gang.

William Ellsworth Lay (known as "Elzy") married early and worked as a cowboy until he connected with Butch Cassidy. When he helped Cassidy rob a payroll in Castle Gate, Utah, in April of 1897, his wife packed up and left him. Elzy was close to Cassidy and supposedly masterminded several of the Wild Bunch robberies.

Elzy wasn't the only gang member to have a woman in his life. Butch Cassidy carried on a longtime romance with his Lander, Wyoming sweetheart, Mary Boyd. They probably would have married had Cassidy not chosen his criminal life-style. It is believed that after she married a Lander cowboy and became Mary Boyd Rhodes, she still continued to see Cassidy when he traveled into the area. Ben Kilpatrick and Will Carver each had lengthy romances with prostitute Laura Bullion. Later, the Sundance Kid's lady love was the storied Etta Place. She was a former schoolteacher whose morality was nebulous. Etta was adventurous, and some say an excellent marksman.

The Hole-in-the-Wall, located in southwestern Johnson County, Wyoming, was a popular hideout for the Wild Bunch and other desperados of the era. A passage, which could be well-protected, led through an opening in the red stone cliffs into a valley which was surrounded by foothills. The secluded valley, with its rugged terrain, hidden canyons, and grassy mountain pockets which could be used for grazing, made the Hole-in-the-Wall an ideal hideaway for the Wild Bunch.

Another hideout used by the gang was the Robbers' Roost in Emery County, Utah. There is evidence that they spent the winter of 1896-97 there, lying low with some of their women. Elzy Lay's new bride Maude Davis was rumored to be there, as was Etta Place, who might have been Butch Cassidy's girlfriend at the time.

The Wild Bunch was a tag that Wyoming newspapers had given Cassidy's gang. In actuality, Cassidy made it a point to avoid needless violence. The outlaw leader often said, "I have never killed a man." Such was not the case with Harvey Logan who dispatched many. "Flat Nose" George Curry stated that he robbed trains "just for the fun of it."

At high noon on April 21, 1897, the Rio Grande Western arrived into Castle Gate, Utah from Salt Lake City. Aboard was the payroll for the Pleasant Valley Coal Company, which totaled over $8,000. E. L. Carpenter, the company paymaster, and T. W. Lewis, a clerk, walked from the Pleasant Valley office to the railroad depot, a distance of approximately fifty yards. They signed for the payroll, and then toted it back toward the office. As they neared their building, Butch Cassidy daringly stepped out in front of the two men and ordered them to drop the sacks. Cassidy passed the payroll sacks up to Elzy Lay, who was on horseback. He then turned and galloped down the street. Cassidy quickly mounted and followed. As they reached the edge of town, the duo cut the telegraph wire, and in so doing they unknowingly dropped a portion of the loot. They rode until they reached a fresh pair of horses, which helped them outdistance the posse that was in pursuit.

On June 28, 1897, at Belle Fourche, South Dakota, several members of the Wild Bunch (excluding Cassidy) staged a bungled robbery on the Butte County Bank. Historians generally agree that the raid was probably performed by Longabaugh, Harvey and Lonie Logan, O'Day, Punteney, and "Flat Nose" George Curry. The exterior of the bank had large plate glass windows. When bank employees and customers were ordered to raise their hands, they did so in plain view of passersby on the street, which alerted the townspeople. Several shots were fired. The gang aborted the robbery and fled leaving $30,000 untouched in the bank safe. Tom O'Day was captured and jailed. The other five escaped. Over three months later, Curry, Harvey Logan, and Sundance were captured near Lavinia, Montana by Lawman Bill Smith and a bounty hunter. The duo surprised the outlaws by creeping between them and their horses. Several shots were fired and Curry took a bullet in one arm. When they realized they were cut off from their horses the gang members surrendered. They were taken to the jail at Deadwood, South Dakota, where they joined Tom O'Day. All were charged with robbing the bank at Belle Fourche. The four escaped from jail on the last day of October when they overpowered the jailer and his wife. They dashed to the edge of town, where saddled mounts awaited them, and then fled to safety. Several months later, O'Day and Punteney were arrested and charged with the robbery of the Butte County Bank. They stood trial but were acquitted.

Many bank and train robberies were attributed to the Wild Bunch. They were probably responsible for most, although some remain in question. Another topic for debate is exactly which gang members carried out certain raids. Could the same gang members rob a train in Wyoming, and then twenty-one days later rob a bank in Nevada? Many uncertainties exist with regard to the Wild Bunch.

At 2:30 a.m. on June 2, 1899, near Wilcox, Wyoming, a gang

member straddled the railroad track, swinging a warning lantern which brought the westbound Union Pacific train to a stop. The gang separated the express car from the rest of the train, and then proceeded to demolish it with dynamite. Once they had cleaned out the contents of the safes, the gang rode north and split up. Three days later, while camping near the Red Fork of the Powder River, Harvey Logan, "Flat Nose" George Curry, the Sundance Kid, and possibly Butch Cassidy and Harvey Ray, were surprised by a posse that was led by Sheriff Joe Hazen from Douglass. Logan grabbed his rifle and shot Hazen in the stomach. Bullets flew in several directions before the outlaws were able to flee. The group made their way to the Emery Burnaugh ranch on Muddy Creek Road, north of Lander. There is a lonely gravesite on the ranch which descendants of Emery Burnaugh say belongs to one of the Wild Bunch who died shortly after the Hazen killing from wounds received during the shoot-out. Speculation is that it is the resting place of Harvey Ray. On August 29, 1900, slightly over 100 miles west of Wilcox, the Wild Bunch robbed another Union Pacific train. This one was near Tipton. It was clearly a carbon copy of the Wilcox heist. In fact, Wells Fargo employee Ernest C, Woodcock was the express messenger who was victimized in both robberies.

After the Tipton raid, the Union Pacific beefed up its forces. They hired a special posse which could be whisked by rail to the scene of a robbery, from where they would be on the culprit's trail within hours.

Following the robbery of the Great Northern Coast Flyer at Exeter, Montana, in July of 1901, the Wild Bunch split up and headed in different directions. Butch Cassidy began to feel the heat. It was time for an extended vacation. Cassidy, Sundance, and Longabaugh's sweetheart Etta Place, traveled to New York, and then sailed to South America. They established a cattle ranch in Argentina which they operated for a few years until Etta developed appendicitis in 1907. Sundance escorted her to a hospital at Denver, Colorado. He then returned to South America and rejoined Cassidy. The two moved on to Bolivia.

On November 3, 1908, Butch and Sundance robbed an Aramayo mining conglomerate mule train which was loaded with bullion. Three days later after traveling to San Vicente, a youth recognized a stolen mule and immediately informed authorities. Bolivian soldiers responded and surrounded the home where the duo was staying. The Bolivian commander ordered the two outlaws to surrender. Sundance shot the capitan, and the two barricaded themselves inside their room.

Desperately needing ammunition, Sundance made a dash for the pack mules shortly after dark. As he returned, Longabaugh was gunned down by soldiers' bullets. Cassidy dashed from the house and dragged his badly wounded comrade inside. A hail of lead continued to bombard the building.

Basically, historians have written three versions to the outcome of this story. One version indicates that the outlaws never lived to see the following morning. Another indicates that after Longabaugh's death, Cassidy managed to escape and eventually returned to the United States. A third has both Butch and Sundance fleeing to the States, where they concealed their identity and "lived happily ever after."

Evidence indicates that Cassidy, under the identity of William Thadeus Phillips, may have returned to the Lander, Wyoming area visiting such acquaintances as his former sweetheart Mary Boyd, while hunting for loot that the Wild Bunch buried years earlier. Phillips, who claimed to be a mechanical engineer from Des Moines, Iowa, and his wife Gertrude lived in Spokane, Washington, from 1910 until he died of cancer in 1937 at the county poor farm. Other evidence, and Butch's sister refute the possibility. Following the 1991 exhumation of the two "unnamed" bodies from the San Vicente cemetery, DNA tests ruled out

Harry Longabaugh (the Sundance Kid) and Etta Place prior to their departure for South America. *Wyoming State Museum.*

the possibility that they were Butch and Sundance. Their demise is still in question.

Lonie Logan had died earlier, on February 28, 1900, at Dodson, Missouri, when a posse led by Pinkerton detective Bill Sayles cornered Logan behind his aunt's home where a gun battle occurred. Pinned down with nowhere to go, Logan reloaded, and then made one final desperate dash for freedom. He met a barrage of lead, collapsed, and died instantly.

"Flat Nose" George Curry met his death less than two months later at Castle Gate, Utah, on April 17, 1900. A posse led by Sheriffs Jesse Tyler and William Preece chased Curry on horseback, for several miles at close range, during which many shots were exchanged. One finally hit its mark and Curry fell from his saddle. Bleeding heavily, he managed to take cover behind some rocks. After a long period of quiet, the posse cautiously moved in. They found Curry propped against a rock, with his rifle in his hands. He was dead.

Ben Kilpatrick and Laura Bullion were captured in St. Louis, Missouri, on November 5, 1901, with a large amount of stolen currency in their possession. Bullion was sentenced to, and served, a five year term in prison. Kilpatrick was imprisoned at the federal penitentiary in Atlanta, Georgia, where he served a term until February of 1912. The following month he and a former cell-mate, Ole Beck, attempted to rob a Southern Pacific train in Texas. While Beck held the train's engineer and fireman at bay, Kilpatrick raided the express car. As he crouched to pick up a package, Kilpatrick was clobbered with a mallet by express messenger Trousdale. He continued to strike the outlaw until he was dead. When Beck headed back to the express car to see what the delay was, he was shot to death by Trousdale.

Harvey Logan ("Kid Curry") was captured in Knoxville, Tennessee, on December 13, 1901, following a pool room brawl and a shootout in which he wounded three policemen. The Knoxville jail wouldn't hold the clever Logan, however. From the binding wire on a broom, he made a lasso which he used to snare a guard by the neck. With the guard's keys he unlocked his cell and escaped. Following a futile train robbery near Parachute, Colorado, in June of 1904, several robbers were cornered by a posse near the town of Rifle. During the shoot-out which ensued, one of the outlaws was badly wounded and subsequently took his own life. He was later identified as Harvey Logan. Others disagreed with the identification. At any rate, Harvey Logan was never heard from again.

During this time Elzy Lay was serving a life term at the New Mexico Territorial Prison. Following a train robbery at Twin Mountains on July 11, 1899, while riding with the Black Jack Ketchum gang, Lay was wounded twice by a posse but managed to escape. He holed up in an isolated cabin to allow his wounds to heal. The following month he was discovered by another posse, knocked unconscious and taken into custody. On January 10, 1906, Elzy Lay was pardoned for helping to calm a prison riot. Elzy never returned to his criminal ways. In 1909 he remarried, raised two daughters, and eventually died on November 10, 1934, in Los Angeles, of natural causes.

Many fearless men rode with the Wild Bunch. They terrorized banks and trains in many states. In doing so they wrote a graphic chapter in the chronicles of western history.

Belton, the county seat of Bell County, as it looked after the Civil War. *Collection of the Bell County Museum.*

Chapter Fifty
Reprisal in Bell County

During the Civil War there were many communities scattered across the western frontier that lacked adequate protection. While most of the young men were off fighting battles, security was often left to older men and young boys. Sometimes they would organize a protection agency to help guard the home front. Such was the case with the Home Guard in Bell County, Texas. Ethics wasn't a strong suit for many Bell County ranchers. Some used the Home Guard as a screen for rustling activities. On a wide-open range it was easy to round up strays that belonged to neighbors who were on a battlefield far away. Upon returning home, some of the owners would "steal" their cattle and horses back. Much hostility grew out of the rustling activity.

The Home Guard was led by John Early, an individual of dubious character who seemed to enjoy the sport of dragging deserters from their hideouts in the rugged bush country to the west. When the war ended, Early's house became headquarters for scalawags and carpetbaggers. Among his cohorts were Republican Dr. Calvin Clark, considered a turncoat by many, and Judge Hiram Christian, leader of the carpetbaggers. The three men, and their circle of friends, were highly disliked by the majority of Bell County citizens—Southern sympathizers, former soldiers of the Confederate States of America, and their kinfolk.

Sam Hasley was a Confederate soldier who carried a huge grudge against John Early. It began prior to the war's end. In early 1865, John Early and members of the Home Guard captured three deserters who were on the run. Accompanied by their prisoners, the group made camp near a place called Reed's Lake. Two companies of Confederate soldiers also pitched camp nearby. The fugitives were secured before Early and his bunch retired for the night. The following morning, the Home Guard awoke to find the deserters hanging by their necks from a pecan tree.

Whether, or not, there was any justification in John Early's actions during the aftermath of the hangings is a question which will probably never be answered. Early singled out several locals, went to their homes, quizzed them, badgered them, and then pushed them around. One of the citizens who was on the receiving end was Sam Hasley's father, Drew. Early shoved Drew Hasley around, then jerked a handful of hair from his white beard.

Sam Hasley was not one to rush right into a fight. He was cool, calm, and calculating. When he returned from the war to find that his father had been insulted and mistreated, he vowed retaliation. It was some time before an opportunity arose. One night, while riding on a desolate road, Sam Hasley encountered a group of scalawags who were traveling in the opposite direction. As he passed the column of riders, the white face of the last horse stood out in the moonlight. Hasley realized it was Early's horse. As they neared each other Hasley spurred his mount, fired point-blank at Early, then raced out of sight. When Hasley heeled his mount it caused Early's horse to shy. When it did, Hasley's bullet struck the horse. The horse died and Early was unscathed. Early, Christian and Clark decided that it was time to make an example out of some prominent Southerners in Bell County. He used the lynching of the deserters as an excuse to do so. A detachment of soldiers arrested several people, including Drew Hasley, and escorted them to the jail at Austin. It was the last straw as far as Sam Hasley was concerned.

Lawlessness in Bell County had never been greater. Not only did the authorities take advantage of the citizens, but horse thieves and cattle rustlers were running rampant. The citizens of Bell County finally took matters into their own hands. A group of vigilantes emerged. Their moves were highly calculated and they executed them to precision. Furthermore, they were masters at covering their tracks. The vigilantes moved swiftly. Six previously dreaded outlaws met their demise in April of 1866. In June, the bodies of two more horse thieves were found floating in the river near Three Forks.

Speculation has it that the vigilantes were composed predominately of former Confederate soldiers, and that their leaders were Sam Hasley and his brother-in-law Jim McRae. Whoever they were, their identities were highly protected.

While working at the courthouse on the 2nd of July, Judge Hiram Christian somehow found out that he was a marked man. That night, under the cover of darkness, Christian fled Bell County. The vigilantes tracked him all the way to Missouri, where they finally caught up with him. The execution of Hiram Christian was swift, and the vigilantes returned to Texas.

Jonathan and Newton Lindley departed from San Antonio with a warrant for the arrest of two Bell County men whose names were Duncan and Dawes. They were wanted for the murder of Jasper Lindley, one of the horse thieves who had been found in the river near Three Forks. Jonathan, who was Jasper's father, and Newton were accompanied by fifteen soldiers when they arrived in Bell County. Confident of their innocence, Duncan and Dawes surrendered to the soldiers and the group headed toward San Antonio. Before they had traveled far, Jonathan Lindley shot the two prisoners out of their saddles. He and Newton then fled the scene.

Jonathan and Newton Lindley were captured and escorted to the Bell County jail where they were locked up. While they were awaiting trial, a mob surrounded the jailhouse and then shot and killed the prisoners. Naturally, nobody recognized any members of the mob, nor did anybody "discover" the bodies any time soon.

David Griffin was a brother-in-law of Jim McRae, who, as we have previously mentioned, was a brother-in-law of Sam Hasley. The Hasley, McRae and Griffin clans were suspected as being the core of the vigilantes. While Sam Hasley stepped softly and took a low profile, Jim McRae was bold and blatant, and a more visible leader. McRae had become John Early's number one target. On July 30, 1869, Early and a posse approached the Griffin residence where a party was in progress. The Griffins, McRaes and Hasleys were having a festive time. Fearing that a confrontation would endanger the women and children Early withdrew his men a short distance back down the road. Before long Jim McRae and David Griffin rode up the trail in the direction of the concealed posse members. As the two riders drew near, Early and his men shot McRae out of the saddle. Griffin whirled his mount and fled. The badly wounded McRae was able to discharge a couple of shots and wounded a posse member named McDaniels. Jim McRae died later that evening.

Following McRae's death the vigilantes broke up and dispersed.

Eight months later, a telegram was received which announced that "Calvin Clark of Bell County, Texas was killed in Arkansas by a desperado named Halsey [sic] who followed him from Texas."

John Early disappeared. Could he also have met his demise by the hand of Sam Hasley? We may never know.

William Mitchell was determined to attain revenge. *Hood County Museum.*

Chapter Fifty-One
The Mitchell-Truitt Conflict

Bill Mitchell was the personification of a tough Texas cowboy. He was a crack marksman and a master with a rope. His leather-beaten face and fine horsemanship were the result of much time spent in the saddle. Bill Mitchell was as imposing an individual as there was in Hood County. He would also become the central figure in the bloody Mitchell-Truitt feud.

William Nelson Mitchell was the seventh child of Nelson "Cooney" Mitchell and his wife Nancy. Bill was born April 16, 1852. Following the Civil War, the Mitchell clan (which consisted of Bill, his parents, two of his brothers and two of his sisters) established a ranch along the Brazos River at a place that would become known as Mitchell's Bend. One day while Bill and Cooney were out rounding up strays they stumbled upon a large family of poor and destitute squatters. It was obvious to the Mitchells that the Truitt family was underfed and needed help. Needing additional hands on his growing ranch, Cooney Mitchell made the Truitts an offer they couldn't refuse. He would help them build a log home and smokehouse and provide them food until they became self-sufficient. In turn, the Truitts would work for the Mitchells.

Part of the Truitt's compensation would pay off their indebtedness to the Mitchells.

Eventually, the Truitts were able to get along without any help. They paid off their debt to the Mitchells (the Truitts at least thought so) and became independent. It wasn't long before they had purchased a piece of property adjacent to Mitchell land. It would be the catalyst for much trouble.

Along the property line where the Truitt land adjoined that of the Mitchells there was a strip which both families claimed to own. Their argument finally wound up in court during March of 1874. The courtroom battle was heated as tempers flew on both sides. The trial (which was ultimately won by the Truitts) aroused a hatred which would quickly turn to violence.

The Truitt boys left the courthouse and had traveled about six miles on their way home when they were confronted by Bill Mitchell, his father, two brothers-in-law and a neighbor. Evidently, the younger Truitts jeered the Mitchells over the outcome of the trial. This action further incensed the Mitchells who opened fire on the Truitts. Sam and Ike Truitt were killed instantly. Jim, the eldest Truitt (who was a minister), was able to take refuge at a nearby house after he was wounded. A few days

James Morgan Truitt was a minister and newspaperman when he met his demise. *Hood County Museum.*

later Cooney Mitchell, his son-in-law W. J. Owens and their neighbor James Shaw were arrested and charged with murder. Bill Mitchell and his brother-in-law Mitch Graves were able to elude the law and became fugitives.

During the ensuing trial, the Reverend Jim Truitt testified against the Mitchells. The jury was convinced that he told the truth. Cooney Mitchell was sentenced to be executed by hanging. Owens and Shaw were also convicted and sentenced to the penitentiary.

One night, while Cooney Mitchell awaited execution, a heavily armed individual attempted to approach the rear of the jailhouse. A guard shot the shadowy figure who toppled down an embankment toward the river. The next morning the body of Jeff Mitchell, Cooney's youngest son, was found. He had been shot through the head.

A crowd gathered for Cooney Mitchell's execution. Before the noose was placed around his neck, Mitchell was asked if he had any last words. Cooney Mitchell called out to his son Bill, wherever he might be, to avenge his father's death. This onus probably didn't make any difference. Bill Mitchell was the kind of individual who would seek revenge anyway.

After the death of Cooney Mitchell the rest of his family left Mitchell's Bend. The Truitts moved on shortly thereafter. Over ten years would pass before Bill Mitchell and Jim Truitt would meet again.

Truitt moved from parish to parish throughout eastern Texas, until he finally wound up at Timpson. There he supplemented his ministry by operating the local newspaper.

Bill Mitchell also moved about during this period. Using the alias of John W. King, Mitchell lived in Fort Stanton, New Mexico, where he worked as a teamster. Although he was not involved in the Lincoln County War, he was there during its worst days. Mitchell returned to Texas and assumed a new alias, John Davis, the name he used when he married Mary Beckett. They lived together, with Mary's father, in an isolated area west of San Antonio. The couple had one child, Maud Jane.

On July 20, 1886, Bill Mitchell rode into Timpson. After receiving directions to the Truitt residence, he walked through the door without knocking. To the horror of Julia Truitt, Jim's wife, and their daughter, Bill Mitchell drew his revolver and shot Jim Truitt through the head. The fugitive then walked outside, mounted his horse and rode away.

It was two full days before Sheriff A. J. Spradley, from Nacogdoches, was summoned and could hit the trail in pursuit of Mitchell. Spradley was not able to track Mitchell very far, so he returned to Timpson.

Twenty-one years passed before Sheriff Swofford of Hood County received a tip that Bill Mitchell was back in Lincoln County, New Mexico, living under his newest alias, Baldy Russell. Swofford and a deputy traveled to New Mexico and located Mitchell. Posing as cattlemen, the lawmen gained his confidence. When the opportunity arose, and Mitchell's guard was down, the lawmen jumped on their prey and handcuffed him. Mitchell was returned to Hood County, Texas, to stand trial for the murders of Ike and Sam Truitt in 1874. An old piece of evidence surfaced which had not been used at Cooney Mitchell's trial. A derringer which belonged to young Ike had one empty chamber. The Mitchells had maintained all along that Ike Truitt fired the first shot. The jury agreed that this was possible, and acquitted Bill Mitchell.

Bill Mitchell was also indicted in the death of Jim Truitt. Mrs. Julia Truitt Bishop, who had remarried and by now was an accomplished writer, traveled from Chicago to identify Bill Mitchell as her ex-husband's murderer. Following a hung jury, the accused was released under a $20,000 bond. Following another hung jury the venue was changed to Cherokee County and once again Bill Mitchell posted bond. He journeyed back to New Mexico from where he furnished sworn affidavits that he was unable to travel to Texas due to illness. His case was continued several times before he finally appeared in court on December 23, 1910. This time he was found guilty, a decision which was upheld two years later by the Court of Criminal Appeals. At the age of sixty-four Bill Mitchell was sent to prison.

After serving just two years of his sentence, Bill Mitchell escaped. Using the alias of John Davis once again, Mitchell eventually settled down in Arizona. At a hospital in San Simon, with Mary at his side, Bill Mitchell died of heart failure on June 26, 1928. He was 76 years old.

Belle Starr was a remarkable equestrienne. In this photograph that was taken at Ft. Smith she sports an ostrich feather in her hat and a pearl-handled revolver. *Oklahoma Historical Society.*

Chapter Fifty-Two
Belle Starr and Her Bad Boys

Myra Maybelle Shirley, the woman that would later be known as Belle Starr, was born in Missouri on February 5, 1848 (although the birth date inscribed on her tombstone is doubted by many). "May," as she was called by her family, was the only daughter of John and Elizabeth "Eliza" Shirley. Myra Maybelle's entire childhood seems to have been spent in Missouri. When she was twelve years old her parents operated a wayside inn at Carthage. Adjacent to the hotel, the Shirleys also managed a livery stable and blacksmith shop. The Carthage Hotel, as the inn was called, had a fine piano in its parlor. Myra Maybelle was educated at a private school where she studied music. She learned to play the piano well. On occasion, she would perform piano recitals for guests at the inn. Her real love, however, was for the outdoors. The family livery stable offered May the opportunity to become an excellent horsewoman. Her older brother, Bud, was a competent rider and an accurate marksman with firearms. From Bud, Myra Maybelle learned how to handle both a rifle and pistol. Her horsemanship and ability to use firearms were very much in keeping with her desire to be daring and wild. May would pick a fight with anybody, boy or girl.

During the Civil War, Bud fought for the Confederate irregulars of William Clarke Quantrill. Myra Maybelle did all she could to assist the guerrillas' cause. In February of 1863, at the age of fifteen, she spent the night at a mansion near Newtonia in order to "spy" on the Union soldiers being sheltered there. The wily youth indicated that she was lost and would like to stay overnight. The ruse worked, and the unsuspecting soldiers took her in. Bud Shirley, who was in Carthage at the time, was high on the Yankee black list. When May learned that a detachment of Union soldiers was heading to Carthage, she knew that her brother would be in danger. At daybreak, she saddled her horse and rode from Newtonia at breakneck speed in order to warn Bud and the other guerrillas of the potential peril. When the Union soldiers arrived in Carthage, May was there but the guerrillas were long gone.

Myra Maybelle Shirley first met Cole Younger in early 1864, while Cole was riding with Quantrill. John and Eliza Shirley were Southern sympathizers who would offer a warm meal and a bed to any Missouri guerrilla. Cole visited the Shirleys, whom he considered friends, at their inn in Carthage. Myra Maybelle became very enchanted with Cole Younger.

Bud Shirley had become one of the Union Army's most wanted guerrillas. In June of 1864, several Company C soldiers heard that Shirley and a friend, Milt Norris, could be found at the Stewart house, near Carthage. As the troopers surrounded the house, Shirley and Norris attempted to escape. As he leaped over a fence, Bud Shirley was shot and killed. Norris received a superficial wound but was able to sprint to safety. According to legend, May strapped on two six-shooters and let it be known that she intended to revenge her brother's death.

Shortly after Bud's death, the Shirley family pulled up stakes and moved south to Scyene, Texas, where they established a homestead above South Mesquite Creek, just over a mile east of town. Members of the James-Younger Gang may have stopped to visit with the Shirleys at Scyene in July of 1866 during a return trip from San Antonio, Texas. Cole and Myra Maybelle may, or may not, have had a sexual relationship during this visit. Belle Starr always claimed that Cole Younger was the father of her daughter Pearl. Cole, who emphatically denied the accusation, claimed that Belle was six months pregnant, and was married to ex-guerrilla Jim Reed, when he saw her next at the Missouri home of

Reed's mother in 1868. There has been much conjecture through the years as to who sired Belle's daughter Pearl, Cole Younger, Jim Reed or some other man.

Myra MayBelle and Jim Reed courted during the days when both of their families lived in Carthage, Missouri. They continued to see each other periodically when Reed rode with Quantrill's guerrillas. After the bushwhackers broke up, Reed served in the famed Sixteenth Cavalry of the Confederate Army. Following the war, and the death of Jim's father, the Reed family moved to Collin County, Texas. Jim and May renewed their relationship. They were married on November 1, 1866, in Collin County, Texas, by the Reverend S. M. Wilkins. Historians disagree on the date which May gave birth to her daughter Rosie Lee, whom she nicknamed Pearl. It is most likely that Pearl was born in September of 1868, twenty-two months after the marriage of May and Jim. Jim spent much time away from home and his bride. He could often be found at the stronghold of Tom Starr on the South Canadian River in Indian Territory. Tom Starr was a tall, muscular Cherokee Indian with skin that resembled leather. He wore clothing trimmed with fur, and a necklace adorned with dried earlobes of men he had killed. He operated a gang of rustlers that included several of his eight sons. It also often included Jim Reed. Cole Younger frequented Tom Starr's place during the Civil War. After the war, Cole and his brothers visited Starr on trips through Indian Territory. It is said that Tom Starr was so impressed with the Youngers that he named the great crook in the Canadian River after his friends—Youngers' Bend.

In 1869, a gunfight occurred in Fort Smith, Arkansas, following a dispute over a horse race. As lead flew between the advisories, Jim Reed's brother, Scott, was killed by mistake. Jim jumped into the affair and gunned down Scott's killer. With the law on his heels, Jim Reed escaped to Tom Starr's place. Feeling the heat, Reed continued on to California. Myra Maybelle and Pearl followed by stagecoach. While in California, May gave birth (on February 22, 1871) to her second child, James Edwin, who was nicknamed Eddie. About a month later, Federal investigators questioned Jim regarding the passing of counterfeit currency. Knowing he was in hot water, Jim Reed fled to Texas with May and Pearl close behind. The girls traveled to Scyene, while Jim took refuge again at Tom Starr's place.

On November 19, 1873, Jim Reed and two accomplices robbed Watt Grayson, a Creek Indian chief, of the savings he had stashed beneath a trapdoor in the floor of his cabin. Grayson had refused to tell the robbers where his gold was stashed, even after they swung him by the neck from a tree limb a half dozen times. When the trio threatened to hang Mrs. Grayson, the Indian chief revealed where his gold was hidden. Estimates of the take were as high as $34,000. Subsequently, Jim Reed had a fifteen-hundred dollar price on his head.

On April 7, 1874, Jim Reed, Cal Carter and William Boswell (alias William Rogers or William Nelson) robbed the Austin-San Antonio stagecoach on its run to Austin. The four-horse stage was stopped about two miles north of the Blanco River. The bandits fleeced the passengers of their jewelry and about $2,500 in cash. They also stole one bag of mail and three of the coach's horses.

Unknown to May, Jim Reed had been sleeping with a girl named Rosa McCommas from Dallas. She often rode with the robbers as they moved from town to town. She never accompanied them, however, while they did their dirty work. When authorities learned that Rosa was visiting at the farm of John T. Morris, a former officer of the law, they staked out the property hoping that Reed would appear. When Reed and a cohort arrived one evening, presumably to spend the night, the posse concluded that it should wait until daybreak before making any move. During the night, some of the lawmen became impatient and decided to approach the house. This confused some of the other posse members who opened fire on their own men. Deputy U. S. Marshal Herseberg was gunned down and would die three days later. Another lawman was wounded in his leg. The gunfire warned Reed and his comrade and they easily escaped.

Following a robbery in the Going Snake District of Indian Territory, which netted Reed and his men nearly two thousand dollars in gold and property, the robbers were pursued by Cherokee police. They surrounded the home of Tom Starr where Reed had taken refuge, but they also came up empty handed as Jim Reed was able to flee. He headed for Texas.

Reed headed back to the home of John T. Morris to see Rosa who was still visiting there. Supposedly, Reed convinced Morris to assist him with a robbery in Arkansas, not realizing that Morris held a special deputy's commission and was intent upon turning Reed in for the reward. On the evening of August 6, 1874, near Paris, Texas, Reed and Morris stopped at a farmhouse to eat supper. So as not to frighten the lady of the house, they left their guns on their horses. While they were eating,

Morris slipped out and got his revolver. Upon returning to the house he attempted to arrest Reed. Reed hurled the dining table and then grabbed Morris. The two grappled until Morris was able to free his revolver at which time he shot Reed twice. Jim Reed slumped to the floor. He was dead.

May's father died at Scyene in June of 1876. Eliza sold the farm and moved to Dallas. Anxious for a change of scenery, Myra Maybelle and Pearl headed to Carthage, Missouri, where they stayed for several months. Eddie also went to Missouri to live with his Grandmother Reed at Rich Hill. At some point during the next few years, May entered into a relationship with Bruce Younger, a half-brother of Cole's father. Bruce had been arrested as a suspect in the train robbery near Otterville, Missouri (July 8, 1876) by the James-Younger Gang. Bruce had an alibi and was released from custody. When he and Myra Maybelle first met is uncertain, but the couple lived as husband and wife in both Joplin, Missouri, and Galena, Kansas, during part of 1879. Whether, or not, their "marriage" was legal is a matter for speculation. The relationship was short-lived, and during that same year Myra Maybelle left Bruce and headed back to Indian Territory where she renewed her friendship with Tom Starr and his family.

Myra Maybelle's next lover and husband was Sam Starr, one of Tom's sons. Sam was 75% Cherokee and several years younger than Myra Maybelle. They were married early in the summer of 1880 in the Cherokee Nation. It was at this time that Myra Maybelle changed her name to Belle Starr. Her new name had a ring to it, and she loved it. Sam Starr's cabin was located on about sixty acres adjacent to the Canadian. Belle named their ranch after the great bend in the river, which had been dubbed Youngers' Bend by her new father-in-law. Regardless of her semi-tough exterior, Belle Starr still had much of the culture she received as a child in Carthage. The Starr home had a fine piano and a library of classics and other good books, which Belle loved to read. Pearl, who lived with her mother, began to use the last name of Starr. Eddie Reed spent time at Youngers' Bend although he continued to live in Missouri.

In July of 1882, warrants were served on Belle and Sam Starr for horse stealing. They appeared in federal court to face the renowned Judge Isaac Parker. Sam was sentenced to one year and Belle two consecutive six-month terms at the House of Correction, a federal rehabilitation center, in Detroit, Michigan. The couple served nine months before being released for good behavior. Belle and Sam headed back to Youngers' Bend.

Belle always had the welcome mat out for an outlaw seeking refuge. Shortly before Christmas, in 1884, John Middleton rode into Indian Territory and went straight to Belle's Place. Middleton had shot and killed Sheriff J. H. Black of Lamar County, Texas, a month earlier and was on the run from the law.

John Middleton was a thief, rustler, arsonist, jailbreaker and killer. He was a member of the Regulators and a companion of Billy the Kid during the Lincoln County War in New Mexico. By no coincidence, Middleton's mother and brother, Jim, set up housekeeping in Indian Territory near Briartown.

While John Middleton was relatively safe at Belle's place because nobody expected him to be there, the same wasn't true for Sam Starr. Sam was on the dodge and could only sneak home occasionally. Belle's dashing personality appealed to John Middleton, whose presence seemed to satisfy Belle's loneliness. John and Belle had an affair that lasted until late spring. Lawmen raided the Starr ranch looking for Sam Starr and John Middleton, but came up empty. Realizing that it was time to move on, Middleton packed up and left. A few days later, the horse which Middleton had been riding was found about twenty-five miles southwest of Fort Smith. The badly decomposed body of a man was found on a river bank about two hundred yards away.

Trouble continued for Sam and Belle Starr. Much of it was of their own making. Sam Starr, Felix Griffin and Richard Hayes were accused of robbing the Andrew J. Moore store and post office at Blaine, on October 30, 1885. Sam had to remain in hiding. He stayed in, and about, the wilderness around Youngers' Bend, where he was protected by many relatives. Occasionally, when the coast was clear, he would venture home for short visits. The horse that had been found near the decomposed body of John Middleton had been given to him by Belle. When it was discovered that the horse was stolen, Belle was indicted. She appeared in court and was acquitted. On September 16, 1886, Sam Starr was involved in a shoot-out with Indian police. Sam was wounded and the horse he was riding (one of Belle's favorites) was killed. Sam's injury was superficial and he was able to escape. Belle convinced Sam that he should turn himself in to federal authorities at Fort Smith, in order to avoid the wrath of the Indian police, and a relentless detective, Frank West. After Sam was charged with breaking into, and larceny of, a post office, Belle posted his bail. Sam was now under the protection of the federal court and the Indian police could not touch him.

On the seventeenth of December, Lucy Surratt gave a Christmas dance at her home near Whitefield. Belle and Sam attended, as did Pearl and Eddie. Belle was playing the organ and Sam was sitting nearby when they received word that Frank West was approaching the house. West had been forewarned that Sam Starr was inside. Sam stepped outside and immediately accused West of shooting his horse (three months earlier). Both men drew their revolvers. Starr fired first, and his ball was deadly. West staggered, but also fired, and his aim was also true. The two men collapsed to the ground. They were both dead. The slug from West's revolver passed through Sam Starr's body, then struck a twelve-year-old boy in the jaw. The youth, Dan Folsom, had been running toward the house when the shooting occurred.

Following the death of Sam Starr, Cherokee authorities believed that Belle should be removed from Indian Territory as she was no longer a Cherokee subject. Belle moved quickly to remedy this problem. Belle and Bill July, an adopted son of Tom Starr, began cohabiting as man and wife, an arrangement that had the approval of the Cherokee nation. Belle was allowed to keep her land. Bill July, who also became known as Jim July Starr, was of mixed Cherokee and Creek blood. He was fifteen years younger than Belle. Like most of Tom Starr's clan, July was a petty horse thief.

Pearl and Eddie resented July and a rift began to grow between them and their mother. Pearl eventually left home. Later, Pearl gave birth to a daughter that she named Flossie. Eddie Reed was in and out of trouble. He was shot and wounded by a former friend. Pearl returned (without Flossie) to Youngers' Bend in order to help nurse her brother's injury. As his wound healed, he and his mother argued more and more. Following two incidents in which Belle lashed him with a whip, Eddie finally moved out. He would not see his mother alive again.

Belle was making a concerted effort to straighten her life out. She let it be known that Youngers' Bend was no longer a haven for wanted men. When Bill July was arrested for stealing a horse, Belle refused to come to his aid. After friends posted his bail, and July returned home, he received a severe tongue-lashing from Belle.

Edgar A. Watson was a sharecropper who rented a tenant farm from Milo Hoyt Jr. near Whitefield, on the opposite side of the Canadian River from the property of Belle Starr. When Watson, who was a mysterious fellow, had difficulty renewing his lease, he was advised to check with Belle Starr on the possibility of sharecropping a portion of her property. Watson signed a lease with Belle and gave her an advanced payment on the agreement, which was to begin in December of 1888. When Belle discovered that Watson was wanted for murder, in Florida, she backed out of the deal and returned the sharecropper's deposit. She gave him no reason for her change of heart and Watson was furious. When Edgar Watson learned that a fellow named Joseph Tate had agreed to sharecrop the same parcel, Watson advised Tate of Belle Starr's countless lawless activities, and frightened him into canceling his agreement with her. When Belle next saw Watson she lost her temper. During heated words she advised him that she knew that he was wanted for murder in Florida.

Bill July was required to appear in court at Fort Smith on the unresolved horse stealing charge. Belle decided to accompany July on part of his trip, then return to Youngers' Bend. The couple departed on February 2, 1889, a Saturday morning. Enroute they settled an outstanding bill (of $75.00) which had been owed to the store on King Creek. They traveled on to the home of Belle's friend, Mrs. Richard Nail, who resided about twenty miles east of Whitefield. There they spent the night. On Sunday morning, July headed toward Fort Smith and Belle turned back toward Youngers' Bend. Late that afternoon she stopped at the house of Jackson Rowe hoping to see her son, Eddie, who had been staying there. Eddie had been there earlier, but he left prior to Belle's arrival. Among the Sunday afternoon visitors at the Rowe place was Edgar Watson. When Watson spied Belle approaching he immediately left for his tenant cabin which was located about one-eighth mile away. Belle visited for half an hour, then departed.

As she passed a fence corner about three hundred yards from Edgar Watson's tenant cabin, a shotgun blast knocked Belle out of her saddle. Her assailant jumped the fence, approached her wounded body, and then fired again. Buckshot had struck her in the back, shoulder, neck and face. Belle Starr died within the hour. The assassin's tracks circled around to a point about one hundred yards from Watson's cabin before they were lost.

Cherokees, Choctaws, Creeks, white sharecroppers and others attended Belle's funeral, which was held on Wednesday, the 6th of February. Among those in attendance were Edgar Watson and his wife. As soon as Belle Starr had been laid to rest, Bill July pointed his

Winchester at Watson and accused him of murder. July and Eddie Reed escorted Edgar Watson to Fort Smith, where July furnished a sworn affidavit that Watson had killed Belle. In court, Watson's attorney was successful in proving that the evidence against his client was circumstantial. Realizing that he was not safe in Indian Territory, Edgar Watson returned home where he and his wife packed their belongings, then immediately left the area.

Many theories exist as to who was Belle Starr's assassin. Speculation has the murder performed by the likes of Bill July (Jim July Starr), Eddie Reed, one of his uncles, Jim Middleton (brother of John), an assassin hired by a local rancher named Hi Early, and even Tom Starr. Most of the evidence seems to indicate that Edgar Watson was the culprit. Watson eventually returned to Florida where he killed several people, including a woman. He was eventually shot to death by peace officers while resisting arrest.

Belle had willed her land to James Starr (Bill July), but July wasn't around to claim the property. He had joined an outlaw gang that hid out in the Chickasaw nation. In January of 1890 he was shot to death by two members of a posse led by Deputy U. S. Marshal Heck Thomas.

Eddie Reed was eventually appointed a deputy U. S. Marshal for

Bluford "Blue" Duck (a Cherokee Indian) and Belle Starr posed for this photograph on May 24, 1886 as part of a campaign by Duck's attorney to have the convicted killer's death sentence committed to life imprisonment. *Oklahoma Historical Society.*

the Western District of Arkansas. He married a schoolteacher, bought a house, and became a dedicated officer of the law. Eddie Reed was shot to death on December 14, 1896, while attempting to arrest Joe Gibbs and J. N. Clark for selling whiskey. Pearl opened a classy brothel in Fort Smith. Her girls plied their wares at prices upwards of two dollars per night. Like her mother, Pearl was in and out of marriages and relationships. She gave birth to four children. After suffering a stroke, Pearl died on July 6, 1925, in Douglas, Arizona.

    As for Belle Starr, the marble tombstone at her gravesite at Youngers' Bend has an inscription that was penned by her daughter Pearl:

>Shed not for her the bitter tear,
>Nor give the heart to vain regret;
>'Tis but the casket that lies here,
>The gem that filled it sparkles yet.

Portrait of Harry Nicholson Morse (ca. 1880 at age 45), a highly efficient lawman and private detective on the West Coast. *California Historical Society.*

Chapter Fifty-Three
Relentless Harry Morse

Harry Morse was a law enforcement officer and detective of much renown. He was directly or indirectly responsible for the capture and/or deaths of many sought-after California fugitives.

Henry Nicholson Morse was born on February 22, 1835 in New York City. As a youth, Morris was large for his age. He worked as a seaman between Liverpool and New York at the tender age of ten. Morse journeyed to San Francisco during the gold rush of 1849. He labored in the mines for a few years, and then worked at several other professions. Harry Morse was appointed deputy provost marshal for Alameda County, California, in 1863, and later that same year was elected sheriff of Alameda County. He quickly became a highly efficient officer of the law.

Tomas Bustamente—known as Procopio—was a nephew of the legendary Joaquin Murrieta (his mother's brother). He also used the aliases of Tomas Redondo, "Red Dick," and Murrieta. Having been convicted of grand larceny, Procopio entered the confines of San Quentin prison about the same time that Harry Morse was elected sheriff. Among the inmates at San Quentin during Procopio's imprisonment was noted outlaw, Tiburcio Vasquez (who was admitted for a second time in 1867 and discharged in 1870). These outlaws would later become a thorn in the side of Harry Morse.

Livermore Valley was a haven for fugitives from the law. Norrato Ponce was hiding there when he was tracked down by Harry Morse. It was late at night when Morse discovered Ponce and a gunfight ensued during which both parties fired at the gun flashes of the other. Ponce was wounded, and had his horse shot out from under him, but was able to scamper to safety in the darkness. Morse and two deputies continued to track Ponce relentlessly. Six weeks later, they found the outlaw at an adobe house in Pinole Valley. The homestead, which belonged to José Rojos, became the scene of another shoot-out. Morse fired several shots as Ponce ran from the house. One of the slugs found its mark. Ponce fell to the ground. He died about five minutes later.

When Joseph Newell killed elderly Morgan Leighton he inherited the wrath of Sheriff Morse. Harry tracked him to the outskirts of Los Angeles, where he arrested him at a railroad worker's tent. The accused was placed in shackles, then transported by Morse via steamship back to Alameda County.

When Jesus Tejada and his cohorts robbed a store near Stockton in December of 1869 five men were killed. Posses combed the countryside but were unable to find the killers. Six months later Morse discovered the location of Tejada's hideout, and arrested him without incident. Soon after his conviction, Jesus Tejada died in jail of natural causes.

In January of 1871, Juan Soto and two accomplices robbed a store in the Sunol Valley. The store clerk was killed by the trio. In mid-May, Harry Morse led a posse which tracked the bandits to a cabin east of Pacheco Pass. Believing that the killers were further along the trail, Morse and a deputy entered the cabin. Suddenly they were face to face with Soto and his men. Harry was fast on the draw, but as he cleared leather a Mexican woman grabbed his arm. The deputy and Morse quickly retreated from the cabin. Soto also dashed outside and attempted to escape. When he did, Morse put a slug into Soto's right shoulder. The enraged outlaw turned and charged at Harry with a pistol in each hand. Sheriff Morse stood his ground and shot the desperado through the forehead.

Tiburcio Vasquez had been released from prison about six months prior to the death of Soto. Once again, he was terrorizing California and was high on Harry Morse's most-wanted list. On March 1, 1871, Procopio was discharged from San Quentin. Before the month was over, he was dodging the law again. Procopio and a companion, Juan Camargo, stole a cow which they slaughtered for food. Camargo was captured, and he identified Procopio as his accomplice. Procopio sought out Tiburcio Vasquez, his old prison acquaintance, and joined his gang.

For several months, Vásquez and his highwaymen robbed stagecoaches and wagons and looted stores. A manhunt for the gang became intense. With the heat on, and the winter of 1871 setting in, Vásquez and Procopio decided to lie low for a while. They headed to Procopio's old home in the Hermosillo area of lower California where Procopio had friends and relatives. About three months later they were back in the San Francisco area. Shortly thereafter, Vásquez and Procopio parted company. Suddenly, each had a budding dislike for the other. A female was reportedly the catalyst for their disdain.

When Harry Morse learned that Procopio frequented a certain brothel on Morton Street in San Francisco he placed the building under surveillance. When Procopio returned on February 11, 1872, Sheriff Morse was alerted and quickly arrived at the scene. Lawmen simultaneously entered the structure through separate doors. Harry Morse grabbed Procopio by the throat before the outlaw had a chance to respond. He was handcuffed and taken to jail. For lack of any other concrete evidence against him, Procopio was charged with stealing a cow.

When word was received, a few months later, that Tiburcio Vasquez, Francisco Barcenas and Garcia Rodriguez had just been involved in a robbery, Sheriff Morse and two other lawmen swiftly responded in order to intercept the outlaws along their escape route. They were able to do so and surprised the bandits on the road to the Arroyo Cantua. During the ensuing gunfight, Barcenas was killed. Vásquez and Rodriguez were seriously wounded, but were able to escape. Rodriguez was captured within a couple of days. He died shortly thereafter in the prison at San Quentin.

More raids were attributed to Tiburcio Vasquez, including attacks on the villages of Tres Pinos and Kingston. Scores of lawmen combed the hills in a massive manhunt. The elusive Vásquez was nowhere to be found. In early 1874, Governor Newton Booth commissioned Harry Morse to establish an elite team of lawmen whose sole purpose was to capture Tiburcio Vasquez. Upon learning of his whereabouts, Morse and his men tracked Vásquez into Southern California. When Morse advised Los Angeles County Sheriff Billy Rowland as to the location of the outlaws, Rowland and his deputies were able to capture Vásquez.

Harry Morse eventually grew tired of spending endless hours in the saddle in pursuit of bandits. In 1878, he retired from public service. Before long he established the Morse Detective Agency in San Francisco. As a private detective Morse was highly successful. As his revenues grew, Harry Morse diversified into many other types of business including mining, real estate and publishing.

Harry Morse and his many agents played an important part in the investigation that ultimately led to the capture of the elusive stagecoach robber Black Bart in 1883. Tom Burns, a Morse agent, was a member of the posse that captured John Sontag, the notorious train robber.

Henry Nicholson Morse, one of California's great lawmen, passed away at his Oakland home on January 11, 1912. He was seventy-six years old.

Aptly named Rowdy Joe Lowe had strict rules in his saloons and brothels and he wouldn't hesitate to enforce them himself. *Kansas State Historical Society.*

Chapter Fifty-Four
Rowdy Joe Lowe

Joseph Lowe and his common-law wife Kate certainly lived up to their nicknames, "Rowdy Joe" and "Rowdy Kate." Following the Civil War, the temperamental couple operated saloons in the boisterous cow towns of Kansas—first in Ellsworth, then Newton, and for a short while in Delano (West Wichita). In actuality, the saloons were dance halls, gambling halls and brothels. Joe was a part-time bartender and gambler who lured customers to his gaming tables. Kate assumed the role of madam to assure that their girls stayed busy either on the dance floor or in back rooms.

Joe, a native of New York State, met Kate in Illinois when they were both teenagers. Joe was eighteen and Kate thirteen. Except for a brief stint by Joe in the Union Army, in 1865, and a short spell in jail, the pair lived together continuously until they separated in 1875.

While working at the railhead in Ellsworth, in 1869, Rowdy Joe and his friend Jim Bush were apprehended for drugging a man and then robbing him of a large sum of money. Authorities were able to return about $750.00 to the victim. During the following year, Joe Lowe was arrested in Ellsworth and transported to Wichita in order to face charges for stealing a mule which was the property of a fellow named Tom McAdams.

Joe and Kate moved on to Newton where they continued to earn their sobriquets. Joe was cited for operating a house of prostitution, but things would get worse. On Sunday night, February 18, 1872, an altercation occurred between Kate and Joe. Evidently a customer had complained to Joe that he had been insulted by Kate. Joe approached Kate and slapped her for treating the customer with disrespect. Incensed, Kate left the premises with another fellow, A. M. Sweet. After much drink, the two slept together at the house of Fanny Grey. The following day, someone tipped Rowdy as to the whereabouts of Kate and Sweet, and furthermore that Sweet had threatened to kill Joe. Joe Lowe headed straight to Fanny Grey's house. Sweet grabbed his six-shooter, but he was too late. Rowdy Joe fired two slugs into Sweet's body before he was able to get off a shot. Joe went to the sheriff's office and turned himself in. Sweet died three hours later.

Joe and Kate packed their bags and moved on to Wichita. In no time they were back in business again. Rowdy Joe was in the news, as well. On July 19, 1872, Joe Lowe seriously injured one of his customers. Having had too much to drink, Joseph Walters became obnoxious and disorderly. In order to quell the disturbance, Joe drew his revolver and proceeded to pistol-whip the drunken Walters until he was senseless.

Saloon owners in western cow towns were normally an ornery lot. Joe's establishment (which was located on Water Street above the west bank of the Arkansas River in Delano) was located adjacent to the saloon of Edward T. "Red" Beard, an old acquaintance from Newton and a ruthless individual in his own right. On June 3, 1873, Red Beard shot two soldiers inside his saloon after one of their comrades had shot, and wounded, one of Beard's prostitutes, Emma Stanley. A group of outraged soldiers returned the following night to torch Red's place. Gunshots were exchanged as the building burned. Emma Stanley received another wound, and a fellow named Charles Leshhart was also shot. Expedient response by the water brigade saved the saloon of Joseph Lowe (that was next door).

Red Beard's saloon was rebuilt. It hadn't been standing long when all hell broke loose again—this time between Rowdy Joe and Red Beard. On the night of October 27, 1873, after consuming much alcohol, Red Beard fired a shot through his saloon window and the window of Lowe's saloon as well. Within moments Rowdy Joe stormed through the door of Beard's place. Kate was right behind him. Joe, who had received a superficial neck wound, asked who shot at him. Red Beard indicated that he had done so. Both men fired simultaneously. Neither of the saloon owners hit their adversary, but Joe's slug shattered the nose of Billie Anderson, a bystander. Beard exited the front door and Lowe the side door as they each took pot shots at the other. Beard reentered the building and became enraged when he couldn't find his shotgun. When his mistress, Josephine DeMerritt, informed him that he had left his shotgun in another building, he accused her of lying and pushed her to the floor. Beard cocked his revolver and aimed it at Josephine. Walter Beebe (Red's bartender) and two other men intervened by restraining Beard. Josephine DeMerritt scampered down the hallway toward the back of the building. When Beebe and the others freed Beard, he headed toward the hall. Moments later he fired a shot. Evidently it was a case of mistaken identity for Red Beard had shot Annie Franklin in the stomach.

    Beard left his saloon and headed toward the Chisholm Trail bridge across the Arkansas River. He was pursued by Rowdy Joe Lowe. Lowe caught Beard near the bridge and cut him down with a shotgun blast. Red Beard, whose right arm and hip were shattered, lived for two weeks before succumbing to a deadly spread of infection.

    During the ensuing trial the jury rendered a verdict of "not guilty" in the death of E. T. Beard. Although he had won this battle the pressure was building on Rowdy Joe. He also faced charges for wounding Billie Anderson and for destruction of property. Somehow Joe Lowe was able to slip out of custody and disappear. A warrant was issued for his arrest. Walter Beebe (Red Beard's bartender) was sentenced to three years for assisting Joe Lowe's escape. As a sidelight to this matter, Josephine DeMerritt was convicted (in December) of forging the deed to one parcel of Red Beard's property and was sentenced to ten years in the penitentiary.

    Rowdy Joe Lowe, using the assumed name of A. A. Becker, was arrested in St. Louis, Missouri, on January 3, 1874. In his pockets Lowe was carrying $8,295.00 in cash. Kansas authorities were immediately notified of the arrest. The cash was returned to Kate Lowe. Artful negotiations by Kate and a writ of habeas corpus brought about the release of Rowdy Joe before Kansas peace officers could travel to

Missouri and take him into custody.

In May of 1875 Joe Lowe was found guilty of assaulting Kate and was fined $100.00. Kate Lowe gradually grew tired of the abuse she received from Joseph and finally left him.

On February 11, 1899, Rowdy Joe Lowe was shot to death in a Denver saloon by a former policeman.

Former confederate soldirer, Bob Lee, was a terror to the Union League following the Civil War. *Wild Horse Collection.*

Chapter Fifty-Five
The Lee-Peacock Feud

Most of the nation laid down their arms after General Robert E. Lee surrendered his Confederate forces at the courthouse in Appomattox, Virginia, in 1865. More than a year later, President Andrew Johnson declared that "there no longer existed any armed resistance of misguided citizens, or others, to the authority of the United States in any, or in all the States ... excepting only the State of Texas." The President's statement reflected the feeling in Washington that Texas was the only state that failed to totally comply with the "rules" of Reconstruction. One of the reasons was the Lee-Peacock feud, which in actuality was not a feud but simply a continuation of the Civil War. The conflict took place, for the most part, in the "Four Corners" region of northeast Texas, where Grayson, Collin, Fannin, and Hunt counties converge. In the midst of this area is a densely wooded 30 square mile (48 kilometers) thicket. It was a refuge for outlaws and deserters during the war.

Bob Lee lived in the northern part of the thicket. Although married, with three children, Lee volunteered for service in the Ninth Texas Cavalry of the Confederate States of America. Lee was not a slave owner. Most of his relatives and friends who served also fought for the

CSA. The Maddox brothers, John, William and Francis, as well as several of the Boren clan had also joined the Ninth Texas Cavalry. A few men from the Four Corners area joined the Union forces, as well.

As the Civil War ended and it was time to head home, Bob Lee was hearing that trouble existed in his region of Texas. The Federal government had established the Union League, an organization created for the protection of former slaves and Union sympathizers. They set up their headquarters at Pilot Grove, just seven miles (11 kilometers) from Lee's home. Additionally, Union troops were in the area to help with the reconstruction effort. Residents of the Four Corners region considered the infringement and new laws as unwanted and unwelcome. When Bob Lee arrived home he was seen as the man who could minimize this new interference from the Feds.

Lewis Peacock was the head of the Union League. He resided just south of Pilot Grove. As he saw a mounting threat from Bob Lee and his followers, Peacock recruited men who were sympathetic to the cause of the Union League. Among those ready to assist Peacock were James Maddox, James Vaught, Hugh Hudson, John Baldock, some of the Boren clan, and a few of the Nance clan. Bob Lee could count on the help of Parson Martin Smith, the Dixon clan, as well as his own relatives of which there were many including his father and his brothers.

Bob Lee was awakened from his sick bed one night when a group of Union soldiers surrounded his house and informed him that he was under arrest for war crimes. They indicated that they had orders to take him to Sherman, Texas and demanded that he come with them. When they reached the Choctaw Creek bottoms, the soldiers took Lee's gold watch, a twenty dollar gold piece, and forced him to sign a $2,000 promissory note. Then they released him. Bob recognized the men who robbed him as Lewis Peacock, James Maddox, Israel Boren, Sam Bier, Hardy Dial, and Doc Wilson. Bob Lee wasn't about to agree to the note and headed to Bonham where he filed a suit in civil court against Peacock and his men. Lee won his case, but the battle had just begun.

In February of 1867, Bob Lee was in a grocery store at Pilot Grove where he came face to face with James Maddox. The two had words. When Lee turned to leave, Maddox fired a shot at the back of his head. The slug grazed his scalp and knocked him unconscious. He was carried to the home of Dr. William Pierce for treatment. A few days later while Lee was still at the Pierce residence, one of Peacock's men, Hugh Hudson, paid a visit. When Dr. Pierce opened his front door he was shot and killed by Hudson. Dr. W. C. Holmes, who was at the Pierce residence, was an eye-witness to the killing and would later travel to Saltillo, in Hopkins County, to identify Hudson (who had been shot) as Pierce's murderer. When Bob Lee swore to avenge the doctor's death, everyone in the Four Corners area armed themselves and locked their doors. The wrath of Bob Lee followed. During 1868 there were casualties on both sides. Among the dead were Billy Dixon, Lige Clark, Dow Nance, Elijah Clark, Dan Sanders, and John Baldock. Lewis Peacock and many others were wounded. Some of the deaths occurred as follows:

The Dixon clan supported Bob Lee. Elijah Clark was a Peacock man. During the spring of 1868, Clark called on Hester Anne Dixon to invite her in person to accompany him to a dance. While in the Dixon home he politely removed his pistol and placed it on a table. When Hester Anne refused the invitation, Clark left in such a huff that he forgot to pick up his weapon. In front of the house he ran into 16-year-old Billy Dixon. Elijah Clark was so disappointed that he grabbed Dixon's gun and shot him. Slightly wounded, Billy Dixon ran into the house, seized Clark's pistol, ran back outside and shot Elijah Clark who tumbled from his horse with a fatal wound.

A few weeks later, Billy Dixon and his cousin Charlie Dixon were transporting a load of cotton when their wagon broke down. They were about twenty miles (32 kilometers) from their respective homes. As they were fixing the buckboard, a group of Peacock's men rode up. One of the men shot and killed Billy at the roadside, and they proceeded to depart leaving Charlie unharmed.

After two of Peacocks men forced two Lee women to feed them a meal, they departed and quickly met their demise when they were blown out of their saddles just a short distance from the house. A meeting of the Lewis Peacock men was held at the Nance farm. When Bob Lee was tipped that the meeting was going to take place he gathered a group of his supporters. Once the Peacock men had assembled at Nance's horse lot, Bob Lee attacked. In the gunfight that followed three of Peacocks followers were slain. The dead men were Dow Nance, Dan Sanders, and John Baldock.

General J. J. Reynolds put a price on the head of Bob Lee. On August 27, 1868, he issued a proclamation offering a reward of $1,000 to anyone who could deliver Lee to the Post Commander at either Marshall or Austin. Three Union sympathizers from Kansas decided to take the general up on his proposition. They were found dead in the middle of the road not far from the Lee house.

Bob Lee was no longer spending nights at home. He knew that his life was in more danger than ever with the reward on his head. He had set up a hideout in the thicket and would only emerge when he was advised that it was safe to do so.

The Boren's were cousins of Bob Lee, but their family was split over their allegiance to the Union and to the Confederacy. They were correspondingly split in their support of the Peacock and Lee conflict. Henry Boren fought for the Union during the war, but the other Borens cast their lot with the Confederacy. Bill rode with William Clarke Quantrill's raiders. Henry Boren was somehow able to find out where the trail was to Bob Lee's hideout in the thicket. He may have overheard a family member's conversation. One day in either May or June of 1869 (there are several conflicting dates) Bob Lee was ambushed and killed by Henry Boren and members of the Sixth Cavalry.

Before Bob Lee had been laid to rest, Bill Boren retaliated. Furious, he went to the home of Henry Boren and after some cross words shot and killed Henry. Bill claimed that Henry was armed and ordered him off his property. He added that he did not draw until Henry "pulled down on me." Bill Boren left the area to be with his friend, John Wesley Hardin. After several years had passed, Bill was enticed back to the Four Corners. He was subsequently killed by Henry Boren's son.

Dick Johnson and Joe Parker were Bob Lee men intent on killing Lewis Peacock. In early July of 1871 one of them (nobody knows which one) climbed a tree at dawn by Lewis Peacock's home. When Peacock came out to get wood for the wood stove he was shot and killed beside his house.

Things eventually settled down in the Four Corners area, and other places, and for the most part Texas abided by the laws and ideals of Reconstruction.

McDade, Texas, as it once looked. The building at right is the Rock Saloon. *McDade Historical Museum, Courtesy of Vicki Nisbett.*

Chapter Fifty-Six
Shootout on Christmas Day

Prior to 1871, McDade, Texas was a sleepy little burg about 34 miles (55 kilometers) east of Austin. That year the Texas Central Railroad arrived and things picked up a bit. A row of brick buildings was constructed, as was a depot right in the middle of town adjacent to the railroad tracks that ran down the main street. The law in Bastrop County was ineffective, as it was in the neighboring counties of Lee and Williamson. The citizens of these three counties were terrorized by a group of rustlers and murderers called the "Notch Cutters," and there was little they could do about it. Occasionally, railroad men were robbed on payday. Ranchers who had sold cattle or horses ran the risk of losing their cash before they could get it to the bank. The Notch Cutters were in the business of selling beef. Rustled, and then butchered cattle could not be identified. It was the Notch Cutters way. Citizens that had the guts to testify against a gang member could be murdered before they ever reached the courtroom. If they were able to testify, in doing so they probably signed their own death warrant. Members of the gang were ranchers themselves scattered throughout the Yegua Creek area of Lee County, in country called the Knobs. Residents of that region, whether respected citizens or not, learned to become excellent marksmen because of constant trouble with the Comanche Indians.

Citizens finally decided to take matters into their own hands and organized a vigilance committee. Nobody knows for certain when it started or who the original organizers were, but it most likely began sometime in late 1873 or early 1874, in McDade. Naturally, the identities of those involved needed to remain a secret. The first "conviction" by the vigilantes was probably on May 4, 1874. The bullet-riddled body of a negro who had killed a white man was found hanging from a tree on that date. Two fellows named Waddell and Land, who were believed to be members of the Notch Cutters, were hanged side-by-side in January of 1875.

The Notch Cutters retaliated. Businessman Horace Alsup had traveled to Lexington, in Lee County, for a work related meeting. On his return trip, he was blasted from his saddle by a shotgun. Twelve slugs were found in his body. Bill Craddock had been an eye witness to cattle rustling. Furthermore, he recognized the culprits and went to court to testify against them. Soon thereafter, while on his way home from a days work at the syrup mill, he was also shotgunned to death. Later, another hanging occurred. A fellow named Howard Cordell, who was part Indian, was hanged (possibly by the vigilantes). Supposedly, it was said that Cordell was a "hereditary horse thief."

One of the larger spreads to have suffered a great deal of cattle rustling was the Olive Ranch in Williamson County, just across the line from Bastrop County. It was operated by the Olive brothers, Jay, John, Prentice, and Jim. On March 22, 1876, on their ranch, somebody discovered skinned and dressed beef, but nobody was around. It is believed that they were sure the rustlers would return for the goods and took cover to await their return. When the rustlers finally appeared, they were gunned down by the men in hiding. The two dead rustlers, James H. Crow and Turk Turner, were left on the prairie. One of Crow's sons departed from his home to search for his father when the latter did not return. Young Crow found the bodies. It is uncertain who did the shooting for there were no other witnesses. The Olive brothers were blamed. When the case went to court, it was quickly dismissed for lack of evidence.

During the evening on August 1, 1876, a large group of Notch Cutters attacked the Olive Ranch. A bloody battle ensued in which Jay and Prentice Olive were seriously injured, as were two of the ranch hands. The ranch house was torched but the glow from the flames made the outlaw gang easy targets. Blood of the attackers was found in several spots the following morning, but the number of outlaw casualties is unknown.

One day two men were found hanging near the Williamson County line. They were both dressed in fine clothes and were carrying a large sum of money that seemed to be untouched. Neither had any identification and nobody in the area had ever seen them before. Later, another dead man was found, naked, lying on a blanket. He was never identified either. No inquiries ever surfaced regarding the unknown dead men. Strange things were known to happen around McDade.

Pat Erhart was a music teacher and bachelor who lived in a settlement called Blue in the Knobs area. He was liked by everyone. Periodically he would host a party and dance at his large home and people would come from throughout the region to partake in the festivities. One of Erhart's parties took place on June 27, 1877. It was mandatory for all guests to check their firearms when they arrived in order to avoid any trouble. At approximately 2 a.m., a group of masked vigilantes surrounded the house. They presented Erhart with a list of five names of the men they wanted to see. The list read Wade Alsup, John Kuykendall, Young Floyd, Beck Scott, and Jim Floyd. All of the men responded with the exception of Jim Floyd. The vigilantes bound the wrists of the four men with rawhide, placed them on horses, and then led them down the road a piece where they were hanged. The lynchings seemed to have an effect on the Notch Cutters because violence was minimal for several years thereafter.

Storekeeper George Milton, who we now know was deeply involved with the vigilantes, was in his place of business on August 23, 1883, when a lad named Bob Young stepped through the front door and fired his shotgun at Milton. Young missed, and then fled. The persistent fellow returned the following day and missed again. This time Milton gunned him down. Two more murders occurred nine miles (14 kilometers) from McDade on November 22, 1883. In the small settlement of Fedor, a storekeeper named Keffel and his clerk were robbed and killed.

While returning from a business trip to Bastrop, Allen Wynn was accosted by members of the Notch Cutters who shot him, robbed him, and then left thinking he was dead. Wynn, who was a partner of George Milton and Thomas Bishop in both the cattle and saloon business, played dead after a bullet wounded him superficially. Although he was losing blood, he was able to drive his buckboard home and then send for Milton and Bishop. Wynn informed them that he had recognized his assailants.

This mistake by the Notch Cutters would cost them dearly.

A few days later, during the evening on December 1, 1883, Deputy Sheriff Isaac Heffington of Lee County was in McDade trying to follow up on the murders in Fedor. The lawman was shot in the chest at close range near the edge of town. His attacker fled. Heffington would die shortly thereafter. This renewed activity by the Notch Cutters raised the ire of the vigilantes. It was time for them to go back into action.

At about 7:30 p.m., on Christmas Eve, 1883, eight masked vigilantes entered the Rock Saloon in McDade, four through the front door and four through the rear door. They stuck their weapons into the guts of Thad McLemore, Wright McLemore, and Henry Pfeiffer. Thad McLemore was one of the men that had been identified by Allen Wynn. The trio had their hands tied behind their backs and were led down the road about a mile (1.6 kilometers) where they were hanged.

Christmas morning found Thomas Bishop, George Milton, and Dr. Vermillion sitting on the porch in front of George Milton's store. Down the street several people were celebrating the holiday at the Rock Saloon. Six men who were related by marriage rode in together and were also having a good time at the Rock Saloon until they were informed that the vigilantes had hanged three of their friends the night before. Jack, Heywood, and Asbury "Az" Beatty, Charley Goodman, Byrd Hasley, and Robert Stevens were shaken by the news. In the conversation that followed, Jack Beatty claimed that Milton and Bishop had accused Heywood Beatty of assisting in the death of Heffington, the deputy sheriff. Furthermore that he intended to kill both of them. Jack Beatty was advised that both Milton and Bishop were sitting on the front porch of Milton's store at that very moment. The six men concocted a quick plan and decided that it was time right then to rid themselves of both Milton and Bishop. Jack Beatty approached George Milton and reminded him that he (Beatty) had $35 on deposit and would like to get his money. Milton agreed and the two entered the store. It was part of the gang members' plan to split Milton and Bishop. While Milton was inside, Bishop was confronted by Az Beatty on the front porch. Az went for his gun, but Bishop beat him to it and fired a shot that hit Az Beatty in the thigh. The two grappled and rolled into the street. When Milton heard the shot he quickly got the drop on Jack Beatty. Bishop fired again and Az Beatty dropped dead. Milton then grabbed his shotgun as he herded Jack Beatty out the front door and into the street. Byrd Hasley and Charlie Goodman were just outside. Gunfire continued with Goodman taking a slug and falling wounded in the street. Hasley fled the scene. Robert Stevens was also wounded. Jack Beatty was shot in the head by both a pistol and a shotgun blast. He was also dead. Willie Griffin ran out of the Rock Saloon and took a bullet in the head from the pistol of Heywood Beatty. Heywood Beatty had been hit several times, but was able to crawl off between buildings and fled to his home and a doctor's care. Both of his brothers were dead, but he would survive. Willie Griffin died the next day. George Milton and Thomas Bishop were unscathed during the battle. They were arrested, as were Goodman and Stevens. All were released on bond. Governor Ireland ordered the Texas Volunteer Guard to McDade to establish order. The fight was already over so they encountered no difficulty.

During a citizens meeting on December 27, 1883, a list of names was established of undesirables. Those people named on the list were given ten days to either leave the region or stay and be hanged. Henceforth the Notch Cutters were nonexistent.

San Augustin Church in Laredo faces San Augustin Plaza circa 1880. *Webb County Heritage Foundation.*

Chapter Fifty-Seven
Laredo: The Botas and Guaraches

Colonel Santos Benavides was a Confederate war hero of legendary status who had established a political base in Laredo, Texas by the end of the Civil War. Dario Gonzales served under Benavides during the war. They were friends and fixtures in the Democratic Party. Gonzales was elected sheriff of Webb County in the election of 1872. The Democratic Party split that year as a result of many election irregularities. Leading the anti-Benavides faction was a wealthy businessman, Raymond Martin. Martin, a Frenchman, had opened a general store east of San Augustin Plaza and had acquired much land in Webb County. Much of his property was purchased, while some of it was seized from farmers and ranch owners who defaulted in their loans. Gonzales switched his allegiance and was reelected sheriff in 1876 as a Martin supporter. By the 1880s the Martin group virtually controlled Laredo and Webb County politics.

Santos Benavides, the banking brothers Daniel and Patricio Milmo, and J. J. Haynes, a prominent Republican, led a reform movement. They adopted the guarache (the sandal) as their emblem, significant as the symbol of the "common man." Not to be outdone, the Martin faction chose the botas (the boot) as their trademark. Each faction now had a name: the Botas and the Guaraches. Both political parties held lectures, parades, and demonstrations to solicit supporters and intimidate the other party.

Dario Gonzales and Raymond Martin had a falling out in 1883. Supposedly, Gonzales had collected more than $2,000 in taxes from Encinal County (now the western portion of Webb County) which was within his jurisdiction. The money never reached the county treasury. Gonzales was sued and fired as sheriff. When the matter reached the Texas Supreme Court, Gonzales was exonerated. He blamed Martin for his debacle and once again joined the group now known as the Guaraches. Dario Gonzales would soon become the leader of the Guaraches.

The Botas swept the 1884 elections, and the hatred by each faction for the opposite party grew. Two years later, on election day, April 6, 1886, with animosity at its peak, the Botas won again, but this time the Guaraches were able to win two seats on the city council. They were making inroads, they thought, and decided to celebrate their small victory. They dug up one of two Civil War cannons that had been partially buried with its muzzle down (it was being used as a hitching post). The Guaraches painted it yellow and fired it on the evening of the 6th as part of their celebration. The partying by the Guaraches infuriated the Botas who decided to hold a funeral procession to bury the Guarache in effigy. Gonzales was angry. He advised his cohorts that he would allow the Botas to parade, but not to bury the Guarache in effigy. Furthermore he was quoted as saying that "someone else was going to be buried."

The Bota funeral procession began at Bota Hall at 3 p.m. on the afternoon of April 7th and was to proceed to the home of Dario Gonzales where a symbolic sandal would be dramatically buried. The funeral cortege included 30 armed horsemen and 120 riflemen on foot. Additionally, the Botas had snipers stationed at various vantage points to protect the route of the two-block long procession. The Guaraches set up a blockade in front of the Botas with their yellow cannon and armed partisans. Somebody squeezed off a shot, and all hell broke loose. It is estimated that in the next thirty minutes some 2,000 rounds were fired. The cannon's fuse was lit and the old weapon blasted a barrel full of nails which did no damage to anything except the church at San Agustin Plaza. Nobody knows for certain how many casualties resulted from the melee. The best estimate might be sixteen dead and scores wounded. Some bodies were dumped into the Rio Grande River and some of the wounded struggled across the border into Mexico. Eight funerals were held on the very day following the shooting.

Botas claimed that a Guarache, Francisco Garcia, fired the first shot. Guaraches claimed that the first shot was fired by a Botas, Concepcion Hererra. The bloodbath in Laredo is another episode during a very violent period in Texas history. By the time the election of 1890 arrived, the Guaraches nearly ceased to exist.

Charles (left) and George Marlow, while shackled to two dead brothers, fought off a mob intent on lynching them. *Marlow Chamber of Commerce, Courtesy of the Marlow Family.*

Chapter Fifty-Eight
The Battle at Dry Creek

George, Charles, Boone, Alfred "Alf," and Lewellyn "Ep" Marlow were brothers. They were sons of Martha Jane and Dr. Wilson Williamson Marlow. Ep was the youngest of the five. The brothers were a courageous and gutsy bunch, and were involved in one of the most amazing gunfights in Texas history.

On April 15, 1886, the year after Dr. Marlow's death, Boone killed a man near Vernon, in Wilbarger County, Texas. Although Boone claimed to have never seen James H. Holston before, it may be that Holston had been carrying an old grudge against Boone. When Holston decided to rid the country of Boone Marlow he made a grave mistake. Holston took Boone by surprise as he was approaching his sister's house, and opened fire on him. Boone grabbed his Winchester and returned the fire with much greater accuracy. James Holston fell dead. Suddenly Boone was a wanted man. The brothers headed to Colorado with the hope that things would cool down.

Two years later they decided that enough time had passed, and that it would be safe to return to the Southwest. They were wrong. The five brothers were arrested for stealing horses in Indian Territory and jailed in Graham, Texas. The charge was later proven to be unfounded. After being freed on bail, they went to live at the O. G. Denson farm in Young County, about 12 miles (19 kilometers) from Graham. Shortly before Christmas, on December 16, 1888, Sheriff Marion DeKalb Wallace and Deputy Sheriff Thomas B. "Tom" Collier rode to the Denson farm with a warrant for the arrest of Boone Marlow in connection with the 1886 murder of James Holston in Wilbarger County. Collier was the first to enter the house. He drew his pistol and fired the first shot. Boone grabbed his Winchester and shot back. His first bullet went through the deputy's hat, and the second struck Wallace as he approached the front door. Boone ran to the door as Wallace tumbled outside on the porch floor. Both of his kidneys were damaged and Sheriff M. D. Wallace died a week later. Boone suddenly had a price on his head. The governor posted a reward of $200 for Boone
Marlow dead or alive. Citizens of Young County added another $1,500 making the total reward $1,700. Feeling the heat, Boone fled the area.

Near a spot called Hell Creek in Indian Territory, twenty miles (32 kilometers) from Fort Sill, Oklahoma, Boone hid out at the place of his ex-sweetheart, Susan Harbolt. The bounty on Boone's head was attractive to Susan's brother, George E. Harbolt, and two cohorts Jim Beavers and John E. Derrickson. They evidently poisoned Marlow and then shot him before carrying his body to Fort Sill and then on to Graham

The five Marlow brothers, (from Left to Right) George, Boone, Alfred, Lewellyn and Charles. *Marlow Chamber of Commerce, Courtesy of the Marlow Family.*

for the reward. After receiving their reward the trio was later arrested and charged with murder. When he died on January 28, 1889, Boone Marlow never knew the fate of his brothers who were involved in an incredible shootout nine days earlier in Texas.

After Boone fled to Oklahoma, Charles, Alf, and Ep Marlow were arrested for complicity in the shooting of Marion Wallace. Ep actually rode to Graham, Texas, to get a physician for Wallace after the shooting occurred. He was arrested and jailed before he could leave town. Charles and Alf were arrested and transported to Graham to stand trial in federal court. When George (and other family members) went to Graham in an effort to clear his brothers, he was also jailed. The citizens of Graham were mad that their sheriff had been killed and they wanted revenge. The Marlows escaped from the jailhouse on January 14, 1889, but were caught and returned to their cell the following morning.

An unruly mob, all masked, wanted to lynch the Marlow brothers and they surrounded the jail on the night of January 17, 1889, but they had no success. They were afraid to fire a shot as it might waken the townspeople, and the prisoners were able to repel the mob with one mighty punch thrown by Charles Marlow, and a piece of water pipe. Charles Marlow's punch knocked the unidentified man unconscious. He was dragged from the scene. Whether by coincidence, or not, one of the local citizens who was in fine health the morning of the 17th, died within a couple of days from "brain fever." Tom Collier, the new sheriff, and others concocted a story that an attempt was made by Boone Marlow and a large group of men to break the prisoners out of jail, but that the effort was resisted by local lawmen. Upon hearing this fabrication at his office in Dallas, Deputy U. S. Marshal Ben F. Cabell ordered the prisoners moved to a safer jailhouse in Weatherford, Texas.

Graham peace officers, in cahoots with the mob, decided that it was time to act again. After dark, on January 19, 1889, the Marlows were put in irons for the trip to Weatherford. George was shackled to Ep, and Charles was shackled to Alf. Two other prisoners, William D. Burkhart and Louis Clift were shackled to each other. There were seven guards, six who were armed, while the driver of the hack carrying the prisoners was not. There was another hack and a buggy in which the armed guards rode. As the group reached Dry Creek, outside of Graham, all hell broke loose. It was approximately 9 p.m. The mob, all masked, had been waiting, and they opened fire. Although shackled together, Alf and Charles jumped over the side of their hack and quickly got to the guards' hack. George and Ep did the same. Alf grabbed somebody's gun barrel, and in the process was riddled by bullets. Meanwhile, the other prisoners were able to wrestle guns away from the guards and turned them on the mob. One guard was killed and two were injured. The prisoners also grabbed the weapons of the fallen guards. The remaining guards ran to escape the barrage of bullets and to join the mob. Ep was blown to shreds by the mob's gunfire. He was dead. His body was so mutilated that it later needed to be bound up with strips of cloth so he could be dressed for his casket. George had been shot in one hand. Charles had been shot in the jaw and the chest. Louis Clift took a slug in one leg. While shackled to their two dead brothers, George and Charles continued to shoot at the mob. The astonished mob retreated into the woods to reorganize. With a knife that was taken from one of the bodies, Charles was able to separate himself from Alf by cutting off his foot. He then came to the aid of George who couldn't handle the knife because of the wound to his hand. Charles proceeded to amputate Ep's foot in order to free George. Charles, George, Burkhart, and Clift climbed into one of the wagons and with Burkhart driving they fled from the scene. The mob was so stunned that it gave no effort to pursue the wagon. They had planned on a "peaceful" lynching, not a gunfight. The guard that was killed, Sam Criswell, was one of the mob's conspirators. The other two riders in the mob that were shot and killed were, Bruce Wheeler and Frank Harmeson. Both were instigators in the mob action. In addition to all the deaths, and the wounds to George, Charles, and Louis Clift, at least three other men had been shot, and the wounded may have totaled five.

The two Marlow brothers headed back to the Denson farm where they agreed to surrender to Deputy U. S. Marshal W. H. Morton who assured them protection. They were taken to Dallas where they were tried and acquitted. After George and Charles were exonerated of any wrongdoing, they both moved to Colorado where they became peace officers and prominent citizens. Charles died in California on January 19, 1941, fifty-two years to the day after the battle at Dry Creek. George died July 3, 1945 in Colorado.

In 1891, several members of the mob were sentenced for their part in the attack on the Marlows. The battle at Dry Creek was extraordinary. It was the only time in the annals of recorded history that unarmed men shackled together were able through amazing courage and guts to hold off a mob intent on lynching them.

The Colt Single-Action Army was introduced in 1873. Commonly known as the "Peacemaker," this solid-frame, six-shot revolver became the most popular handgun on the western frontier. *Wild Horse Collection.*

Chapter Fifty-Nine
Chronology of Frontier Firearms

From the days when our ancestors first set foot on the New Land, America has been a gun-owning society. Prior to the California gold rush, most of the western frontier was vast wilderness, sparsely inhabited by Indian tribes. White men who ventured into this virgin territory were predominately trappers, fur traders and explorers. In 1849 thousands of people migrated to the West Coast hoping to fulfill their dreams of riches. They faced many perils in the hinterland. Pioneers felt the necessity to carry firearms with them at all times as a means of protection. Our "right to bear arms" was probably never more evident than during the half-century between the California gold rush and the turn of the century. Gun manufacturers provided a wide variety of models from which an individual could choose.

The step from inconsistent flintlocks to the more dependable percussion caps was a major breakthrough in the development of weaponry. The following chronology highlights the evolution of firearms during the developmental years between 1835 and 1897:

1835	Sam Colt patented a mechanically revolving cylinder in England, and the following year in the United States. He mass produced handguns in both countries with advanced technological methods.
1837	Ethan Allen patented a self-cocking mechanism. Allen was one of the forerunners in the development of repeating handguns. He, and Henry Deringer, Jr., were leaders in the manufacture of pocket arms. Allen later developed pistols with revolving barrels called "pepperboxes."

1839	The government of Texas purchased 180 .36 caliber Paterson Colt revolvers from the Patent Arms Manufacturing Company. Most of these handguns were issued to the Texas Rangers. The Patent Arms Manufacturing Company would eventually fail, but the Rangers had helped establish the efficiency of Colt's revolvers.
1847	Sam Colt, with the assistance of Captain Samuel Walker, obtained a government contract for 1000 .44 caliber Walker Colt revolvers which were earmarked for the Mexican War. Although Eli Whitney, Jr. originally manufactured the Walker Colt for Sam Colt, the latter eventually purchased Whitney's equipment and established his own manufacturing plant at Hartford, Connecticut.
1848	Allen & Thurber had sold more than 10,000 pepperbox models during a three year period. The pepperbox (with its revolving barrels) actually exceeded the total sales of Colt products for a while.
	Christian Sharps patented his vertically sliding block design. He began producing a breech loading single-shot rifle which had a high degree of accuracy. Although the muzzle-loading rifle remained popular for many years, the breechloader could be reloaded much more rapidly. Sharps manufactured rifles up to .60 caliber. His .50 caliber rifle was a favorite of buffalo hunters.
1851	Colt began manufacture of its Model 1851 Navy. The Navy revolver would become a popular handgun during the late 1850s.
1854	Smith and Wesson patented a lever-action repeating pistol.
1855	Smith and Wesson sold its rights to the lever-action pistol to the Volcanic Repeating Arms Company. Oliver Winchester was a Volcanic stockholder.
1856	Following the demise of the Volcanic Repeating Arms Company, the New Haven Arms Company was established with Oliver Winchester as president and Benjamin Tyler Henry as plant superintendent.
1857	Smith and Wesson produced a seven-shot .22 caliber single-action handgun with a bored-through chamber. After realizing that Rollin White had patented such a chamber two years earlier, Smith and Wesson purchased his patent rights.
	Benjamin Tyler Henry patented his design of a lever-action rifle

with a rim-fire cartridge. The Henry rifle, which achieved much success on the Western Frontier, was the predecessor of the famed Winchester.

1858 E. Remington & Sons began production of a revolver that was designed by Fordyce Beals.

1860 Christopher M. Spencer patented a repeating rifle which became very popular as a combat weapon during the Civil War.

The New Haven Arms Company began producing B. Tyler Henry's .44 caliber, lever-action, brass-framed Henry rifle that was patented three years earlier. They would soon change their name to the Henry Repeating Rifle Company.

Colt introduced its Model 1860 Army which was to become a popular handgun.

1861 Smith and Wesson began production of a .32 caliber handgun, many of which reached the Western Frontier.

1863 The advent of rim-fire and center-fire cartridges was a significant development in the evolution of firearms. By about 1863, the more popular gun dealers in the Old West offered a wide variety of firearms, both percussion and cartridge. Metallic cartridges made loading considerably faster and safer.

1865 The U. S. Army had been searching for a method to convert its thousands of muzzle-loading muskets to breechloaders. When Erskine S. Allin, of the Springfield Armory, patented his conversion method, he solved the government's dilemma. The Model 1865 Springfield, which was popularly known as the "needle gun" or "Allin's Alteration," was the first government conversion.

1866 A new design by Erskine S. Allin made the Model 1866 Springfield even more efficient than its predecessor.

The Henry Repeating Rifle Company (originally the New Haven Arms Company) changed its name again to become the Winchester Repeating Arms Company.

Nelson King, Winchester's superintendent, patented a revolutionary new magazine tube which could be loaded with 15 cartridges.

Cartridges were simply pushed through a spring-tempered loading gate located in the right side of the receiver. The design was incorporated into the first rifle to bear Winchester's name—the Model 1866. A brass receiver was added to the weapon which was also available as a carbine.

1867   Charles and John Parker began manufacturing one of the more popular shotguns. Parker shotguns were available in 10, 11 and 12-gauge. The brothers ran advertisements, which could be seen in many western newspapers, promoting Parker shotguns from $50 to about $200 for a well-adorned version.

1869   There was an ever-expanding market for weapons which could be easily concealed by hiding them in a pocket, or elsewhere. Henry Deringer had so popularized short-barrel single-shot pocket pistols that they became known as "derringers" (spelled with an added "r"). Colt began producing derringers in 1869.

The Colt and Remington .44s were extremely popular in the western civilian market.

1870   Smith and Wesson introduced their Model 3, the first large-bore (.44 caliber) metallic cartridge revolver to be manufactured. Its extractor reduced reloading time by nearly one-half, by ejecting the previously fired shells when the handgun was opened for reloading. This feature made the handgun a favorite of many outlaws—including Jesse James. Major George W. Schofield of the Tenth Cavalry redesigned the Model 3 and the Schofield name became an integral part of ensuing Smith and Wesson models.

The Model 1870 Springfield would become the preferred infantry rifle, and would remain so through about 1873.

The seven-shot Spencer carbine was used by mounted troops during post-war Indian fighting.

1871   Remington produced a .50 caliber single-shot pistol, its Model 1871, using the rolling-block design it popularized on rifles and carbines during the 60s.

1873   Colt introduced its Single-Action Army revolver, which was more commonly known as the "Peacemaker." The model, which was destined to become the most famous handgun of its era, had a solid frame with a six-shot cylinder that opened to the side. It was initially chambered for a new .45 caliber center-fire cartridge. The revolver was rugged, easy to handle, would cock rapidly, and had excellent handling qualities.

The legendary Winchester Model 1873 was introduced. The rifle boasted a center-fire .44-40 cartridge (.44 caliber plus 40 grains of powder) and an iron receiver. The popular Model 1873 was produced continuously until 1919. The Winchester Model 1876 was modified to receive .45-70 or .45-75 cartridges.

1877	Shotguns played an important role in the firearms of the Old West. It was often the preferred weapon when a gunfight was inevitable. Stagecoach drivers were equipped with shotguns. Wells Fargo messengers often carried sawed-off shotguns. Remington offered a variety of models which were competitively priced with Parker.
	Although they never rivaled the dominance of Parker and Remington, Stevens and Colt entered the shotgun market in 1877 and 1878 respectively. Both offered 10 and 12-gauge models.
1883	Harrington & Richardson introduced a hammerless double-barreled shotgun. Ithaca and L. C. Smith successfully manufactured shotguns, as well.
1885	The Winchester Model 1885 High Wall was introduced. It was the first of 44 John Moses Browning designs to be purchased by Winchester.
1886	The Winchester Model 1886, another Browning design, was stronger and superior to any Winchester previously manufactured. The popular "86" could handle the .45-70 and various other calibers, and was sold by gun dealers across the Old West.
1887	Winchester introduced a lever-action shotgun, another product of the ingenious John Moses Browning. The Model 1887 was available in both 10 and 12-gauge.
1889	Marlin was Winchester's only major competitor in the lever-action market. John Marlin's Model 1889 introduced a solid-top, side-ejection receiver through which fired shells ejected from the upper right side of the receiver.

	Colt introduced its .38 caliber double-action revolver. This model, which was issued by the U.S. Navy, had a swing-out cylinder.
1892	The Winchester Model 1892 lever-action rifle was introduced. This successful repeating rifle was manufactured in calibers of: .44-40, .38-40, .32-20 and .25-20.
1893	Winchester began marketing another Browning invention—a pump shotgun.
1894	Winchester introduced its Model 1894 lever-action rifle.
1895	Another Browning-inspired Winchester, the Model 1895 lever-action rifle was introduced.
1896	Arthur Savage marketed a new hammerless, lever-action repeater with his .303 caliber Savage Model 1896.
1897	Winchester's Model 1897 (a perfected version of the Model 1893) became one of the best selling repeating shotguns ever manufactured.

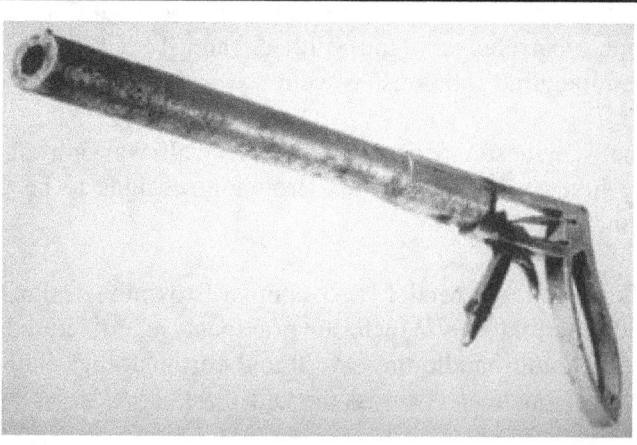

John Moses Browning was truly the greatest gun inventor of all time. Over eighty different firearms developed from 128 Browning patents. His designs were used by many manufacturers, including Winchester, Colt, Remington, Fabrique Nationale (Belgium), Savage, Stevens, Ithaca, and his own company, Browning. This photograph shows one of Browning's early experimental models which never went into production. *Browning.*

Acknowledgements

Chip Southworth
Madeline Meehan
Sue Anderson
Ruth S. Bennett
Teresa Bond
Nancy Flanders
Becky Lintz, Colorado Historical Society
Oklahoma Historical Society
David N. Kloppenborg, Boot Hill Museum
Christie Stanley, Kansas State Historical Society
Bonnie Morgan, Montana Historical Society
Bill Hubbs, The Barney Hubbs Collection
Dorinda Venegas, West of the Pecos Museum
LaVaughn Bresnahan, Wyoming State Museum
Bob Chandler, Wells Fargo Historical Services
Center for American History, University of Texas at Austin
John R. Lovett, Western History Collections, University of Oklahoma Library
John W. Anderson, Archives, Texas State Library
University of New Mexico, Zimmerman Library
Museum of New Mexico
Arizona State University, Hayden Library
Bruce Hanson, Western History Department, Denver Public Library
Bill Waltz
Dean Nelson, Museum of Connecticut History
Lee Good and Sandra Thompson, J. M. Davis Arms & Historical Museum
Elizabeth Holmes, Buffalo Bill Historical Center
Kim Murphy, Colt's Manufacturing Company, Inc.
Connecticut State Library
El Paso Museum of History
UTEP Library, University of Texas at El Paso
Colt Collectors Association
Deedra Braner, Browning
Becky Costello, Winchester Arms
Remington Arms Company, Inc.
Western Heritage Museum, Union Pacific Railroad Collection
Texas Ranger Museum
Elizabeth Holmes and Paul Sees, Buffalo Bill Historical Center
Mary Nelson, Special Collections, Wichita State University
Molly Freeman, Austin Public Library History Center

Jim Bradshaw, Nita Stewart Haley Memorial Library
Mario Einaudi, Arizona Historical Society
Sheila Holder, Tulare County Library
Dawn Rodrigues, California State Library
Kelly Hobbs, Fresno City and County Historical Society
Doug Wickland, National Firearms Museum
Nancy Sherbert, Kansas State Historical Society
Jane Hoerster, Mason County Library
Grace Rae Davenport
Don DeCoss, Wells Fargo Museum
Juliet L. Galonska and Bill Black, Fort Smith National Historic Site
Hayes Colburn
Elvis Fleming and Annette Lucero, Historical Center for Southeast New Mexico
Beverly Hammond and Drew Gomber, Lincoln Heritage Trust
Barbara Smith-LaBorde, University of Texas at Austin
Jodi Wright, Bell County Museum
Berneta Peoples and Gene Bigham, Belton Journal
Belton City Library
George Anne Cormier, Calhoun County Museum
Connie Todd, Texas State University
Lynda Hatch
W.M. Von-Maszewski and Debbie Shoemaker, George Memorial Library
Vircenoy Macatee and Nevin Foster, Hood County Museum
Anna and Bill Crawford
Ben Evridge, Comanche County Museum
Katherine Roberds Cox
D. Ray Blakeley, Herzstein Museum
Mary Robertson and Jackie bean, Yuba County Library
Karen Burrow, Mary Aaron Museum
Placer County Museum
Patricia Akre, San Francisco History Center, San Francisco Public Library
Union County Historical Society
Cora Wilson, Jackson County Historical Society
Emily Wolff, California Historical Society
José Villegas, New Mexico State Records Center and Archives
Alissa Rosenberg, Minnesota Historical Society
Jed Howard
Myrtle Fritschy
Rebecca Sue Burdsal
John Burdsal
Paul Sees, Buffalo Bill Historical Center
Gene Franklin

Bibliography

BOOKS

Adams, Ramon F. *A Fitting Death for Billy the Kid.* Norman: University of Oklahoma Press, 1960.

Adams, Ramon F. *Six-Guns & Saddle Leather: A Bibliography of Books & Pamphlets on Western Outlaws and Gunmen.* Norman: University of Oklahoma Press, 1969.

Ashbaugh, Don. *Nevada's Turbulent Yesterday.* Los Angeles: Westernlore Press, 1963.

Baker, Pearl. *The Wild Bunch at Robber Roost.* Los Angeles: Westernlore Press, 1963

Ballert, Marion, with Carl W. Breihan. *Billy the Kid: A Date with Destiny.* Seattle: Superior Publishing Co., 1970.

Bartholomew, Ed. *Black Jack Ketchum: Last of the Hold-Up Kings.* Houston: Frontier Press of Texas, 1955.

Bartholomew, Ed. *Wyatt Earp: The Man & the Myth.* Toyahvale, TX: Frontier Book Co., 1964.

Beebe, Lucius, and Charles Clegg. *U.S. West: The Saga of Wells Fargo.* New York: E. P. Dutton & Co. 1949.

Bird, Allan G. *Silverton: Then and Now.* Englewood, CO: Access Publishing, 1990.

Blair, Edward. *Everybody Came to Leadville.* Leadville: Timberline Books, 1971.

Block, Eugene B. *Great Train Robberies of the West.* New York: Coward-McCann, Inc., 1959.

Boessenecker, John. *Badge and Buckshot: Lawlessness in Old California.* Norman: University of Oklahoma Press, 1988.

Breihan, Carl W. *Great Lawmen of the West.* New York: Bonanza Books, 1963.

Breihan, Carl W. *Ride the Razor's Edge.* Gretna, LA: Pelican Publishing Co., 1992.

Breihan, Carl. *Younger Brothers.* San Antonio: The Naylor Co., 1972.

Brown, John Henry. *History of Texas, from 1685 to 1892. Volume One.* St. Louis, MO: Beckktold & Co., 1892.

Burrows, William E. *Vigilante!* New York: Harcourt Brace Jovanovich, 1976.

Burton, Jeff. *Dynamite and Six-shooter.* Santa Fe: Palomino Press, 1970.

Calvert, Robert A. and Arnoldo De Leon. *The History of Texas.* Second Edition. Wheeling, IL: Harlan Davidson, Inc., 1996.

Castleman, Harvey N. *Sam Bass: The Train Robber.* Girard, KS: Haldeman-Julius Publications, 1944.

Chamblin, Thomas S., ed. *The Historical Encyclopedia of Texas.* Austin: The Texas Historical Institute, 1982.

Chrisman, Harry E. *The Ladder of Rivers.* Denver: Sage Books, 1962.

Coe, George W. *Frontier Fighter.* Albuquerque: University of New Mexico Press, 1934.

Coolidge, Dane. *Fighting Men of the West.* New York: E.P. Dutton, 1932.

Cossley-Batt, Jill. *The Last of the California Rangers.* New York and London, Funk and Wagnalls Co., 1928.

Coursey, O.W. *Wild Bill: James Butler Hickok.* Mitchell, SD, Educator Supply Co., 1924.

Cox, William R. *Luke Short and His Era.* Garden City, NY: Doubleday and Co., Inc., 1961.

Crofutt, George A. *Crofutt's Grip-Sack Guide of Colorado.* Boulder: Johnson Books, 1885.

Croy, Homer. *Jesse James Was My Neighbor.* New York: Duell, Sloan and Pearce, 1949.

Croy, Homer. *Trigger Marshal: The Story of Chris Madsen.* New York: Duell, Sloan and Pearce, 1958.

Dalton, Emmett. *Beyond the Law.* Coffeyville, KS: The Coffeyville Historical Society, 1918.

DeArment, Robert K. *Bat Masterson: The Man and the Legend.* Norman: The University of Oklahoma Press, 1979.

Dimsdale, Thomas J. *The Vigilantes of Montana.* Norman: University of Oklahoma

Press, 1953.

Elliot, David S., and Ed Bartholomew. *The Dalton Gang and the Coffeyville Raid.* Fort Davis, TX: Frontier Book Co., 1968.
Elliot, David Stewart. *Last Raid of the Daltons.* Freeport, NY: Books for Libraries Press, 1971

Elman, Robert. *Badmen of the West.* Scaucus, NJ: Ridge Press, Inc., 1974.

Ernst, John. *Jesse James.* Englewood Cliffs, NJ: Prentice-Hall, Inc., 1976.

Erwin, Allen A. *The Southwest of John H. Slaughter, 1841-1922: Pioneer Cattleman and Traildriver of Texas, the Pecos, and Arizona and Sheriff of Tombstone.* Glendale, CA: Arthur II. Clark Co., 1965.

Ewell, Thomas T. *History of Hood County.* Granbury, TX: Frank Gaston, Publisher, 1895. Reprinted by the Junior Woman's Club, Granbury, TX, 1956.

Fisher, O.c, and J.C Dykes. *King Fisher: His Life and Times.* Norman: University of Oklahoma Press, 1960.

Forrest, Earle R. *Arizona's Dark and Bloody Ground.* Caldwell, ID: Caxton Printers, Ltd., 1952.

Fossett, Frank. *Colorado.* New York: C.G. Crawford, 1880.

Garavaglia, Louis A. and Charles G. Worman. *Firearms of the American West, 1803-1865.* Albuquerque: University of New Mexico Press, 1984.

Garavaglia, Louis A. and Charles G. Worman. *Firearms of the American West, 1866-1894.* Albuquerque: University of New Mexico Press, 1985.

Gard, Wayne. *Frontier Justice.* Norman: University of Oklahoma Press, 1949.

Gard, Wayne. *Sam Bass.* Boston and New York: Houghton Mifflin, 1936.

Garrett, Patrick F. *The Authentic Life of Billy, the Kid: The Noted Desperado of the Southwest, Whose Deeds of Daring and Blood Made His Name a Terror in New Mexico, Arizona, and Northern Mexico.* Norman: University of Oklahoma Press, 1954.

Glasscock, C. B. *Bandits and the Southern Pacific.* New York: Frederick A. Stokes Co., 1929.

Graves, Richard S. *Oklahoma Outlaws: A Graphic History of the Early Days of Oklahoma.* Oklahoma City: State Printing Co., 1915.

Grimes, Roy. *300 Years In Victoria County.* Victoria, TX: The Victoria Advocate

Publishing Co., 1968.

Haley, J. Evetts. *Jeff Milton: A Good Man With a Gun.* Norman: University of Oklahoma Press, 1948.

Hall, Frank. *History of the State of Colorado.* 4 Vols. Chicago: Blakely Printing Co., 1895.

Hall, Sarah Harkey. *Surviving on the Texas Frontier.* Austin: Eakin Press, 1996.

Hamlin, William Lee. *The True Story of Billy the Kid.* Caldwell, ID: Caxton Printers, Ltd., 1959.

Hardin, John Wesley. *The Life of John Wesley Hardin as Written by Himself.* Norman: University of Oklahoma Press, 1961.

Harkey, Dee. *Mean as Hell.* Santa Fe, NM: Ancient City Press, 1989.

Hertzog, Peter. *A Dictionary of New Mexico Desperadoes.* Santa Fe, NM: Press of the Territorian, 1965.

Horan, James D. *Across the Cimarron.* New York: Crown Publishers, Inc., 1956.

Horan, James D. *The Authentic Wild West: The Gunfighters.* New York: Crown Publishers, Inc., 1976.

Horan, James D. and Howard Swiggett. *The Pinkerton Story.* New York: G. P. Putnam's Sons, 1951.

Horn, Tom. *Life of Tom Horn, Government Scout and Interpreter, Written By Himself, Together with His Letters and Statements by His Friends.* Norman: University of Oklahoma Press, 1964.

Hunter, J. Marvin and Noah H. Rose. *The Album of Gunfighters.* San Antonio: Hunter and Rose, 1951.

Jahns, Pat. *The Frontier World of Doc Holliday.* New York: Hastings House, 1957.

James, Jesse, Jr. *Jesse James, My Father.* Independence, MO: Sentinel Publishing Co., 1899.

James, Vinton Lee. *Frontier and Pioneer Recollections of Early Days in San Antonio and West Texas.* San Antonio: Vinton Lee James, 1938.

Jennings, N.A. *A Texas Ranger.* New York: Charles Scribner's Sons, 1899.

Kirby, Edward M. *The Saga of Butch Cassidy and the Wild Bunch.* Palmer Lake, CO:

The Filter Press, 1977.

Lake, Stuart N. *Wyatt Earp: Frontier Marshal.* Boston and New York: Houghton Mifflin, 1931.

Lamar, Howard R. (Ed.). *The Reader's Encyclopedia of the American West.* New York: Thomas Y. Crowell Co., 1977.

Langford, N.P. *Vigilante Days and Ways.* Missoula, MT: Montana State University, 1957.

Larson, T.A. *History of Wyoming.* Lincoln: University of Nebraska Press, 1965.

Latta, Frank F. *Dalton Gang Days.* Santa Cruz, CA: Bear State Books, 1976.

Llewellyn, Karl N., and E. Adamson Hoebel. *The Cheyenne Way: Conflict and Case Law in Primitive Jurisprudence.* Norman: University of Oklahoma Press, 1941.

Lucia, Ellis. *Tough Men, Tough Country.* Englewood Cliffs, NJ: Prentice-Hall, Inc., 1963.

Malone, Dumas, ed. *Dictionary of American Biography.* New York: Charles Scribner's Sons, 1943.

Malone, Michael P. and Richard B. Roeder. *Montana: A History of Two Centuries.* Seattle: University of Washington Press, 1988.

Maxwell, Hu. *Evans and Sontag. The Famous Bandits of California.* Fresno, CA: Panorama West Books, 1981.

McNeal, T.A. *When Kansas Was Young.* New York: The Macmillan Co., 1922.

McReynolds, Edwin C. *Oklahoma: A History of The Sooner State.* Norman: University of Oklahoma Press, 1954.

Metz, Leon C. *Dallas Stoudenmire.* Norman: Universirty of Oklahoma Press, 1979.

Metz, Leon C. *John Selman, Gunfighter.* Norman: University of Oklahoma Press, 1980.

Metz, Leon C. *Pat Garrett: The Story of a Western Lawman.* Norman: University of Oklahoma Press, 1973.

Miller, Floyd. *Bill Tilghman: Marshal of the Last Frontier.* New York: Doubleday and Co., Inc., 1968.

Miller, Joseph. *The Arizona Rangers.* New York: Hastings House Publishers, 1972.

Miller, Nyle H., and Joseph W. Snell. *Great Gunfighters of the Kansas Cowtowns, 1867-1886*. Lincoln: University of Nebraska Press, 1967.

Moody, Ralph. *Stagecoach West*. New York: Thomas Y. Crowell Co., 1967.

Nash, Jay Robert. *Encyclopedia of Western Lawmen & Outlaws*. New York: Paragon House, 1992.

Nix, Evett Dumas. *Oklahombres: Particularly the Wilder Ones. As told to Gordon Hines*. St. Louis: E.D. Nix, 1929.

Nolan, Frederick. Bad Blood: *The Life and Times of the Horrell Brothers*. Stillwater, OK: Barbed Wire Press, 1994.

Nolan, Frederick. *The Lincoln County War: A Documentary History*. Norman: University of Oklahoma Press, 1992.

Nordyke, Lewis. *John Wesley Hardin: Texas Gunman*. New York: William Morrow & Co., 1957.

Olmstead, Frederick Law. *A Journey Through Texas; or, a Saddle-trip on the Southwestern Frontier: with a Statistical Appendix*. New York: Dix, Edwards and Co., 1857.

O'Neal, Bill. *Encyclopedia of Western Gunfighters*. Norman: University of Oklahoma Press, 1979.

Paine, Lauran. *Texas Ben Thompson*. Los Angeles: Westernlore Press, 1966.

Paine, Lauran. *Tom Horn: Man of the West*. Barre, MA, Barre Publishing Co., 1963.

Parker, Watson. *Deadwood: The Golden Years*. Lincoln: University of Nebraska Press, 1981.

Parsons, Chuck. *Clay Allison: Portrait of a Shootist*. Seagraves, TX, Pioneer Book Publishers, 1983.

Parsons, Chuck. *Robert Clay Allison: Gentleman Gunfighter*. Pecos TX, West of the Pecos Museum Press, 1977.

Patterson, Richard. *Historical Atlas of the Outlaw West*. Boulder, CO: Johnson Books, 1985.

Patterson, Richard. *Wyoming's Outlaw Days*. Boulder, CO: Johnson Books, 1982.

Poe, John William. *The Death of Billy the Kid*. Boston and New York: Houghton

Mifflin Co., 1933.

Polk, Stella Gipson. *Mason and Mason County: A History.* Austin: The Pemberton Press, 1966.
Prassel, Frank Richard. *The Western Peace Officer: A Legacy of Law and Order.* Norman: University of Oklahoma Press, 1972.

Preece, Harold. *The Dalton Gang: End of an Outlaw Era.* New York: Hastings House, 1963.

Rathmell, William (Edited by). *Life of the Marlows, A True Story of Frontier Life of Early Days.* University of North Texas Press, 1984.

Rennert, Vincent Paul. *Western Outlaws.* New York: Crowell-Collier Press, 1968.

Rickards, Colin. *Mysterious Dave Mather.* Santa Fe, NM: Press of the Territorian, 1968.

Roberton, Frank C., and that Beth Kay Harris. *Soapy Smith, King of the Frontier Con Men.* New York: Hastings House, Publishers, 1961.

Rosa, Joseph G. *Age of the Gunfighter: Men and Weapons on the Frontier 1840-1900.* Norman: University of Oklahoma Press, 1995.

Rosa, Joseph G. *They Called Him Wild Bill: The Life and Adventures of James Butler Hickok.* Norman: Univerity of Oklahoma Press, 1964.

Rose, Victor M. *The Texas Vendetta; or, The Sutton-Taylor Feud.* New York: J. J. Little and Co., 1956.

San Saba Historical Commission. *San Saba County History: 1856-1983.* San Angelo, TX: News Foto, 1983.

Schultz, Vernon B. *Southwestern Town: The Story of Willcox, Arizona.* Tucson: University of Arizona Press, 1964.

Secrest, William B. *Dangerous Trails: Five Desperadoes of the Old West Coast.* Stillwater, OK: Barbed Wire Press, 1995.

Secrest, William B. *Lawmen & Desperadoes.* Spokane: The Arthur H. Clark Company, 1994.

Settle, William A., Jr. *Jesse James Was His Name.* Columbia: University of Missouri Press, 1966.

Shirley, Glenn. *Belle Starr and Her Times.* Norman, OK: University of Oklahoma Press, 1982.

Shirley, Glenn. *Heck Thomas: Frontier Marshal, The Story of a Real Gunfighter.* Philadelphia and New York: Chilton Co., 1962.

Sonnichsen, C.L. *I'll Die Before I'll Run.* New York: The Devin-Adair Co., 1962.

Sonnichsen, C.L. *Outlaw. Bill Mitchell alias Baldy Russell. His Life and Times.* Denver: Sage Books, 1965.

Sping, Agnes Wright. *The Cheyenne and Black Hills Stage and Express Routes.* Glandale, CA: The Arthur H. Clark Co., 1949.

Stanley, F. *Clay Allison.* Denver: World Press, Inc., 1956.

Stanley, F. *Jim Courtright: Two Gun Marshal of Fort Worth.* Denver: World Press, Inc., 1957.

Steckmesser, Kent Ladd. *The Western Hero in History and Legend.* Norman: University of Oklahoma Press, 1965.

Steele, Phillip W. *Jesse and Frank James: The Family History.* Gretna, LA: Pelican Publishing Co., 1991.

Stewart, George. *Committee of Vigilance.* Boston: Houghton Mifflin Co., 1964.

Stiles, T.J. *In Their Own Words: Warriors and Pioneers.* New York: The Berkley Publishing Group, 1996.

Sreeter, Floyd B. *Ben Thompson: Man With A Gun.* New York: Frederick Fell, Inc., 1957.

Summerfield, Charles. [Alfred W. Arrington]. *The Desperadoes of the Southwest: containing an account of the Cane-Hill murders, together with the lives of several of the most notorious regulators and moderators of that region.* New York: W.H. Graham, 1847.

Sutton, Fred Ellsworth. *Hands Up!: Stories of the Six-Gun Fighters of the Old Wild West. As told to A.B. McDonald.* Indianapolis: Bobbs-Merrill, 1927.

Sutton, Robert C., Jr. *The Sutton-Taylor Feud.* Quanah, TX: Nortex Press, 1974.

Swallow, Allen. ed. *The Wild Bunch.* Denver: Sage Books, 1966.

Tanner, Karen Holliday. *Doc Holliday: A Family Portrait.* Norman: University of Oklahoma Press, 1998.

Thompson, Dr. Jerry D. *Laredo: A Pictoral History.* Virginia Beach: The Donning Company, 1986.

Thrapp, Dan L. *Encyclopedia of Frontier Biography:* Vols I, II, III, IV. Lincoln: University of Nebraska Press, 1988.

Tilghman, Zoe A. *Marshal of the Last Frontier: Life and Services of William Matthew (Bill) Tilghman for 50 years one of the greatest peace officers of the West.* Glendale, CA: Arthur H. Clark Co., 1964.

Trachtman, Paul. ed. *The Gunfighters.* New York: Time-Life Books, 1974.

U.S. Bureau of the Census, Revised by the Social Science Research Council. *The Statistical History of the United States from Colonial Times to the Present.* Stanford: Fairfield Publishers, Inc., 1965.

Vestal, Stanley. *Queen of Cowtowns: Dodge City.* New York: Harper & Brothers, 1952.

Waters, Frank. *The Earp Brothers of Tombstone.* London: Neville Spearman, Ltd., 1962.

Webb, Walter Prescott. *The Great Plains.* New York: Grosset and Dunlap, 1931.

Webb, Walter Prescott. *The Texas Rangers: A Century of Frontier Defense.* Austin, University of Texas Press, 1965.

Wellman, Paul I. *A Dynasty of Western Outlaws.* Lincoln, NE: The University of Nebraska Press, 1985.

Wilkins, Frederick. *The Legend Begins: The Texas Rangers, 1823-1845.* Austin: State House Press, 1996.

Wilson, Neill Compton. *Treasure Express: Epic Days of the Wells Fargo.* New York: Macmillan, 1936.

Wilson, Rufus Rockwell. *A Notable Company of Adventurers.* New York: B. W. Dodge and Co., 1908.

Winther, Oscar Osburn. *The Old Oregon Country.* Stanford: Stanford University Press, 1950.

Wolle, Muriel Sibell. *Stampede to Timberline.* Denver: Sage Books, 1962.

Yost, Nellie Snyder. *Medicine Lodge.* Chicago: Sage Books, 1970.

Younger, Coleman. *The Story of Cole Younger, by Himself.* Chicago: Henneberry Co., 1903.

NEWSPAPERS

Alameda County Gazette
Albuquerque Review
Black Hills Daily Times (Deadwood, SD)
Black Hills Pioneer (Deadwood, SD)
Central City Register-Call
Colorado Springs Gazette
Daily Citizen (Tucson, AZ)
Daily Free Press (Atchison, KS)
Dallas Times-Herald
Denver Post
Dodge City Times
Dolores News (Rico, CO)
Durango Herald
Fairplay Flume
Hays Daily News
Herald (San Francisco, CA)
Herald Democrat (Leadville, CO)
Jacksonian, The (Cimarron, KS)
LaPlata Miner, The
Larned Press, The
Las Cruces Rio Grande Republican
Lincoln County Leader
Marysville Appeal-Democrat
Marysville Herald
Mineral County Miner (Creede, CO)
Mesilla Valley Independent (Las Cruces, NM)
Missouri Republican, The (St. Louis, MO)
Mountain Messenger (Idaho Springs, CO)
Oklahoma State Capital (Oklahoma City, OK)
Omaha Republican
Oregonian, The (Portland, OR)
Pawnee Herald (Larned, KS)
Prescott Courier
Republican (Telluride, CO)
Rocky Mountain News (Denver, CO)
Sacramento Times
San Francisco Call
San Francisco Chronicle
San Francisco Examiner
San Juan Herald, The
Santa Fe New Mexican
Silverton Democrat
Silverton Standard
Steamboat Pilot (Steamboat Springs, CO)
Telluride Journal

Trinidad Enterprise, The
Tombstone Epitaph
Trinidad News
Wichita Eagle

ARTICLES

Adams, Paul. "The Unsolved Murder of Ben Thompson, Pistoleer Extraordinary," Southwestern Historical Quarterly, Vol. XLVII, No. 3 (January 1945), 321-29.

Berrier, Deborah. "Clay Allison Never Killed a Man Willingly." American History Illustrated, Summer, 1982.

Berrier, Deborah. "Clay Allison: Shootist." American History Illustrated 1982 17(4): 38-39.

Best, J.D. "Where the Daltons Stopped." True West, April, 1983.

Bocock, Pamela S. "Camp Guthrie: Urban Outpost in the Territory, 1889*1891." Chronicles of Oklahoma 1984 62(2): 166-189.

Bossennecker, John. "Bob Devine: 'We Raided Hole-in-the-Wall.' " Real West, January 1980.

Brown, Dee. "Butch Cassidy and the Sundance Kid." American History Illustrated, Summer, 1982.

Carlson, Paul H. "Panhandle Pastores: Early Sheepherding in the Texas Panhandle." Panhandle-Plains Historical Review 1980. 53: 1-15.

Castel, Albert. "Men Behind the Masks: The James Brothers." American History Illustrated, Summer 1982.

Cawelti, John G. "The Gunfighter and Society," The American West, Vol. V, No. 2 (March 1968), 30-35, 76-78.

Cline, Don. "Secret Life of Billy the Kid." True West, April 1984.

Clum, John P. "It Happened in Tombstone," Arizona Historical Review, Vol. II, No. 3 (October 1929), 46-72.

De Mattos, Jack. "Those Guns of Bat Masterson." Frontier Times, February-March 1977.

Hensen, George W. "The True Story of Wild Bill – McCanles Affray in Jefferson County, Nebraska, July 12, 1861," Nebraska History Magazine, Vol. X, No. 2 (April-June, 1927), 71-112.

Hendrix, Janey B. "Redbird Smith and the Nighthawk Keetoowahs." Journal of Cherokee Studies. 1983 8(1): 22-39.

Holden, W. C. "Law and Lawlessness on the Texas Frontier, 1875-1890," Southwestern Historical Quarterly, Vol. XLIV, No. 2 (October 1940), 188-203.

Jensen, Jody. "Birth of the Arizona Rangers." Old West, Spring 1983.

Kildare, Maurice. "Fastest Gun in Phoenix." Frontier Times, December-January 1968.

Koop, Waldo E., "Enter John Wesley Hardin, A Dim Trail to Abilene." The Prairie Scout, Vol. II, ed. by The Westerners. Ives Printing Co., 1974.

Kubista, Bob. "This Robber Made It Back to His Cache." Frontier Times, December-January 1968.

McCarthy, Donald. "Bill Brazelton, Stage Robber." Frontier Times, January 1980.

McGinty, Brian. "John Wesley Hardin: Gentleman of Guns." American History Illustrated, Summer 1982.

Mills, James R. "End of the Murrietta Gang." True West, March-April 1958.

O'Neal, Bill. "Medicine Lodge Bank Robbery." True West, August 1983.

Perrigo, Lynn I. "Law and Order in Early Colorado Mining Camps," Mississippi Valley Historical Review, Col. XXVIII, No. 1 (June 1941), 41-62.

Robbins, Peggy. "Sam Bass: The Texas Robin Hood." American History Illustrated, 1982 17(4): 37.

Rockwell, Nelson. "The Case of the Bungling Bank Robbers." Frontier Times, Fall 1960.

Rohrs, Richard C. "The Study of Oklahoma History During the Territorial Period: An Alternative Methodological Approach." Chronicles of Oklahoma, 1982 60(2): 174-185.

Sanchez, Lynda A. "They Loved Billy the Kid." True West, January 1984.

Simmons, Marc. "Billy the Kid and the Lincoln County War." American History Illustrated, Summer 1982.

Soltysiak, Harry A. "The Pinkerton Bomb." American History Illustrated, 1992 27(2): 52-53.

Stanchack, John. "Charles 'Black Bart' Boles." American History Illustrated, Summer 1982.

Walker, Dale I. "Buckey O'Neill and the Holdup at Diablo Canyon." Real West Annual, 1980.

Weiss, Harold J., Jr. "Western Lawmen: Image and Reality." Journal of the West, 1985 24(1): 23-32.

West, Elliott. "Wicked Dodge City." American History Illustrated, Summer 1982.

Wharton, Clarence. "Early Judicial History of Texas," Texas Law Review, Vol. XII, No. 3 (April 1934), 311-25.

OTHER SOURCES

Arizona Pioneers' Historical Society, Tucson, AZ: Arizona Rangers: Good History and Records, Manuscript File.

Austin Public Library History Center

Colorado State Archives, Denver, CO: Calvert, Charles E., "United States Marshals: Territorial and State."

George Eastman House Collection.

G. R. Fardon Photo Files.

Federal Records Center, Denver, CO:

Criminal Dockets, First Judicial District, New Mexico Territory, August 1, 1882--March 26, 1912.

Records of the U.S. District Court, Territory of New Mexico, Fifth Judicial District, 1890-1911.

Records of the U.S. District Court, Territory of New Mexico, First Judicial District, 1896-1909.

Hubbs Enterprises, Pecos, TX: Barney Hubbs Collection, Clay Allison Files.

Robert G. McCubbin Collection, El Paso, TX.

Lincoln County, NM: Estate Records, Contracts and Leases.

Oklahoma Historical Society, Oklahoma City, OK: Foreman, Grant -- U.S. Marshal, Vertical File.   Indian-Pioneer History (W.P.A. Project, 1937).

Oklahoma Historical Society, Oklahoma City, OK: Madsen, Chris, "United States Deputy Marshals," Manuscript File.

United States Geological Survey, Maps, U.S. Department of the Interior, Federal Center, Denver.

University of Arizona Archives, Tucson, AZ: Slaughter, [John], Manuscript File.

University of Oklahoma Archives, Norman, OK: Tilghman, [Mr. and Mrs.] William, Manuscript File.

University of Texas at Austin, The Dolph Briscoe Center for American History, Special Collections.

University of Wyoming Western History Center, Laramie, WY: Canton, Frank M., Manuscript File.

University of Wyoming Western History Center, Laramie, WY: LeFors, Joe, Manuscript File.

Wichita State University: Special Collections.

Wild Horse Collection, Round Rock, TX.

Index

A

Abilene, Kansas 75, 146
Acme Saloon 77, 78
Ada, Oklahoma 229, 230
A. D. Walsh's Can Can Lunch and Eating Counter 40
Albuquerque, Texas 264
Alder Gulch, Montana 136, 168
Alexander Mitchell and Company 15
Alhambra Saloon 40
Allen, Billy 43, 44
Allen, Ethan 363
Allen, J. S. 23
Allensworth, Billy 192
Allin, Erskine S. 365
Allison, John 151, 152
Allison, Robert Clay 151, 152, 158
Alton, Illinois 13
Alvord, Burt 141, 287 - 290
Alvord-Stiles Gang 287 - 290
Anderson, "Bloody" Bill 13, 14, 17
Anderson, Hugh 75, 95 - 97
Anderson, Tom. *See* Christian, Bob
Antrim, Henry. *See* Billy the Kid
Antrim, William. *See* Billy the Kid
Antrim, William Henry Harrison 79
Appomattox, Virginia 345
Arapaho, Oklahoma 102
Ardmore, Oklahoma 102
Arizona Rangers 139 - 143, 289, 290
Arizona Territory 37, 38, 52, 80, 140, 141
Armstrong, John 76
Arnold, Mace "Winchester Smith" 271
Arroyo Cantua 239, 240, 339
Askew, Daniel 20, 21
Aspen, Colorado 300
Atchison, Topeka & Santa Fe Railway 157
Aten, Ira (Sergeant) 207, 209 - 211
Atkins, Dave 131, 132, 134
Atlanta, Georgia 317
Aurora, Nevada 127, 128, 241 - 244
Austin, Texas 77, 251, 295

Axtell, S. B. (Governor) 80
Aztec Land and Cattle Company 52, 53, 140. 180

B

Bailey, Ed 35
Baker, Cullen Montgomery 273, 274, 276
Baker, Frank 82, 84
Bank's Saloon and Billiard Parlor 262, 264
Bannack, Montana 137, 167 - 170
Barber, Amos (Governor) 234
Barnes, Seaborn 163 - 165
Barrickman, Alec 266, 269
Bassett, Charlie 108, 158
Bassham, Tucker 26
Bass, Sam 163 - 165, 309
Battle of the Little Big Horn 308
Beard, Edward T. "Red" 342, 343
Beard, Mose 216
Beatty, Az 352
Beatty, Jack 352, 353
Beaver, Oscar 69
Beavers, Jim 360
Beaver Smith's Saloon 79, 91
Beckwith, Robert 86, 89, 93, 116
Beeson, C. M. "Chalk" 100
Behan, John (Sheriff) 38, 40, 42
Beidler, John X. 168
Bell County, Texas 319 - 322
Bell, C. S. (Captain) 251 - 253, 261
Belle Fourche, South Dakota 314
Bell, J. W. (Deputy) 93
Bell, Tom (Dr. Thomas Hodges) 103 - 105
Benavides, Santos (Colonel) 355
Ben Hur 91
Beni, Jules 135, 136
Bennett, Thomas M. 282
Bergh House, the. *See* Fairplay Hotel, the
Berry, Alpheus W. 195 - 199
Berry, Beach D. 195 - 199
Berry, Burchard B. 195 - 199
Berry, Daniel P. 195 - 199
Berry, Harriett M. "Hattie" 195 - 199
Berry, Viola 196
Berry, William Roy 195, 198
Bigler, John (Governor) 238
Big Springs, Nebraska 163
Billy the Kid (Henry McCarty, Henry Andtrim, William H. Bonney) 7, 52, 79 - 94,
    153, 191, 332

Bishop, Thomas 351 - 353
Black Bart (Charles E. Boles) 201 - 204, 340
Black Jack Ketchum Gang 129-134, 318
Blakely, Jake 206, 210
Blake, William "Tulsa Jack" 99
Blazer, Doc 85
Blazer's Mill 85
Blevins, Charles 52 - 54, 57
Blevins, Eva 55, 56
Blevins, Hampton 52, 53
Blevins, John 54 - 56
Blevins, Mart 52, 53
Blevins, Sam Houston 52, 56
Bligh, D. G. 16
Bliss, Jack 191
Bobbitt, Gus 230
Bodie, California 245 - 248
Bodie Mining District, the 245
Bolds, George 190, 191
Boles, Charles E.. *See* Black Bart
Bonham, Texas 73
Bonney, William H.. *See* Billy the Kid
Boot Hill 107, 157, 161, 171, 221, 225, 369
Booth, Newton (Governor) 339
Boren, Bill 348
Boren, Henry 348
Botas, the 355 - 357
Bowdre, Charlie 83, 85, 86, 88, 92
Bowen, Bill 113, 117, 118
Bowen, Emma 226
Bowen, Jane *See* Hardin, Jane
Boyd, Mary 313, 316
Boyer, Joseph 53
Boyle, John 20
Brady, William (Sheriff) 82, 83, 86
Brahma Bull and Red Hot Bar 206, 207, 210
Brewer, Dick 83 - 85
Bristol, Warren H. (Judge) 92
Broadwell, Dick 45 - 48
Brooks, Ed 191
Brooks, William L. "Billy" or "Bully" 171 - 173
Brown and Cort's Saloon 281
Brown, Bob 288, 289
Brown, Henry Newton 83 - 90, 153 - 155
Browning, John Moses 367, 368
Brown, Neil 191
Brown's Hole, Colorado 299
Brunot Treaty 280

Buffalo Bill's Wild West Show 142
Buffalo, Wyoming 233
Bullion, Ed 131, 134
Bullion, Laura 131, 313, 317
Bull's Head Saloon 147
Bunton, Bill 169, 170
Burkhart, William D. 361
Burns, Dick 16
Burns, Tom 70, 72, 340
Burton, Amos 45, 49
Bushwhackers, the 9

C

Cahill, Frank "Windy" 80
Calamity Jane 284
Caldwell, Kansas 153 - 155
California Rangers 239, 240
Campbell, Billy 90
Camp Brown 276, 277
Camp Grant 80
Canton, Frank M. 231 - 235
Carlsbad, New Mexico (formerly Eddy, New Mexico) 133, 177, 178
Carrington, Bob 53
Carthage, Missouri 327 - 329, 331
Carver, Will 129 - 134, 310 - 312
Cassidy, Butch (Robert Leroy Parker) 7, 129, 133, 311 - 317
Castle Gate, Utah 313, 317
Catron, Thomas B. (U. S. District Attorney) 83
Centralia, Missouri 14
Chacón, Augustine 141
Chadwell, Bill. *See* Stiles, Bill
Champion, Nathan D. 231 - 233, 235
Chapman, Houston 90
Chaves, José Chaves y 89
Chaves, Martin 87, 88
Checotah, Oklahoma 102
Cherokee Indians 181
Cherokee Strip, the 45, 49
Cheyenne, Wyoming 151, 232, 235, 293, 307 - 309
Cheyenne and Black Hills Stage, Mail and Express Line 307
Cheyenne Club 231
Cheyenne County, Kansas 193, 195, 198
Cheyenne Indians 219, 220
Chicago and Alton Railroad 26, 27
Chicago, Rock Island & Pacific Railroad 19, 27
Chickasaw Indians 181, 335
Chisholm Trail 165, 343
Chisum, John Simpson 81, 83

Choate, Crockett 252, 256, 258
Choate, John 252, 254, 255, 257, 258
Choctaw Indians 181
Christian, Bob (Tom Anderson) 130
Christian, Hiram (Judge) 319, 321
Christian, Will "Black Jack" 130
Christie, Ned 184 - 187
Cimarron, Kansas 7, 189 - 192, 220, 221
Cimarron, New Mexico 151
Civil War, the (War Between the States, the) 8, 9, 14, 16, 17, 21, 59, 111, 147, 182, 213, 250, 273, 283, 303, 319, 323, 328, 329, 341, 345, 346, 355, 356, 365
Claiborne, Billy 41
Clanton, Billy 40, 41
Clanton, Ike 38, 40 - 43
Clark, Dr. Calvin 319, 322
Clark, Elijah 347
Clay County Savings Bank 15
Clayton, New Mexico 134
Cleary, Harry 281
Clements, Emmanuel "Mannen" 76, 77, 263
Clements, Sallie 77
Clift, Louis 361, 362
Clifton, Dan "Dynamite Dick" 99
Clinton, Texas 265
Cloverdale, California 202
C. M. Condon & Company Bank 46
Cochise, Arizona 288
Coe, Frank 85, 86
Coe, George 84, 85, 88, 89
Coe, Phil 147
Coffeyville, Kansas 45, 47, 67, 99
Cole Younger, By Himself 30
Collier, Thomas B. "Tom" (Deputy Sheriff) 360, 361
Collins, Joel 163
Collis Station, California 67, 69
Colt, Sam 363, 364
Columbia Deposit Bank 18
Columbia, Kentucky 18
Comanche Indians 349
Comanche, Texas 76, 266, 268, 269, 272
Connelly, Charles T. (City Marshal) 48
Connors, Bill 280
Cooley, Scott 214 - 217
Cooper, Andy 52 - 56, 58
Copperopolis, California 202, 203
Corinth, Mississippi 20
Corydon, Iowa 18
Council Bluffs, Iowa 19

Courtright, Jim (Timothy Isaiah Courtright) 7, 59 - 63
Cox, George 100
Coy, Jacob 296
Craddock, Billy 350
Crane, Jim 38, 39
Creek Indians 181, 329
Creekmore, Milo 186
Crittenden, Thomas T. (Governor) 28
Crumpton, Zachariah 114
Cruz, Florentino 42
C. S. Fly's Gallery 41
Cuero, Texas 260, 262, 263, 264, 266, 268, 270, 271
Cummings, Doc 304, 305
Curry, "Flat Nose" George 312 - 315, 317
Custer, George (General) 308

D

Daggs Brothers, the 53
Daggs, P.P. 53
Dallas, Texas 34
Dalton, Bill 66, 99 - 102
Dalton, Bob 45 - 48, 66, 99
Dalton, Emmett 45 - 49, 66, 67, 99
Dalton Gang, the (the Dalton Brothers) 7, 45, 46, 66, 67, 99
Dalton, Grat 45, 46, 48, 66, 99
Daly, George 246, 247
Daly, John 241 - 243
Daniels, Ben 191
Daugherty, Roy. *See* Jones, Tom "Arkansas"
Daviess County Savings Bank 17
Davis, Edmund J. (Governor) 258, 259
Davis, Maude 313
Day, Alfred Hays 262
Deadwood, Dakota Territory 148, 309
Deadwood Stage 307 - 310
de Billier, Frederick O. 231
DeMerritt, Josephine 343
Denton, Texas 163
Denver, Colorado 315
Deringer, Henry Jr. 363, 366
Dermody, James 280, 281
Dermody, Pete 280
Derrickson, John E. 360
Devers, James 16
Dewey, A. P. 193, 194
Dewey-Berry Feud 193 - 199
Dewey, Chauncey 193 - 199
Dewey, C. P. 194, 198

DeWitt County, Texas 251 - 254, 256, 259 - 261, 265, 266, 269, 272
Dietz, Lewis 49
Dixon, Bill 76
Dixon, Billy 347
Dobbins, California 202
Dodge City, Kansas 35, 37, 61, 107 - 109, 157 - 161, 172, 189 - 191, 220
Dodge City Peace Commission 160
Dodge City Times 35
Dodge House 35
Dolan, James Joseph "Jimmy" 81, 82, 83, 86 - 88, 90, 92, 115
Doolin, Bill 99 - 102, 221, 222
Doolin Gang, the 99 - 102, 221
Dover, Oklahoma 102
Drum's Saloon 147, 223, 224
Dry Creek 104, 359 - 362
Dudley, Nathan A. (Colonel) 88
Duncan's Mills, California 201, 202
Dunlap, "Three-Fingered" Jack 288, 289
Dunn, Bill 102
Durango, Colorado 282, 380

E

Early, John 319 - 322
Earp, Allie 37
Earp, Hattie 40
Earp, James 37, 40
Earp, Mattie 37
Earp, Morgan 39 - 42
Earp, Virgil 37 - 42
Earp, Warren 39, 42
Earp, Wyatt 7, 33 - 40, 42, 44, 61, 158, 160
Eddy, New Mexico. *See* Carlsbad, New Mexico
Edwards, John Newman (Major) 17
Elder, Kate "Big-nose Kate" (Mary Katherine Haroney) 34 - 37, 39 42, 44
Elliot, Richard E. 38
Ellsworth, Kansas 341
El Paso, Texas 77, 78, 116, 303, 304, 305
English, J. W. 191, 221
E. Remington & Sons 365
Erhart, Pat 351
Eskridge, Dyson 281
Estabo, Tranquellano 179
Eureka Springs, Arkansas 222
Evans, Christopher 65, 67 - 72
Evans, Jessie 80 - 82, 85, 87, 89, 90
Evergreen, Texas 275
Exeter, Montana 315

F

Faber, Charles (Deputy Sheriff) 152
Fairhurst, Ed 191
Fairplay Hotel 282
Faribault, Minnesota 25
Farmers and Merchants Bank 284
Farr, Edward (Sheriff) 132
First National Bank of Coffeyville 46, 47
First National Bank of Northfield 23 - 26
Fisher, John King 295 - 297
Five Civilized Tribes 181, 182
Fly, Camillus S. 40, 41
Fly, Mollie 40
Folsom, New Mexico 131, 132
Folsom Prison 67
Forbes, Charley 168
Ford, Charles 27
Ford County Bank 99
Ford, Robert Newton "Bob" 28, 284, 286
Fort Dodge, Kansas 157, 158, 161
Ft. Griffin, Texas 34
Fort Hays 225 - 227
Fort Laramie 308
Fort Mason, Texas 213, 251
Fort McKinney 235
Fort Ross, California 201, 202
Fort Sill, Oklahoma 360
Fort Smith, Arkansas 182 - 188, 329
Fort Stanton, New Mexico 83, 85 - 89, 114, 325
Fort Sumner, New Mexico 79, 91 - 93
Fort Worth, Texas 60, 108, 160
Foster, Joe 295 - 297
Fountain, Albert J. (Colonel) 80
Frazer, G. A. "Bud" (Sheriff) 229
Fremont Street 41
French, Jim "Big Jim" 83, 84, 120
Frost, H. H. 206, 207, 210

G

Gallagher, Jack 168, 170
Gallatin, Missouri 17
Galveston, Texas 211, 252, 254, 267 - 269, 272
Garcia, "Three-Fingered" Jack 237, 240
Gard, George (U.S. Marshal) 70, 72
Garrett, Pat (Sheriff) 7, 91 - 94
Garvey, Jim (Sheriff) 206, 210, 211
Geppert, George 154

Gibson, Ned 208, 209, 211
Gibson, Volney 205, 208 - 211
Giddings, Marsh (Governor) 115
Giddings, Texas 275, 277
Gillespie, Bob 53, 54
Gilmer & Salisbury 307 - 310
Gladden, George 215, 216
Glendale, Missouri 26
Glenwood Springs, Colorado 44
Globe, Arizona 37, 58
Goff, John 246, 247
Going Snake District 330
Gonzales, Dario 355, 356
Gonzales Enquirer 265
Gonzales, Ignacio 85, 89
Gosper, John J. 38
Graham, Billy 54, 57
Graham, Dayton 140, 141
Graham, John 54, 57
Graham-Tewksbury Feud 51 - 58
Graham, Texas 360, 361
Graham, Thomas 56 - 58
Graham, Will Hicks 125 - 128
Grant, Joe 91
Grant, Ulysses S. (President) 182
Grasshopper Creek 167
Gray County, Kansas 189 - 192, 220
Great Northern Coast Flyer 315
Gregg, William 11
Griffin, David 321
Griffin, Frank 16
Griffin, Georgia 33
Grimes, A. W. (Deputy Sheriff) 164
Gristy, Bill 103 - 105
Guaraches, the 355 - 357
Gunnison, Colorado 43, 108, 284
Gustavson, Nicholas 23, 25
Gutierrez, Celsa 93
Gylam, Jacob L. "Jack" (Sheriff) 114

H

Hahns Peak, Colorado 300
Harbolt, George E. 360
Harbolt, Susan 360
Hardin, Jane 75, 263
Hardin, Joe 266, 269
Hardin, John Wesley "Wes" 7, 73 - 78, 89, 263 - 269, 272, 348
Harkey, D. R. "Dee" 175 - 180

Harkey, Joe 176, 177
Harkey, Sophie New 175, 177
Harlem, Kansas 14
Haroney, Mary Katherine. *See* Elder, Kate
Harrell, George (Texas Ranger) 165
Harris, Charles 226
Harris, Jack 295, 296
Harris, W. H. 160
Hart, Edward "Little" 115
Harwood House 41
Hash Knife outfit, the. *See* Aztec Land and Cattle Company
Hash Knife Ranch 52, 53, 140, 180
Hasley, Sam 319 - 322
Hat Creek Station 309
Hayes, Rutherford B. (President) 90
Hayes, Upton B. (Colonel) 11
Haynes, J. J. 355
Hays, Kansas (originally Hays City) 147, 225 - 227
Hazen, Joe (Sheriff) 130, 315
Helm, Boone 169, 170
Helm, Jack 76, 251 - 256, 258, 260, 261, 263, 264
Henry, Benjamin Tyler 364
Heywood, Joseph 24
Hickok, James Butler "Wild Bill" 7, 60, 75, 145 - 148
Higgins, John Calhoun Pinckney "Pink" 117 - 123
Hill, Tom 82
Hindman, George 84, 86
Hite, Clarence 27
Hite, Wood 26, 27
Hoch, Edward W. Hoch (Governor) 49
Hodges, Thomas (Dr.). *See* Bell, Tom
Hoerster, Dan 215
Holbrook, Arizona 54 - 58
Hole-in-the-Wall, Wyoming 232, 313
Holliday, John Henry "Doc" 7, 33 - 43, 158, 287
Holstein, Sim 261, 262
Holston, James H. 359
Hoodoo War, the (the Mason County War) 123, 213 - 217
Hoover, John J. 282
Horn, Tom 291 - 293
Horrell, Ben 111 - 115
Horrell-Higgins Feud 111 - 124
Horrell, Mart 111 - 124
Horrell, Merritt 111 - 118
Horrell, Sam 111 - 124
Horrell, Tom 111 - 124
Horrell War 111, 113 - 117
Hotel Glenwood 44

Houck, James D. 54
"House," the 81
Houston Telegraph 265
Hoy, Valentine 299, 300
Hudson, Dick (Deputy Sheriff) 271
Hudson, Hugh 346
Hueston, Thomas J. 100
Hughes and Wasson Bank 16
Hume, Jim 202, 203
Hunter, Kit 271
Hunter, Luke (Sheriff) 281

I

Indian Charley 42
Indianola, Texas 250, 266
Indian Territory 181 - 185, 187, 219, 329 - 333, 335, 360
Ingalls, Kansas 7, 189 - 192, 220, 221
Ingalls, Oklahoma 99 - 102
Innocents, the 167 - 170
Iron Clad, the 309, 310
Isham Brothers' hardware 46, 48, 49
Isham, Henry H. 49

J

Jackson, Andrew (President) 181
Jackson County 10, 16, 26
Jackson, Frank 163, 164, 165
Jackson, Fred 70, 72
Jacksonville, Florida 143
Jacobs, William 53, 54
James, Alexander Franklin "Frank" 7, 10 - 30
James, Annie Ralston 21
James, Jesse Woodson 7, 9, 11 - 27, 31, 284, 366
James, Robert 11
James, Susan 11
James-Younger Gang 9 - 30
James-Younger Wild West Show 30
James, Zerelda. *See* Samuel, Zerelda
James, Zerelda "Zee" Mimms 14, 20, 21, 26
Jarrette, John 11, 12, 13, 15, 16
Jaybirds, the 205 - 211
Jaybird-Woodpecker Conflict 205 - 211
Jayhawkers 10, 11
Jerry Scott's Matador Saloon 112, 113
J. J. Dolan & Company 83
Johnson, Andrew (President) 345
Johnson, A. V. E. (Major) 14

Johnson, Billn 304
Johnson County Invasion 231 - 235
Johnson, Dick 348
Johnson, Jack "Turkey Creek" 42
Johnson, Jake 61
Jones, John B. (Major) 120 - 123, 216
Jones, Payne 16
Jones, Tom "Arkansas" (Roy Daughterly) 99
Joyce, Milt E. 38
Julesburg, Colorado 135
July, Bill (Jim July Starr) 333 - 335

K

Kansas City Times 17
Kansas Daily Commonwealth 172
Kansas-Nebraska Act of 1854, the 9
Kansas Pacific Railroad 20
Kansas State Fair 18, 19
KC Ranch 232, 233
Kearney, Missouri 11, 14, 17, 18, 20, 30, 31
Keetoowah Society 184
Kerry, Hobbs 21
Ketchum, Samuel W. "Sam" 129 - 134
Ketchum, Thomas Edward "Black Jack" 129 - 134
Killarney Kate 284
Kilpatrick, Ben 311, 312, 317
King, Martin 271
Kinney, John W. 80
Kloehr, John J. 45, 48

L

La Cananea, Sonora 142
Lackey, John 75
Ladd, Jack 21
Lady Gay Saloon 109, 159
Lake, Agnes 148
Lake Valley, New Mexico 60
Lampasas, Texas 111 - 113, 117 - 120, 122
Lanahan, Peter (Sheriff) 226
Lane, "Club Foot" George 169, 170
Langford, Nathaniel 168
Lant, David 299, 300
LaPlata Miner 280
Laredo, Texas 355 - 357
Las Animas, Colorado 152
Las Cruces, New Mexico 111
Las Vegas, New Mexico 36, 39, 107, 108

LaTourette, Koertenius "Charley" 283, 284
Lavinia, Montana 314
Law, George 285
Lawrence, Kansas 12
Lawson, Oklahoma 102
Lay, Elzy. *See* Lay, William Ellsworth "Elzy"
Lay, William Ellsworth "Elzy" 129, 132, 133, 312 - 315, 318
Leadville, Colorado 43, 61, 283
Leavenworth, Kansas 276
Lee, Bob 312, 345 - 348
Lee-Peacock feud 345 - 348
Lee, Robert E. (General) 249, 345
Lee's Summit, Missouri 10, 30
LeFors, Joe (Deputy U. S. Marshal) 293
Lemon, George Frank 126, 127
Levagood, Maude 154
Lexington, Missouri 14, 15
Lexington, Texas 276
Liberty, Missouri 15, 20
Liddil, Dick 26, 27
Life of John Wesley Hardin as Written by Himself 77
Lighthorse, the 182, 185
Lincoln County War 7, 52, 79 - 93, 153, 325, 332
Lincoln, New Mexico 7, 52, 59, 79 - 94, 111, 113 - 115, 153, 221, 302, 325, 326, 332
Little Rock, Arkansas 60
Little, Thomas 16
Logan, Harvey "Kid Curry" 130, 132, 191, 312 - 315, 317
Logan, John "Blackjack" (General) 59
Logan, Lonie 312, 314, 317
Longabaugh, Harry Alonzo "the Sundance Kid" 311 - 316
Long Branch Saloon 61, 159, 160
Long, John "Jack" 84, 87
Longley, Cale 277
Longley, William Preston 275 - 277
Los Angeles, California 44
Love, Harry (Captain) 239, 240
Love, W. H. (Deputy U.S. Marshal) 132
Loving, "Cockeyed" Frank 159
Lowe, Joseph "Rowdy Joe" 341 - 344
Lowe, Kate "Rowdy Kate" 341 - 344
Lynn, Wiley 222
Lyons, Hayes 168

M

MacNab, Frank 83 - 86
Maddox, Francis 346
Maddox, John 346
Maddox, William 346

Madsen, Chris (Deputy U.S. Marshal) 221
Maledon, George 183
Manning, Doc 305
Manning, Frank 305
Manning, Jim 305
Manning, John 305
Maples, Dan (Deputy U. S. Marshal) 185, 187
Maples, Sam 187
Marcus, Josephine (Josie Earp) 38, 44
Marlow, Alfred "Alf" 359 - 362
Marlow, Boone 359 - 361
Marlow, Charley 359 - 362
Marlow, George 359 - 362
Marlow, Lewellyn "Ep" 359 - 362
Martinez, Atanacio (Constable) 83
Martin, Juan (Constable) 114
Martin, Raymond 355, 356
Marysville, California 103, 104, 202
Mason, Texas 215
Masterson, Ed 158
Masterson, James "Massey" 243
Masterson, Jim 7, 100, 101, 159, 160, 189 - 192, 220, 221
Masterson, William Barclay "Bat" 7, 33, 43, 61, 158, 160, 161, 192, 223, 284
Matagorda Bay 270
Mather, Josiah 107, 109, 110, 161
Mather, "Mysterious" Dave 107 - 109, 160
Mathews, Billy 84, 86, 87, 90
Maxwell, Pete 93, 94
McBride, William J. 195 - 198
McCall, John "Broken Nose Jack" 149
McCanles, Dave 146, 147
McCarty, Bill 279, 284
McCarty, Catherine 79
McCarty, Fred 279, 285
McCarty, Henry. *See* Billy the Kid
McCarty, Michael 79
McCarty, Tom 284, 285
McClain, John (Judge) 15
McClurg, Joseph (Governor) 17
McCluskie, Arthur "Art" 96, 97, 368
McCluskie, Mike 95, 96
McCullough, Robert (Sheriff) 197
McDade, Texas 349
McDougal, Cattle Annie 222
McDowell, John "Three-Fingered Jack" 241
McGinnis, Andy (Deputy Sheriff) 69
McGuire, A. J. "Yank" 128
McGuire, Andy 15, 16

McIntire, Jim 60, 61
McKemma, Robert 309
McKinley, William (President) 134
McLaury, Frank 38, 40, 41
McLaury, Tom 38, 40, 41
McMasters, Sherman 42
McNelly, Leander H. (Captain) 269, 272
McRae, Jim 320, 321
McSween, Alexander Anderson 81, 86 - 89
McSween, Susan E. 81, 89, 90
Medicine Lodge, Kansas 96, 97, 153 - 155
Melvin, Silas 34
Merrill, Dave 300, 301
Mescalero Apache Indian Reservation 85
Mesilla Valley Independent 80, 380
Middleton, John 83 - 86, 90, 332
Miller, Clell 18, 19, 21, 23 - 25
Miller, Ed 26, 27
Miller, Jim "Deacon" 7, 77, 175, 229, 230
Milligan, Tom 280
Mills, Alexander H. "Ham" (Sheriff) 114
Milmo, Daniel 355
Milmo, Patricio 355
Milton, George 351 - 353
Milton, Jeff Davis (Chief) 78, 131, 287, 289
Mimms, Mrs. John 14
Mimms, Zerelda "Zee" *See* James, Zerelda "Zee" Mimms
Missouri Pacific Railroad 21
Mitchell, Nelson "Cooney" 323, 325, 326
Mitchell, Robert "Bob" 118 - 120, 123
Mitchell, William Nelson 323 - 326, 378
Mogollon Rim, Arizona 52 - 54
Montana Vigilantes 168
Montaño, José 115
Morose, Helen Buelah 77
Morose, Martin 77
Morrell, Ed 71
Morris, Harvey 89
Morse Detective Agency 340
Morse, Henry Nicholson "Harry" 203, 337 - 340
Morton, Buck 82 - 84
Morton, W. H. (Deputy U. S. Marshal) 362
Mossman, Burton 140 - 142, 289, 290
Mount Olivet Cemetery 31
Mulvenon, William (Sheriff) 54, 57
Muncie, Kansas 20
Murphy, Jim 163 - 165
Murphy, Lawrence Gustave "L. G." 81, 82, 115

Murrieta, Jesus 238
Murrieta, Joaquin 237 - 240, 337
Muscle Shoals, Alabama 26

N

Napavine, Washington 301
Nation, Carry 206
Navajo Springs, Arizona 55
Ned's Fort Mountain 186
Neiman, Charles (Sheriff) 300
Nevada City, California 104, 167
Newcomb, George "Bitter Creek" 99 - 101
New Mexico Territorial Prison 132 - 134, 318
New Mexico Territory 80, 93
New, Sophie. *See* Harkey, Sophie
Newton, Kansas 95, 96, 341
Newton's General Massacre 96
Nickell, Kels P. 293
Nickell, Willie 293
Nighthawk Keetoowahs 185, 186
Nite, Jim 179, 180
Nix, E. D. (U. S. Marshal) 100
Nixon, Thomas C. (Assistant Marshal) 108
Northern Wyoming Farmers' and Stock Growers' Association 232
Notch Cutters 349 - 353

O

Oakwood Cemetery 63
Ocobock Brothers' Bank 18
O'Day, Tom 312, 314
O'Folliard, Tom 89 - 92
Ogsbury, D. C. "Clate" 281
O. K. Corral 41, 287
O'Kelley, Ed 284
O. K. Hotel 100
Oklahoma District Land Rush in 1889, the 221
Oklahombres, the. *See* Doolin Gang, the
Olinger, Robert (Deputy) 93
Olive Ranch 350
Olympic Dance Hall 152
Opera House Saloon 109
Oregon State Penitentiary 300, 301
Oregon Trail 146
Organic Act 100
Oriental Saloon 38, 42, 43, 61
Oroville, California 104, 202
Otterville, Missouri 21, 331

Outlaw, Bass (Deputy U. S. Marshal) 78
Overland Stage Company 135, 136
Owens, Commodore Perry (Sheriff) 7, 54, 55
Owens, George 289
Owens, Louis 288, 289

P

Paddleford, Walter 179
Paine, John 52, 53
Parker, Isaac Charles (Judge) 181 - 183, 185, 187, 188, 331
Parker, James Wesson (Judge) 206, 209 - 211
Parker, Joe 348
Parker, Robert Leroy. *See* Cassidy, Butch
Parris, John 185
Patrón, Juan 114, 115
Payne, E. Wylie 154
Peacock, Lewis 346 - 348
Pecos, Texas 152
Pence, Bud 15, 16
Pence, Donny 15, 16
Pensacola, Florida 76, 272
Peppin, George 84, 86, 87, 90
Perry, Joab 15
Pett's Ferry 274
Phoenix, New Mexico 178, 179
Pickett, Tom 52, 92
Pierce, A. H. "Shanghai" 251
Pierce, Charles 99
Pierce, Dr. William 346
Pillsbury, John (Governor) 24
Pilot Grove, Texas 346
Pinkerton National Detective Agency 19 - 21, 26
Pitts, Charlie 21 - 24
Place, Etta 313, 315, 316
Pleasant Valley, Arizona 7, 8, 51 - 58, 180
Pleasant Valley War 7, 8, 51 - 58, 180
Plummer, Amos Henry (Sheriff) 137, 167 - 170
Pond, the 241, 242
Pool, Dave 15
Pool, John 15
Posse Comitatus Act 88
Powell, Buck 87
Powers, Bill 45, 46, 48
Prather, Ed 220
Preece, William (Sheriff) 317
Pridgen, Bolivar 261, 265, 266, 269, 272
Pridgen, Jim 265
Pridgen, Wiley 265

Procopio (Tomas Bustamente) 337 - 339
Puerco River 55
Punteney, Walt 312

Q

Quantrill, William Clarke 10 - 14, 328, 348
Quinn, Mary 177

R

Rabbit Trap Canyon 186
Raidler, William "Little Bill" 99, 222
Ralston, Annie *See* James, Annie Ralston
Randlett, James (Captain) 117
Ransom Saloon 99, 100
Rapelji, Hi (Deputy Sheriffs) 70, 72
Ray, Harvey 312, 315
Ray, Ned 168 - 170
Ray, Nick 233, 235
Real Del Monte 241, 242, 244
Reconstruction Acts 249
Redding, California 202
Reddy, Patrick 245 - 248
Reed, Eddie 188, 331, 333, 335, 336
Reed, Jim 17, 328 - 331
"Regulators," the 83
Reicheldeffer, Charlie 191
Reynolds, J. J. (General) 347
Richardson, Levi 159
Richards, William (Governor) 312
Richland Springs, Texas 175, 177
Richmond, John 60
Richmond, Missouri 16
Richmond, Texas 205, 210
Riley, Jim 95, 96
Riley, John Henry 81
Ringo, Johnny 42
Rio Grande River 356
Rio Grande Western 313
Rio Hondo 116
Rivers, Frank. *See* Long, John "Jack"
Rivers, Harry (Marshal) 283, 284
Robbers' Roost, Utah 313
Roberts, Andrew L. "Buckshot" 85
Roberts, Jim 53, 58
Roberts, Mose 56
Robertson, Ben. *See* Wheeler, Ben
Rock Island Railroad 180

Rock Saloon 349, 352, 353
Rocky Cut, Missouri 21
Roosevelt, Theodore (Teddy Roosevelt's Rough Riders) 142
Roswell, New Mexico 116
Rowland, Billy (Sheriff) 339
Rudabaugh, Dave 91, 92, 108
Rulo, Nebraska 14
Rusk, Dave (Deputy) 186
Ryan, Bill 26
Rynerson, William L. (District Attorney) 83
Rynning, Thomas H. 142

S

St Joseph, Missouri 27, 276
St. Louis, Missouri 317, 343
Ste. Genevieve Savings Association 19
Salazar, Yginio 89, 93
Saloon No. 10 148
Salt Lake City, Utah 313
Samuel, Archie 11, 21
Samuel, Dr. Reuben 11
Samuel, Fannie 11, 26
Saumel, John 11
Samuel, Sallie 11, 77
Samuel, Zerelda 10, 11, 14, 20, 22
San Antonio, Texas 20, 176, 250, 251, 255, 261, 264, 295, 296, 321, 325, 328, 330
San Augustin Church 355, 356
San Augustin Plaza 355, 356
Sanders, Wilbur Fisk (Colonel) 168
San Joaquin Valley, California 65 - 71
San Juan Herald 281, 380
San Miguel Valley Bank 311
Santa Fe, New Mexico 79
Santa Fe Railroad 95
Santa Fe Trail 146, 157
Savage, Arthur 368
Savage, Peter 247, 248
Savannah, Missouri 15
Sayles, Bill 317
Scarborough, George (Deputy U. S. Marshal) 78, 131
Scott, Jerry 112, 113, 115, 117, 118
Scurlock, Josiah "Doc" 83, 85 - 90
Sears, James 241, 242
Selman, John 77, 78, 89
Selman, John Jr. 78
Selman, Tom 89
Seminole Indians 181
Seven Rivers 83, 86, 87, 116

Shadley, Lafayette "Lafe" 100
Sharps, Christian 364
Shaw, John (Mayor) 16
Sheets, John (Captain) 17
Shepherd, George 15, 16
Shepherd, Oliver 15, 16
Shirley, Bud 328
Shirley, Jim 285, 286
Shirley, John 17
Shirley, Myra Maybelle. *See* Starr, Belle
Short, Luke Lamar 7, 59 - 63
Silver City, New Mexico 60, 61, 80
Silverton, Colorado 143, 280 - 282
Simms, Benjamin 11
Simms, Billy 295, 296
Simms, Cicero 282, 283
Simpson, W. Ray 279, 284, 285
Singer, Fred (Sheriff) 158, 160, 191, 192
Sioux Indians 61, 307, 308
Skidmore, F. O. 252, 256
Skinner, Cyrus 167, 168, 169, 170
Skinner's Saloon 137, 168
Slade, Joseph Alfred "Jack" 135 - 137
Slade, Virginia 137
Slaughter, Gabriel 266, 272
Slaughter, John (Sheriff) 287
Smith and Wesson 364 - 366
Smith, Bill 140, 141, 314
Smith, Charles 49
Smith, James Madison 11
Smith, Martin (Parson) 346
Smith, Sam 83, 87 - 89
Smith, "Soapy Smith" Jefferson Randolph 284, 377
Smith, Tom C. 232
Smith, Van C. 116
Smith, Will 66 - 68, 70
Smith, William "Billy" 153, 154
Sonora, Mexico 179, 239, 240
Sontag, George 67 - 71
Sontag, John 67 - 72, 340
Soule, Asa 190, 220
Southern Bank of Kentucky 16
Southern Pacific Railroad 66, 68, 69, 288
Spanish-American War 142
Spearville, Kansas 99
Speed, Dick 100
Spencer, Christopher M. 365
Spencer, Pete "Spence" 38

Spicer, Justice Wells 41
Springfield, Missouri 147
Starr, Belle (Myra Maybelle Shirley) 17, 187, 188, 327 - 336
Starr, Jim July *See* July, Bill
Starr, Sam 187, 188, 331 - 333
Starr, Tom 329 - 331, 333, 335
Steins Pass, Arizona 134
Stevens, Jennie "Little Britches" 222
Stiles, Bill 21 - 24
Stiles, William Larkin "Billy" 141, 288 - 290
Stillwater, Oklahoma 100
Stillwell, Frank 38, 42
Stinking Springs 92
Stinson, Buck 168 - 170
Stoudenmire, Dallas 303 - 305
Sughrue, Patrick F. (Sheriff) 108
Sutter's Mill 125
Sutton, Bill 258 - 263, 265 - 272
Sutton, Laura 264, 266, 267
Swan Land and Cattle Company 292

T

Tahlequah, Indian Territory (later Oklahoma) 181, 185, 186
TA Ranch 231, 234, 236
Taylor, Amanda 260, 261
Taylor, Bill 266, 268 - 272
Taylor, Charley 259, 260
Taylor, Creed 249, 250, 252 - 255
Taylor, Hays 250, 251, 254
Taylor, Jim 76, 262, 264, 266 - 268, 270, 271
Taylor, Phillip "Doboy" 251, 252, 259, 261
Taylor, Pitkin 259 - 262
Taylor, Susan Cochran Day 259
Taylor, William Riley Jr. "Buck" 251, 259
Telluride, Colorado 311, 380
Terry, Kyle 208, 209, 211
Tewksbury, Ed 53, 54, 58
Tewksbury, Jim 53, 58
Texas Central Railroad 349
Texas Flyer 131
Texas & Pacific Railway 132
Texas Rangers' Frontier Battalion 120 - 123, 216
Texas Rangers, the 60, 76, 118, 120, 123, 164, 207, 209, 215 - 217, 230, 258, 269,
    272, 304, 364
Texas Supreme Court 356
Thacker, John E.131
Thomas, Heck (Deputy U. S. Marshal) 102, 185 - 187, 221, 335
Thompson, Ben 147, 148, 295, 296, 297

Thompson, Billy 158
Thompson, H. A. "Hi" 100
T.I.C. Commercial Detective Agency 61
Tilghman, William Matthew Jr. "Bill" 7, 108, 158, 189, 191, 219 - 223
Tin Cup, Colorado 283, 284
Tishimingo Savings Bank 20
Tolbert, Paden (Deputy U. S. Marshal) 186
Tombstone, Arizona 36 - 43, 61, 116, 160, 287, 289
Tommy Drum's Saloon 147, 225, 226
Tonto Basin, Arizona 51, 52, 54
Tracy, Harry (Harry Severns) 299 - 302
Trail of Tears 181
Trinidad, Colorado 36, 42, 132
Truitt, Jim (Reverend) 325, 326
Tucker, Tom 52 - 54, 180
Tunstall, John Henry "the Englishman" 81
Turner Hall Opera House 296
Tutt, Dave 147
Tuttle Dance Hall 95, 97
Tuttle, Perry 95
Tyler, Jess (Sheriff) 317
Tyler, Johnny 38, 43

U

Union League 345, 346
Union Pacific Railroad 140, 226, 232, 291, 307, 309, 310, 315
U.S.-Mexican War 238
Ute Indians 277, 280

V

Vail & Company 173
Valenzuela, Joaquin 237, 238, 240
Van Buren, Arkansas 182
Vanhorn, J. J. (Colonel) 235
Van Sant, S. R. (Governor) 29
Vasquez, Tiburcio 337 - 339
Vaudeville Theatre and Gambling Saloon 295, 296
Vaughan, J. F. 124
Vigilance Committee, the (Montana) 126, 127, 137
Virginia City, Montana 136, 137, 168, 170, 247
Visalia, California 65, 67, 68, 70, 71

W

Wabash, St. Louis & Pacific Railroad 14
Waco, Texas 74, 124, 263
Wagner, Jack 159
Waite, Frank 83

Walker, William 125
Wallace, Lew (Governor) 90
Wallace, Marion DeKalb (Sheriff) 360, 361
Walley, Irvin 11
War Between the States, the. *See* Civil War, the
Ward, Hiram 280, 281
Ware, Dick (Texas Ranger) 165
War of 1812 55
Warrensburg, Missouri 16
Watonwan River 24
Watson, Edgar A. 333
Watson, Newt 191, 192
Weaverville, California 202
Webb, Charles (Deputy Sheriff) 76, 77, 268, 272
Weeks, Sarah Elizabeth "Betty" 60
Weightman, George "Red Buck" 99
Wells Fargo 38, 57, 65 - 67, 104, 131, 201 - 203, 289, 315, 367
Wells, Sam. *See* Pitts, Charlie
Wesley, John 153 - 155
West, "Little" Dick 99
Western Stage Company 309
Westfall, William 27
Wheeler, Ben (Ben Robertson) 153 - 155
Wheeler, Henry 23, 24
Wheeler, Henry Cornwall 142
White, Bill. *See* Gristy, Bill
White, Charlie 37
White Elephant Saloon 61
Wichita, Kansas 342
Wilburn, Aaron O. 116
Wilcox Canyon 71
Wilcox, Wyoming 314
Wild Bunch, the 99, 129, 133, 191, 311 - 318
Wilkerson, James 15
Wilkinson, Burt 281
Williams, Mike 148
Williamson, Tim 214, 215
Wilson, Billy 92
Wilson, Clyde 196 - 198
Wilson, Vic (Deputy U.S. Marshal) 69
Wincher, John 20
Winchester, Oliver 364
Winchester Repeating Arms Company 365
Wolcott, Frank (Major) 231, 233, 236
Wolf, Arch 186, 187
Woodpeckers, the 205 - 211
Worley, John (Deputy Sheriff) 214, 215
Wortley Hotel 87, 93

Wren, Bill 118 - 120
Wren, William. *See* Wren, Bill
Wynn, Allen 351, 352
Wyoming Stock Growers Association 231 - 233, 292

Y

Yantis, Oliver "Ol" 99
Yavapai County, Arizona 116
Yeager, Red 137, 169, 170
Yoas, Bravo Juan 288, 289
Yorktown, Texas 276
Younger, Bob 14, 18 - 30
Younger, Bruce 331
Younger, Bursheba 12, 16, 17
Younger, Caroline 12
Younger, Cole 7, 9 - 30, 328, 329
Younger, Henry Washington 9, 11
Younger, Jim 13, 14, 16 - 29
Younger, John 18 - 20
Younger, Josie 12, 26, 44, 79
Younger, Rosie Lee "Pearl" 328, 329
Younger, Sally 12
Yreka, California 202
Yuma, Arizona 290

Z

Zulick, C. Meyer (Governor) 57

www.ingramcontent.com/pod-product-compliance
Lightning Source LLC
Chambersburg PA
CBHW071214080526
44587CB00013BA/1367